Scaffolding Emergent Literacy

A Child-Centered Approach for Preschool through Grade 5

SECOND EDITION

Anne K. Soderman

Michigan State University

Kara M. Gregory

Michigan State University

Louise T. McCarty

Hugger Elementary School

Boston • New York • San Francisco
Mexico City • Montreal • Toronto • London • Madrid • Munich • Paris
Hong Kong • Singapore • Tokyo • Cape Town • Sydney

Series Editor: Aurora Martínez Ramos
Editorial Assistant: Erin Beatty
Senior Marketing Manager: Elizabeth Fogarty
Editorial-Production Service: Omegatype Typography, Inc.
Manufacturing Buyer: Andrew Turso
Composition Buyer: Linda Cox
Cover Administrator: Kristina Mose-Libon
Electronic Composition: Omegatype Typography, Inc.

For related titles and support materials, visit our online catalog at www.ablongman.com.

Library of Congress Cataloging-in-Publication Data

Soderman, Anne Keil.
    Scaffolding emergent literacy : a child-centered approach for preschool through grade 5 / Anne K. Soderman, Kara M. Gregory, Louise T. McCarty.—2nd ed.
      p. cm.
    Includes bibliographical references and index.
    ISBN 0-205-38643-1
    1. Language arts (Early childhood)   2. Language arts (Elementary)   3. Child development. I. Gregory, Kara M.   II. McCarty, Louise T.   III. Title.

LB1139.5.L35S63 2005
372.6—dc22

2004043671

Photo Credits
pp. 7, 8, 13, 16, 18, 21, 24, 38, 41, 43, 45, 47, 48, 49, 53, 54, 58 (left and right), 61, 69, 74, 79, 80, 82, 83, 86, 92, 111, 115, 118, 123, 128 (top and bottom), 129, 133, 137, 154 (top and bottom), 155, 175, 181, 194: Erin Groom; pp. 15, 126: T. Lindfors/Lindfors Photography; pp. 81 (top and bottom), 233: Kara M. Gregory; pp. 216, 217: Louise T. McCarty

Printed in the United States of America

10 9 8 7 6 5 4 3 2   09 08 07 06 05

Contents

Preface   vii

PART 1   Setting the Stage:
Appropriate Practices, Processes, and Contexts

CHAPTER 1

Developing Literacy in the Young Child: Antecedents, Transactions, and Outcomes   1

Antecedents in Developing Literacy   2
Chronological Age Differences   3
Gender Differences   3
Variations in Brain Organization   4
Supporting Children Who Are English Language Learners   6
Sociocultural Influences   8

Transactions: Theoretical Transformations in the Home and School Contexts   9
A Theoretical Perspective for Developing Literacy   9
Developmentally Appropriate Practices   15
Current Approaches to Literacy Practice in the Primary Classroom: How Developmentally Appropriate Are They?   17
Integrating Learning across the Curriculum   20
The Role of Technology in Literacy Development   20

Outcomes: Measuring Literacy Growth in a Developmentally Appropriate Context   22

Final Thoughts   23

Challenge Yourself   24

Suggested Sources for Additional Information   24
Popular Literacy-Promoting Software for Children   24

CHAPTER 2

Literacy Links and Processes   26

A Look at Literacy   26
A Glimpse of Literacy: Philosophies and Definitions   26

Language and Literacy   27
Oral Language   27
Written Language   28

Functions of Oral and Written Language   29
Oral Language Functions   29
Written Language Functions   29

Concepts of Written Language   30

Methods of Organizing Literacy Instruction   31
Critical Core Components of Literacy   32

The Role of Oral Language   32

The Role of Phonological Awareness   34

The Role of Print   38
The Role of Word Awareness   38
Knowledge about Words   38
Concepts about Words   39
The Role of Alphabet Knowledge   40
The Role of Writing   41
Production of Print   42
The Role of Books in the Classroom   46
The Role of Comprehension   49

Final Thoughts   50

Challenge Yourself   51

Suggested Sources for Additional Information   51
Organizations   51

CHAPTER 3

Organizing for Literacy   52

Exploring the Literate Environment   52

The Physical Structure: Classroom Design and Layout   53
Spatial Area Guidelines   53

Creating Interest Areas   57

Places to Learn and Explore   57
Classroom Library   57
Listening Center   58
Writing Center   58

Dramatic Play Area 59
Music Area 59
Block Area 59
Storytelling Area 60
Puzzles and Manipulatives 60
Science Area 60
Meeting Area 60

**Structural Support: Materials for
a Literate Environment** 60
Literacy Props 60
The Print-Rich Classroom 62
Environmental Print 63

The Structure of Time 66
Integrating Subject Matter 66
Planning Your Day 66
Routines: Guiding and Facilitating Instruction 66

**Structuring Connections: Linking Home
and School** 69
The Teacher Role 69
The Connecting Piece: Strengthening Parental Support 70

Final Thoughts 71

Challenge Yourself 71

Suggested Sources for Additional Information 71

PART 2 Linking Theory and Practice:
Recipes for Success

CHAPTER 4
Emerging Literacy: A Nurturing Classroom Context 72

Exploring the Emerging Phase of Literacy 72
Children's Emerging Literacy Behaviors 73
Emerging Writing Behaviors 75
Emerging Oral Language Behaviors 75

Emerging Literacy Resources 78
Factors Linked to Future Literacy Success 78
Play and Emerging Literacy 80
The Adult's Role in Emerging Literacy 82
Guidelines to Support Emerging Literacy 82

**CLASSROOM APPLICATIONS TO SUPPORT
EMERGING LITERACY** 85
Language Experience Approach (LEA) 85
Scaffolded Writing 88
Planning Play "Sets" with Children 89
Shared Reading 92
Journal Writing 94
Predictable Charts 96
Reading around the Room 98
Author! Author! 98
Pocket Chart Songs and Chants 99
Daily Message—Daily News 100
Using Nursery Rhymes 102
Surprise Box 104
Labeling the Classroom 105
Enjoying Environmental Print! 106
Name Games 107

Final Thoughts 109

Challenge Yourself 109

**Suggested Sources for
Additional Information** 109

CHAPTER 5
Early Literacy: A Supportive Classroom Context 110

**Children in the Early Primary Grades:
Primed for Developing the "Tools of
the Tribe"** 110
*The Adult's Role in Early Literacy: Strategies for Providing
Needed Support* 113
Children Who Experience Literacy Problems 117

**CLASSROOM APPLICATIONS TO SUPPORT
EARLY LITERACY** 121
Interactive Reading/Writing Activities 121
Word Wall 122
Guided Reading/Supported Reading 124
Read-Alouds 125
Book Making and Other Creative Writing 127
PowerPoint Presentations 130
Making Words 132
Challenge Words 134
Retellings 136
Story Mapping 137
Theme/Concept Charts 139
Interactive Journals 140
Process Writing 141
Self-Selected Reading 143
Onsets and Rimes/Word Families 144
Author's Chair and Author's Night 145

Final Thoughts 147

Challenge Yourself 148

Suggested Sources for
Additional Information 148

Children's Technology 148

CHAPTER 6

Moving toward Fluency: Developing Greater Self-Efficacy in Literacy 149

Almost There: Children on Their Way to Fluency 149

Fluent Readers 150

The Fluent Writer 152

Those Who Are Not "Getting It": Children with Learning Problems and Disabilities 152

The Role of the Teacher in Developing Learning Contexts That Promote Continued Skill and Concept Attainment 153

CLASSROOM APPLICATIONS TO MOVE CHILDREN TOWARD FLUENCY 157

Spelling Pattern Recognition Teams 157

Buddy Biographies 158

Language Detectives 160

Writer's Workshop with Peer Conferencing 162

Response Journals and Logs 166

KWHLH 169

Sort, Search, and Discover (SSD) 171

Graphic Organizers 173

Reader's Theater 176

Directed Reading/Thinking Activity (DRTA) 177

SQ3R 179

Literacy Circles 181

Final Thoughts 184

Challenge Yourself 185

Suggested Resources for
Additional Information 185

Books 185

Children's Technology 185

PART 3 Evaluating and Directing Learning: A Reflective Process

CHAPTER 7

Documenting Skills and Competencies 186

A Quality Assessment Package: What Does It Look Like? 187

Developmentally Appropriate Assessment and Evaluation 187

Principled Data Gathering 187

Assessing Language and Literacy Acquisition 188

Becoming a Kid-Watcher: Systematic Observation 188

Recording Inferences, Judgments, and Reflections: Rating Scales and Rubrics 191

Children's Art as an Observational Literacy Assessment Tool 192

Assessing Reading Accuracy and Comprehension 193

Assessing Spelling and Writing Acquisition Skills 197

Self-Appraisal by the Child 199

The Status of Standardized Testing 202

Final Thoughts 207

Challenge Yourself 207

Suggested Sources for
Additional Information 208

CHAPTER 8

Portfolios and Student-Led Conferencing: Celebrating the Stages of Development 209

Portfolios: Empowering the Learner 209

What Is a Portfolio? 209

Who Can Use a Portfolio? 210

What Are the Benefits of Portfolios? 210

The Portfolio Approach: Stepping in the Right Direction 211

How Do Portfolios Work? 211

What Goes into a Portfolio? 212

What Are the Various Types of Portfolios? 213

Working Portfolios 213

Showcase Portfolios 216

Electronic Portfolios 216

How Do You Get Started? 216

How Can You Introduce the Portfolio Concept? 217

How Can You Manage Storage and Time Issues? 217

Here We Go . . . Implementing Portfolios 218

Portfolio Evaluation: Reflecting and Responding 219

Teaching Self-Reflection 219

Teaching Goal Setting 221

**Sharing the Portfolio: A Celebration
of Learning 221**

Student-Led Conferencing 221
Preparing for the "Big Day" 225
Student Preparation 226
Role Playing with Older Students 226
Student-Led Conferencing Procedures and Goals 228
Scheduling Conferences 229
Conference Attendance 230
Three-Way Conferences 230
Take-Home Portfolio Conferences 230
Storyboards (Presentation Boards) 230
End of the Year Literacy Learning Celebrations 233

Parents and Portfolios 233

Final Thoughts 234
Wishing You Success 234
Challenge Yourself 234
**Suggested Sources for
Additional Information 235**
Organizations 235

APPENDIX
**Alphabetical Listing of the First Thousand
Words for Children's Reading 236**

References 239

Index 244

You just can't escape the imagination that happens when you are reading. You see the movie in your head . . . and it's your movie. Everyone's movie is unique. There is nothing like it.—Sarah

Even in our high-tech era, the special excitement and mystery of reading are alive and well. This is the enthusiasm for literacy that we want to inspire in the children with whom we work. We want them to be swept away by the story or fascinated by the facts. We want them to have the skills and knowledge to pursue their areas of interest as well as the ability to communicate their ideas to others in creative and engaging ways.

For these things to occur, children must possess the fundamentals of literacy. It is our responsibility as educators to lay the groundwork and help children develop the necessary tools to retain a lifelong zest for learning and literacy. How do we do this? Is there a specific recipe? What are the fundamental ingredients of literacy instruction?

Children arrive on their first day, bright-eyed and enthusiastic about learning to read in this sacred place called "school." Whether it is preschool or elementary school, they just "know" that this is where *it* is learned. They seem to know that *it* is the ultimate cultural accomplishment . . . *it* will make them powerful . . . *it* will unlock doors for them. We must make sure that they leave not only with that same enthusiasm for *it* but also with the tools for using and making sense of *it,* too!

In this book, we will discuss many avenues to follow while we help children in their journey toward reading. We will also discuss the other components of literacy (speaking, writing, listening, and viewing) that help children accomplish a variety of everyday language and communication tasks.

The key to teaching literacy is not only our attitude or philosophy about how children become literate, nor is it solely how we set up the classroom environment to support literacy, nor is it our knowledge of the literacy process and activities, nor is it primarily how we assess children. None of these alone determines our success in teaching and fostering literacy behaviors. Rather, it is the *dynamic contribution* of all of these factors that will help children create the links between the literacy processes of reading, writing, speaking, listening, and viewing.

Stop for a moment and consider all of the links it takes for a child to become a fluent lifelong user of literacy. You, the teacher, play a great role in forming these links. Before the child ever enters your classroom on the first day of school, you've already begun facilitating the linking process in the ways you've set up your classroom to support literacy. Each day, by what you say and do, you send messages to children about the links between language, literacy, and their lives. You help children make sense out of what puzzles them and encourage them to go beyond what they can currently do to continue in their literacy growth.

You also link literacy with their homes. You share your knowledge of literacy with families to help them support their children's progress. You offer suggestions for at-home activities, not only to help children practice literacy behaviors but also to help them see the link between what is done at home and in school.

This is an enormous undertaking for any teacher. It also places serious pressure on all of us in the teaching profession. In our work as classroom teachers, early childhood consultants, and teacher educators, we are well aware of the time it takes to put together and maintain a cohesive educational environment. The purpose of this book is to help classroom teachers, student teachers, and paraprofessionals better understand the process of literacy development within the framework of developmentally appropriate practice. Although we provide some theoretical background on literacy, the main focus of the book is on the practical application of the theory with real children in preschool through fifth-grade classrooms.

Coming from a child development perspective, we advocate a child-centered approach. We examine ways literacy affects the entire child. We are concerned with the social, emotional, cognitive, and physical aspects of literacy. We recognize the differences between individuals that stem from maturation and experience. We recognize that children come to school with a variety of experiences, from different family and cultural contexts. We recognize the role of play in literacy and advocate active learning experiences for children of all ages, with an emphasis on the social aspect of learning. Finally, we believe that children develop and learn best in environments in which they feel safe and secure.

This book has been designed to be informative and to the point. Theory and relevant research are presented in each chapter to support what we are advocating. These are followed by specific strategies for applying what this means for daily practice in the classroom.

In Part One, "Setting the Stage: Appropriate Practices, Processes, and Contexts," there are three chapters. Chapter 1, "Developing Literacy in the Young Child: Antecedents, Transactions, and Outcomes," explores what our knowledge of child development and developmentally appropriate practice means relative to literacy development. Chapter 2, "Literacy Links and Processes," discusses the dynamic process of literacy development and provides general suggestions for classroom implementation for key concepts in literacy learning. Chapter 3, "Organizing for Literacy," discusses the physical structuring of the classroom environment, important materials to consider, the structure of time, and links between home and school to support literacy development.

In Part Two "Linking Theory and Practice: Recipes for Success," we expand on the three phases of literacy: emerging, early, and fluent. The three chapters, "Emerging Literacy: A Nurturing Classroom Context" (Chapter 4), "Early Literacy: A Supportive Classroom Context" (Chapter 5), and "Moving toward Fluency: Developing Greater Self-Efficacy in Literacy" (Chapter 6) further explore theory and research relevant to that phase of development and provide numerous strategies to enhance children's literacy development. The strategies are presented first in a general form, followed by direct classroom examples of the strategies in action. The strategies, though presented within a specific chapter, can be easily adapted to fit into the other phases.

Finally, we explore a variety of ways to evaluate literacy development in Part Three, "Evaluating and Directing Learning: A Reflective Process." Chapters 7 and 8 explore methods of evaluating children's literacy development to document current progress, plan for future instruction, and set new goals. Chapter 7 explores the variety of avenues classroom teachers can use to evaluate their students' literacy progress. Chapter 8 focuses specifically on the use of portfolios and on conducting student-led conferencing to share authentic assessment with parents.

In this book, we have tried to include much of the latest information on literacy in an accessible form. We have included a variety of strategies, both cutting edge and tried and true. These strategies and activities can be used in concert with any curriculum and across numerous content areas.

New to This Edition

There has been an explosion in the general understanding of literacy learning since the publication of the first edition. While keeping on top of the latest relevant research, this edition also offers readers some timely information regarding "hot" topics such as "How do you help English language learners acquire literacy skills and concepts?" and "What is the role for developmentally appropriate practice in today's educational environments for literacy?" In addition to some new activities, we've added photos to help illustrate some key points and activities along with more information on the use of technology. We are excited about the changes and hope that you find them informative and, most importantly, useful.

In the end, our goal for children is that they become healthy, happy, productive, well-adjusted members of society. One of the best ways we can help ensure their success is to help them become more fluent in the literacy process and develop lifelong literacy behaviors. We all know how much educators can make a difference when we work with children and their families toward this goal. We wish you many successes as you continue on your path of literacy education.

Acknowledgments

Numerous individuals and schools helped us create this book. We owe them our appreciation.

First, we'd like to thank specifically the staff and students at the following schools: Hugger Elementary, Rochester, MI; Sheridans Elementary School, Yokosuka, Japan; DoDDs Elementary Schools, Yokota, Japan; Gundry Elementary, Flint, MI; Loon Lake Elementary, Walled Lake, MI; International School, Manila, Philippines; Central Elementary, Petosky, MI; Michigan State Child Development Laboratories, East Lansing, MI; Allen Street School, Lansing, MI; Hampton Elementary, Rochester Hills, MI; Kaiser Elementary, Houston, TX; Village Community Preschool, Pinckney Schools, Pinckney, MI; and Char-Em Intermediate School District, Charlevoix, MI. Thanks are also in order to Dr. Linda Ayres, Walled Lake, MI; Bill Laetner, *Detroit Free Press*; Julie Carpenter, kindergarten teacher, Grand River Elementary School, Lansing, MI; Nancy Navarro, director of early childhood education, Port Huron Schools, Port Huron, MI; Dr. Patricia Kostell, educational consultant, South Carolina; Erin Groom, photographer, Instructional Media Center, Michigan State University; Patricia Brockway, preschool teacher, Pinckney, MI; and Stephanie Parenthesis, College of Human Ecology Librarian, Michigan State University.

Second, our thanks to Aurora Martinez and the Allyn and Bacon staff, and to Karla Walsh and the team at Omegatype Typography. We also wish to thank the reviewers for this edition: Vi Alexander, Stephen F. Austin State University; Deborah Allen, Kean University; Verlinda Angell, Southern Utah University; and Nancy Hansen-Krening, University of Washington.

Of course, we owe an unending debt of gratitude to our families who served in numerous and quite important capacities throughout the birth and the revisions of this text. Only you know what we put you through! Gracias!

Finally, we'd like to thank the parents, teachers, and children we have worked with over the years, who have helped us to shape and refine our literacy understanding.

1

Developing Literacy in the Young Child
Antecedents, Transactions, and Outcomes

Alexander is not yet three years old. As he rides home from his child care setting on the familiar route taken every day, his mother entertains him: "Look for one of your signs, Alexander. See if you can see McDonald's."

As they pass signs that he recognizes, he calls them out: "Mobil . . . with a red O!" "McDonald's!" "Burger King!" "Kmart!" "Applebee's!" "Target!" "Home Depot!" "Taco Bell!"

"You can read!" encourages his mother. "Look at how many signs you can read."

Already, Alexander is coming to differentiate between the many signs and symbols in his world and to communicate that knowledge to others. He enjoys games such as finding familiar signs, colors, and objects, and he likes being read to. He has learned how to use the family's VCR to watch his favorite videos, and he needs only a little assistance at the child care center's computer to operate a software program that he particularly likes. He is growing in his ability to remember and repeat the songs, nursery rhymes, and fingerplays shared with him by the adults who care for him, and he also imitates those adults by "reading" picture books to his Elmo doll. When Alexander thinks about creating or representing something, he does so with blocks, clay, wire, and a variety of other materials. More frequently, he is asking for markers and paper; he is not at all bothered that his scribbles cannot be interpreted by others. His interest in that will come later, as he moves through the emerging and early stages of literacy, gaining more sophisticated concepts of print on his way to fluency and a literate future.

Becoming **literate** today is a more complex task than it used to be. Rather than just learning how to read, it means that Alexander and other children must eventually develop reading and writing skills that are sophisticated enough for competency in the workplace. They will need oral skills to articulate effectively to others and visual skills to draw meaning from the illustrations they see. Their literacy will have to extend to technology, the ability to read and understand scientific literature, and the ability to comprehend other cultures. Tompkins (2001) draws all of these needed competencies together by defining literacy as a *tool*, a way to come to learn about the world and a means to participate more fully in society.

According to Whitehurst and Lonigan (2001:12–13), emergent and conventional literacy abilities are dependent on two very essential and interdependent information systems:

1. **Outside in.** These are sources outside the printed word that directly support children's understanding of the meaning of print. They include vocabulary, phonological-processing skills, conceptual knowledge, story schemas, and semantic sense within contexts.

2. **Inside out.** These are sources within the printed word that support the ability to translate print into sounds or sounds into print. Included are phonemic awareness, letter knowledge, links between letters and sounds, decoding strategies, punctuation and sentence grammar, and memory to organize elements into correct sequences.

As can be seen in Figure 1.1, there are periods in children's developing literacy when one of these systems may become more dominant. For example, building phonological awareness and an adequate store of vocabulary in the preschool years during the emerging phase of literacy prepares the child for the decoding tasks that will dominate the early phase. Strongly developed decoding abilities and

Figure 1.1 Emergent literacy abilities, emerging to fluent phases; relation to outside-in and inside-out information systems.

Source: Adapted from Whitehurst and Lonigan (2001).

automaticity during the early phase then allow the child to mentally concentrate in the final stage of literacy on outside-in components such as making sense of what is being read.

Although this book is directed primarily toward describing the developing literacy of young children in general and providing effective strategies to support and evaluate it, we believe that this process is dynamic and highly individual for each child. Three major factors must be considered in helping each child build a qualitatively useful repertoire of literacy skills in any formal learning context. The first factor takes into consideration all of the various **antecedents** that a child brings into the classroom, including chronological age differences, gender differences, cognitive organization, primary language, and sociocultural differences. The second factor consists of all the **transactions** related to literacy skill building that go on both inside and outside the classroom during the child's preprimary and elementary years. These are influenced by how the philosophical understandings of administrators and teachers are played out practically in the classroom. A child's perception of how meaningful and useful classroom experiences and activities are, and how comfortable he or she feels in the constructed learning community, will be of utmost importance. Also essential will be continued parental involvement related to literacy in both the home and school contexts. **Outcomes** are the third factor that must be considered. Central here is how well a child's continuous progress is monitored and shared effectively with others who can use the information to address the child's developmental needs. The extent to which inputs and desired outputs are matched carefully will play a critical role in the child's success.

In this chapter, you will learn more about these three major components that underscore ongoing literacy development. Information we have gained from research conducted in the last couple of decades about human development as well as best practices in the preprimary and primary classroom will be central to our discussion.

As you read, think about these questions:

- In what general ways do young children differ from one another? How do these differences affect their literacy acquisition?
- What do you believe constitutes an appropriate and effective learning context to support children's emerging literacy? What would you *expect* to see?
- How can parents be drawn more fully into the process after a child has entered the formal learning setting?
- How should we be documenting children's literacy progress? How should we use the data that are collected?

These questions and related issues will be addressed in the pages that follow. The chapter has been divided into three parts looking at the many antecedents, transactions, and outcomes that work in synergy over time to form a child's long-range literacy capability.

Antecedents in Developing Literacy

Right from birth, children are language users as they move from listening and speaking to subsequent literacy skills in reading and writing. These language processes always develop in a cyclical, interdependent manner and in concert with oral language. Each informs and supports the other as children experience conversation with others, have contact with books, see a variety of print in their everyday world, and attempt to recreate print for their own purposes (Strickland & Morrow, 2000).

Rather than discontinuous leaps, emerging literacy simply keeps emerging as children imitate adults using literacy skills for purposeful, goal-directed activity. It is viewed as a "complex sociopsycholinguistic activity," where children learn in the home and the community as well as in the formal classroom. Children do not suddenly come to a "readiness point" at which they are ready to begin reading and writing; rather, they slowly and gradually add to the experiences they bring with them to school. These accumulated sets of experiences then serve as a springboard from which children dive into formal literacy instruction (Strickland & Morrow, 1989a:v–2).

Clearly, in the early years, movement from one stage of emerging literacy to the next may be age-related but somewhat variable for each child. This is because children vary significantly with respect to numerous factors such as age, gender, primary language, culture, brain organization, and experience. Each of these has an impact on their abilities and capabilities for dealing effectively with formal literacy tasks. At no other time in the school experience will there be so many subtle and explicit differences as in a specific cohort group of preprimary or primary children. Let's take a closer look at some of the differences you may see in the children in your classroom.

Chronological Age Differences

Because of a number of factors, the chronological age of children in any particular grade can range from less than a month to more than two years' difference. Parents of children with summer or fall birth dates, particularly when they are boys, may be reluctant to send them to school. Instead, the parents may hold them out and keep them in a less demanding preprimary setting until the next school year. Others who may not be able to afford child care or a preschool for another year may send their child to kindergarten, even though he will be much younger than his peers. No matter what state legislatures do to minimize these differences by bringing the entrance cut-offs closer to fall entry dates, there will continue to be children entering school who are significantly older or younger than their grade-level peers. As children progress through the primary grades, these differences may be increased when children are retained or placed in multiage settings.

There are other differences in children that may have a greater impact on their ability to function well in a formal learning setting than does chronological age, but they are often age-related if not age-dependent. These include visual and auditory memory, cognitive reasoning, episodic and semantic memory, ability to note detail or likenesses and differences, eye–hand coordination, and fine motor abilities. An example of such differences (see Figures 1.2 and 1.3) can be seen in the drawings made by two boys sitting next to one another in a first-grade classroom. They had just come back from an assembly where Ronald McDonald had presented a magic show, and their abilities to

reconstruct what they had seen seemed to be connected at least in part to the year's difference in their ages (6 years, 9 months, vs. 7 years, 10 months). The variations in detail that each child depicted from short-term memory are significant. So is the correlation among the sophistication of their drawings, relative hand strength and steadiness in producing the figures and letters, and their ability to write conventionally.

When viewing the work of these two children, it's important to keep in mind the age differences. Expecting the same output simply because they are both first graders can lead to a classification in the younger child of pseudo-slowness. These early labels often follow children through their school careers. The younger the child in a preprimary or early primary classroom, the greater the chance he or she may be classified as "low" or "slow." The opposite is also true; that is, older children with more advanced skills can be falsely identified as gifted or talented, a reputation that can inappropriately *heighten* expectations for a child. When, in the long run, such children cannot live up to those expectations, they may be seen as lazy, unmotivated, or not living up to their potential.

Gender Differences

When gender differences are added to the picture, it becomes even more complex. Young males, on average, can be cognitively anywhere from 6 to 18 months behind their female counterparts at the same age, according to brain-growth periodization studies (Epstein, 1978; Thatcher, Walker, & Guidice, 1987). Boys have been shown to be at

Figure 1.2   Joel, 6 years, 9 months, grade 1: "I went to assembly to see Ronald McDonald."

Figure 1.3   Matthew, 7 years, 10 months, grade 1: "I went to see Ronald McDonald today. I liked when he did magic."

greater risk for language disorders and are three to five times more likely to have reading and spelling difficulties, oral language problems, attention–concentration deficiencies, directional confusion, memory sequencing problems, and deficiency in ability to retrieve linguistic representations. Boys are also more often delayed with respect to ocular development and have somewhat more trouble with the rapid eye fixations, release, and convergence that are necessary to track abstract figures on a printed page without losing their place (Soderman et al., 1995).

In the early years, the tendency toward nonsymmetrical development in the hemispheres is found more often in males, leading to both special abilities and special areas of difficulty—learning disorders, hormonal effects, handedness, delayed maturation, allergies, and various developmental diseases. There are many famous examples of males who were notably unsuccessful in their early schooling because of slowly developing language and literacy skills but who were particularly facile with respect to a powerful visual imagination. This is a combination that, more often than not, comes at a heavy cost in the school environment, as was demonstrated all too well by Michael Faraday, Hans Christian Andersen, Albert Einstein, Thomas Edison, Auguste Rodin, Leonardo da Vinci, Winston Churchill, and George Patton, among many others (West, 1997).

It is important to point out here that most young males experiencing these differences in brain wiring do *not* eventually become famous. Rather, they serve to overpopulate our K–12 special education classrooms for the emotionally impaired and learning disabled at a 7:3 ratio to females. And, although for most children the lags may

be lessened significantly by second or third grade, they may already have had some fairly negative experiences in primary classrooms where expectations or instructional strategies are inappropriate. Unfortunately, by the time they are developmentally and constitutionally ready for age-related literacy experiences, they often are visibly turned off to learning—and their teachers may be equally turned off with them.

Variations in Brain Organization

Gavin, a third grader, is known as a poor reader. He reads words in a simple story—when he can decode them—as if he were reading words from a shopping list. He does this so slowly that his comprehension is severely affected. When asked to do a reading task or work with an assigned tutor, he balks. Adults, trying to help him, have had him tested for visual acuity, intelligence, motivation, and attention deficit disorder. None of these appear to be a problem. Lately, it has been suggested that he just isn't trying hard enough.

Unlike Gavin, many young children learn to read easily and naturally—a few before they even enter the formal classroom. These children easily develop a sight vocabulary and seem to slide smoothly into reading increasingly sophisticated material. They come to understand that there is a distinct message in the print that is before them, that it is "preserved there in a verbally invariable way—that the story as read today will be verbally identical with the story as read yesterday" (Holdaway, 1979:56). By watching other children and adults and then engaging in self-regulated, self-correcting, and self-sustaining reading-like behaviors, they become acquainted with a variety of factors necessary for early reading and writing. Finally, with experience, they come to understand that print is a system of visual symbols organized by complex conventions of directionality, punctuation, and letter–sound associations, and that these cues are related to even wider systems of language cues that can be mastered (Holdaway, 1979:56).

Other children, such as Gavin, struggle. They require extra support and eventually may be labeled as "learners with special needs" (Waring, 1995). Some never completely master reading and writing skills, but grow to adulthood with only a rudimentary knowledge of how to use these important processes. Although all children who struggle cannot be lumped into a single category, it has been estimated that as many as 15 percent of children in the United States have some type of reading disability that requires remedial and clinical intervention; in about 3 percent, the condition is severe (McCormick, 2003).

As we try to sort out some of the reasons for these differences in young children, at least part of the explanation can be found in recent brain research. Reading requires the smooth, speedy firing of neurons from one part of the brain (the primary visual cortex), where individual letters are identified (e.g., *d-o-g*), to another (the angural gyrus), where the letters are interpreted phonologically (e.g., /d/ /ô/ /g/), to still another area (the superior temporal gyrus), where the word is given meaning, depending on how it is used in a sentence (see Figure 1.4). All of this takes place in normal readers in less than 40 milliseconds. Absolutely mind-boggling, isn't it?

For some children, this amazing feat, which is so normal in others, is *indeed* mind-boggling. These children, who have great difficulty in reading that cannot be explained by a lack of intelligence or other specific causes, have been termed *dyslexic* (McCormick, 2003). Some may take twelve times as long as average children to decode a word; still others struggle and can't decipher the word at all, no matter how long they take. Think of something that would be twelve times as hard for you as for anyone else—or simply impossible. How motivated would you be to continue doing it? Would it be something you would *prefer* to do in your leisure time? What if this were something you were forced to struggle with every day? When others could see how deficient you were, how would it affect your self-esteem?

The codirectors of the Yale Center for Learning and Attention at Yale University, Dr. Sally Shaywitz and her husband, Bennett Shaywitz, have been interested in this phenomenon called dyslexia for years. Now, with the aid of functional magnetic resonance imaging (fMRI), they have identified a specific neural pathway in the brain that good readers use for reading. Poor readers, it seems, have a glitch in the wiring. They have marked difficulty in processing what they see and, apparently, don't even use the

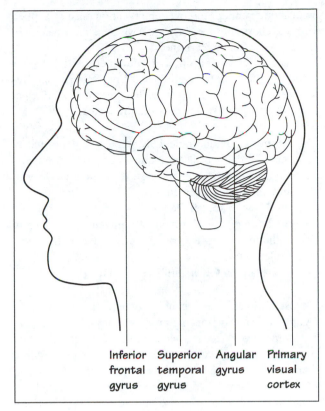

Figure 1.4   From functional magnetic resonance imaging, we have identified the differences between dyslexia and normal pathways followed during a reading task.

Source: Adapted from Kolata (1998) reporting on the work of Dr. Sally Shaywitz and Dr. Bennett Shaywitz.

same neural pathway as other children. When they are given a reading task, the inferior frontal gyrus becomes overstimulated, and there is a complementary *understimulation* in crucial portions in the center and back of the brain (note again the primary visual cortex, superior temporal gyrus, and angural gyrus in Figure 1.4). This study is the first to demonstrate the neurological flaw that affects literally all the neurobiological components for reading. In our earlier example, *dog,* we can easily break the word down into three distinct sounds (/d/ /ô/ /g/) if asked to do so. As we read the word, however, we don't normally do that. We simply read it as one sound—*dog*—and our brain does the rest, flashing what is needed linearly, easily, and quickly (Kolata, 1998; Shaywitz, 2003).

Despite this new evidence, dyslexia remains a complex phenomenon. We must be careful about oversimplifying the diagnosis or assigning a prescribed intervention for any particular child. The bottom line, of course, is that the difficulty a child is experiencing must be modified as much as possible. Everything and anything that is at our disposal for this task should be considered, keeping in mind that what works in one case may not be effective with another child. Moreover, intervention must be applied over the course of time, because developmental changes in a child will affect the prognosis.

The chief of the child development and behavior branch of the National Institutes of Child and Human Development, G. Reid Lyon, notes that there are four distinct stages in the process whereby children learn to read:

1. Beginning phonological awareness and an understanding that words are made up of different sounds
2. An initial knowledge of linguistics (sound to letters) and phonics (letter to sounds), associating those sounds with specific letters
3. Becoming increasingly able to match letters quickly with the appropriate sound—that is, becoming a *fast* reader
4. Centering on the *meaning* of words

Breakdowns can occur anywhere in this process. Lyon advocates identifying problems early, because there are "sensitive periods when children can learn to read more easily, just like there are windows when children learn foreign language easier." His timetable—*by the end of the second grade*—fits our definition of when cautious concern should shift to more intense intervention. Early warning signs that a child may have a learning disability and need professional diagnosis include the following (Wingert & Kantrowitz, 1997:58–60):

Preschool/Kindergarten
- Starts talking later than other children
- Has pronunciation problems
- Has slow vocabulary growth
- Is often unable to find the right word
- Has trouble learning numbers, the alphabet, days of the week
- Has difficulty rhyming words
- Is extremely restless and distractible
- Has trouble interacting with peers
- Displays a poor ability to follow directions or routines
- Avoids puzzles, drawing, and cutting

Kindergarten through Fourth Grade
- Has a slow recall of facts
- Makes consistent reading and spelling errors, including letter reversals (*b/d*), inversions (*m/w*), transpositions (*felt, left*), and substitutions (*house/home*)
- Is slow to learn the connection between letters and sounds
- Transposes number sequences and confuses arithmetic signs (+, −, ×, /, =)
- Is slow to learn new skills
- Relies heavily on memorization
- Is impulsive and lacks basic planning skills
- Has difficulty following directions or routines

- Has an unstable pencil grip
- Has trouble learning about time

Very few children fall into the categories discussed in this section. However, with children who move into the primary years demonstrating literacy progression that is noticeably different than that of other children, teachers will want to alert other professionals to interact with these children as early as possible. These are children who, despite our best attempts to present skill and concept building in an engaging way for them, are making little visible progress—even in emerging literacy.

Because children with dyslexia and other learning disabilities differ from one another as much as children without these conditions, each child requires his or her own unique approach to support literacy learning. Sometimes additional support must come in terms of greater concentration on activities related to the *visual* aspects of literacy; in other cases, an *auditory* approach or a combination of both may produce better results for a child. This is where the circle of support we provide must be widened to include our colleagues with expertise in disabilities.

Supporting Children Who Are English Language Learners

Immediately upon entering the old brick building that houses the North School, one encounters evidence that this is a school community that celebrates the linguistic and cultural diversity of its students. A graph of native languages spoken by each grade level covers one wall. Large photographs of students from a variety of ethnic backgrounds cover another. Handwritten greetings in many languages welcome visitors and signal the entrance to the Learning Center, which houses the English as a Second Language (ESL) program. The noise level in the Learning Center is high. Leah, the ESL teacher, smiles and shakes her head, "You know, sometimes my students come into the Learning Center, and they talk and talk and talk, and I try to calm them down, and they say, "But you don't understand. I don't talk all day." (Coppola, 2003:182)

Almost every classroom in the United States now has at least one or more children whose first language is not English. If you teach in a state such as California, Arizona, and Florida, you may have a majority of children in your classroom who have little English proficiency when they enter. As the United States becomes increasingly diverse and multilingual, greater numbers of teachers are expected to meet the needs of children whose primary language is not the same as that used in the monolingual classroom. Yet, when they are asked, fewer than 20 percent of these teachers say they feel adequately prepared to do so (National Center for Educational Statistics, 1999).

Because of tight educational budgets and the disappearance of bilingual programs, teachers who have had

Respecting diversity in the monolingual classroom.

little experience in teaching English language learners are scrambling to find resources to help these children build the language skills they need. Dilemmas frequently described include the likelihood that the teacher has no knowledge whatsoever of the child's primary language and only limited knowledge of language acquisition in general. Teachers talk of increased stress when trying to consider the language-learning needs of some of the children in addition to the content of classroom teaching and feel deficient in terms of actual techniques to help children assimilate successfully and quickly. Additional challenges noted involve communicating with the children's parents, assessing how much an English learner really understands about what is being taught, making classroom activities meaningful for such a child, and modifying oral input sufficiently so that an English learner can understand at least *some* of what is being said.

In meeting these real challenges, effective teachers scaffold their way initially by learning as much as possible about the child's linguistic, cultural, and educational background. What is the child's full name and how is it written in his or her home language? What name does the child prefer for classroom use? Who are the persons who live with the child at home, and what are their names? Which languages are preferred for oral communication at home? In what language are there written materials in the house? Where did the child attend school previously, and have there been any breaks in education due to travel or health? Are there any special dietary, clothing, or religious requirements that must be observed? These teachers make the effort to learn at least a few words in the child's language ("Good morning," "Good job," "See you tomorrow"). They may label areas of the classroom in the child's language or incorporate names of the child's family members into the stories they tell (Smyth, 2003).

To encourage the class's respect for various languages, samples of written script in other languages can be displayed in the classroom, and copies of familiar books (such as *Rainbow Fish*) that have been written in other languages can be placed in the reading corner. Whenever possible, books should be purchased that are written in English, but with a facing page in the child's primary language. These books are valuable additions for both English learners and English-proficient children.

Instructional scaffolding techniques include using a child's native language when possible for clarification of vocabulary, directions, or key concepts; providing "think-alouds" and modeling when explaining an upcoming activity; providing learning strategy objectives; tapping the child's prior knowledge; using visuals and manipulatives; teaching key vocabulary; and adjusting your speech (e.g., facing the child, pausing more frequently, paraphrasing, using shorter sentences, increasing waiting time for children to answer, and focusing on the child's meaning rather than on grammar) (Laturnau, 2003).

Along with the use of more formal strategies to build a foundation in the English language, English-speaking buddies can be paired with English learners to help them in class, in the lunchroom, and on the playground. These dyads should be changed often enough to avoid overloading one child and also to foster rapport-building among all English learners and English-speaking children in the classroom.

Above all, we need to avoid the trap of having low expectations for these children, keeping in mind that, like all children, English learners always know a great deal more than they are able to share in the classroom. The best way to motivate their literacy learning is to have them read or write about what they have some knowledge of and interest in. The teacher's job is to link that knowledge and interest to the school curriculum in ways to enhance needed skills and concepts.

Research indicates that instead of simply allowing language acquisition to evolve naturally for the child or teaching systematic word recognition, comprehensive

English-speaking and English-learning buddies.

classroom instruction should incorporate both informal and formal language learning opportunities (Dutro & Moran, 2003). Since true learning is interactive, learning English efficiently requires conversation, creative and collaborative experiences, discussion, games, and interaction between teacher and child and child and peers. In schools where teachers are required to strictly follow adopted reading programs without any deviation and using only "approved" materials, the task of supporting an English-learning child will be made more difficult.

Sociocultural Influences

Mr. Kantrall teaches a "normal" class of 27 fourth graders in a school that is considered high risk. Fourteen of the children have already seen their parents separate, divorce, or remarry. Three have had chronically unemployed parents, and Mr. Kantrall knows of at least two families who have had visits from protective services. He hears Cierra describing last night's scene at 3:00 A.M. when her "Dad came home drunk and started messin' with my mom and breaking everything in the house." In awe, he notes that despite all that, she got herself to school on time and is glad to be there. Six of the children use nonstandard dialects of English consistently, and one of them is struggling with English as a second language. One child included in the class, who has been given the label "neurologically handicapped," is said to have had a prenatal history of heavy drug use by his mother. If things go as they have for the past several years, the makeup of Mr. Kantrall's class will not be the same at the end of the year. Because of the high mobility that characterizes high-risk families and communities such as his, he will lose at least 40 percent of the children who started in September and will gain others funneling in from other schools throughout the school year.

By the time young children enter school, any number of sociocultural influences have already begun to positively or negatively shape their approach to other people and to their world. These reflect the variety of family and community contexts from which children come, and it is clear that positive precursors to literacy are not evenly distributed across all children. Sociocultural influences can be highly positive when the child has had the benefits that come from a stable and loving family and an enriched bank of experiences prior to and after school entrance. There is no doubt whatsoever that single-parent families can provide these supports for their children just as well as intact families if there are not financial difficulties and if the children continue to have access to both parents and extended family members. The bottom line is that whether children are read to, have access to books, see literacy models, and have opportunities to talk with adults and other children in the preschool years predicts how well they will do later in school-based literacy tasks.

Conversely, multiple factors such as financial stress, violence, substance abuse in caregivers, mobility of parents, multiple and troublesome family transitions, sexual and physical abuse, and the greediness of the workplace in consuming parents' time are increasing for growing numbers of young children and can be found today at every socioeconomic level. When children are struggling to cope with these negative antecedents to learning, they often don't have enough energy left over to attend adequately to what's going on in the classroom. Teachers who succeed in moving all children in their classroom forward are those who are sensitive to these individual differences in children but continue to value the language and literacy potential in every child. They approach each new group of children and new school year by constructing a learning environment that is always a come-as-you-are party, a place designed to accept children where they are but with the full intention of having them grow as much as possible during the next school year.

APPLICATIONS FOR RESPONDING TO ANTECEDENT VARIATIONS IN CHILDREN

1. Recognize that children differ chronologically and also with respect to brain organization, gender, language, and sociocultural experiences. Respect every child's ability to become literate.

2. Find some mechanism to become familiar with what goes on in a child's world outside the classroom. This could be a home visit or having a parent complete an ecomap (see Figure 1.5) at your first meeting early in the school year. This provides an opportunity for the parent to share information with the teacher about who the significant other people are in the child's life. It promotes discussion about activities in which the child is involved and most interested. Also important are the facts presented as the parent constructs a time line of critical events in the child's life.

3. Design a classroom climate and learning community that will boost children's motivation to learn and move their performance in a positive direction.

4. Match the children's individual needs as closely as possible with the strategies provided in Part Two of this book to support skill and concept building. Develop learning activities that take into consideration children's cultural, experiential, primary-language, cognitive, chronological age, and gender differences.

5. Use the evaluation strategies suggested in Chapters 7 and 8 of this book to determine children's baseline literacy strengths and weaknesses. Evaluate each child's progress against his or her own rate of growth rather than against that of other children in your classroom.

6. When children need diagnosis or extra support that is outside your scope of expertise, consult with other professionals about a speedy referral, and then follow up to see that it is done in a timely manner.

Transactions: Theoretical Transformations in the Home and School Contexts

Melanie, a third-year teacher in a large school district, is attending an inservice for all primary teachers. Although the topic is "A Developmentally Appropriate Approach to Literacy," the presenter initially challenges the participants to talk with one another about theoretical perspectives they hold related to the transmission of literacy knowledge: "Share with each other the conditions under which you believe children best *become literate."*

Realizing she's never really thought about it before, Melanie turns to the colleague next to her, laughs nervously, and says, "Whoa, this is a big order. Feel free to go first."

Why bother to think about theoretical perspectives related to the transformation of knowledge? What does this have to do with the everyday exchanges and transactions that underlie the experiences we structure for children who are building literacy knowledge? How do our theoretical perspectives influence our decision making relative to how we define learning, our role in the classroom, teaching strategies we employ or reject, materials we purchase, interactions we encourage or discourage, and the way we structure and measure outcomes?

In this next section, we offer a theoretical perspective that we think explains how literacy is transformed most effectively in the preprimary and elementary classroom. We will also take a look at the practices we believe best support a literate environment for learners and teachers and at how parents can be made stronger partners in the overall literacy venture.

A Theoretical Perspective for Developing Literacy

A theoretical perspective is useful because it serves as a tool for making sense of a particular phenomenon and then as a guide for decision making. It helps us to articulate to

Critical Events

9/10/94	Birth, 3 weeks premature (4 lb., 10 oz.; Casper, Wyoming)
8/27/96	Birth of sister Caetlyn
4/97	Severe chicken pox (convulsions/hospitalization)
7/97	Parents separate and divorce
8/97	Attends Kinder-Care Mother employed
1/98	Moves to Dansville, MI, with mother and sister to live with maternal grandparents Attends Tiny Tots Child Care Mother employed
3/98	Chronic ear infection (hospitalized/tonsils out)
5/98	Moves to apartment with mother and sister (Lansing, MI) Attends family day care over summer and next year
9/98	Begins kindergarten (Lansing, MI, schools)
2/99	Kindergarten teacher begins pregnancy leave Substitute teacher
6/00	Mother remarries
8/00	Family moves to Southfield, MI
9/00	Attends 1st grade to March of 3rd grade, Southfield, MI
3/03	Mother and stepfather separate and divorce (moves with mother and sister back to Dansville to maternal grandparents' home)
4/03	Finishes third grade in Dansville
6/03	Attends summer school in Dansville
9/03	Begins grade 4 in Dansville
1/04	Assigned to L.D. category

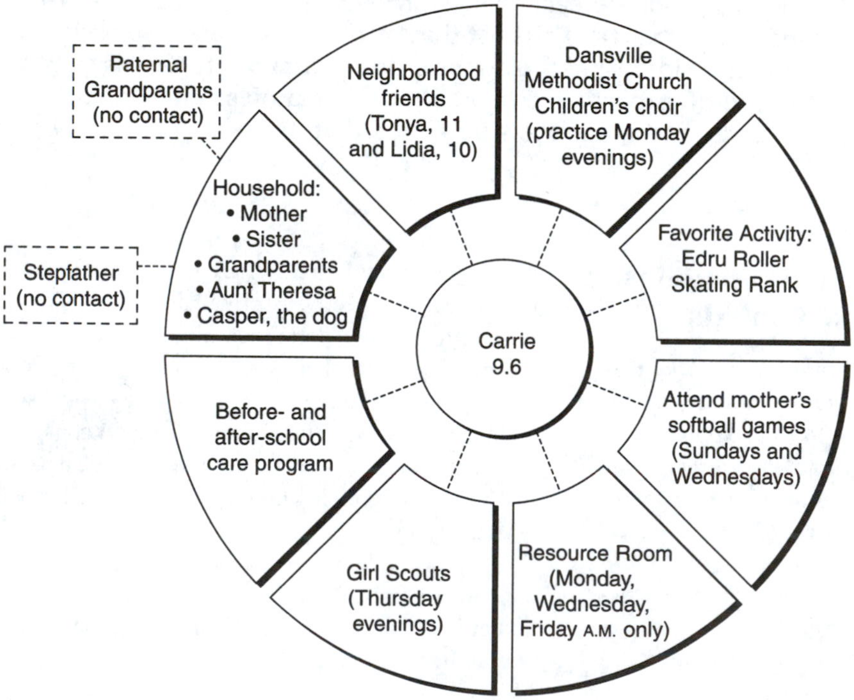

Figure 1.5   Ecomap of Carrie, 9 years old, fourth-grader.

others what we believe and provides an explanation for connecting cause and effect. With respect to literacy transformation in children, it should serve as an explanation for what we elect to do or *not* do on a day-to-day basis in our classrooms as we work with children and parents toward desired outcomes. A well-developed theory base helps us develop a congruent set of principles and practices to guide our teaching.

One of the best explanations of how children construct knowledge, including all of their understandings about literacy, is that of Lev Vygotsky, a Russian psychologist. In the 1920s and 1930s, he wrote about the connections he saw between children's relationships and their psychological and cognitive development. Called **social-constructivist** theory (or, sometimes, sociocultural collectivist theory), Vygotsky's perspective was that individuals pay attention to what goes on around them and are motivated to learn what they feel they need in order to function well in their world. Through guidance from others and practice, they then incorporate these skills into their own behavioral repertoires. In short, the social context is all important in human intellectual growth.

Although Vygotsky was a contemporary of Piaget, the two differed theoretically. Both were constructivists. However, Piaget, who was a **developmental constructivist,** saw *development leading learning,* with cognition influenced by both maturation and experience as children pass through a series of stages. Conversely, Vygotsky saw *learning leading development.* Both differed from the **behaviorists,** who saw learning and development as virtually one and the same—simply the accumulation of more and more information (Brewer, 2001).

Vygotsky's theory is particularly applicable to the transformation of knowledge related to literacy because he saw a child's capacity to use language to regulate thought and action as central to his theory. Berk and Winsler (1995:13) write:

> Because Vygotsky regarded language as a critical bridge between the sociocultural world and individual mental functioning, he viewed the acquisition of language as the most significant milestone in children's cognitive development. . . . the theory is unique in highlighting not only the role of important people in the child's life but the importance of schooling in leading development forward.

Obviously, there isn't room here to present a detailed description of Vygotsky's views on development or all of his ideas about the importance of shared language. For a more in-depth account, we refer the reader to Berk and Winsler's text (see the "Suggested Sources" at the end of this chapter). However, there are several aspects of the theory that we believe are necessary to share with you here.

ZONE OF PROXIMAL DEVELOPMENT (ZPD)   Vygotsky believed in a learning continuum (see Figure 1.6) that was characterized by the distance between (1) a child's ability to solve a problem independently and (2) the child's "maximally assisted" problem-solving ability under adult guidance or in collaboration with more capable peers (Vygotsky, 1978, 1986). He called this area the zone of proximal development, or ZPD. For example, 6-year-old Tina is currently at an independent level with respect to reading and writing a number of simple three- and four-

letter words, including the word *will.* However, when her teacher notes her inability to sound out the word *fill,* he knows she is not yet using the concept of word families or onset and rime (described in Chapter 5) to decode unfamiliar words that share the same vowel and ending letters and also rhyme. Understanding that this knowledge will help Tina unlock a major decoding strategy and significantly increase the number of words she can read, her teacher takes the time to explain and play the Word Family Game with Tina. On a small white board nearby, he prints the word *will* and asks Tina if she knows the word. When she responds positively, he wipes away the onset—*w*—and replaces it with a few other letters, first *b,* then *k.* Tina lights up with her newly gained skill and calls out the transformed words. Her teacher then gives Tina a chance to take over. He asks her if she can think of some other letters that could produce still another new word. She thinks for a moment and suggests, tentatively, "*t?*"

"You bet," he says, erasing *k* and substituting *t.* Confirmed and encouraged, Tina offers *m, J, f,* and *h.* "I think you have it," says her teacher. "These words are all in the *ill* word family, aren't they? They all rhyme and have exactly the same ending. That's why we say they're a family. Let's go back to what we were doing."

They return to the text and, when asked to decode the word *fill,* Tina remarks, "That's easy! It says *fill.*" Later that day, her teacher approaches with the white board, returns to the concept, and asks Tina if *she* can think of any other word families. He wants to see whether she is able to go further with the concept or needs more practice before moving forward.

Vygotsky believed that it was important not to work *outside* of the child's ZPD—what a child can do independently and with the help of a more experienced peer or adult. However, he was also certain that it was important not to have children spending time on what they had already mastered. Adults, he believed, needed to be constantly nudging children to move along on the developmental pathway toward more complex learning.

SCAFFOLDING   This term was not invented by Vygotsky but by Wood and Middleton (1975). It consists of getting children involved in joint problem solving with another peer or an adult. As the two work together toward a common goal (e.g., having Tina understand about word families), the child stretches to understand the new information and, at the same time, is helped by the teacher pointing out the connection between what the child already understands and the new skill or concept.

The concepts of scaffolding and ZPD are highly interdependent, as was illustrated in our previous example. Tina's teacher introduced her to the concept of word families and coached her along toward understanding and application. He was careful to start at a point where Tina could function independently and then build with her a more sophisticated concept that could be applied in other

Scaffolded Assistance in Emerging Literacy: The Teacher's Role

1. Determine child's current ability relative to a particular skill to be learned or expanded on.
2. Help child select an appropriate activity or experience that will improve the skill.
3. Modify the difficulty of the task to an appropriate level of challenge by adjusting the activity downward or upward.
4. Structure a joint problem-solving experience with the child by demonstrating the steps needed to perform the activity, allowing the child to control the activity as much as possible.
5. Decrease the level of adult or knowledgeable peer assistance as the child demonstrates capable performance, allowing the child to take the lead when indicated. Provide adequate opportunity for practice.
6. Follow up to determine whether the skill has been truly mastered.
7. Include the child in setting a new target for moving forward to an increased skill or concept level.

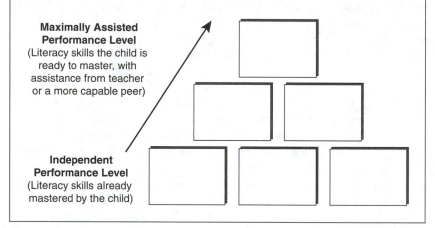

Maximally Assisted Performance Level (Literacy skills the child is ready to master, with assistance from teacher or a more capable peer)

Independent Performance Level (Literacy skills already mastered by the child)

Figure 1.6 L. Vygotsky's zone of proximal development (ZPD).

situations. When he thought she was at a point that she understood the new information, he backed away and let her take over. Scaffolding is more likely to be successful if the following are true:

- Rapport has been established between the teacher and the learner.
- The coaching adult or peer is sensitive to the child's responses.
- The task is neither too tough nor too easy.
- The adult or older peer knows when to let the child take the next step.
- The coach lets the child control the activity as much as possible.

IMAGINATIVE PLAY We can't stress enough the role of play in developing children's cognitive, social, and creative selves. It advances cognitive development because it requires the use of abstract thought and strength-

ens memory. Children develop more sophisticated language and social skills as they reason with others about play situations, express varying points of view, handle disputes without dominance from adults, and persuade others to their own point of view. The boundaries between fantasy and reality that are often obscure in the early years disappear as children transform objects from real to pretend and back again. When we think about each of these contributions to a child's overall development, we can understand why Vygotsky accorded imaginative play such a prominent role in his theoretical perspectives. Children with poorly developed imaginations will have a tougher time when asked to summarize, paraphrase, image text, or create their own stories and reports.

CHILDREN WITH SPECIAL NEEDS As would be expected, Vygotsky believed strongly in inclusion for children with special needs. He was particularly concerned about deaf children because he felt that language

Children creating their own meaning.

was so crucial in social skill and concept development. In his later writings, he became an advocate for sign language, which he thought would facilitate the communication that these children—and all children—need for scaffolding opportunities and language learning. His theory has been found helpful in treating children diagnosed with ADHD (attention deficit hyperactivity disorder), teaching them to use verbal self-talk strategies for self-instruction and self-regulation of behavior.

How *easy* is it to apply constructivist theory in the real classroom? Airasian and Walsh (1997:447–449) say, realistically, that it can be tough because few of us were trained to work with children using such principles. They propose a few cautions. First, a constructivist theory is just a theory. It does not come with an instructional approach for implementing it. It does emphasize "non-rote tasks and active child participation in the learning process (e.g., cooperative learning, performance assessments, product-oriented activities, and hands-on learning as well

as reciprocal teaching and evaluation methods)." However, all of these must be carefully and appropriately matched to identified outcomes. Second, teachers should not "assume that a constructivist orientation will make the same demands on teaching time as a nonconstructivist approach." Both teachers and students have to learn a number of roles that are not found in traditional classrooms. "Teachers have to learn to guide, not tell . . . to create environments in which students can make their own meanings rather than be handed them by the teacher . . . to not have children search for the one 'right' answer."

On the other hand, children have to learn to think for themselves and not wait for the teacher to tell them what to think. They must learn to articulate their ideas clearly and revisit and revise their constructions. In the social-constructivist classroom, they will do this with the sensitive aid of a teacher who will use individual and small-group interaction as the primary teaching mode. Many of these approaches will be discussed in Chapter 2.

APPLICATIONS FOR APPLYING CONSTRUCTIVIST-BASED TRANSACTIONS IN THE CLASSROOM

1. Provide many opportunities and enough time for meaningful discussions and explorations—both teacher–child and child–child interaction. Cooperative and collaborative learning are essential to promote collegiality and rapport, cognitive and literacy growth, and social-emotional strength. Activities should be related to the curriculum and

designed to be engaging, meaningful, and useful to the children participating in them.

2. Structure your day to include one-on-one and small-group instruction as much as possible. Ask questions that are open-ended and that call for elaborate, thoughtful answers rather than expecting a bottom-line correct answer. For example, when evaluating how well a child comprehends a story, ask questions such as "What do you think that story was all about?" rather than asking, "What kind of puppy did Peter's parents want to buy?"

3. Create a highly literate classroom setting (see Chapters 2 and 3) where literacy activities pervade all areas of the curriculum, where oral and written language are primary tools for constructing and sharing meaning.

4. Plan a balance of oral language, reading, and writing activities into the daily block and overall schedule.

5. Respect each child's ZPD when you provide help to children. Be responsive to current functioning but also lead children further in skill and concept building, as indicated by their responses. Challenge them appropriately to stretch their current levels of understanding.

6. Shape the classroom into a harmonious community of learners where adults and children are independent, contributing to one another's understanding in culturally meaningful literacy activities. Foster peer interactions by structuring mixed-age and mixed-ability groups. Encourage children who understand a skill or concept very well to serve as scaffolders for children who need additional help, moving each child ahead in skill and concept building as rigorously as possible.

7. Use dynamic assessment strategies to know where each child is on the learning continuum. These involve purposeful teaching within the testing situation. Rather than static assessment procedures that center on what a child *already* knows or doesn't know, dynamic assessment measures the breadth of a child's ZPD, using a **pretest–intervene (scaffold)–retest methodology** that allows the teacher to learn what practices work most effectively with any particular child. For example, the teacher who was listening to Tina read a passage was "retesting" her ability to use strategies to decode by simply observing which strategies she used and did not use. He then taught her a strategy she was not using—word families. In this way, he was intervening or scaffolding. When he went back later in the day to see if she really understood and could still apply the strategy, he was "retesting."

8. Teach children the value of self-talk and encourage them to use it for talking themselves through a challenging problem or in regulating their own behavior. For example, Raymond, a first grader, was constantly asking other children how to spell a word rather than sounding it out himself during journal writing. His teacher explained the value of "doing his own headwork" rather than staying dependent on others, and assured him that thinking the word through would eventually result in better spelling capability. She asked him to tell himself the following when he was struggling with a word: (1) "Just give it a try." (2) "Think of other words I know that sound almost the same." (3) "Write as many letters as I can think of in the word." She had him repeat each step after her and then had him tell her the whole sequence a couple of times. She then gave him a word she thought would be moderately difficult for him and asked him to spell it. When he didn't know exactly how to spell the word, he practiced the process they had agreed on. Eventually, he developed greater autonomy in his writing as well as increased fluidity and ability to spell words conventionally.

Challenge children appropriately in order to stretch their understanding.

Developmentally Appropriate Practices

Woodrow Wilson, who had been a schoolteacher before becoming president, once quipped that it was easier to move a cemetery than to change curriculum. In the 1970s and 1980s, many of the criticisms of education and calls for reform were focused on primary curriculum and instruction. Critics felt that widespread practices ignored what we knew about how children develop and learn and also the sociocultural factors affecting the children who were coming to school. Teaching methods were viewed as particularly injurious to children because they had become increasingly didactic and age-inappropriate.

Out of the many discussions that took place among educators and other stakeholders, a powerful idea began to take shape—that of developmentally appropriate practices (DAP). Defined and then redefined by the National Association for the Education of Young Children, the practices are as follows:

a. Developmentally appropriate curriculum provides for all areas of a child's development: physical, emotional, social, linguistic, aesthetic, and cognitive.

b. Curriculum includes a broad range of content across disciplines that is socially relevant, intellectually engaging, and personally meaningful to children.

c. Curriculum builds upon what children already know and are able to do (activating prior knowledge) to consolidate their learning and to foster their acquisition of new concepts and skills.

d. Effective curriculum plans frequently integrate across traditional subject-matter divisions to help children make meaningful connections and provide opportunities for rich conceptual development; focusing on one subject is also a valid strategy at times.

e. Curriculum promotes the development of knowledge and understanding, processes and skills, as well as the dispositions to use and apply skills and to go on learning.

f. Curriculum content has intellectual integrity, reflecting the key concepts and tools of inquiry of recognized disciplines in ways that are accessible and achievable for young children, ages 3 through 8. . . . Children directly participate in study of the disciplines, for instance, by conducting scientific experiments, writing, performing, solving mathematical problems, collecting and analyzing data, collecting oral history, and performing other roles of experts in the disciplines.

g. Curriculum provides opportunities to support children's home culture and language while also developing all children's abilities to participate in the shared culture of the program and the community.

h. Curriculum goals are realistic and attainable for most children in the designated age range for which they are designed.

i. When used, technology is physically and philosophically integrated in the classroom curriculum and teaching (Bredekamp & Copple, 1997:20–21).

These practices can be seen in preprimary and primary programs that (1) match how children develop and learn with engaging activities in the classroom; (2) allow for individual, small-group, and large-group instruction, treating children as individuals rather than as a cohort group; and (3) treat all children and their families with respect (Kostelnik, Soderman, & Whiren, 2004).

All of this makes a great deal of sense to those of us who have spent time in real classrooms with real children. Today, however, these hard-earned and thoughtful practices are being challenged as ideological conflicts grow about teaching children to read. What we have learned about best practice and the need for balanced literacy is giving way to a pronounced failure to distinguish the importance of acquiring decoding skills (inside-out information systems) from the equally important and more expansive process of developing comprehension abilities (outside-in information systems). As noted previously, both are essential.

Policymakers seem to have centered on the acquisition of decoding skills as a panacea for all academic underachievement (Cummins, 2003). Thus, some school districts have erroneously replaced good whole-language programs (which included the development of phonemic awareness and phonological skill building in a variety of ways) with narrowly focused phonics programs and high-stakes standardized assessment.

Unless the pendulum moves somewhat back to center, children potentially have a great deal to lose. Once they have developed fluent decoding skills that are central to

these programs, they may experience a significant inability in comprehension capability unless we again reshape a more reasonable approach. In addition, the troublesome school drop-out rates we see today in the United States may increase if the real needs of at-risk children are ignored in pursuit of a highly prescribed, one-size-fits-all approach to learning. We can build the best curricular programs in the world but they will do us little good if children do not have the prerequisites needed to understand the prescribed level of material. We can rigorously assess children with standardized tests, but that will do us little good unless the results provide clues about how to shape more effective instruction for a particular child.

We continue to believe that we should not lose the gains made in the last decade with respect to making programs for children more responsive to individual needs. At the same time, we are proponents of rigorous concept and skill building in the early years that creates as much literacy strength as possible in each developing child. This is a perspective that melds extremely well with the social-constructivist theory that underscores this entire text.

Teachers in developmentally appropriate classrooms act more as facilitators and guides for children's learning than as veritable fonts of wisdom and keepers of "correct" answers. They use children's interests and ways of learning as a guide and provide concrete materials and activities to introduce new information. They encourage children to pose their own questions and model strategies for finding answers to those questions, organizing the information, and articulating it to others, making academics

Encourage children to pose their own questions about texts.

an integral part of classroom life. Teachers who practice DAP acknowledge that the children who come into their classrooms vary dramatically from one another and that a one-size-fits-all approach to literacy and learning is not the best we can offer to them in the critical early years. Children are given choices in these classrooms about what they will do and with whom they will do it—but the choices they make are expected to be good *learning* choices—that is, ones that have educational value.

A classroom climate that encourages children to interact frequently with one another and with the adults in the setting promotes DAP and, in turn, literacy development. "Mixing it up"—having heterogeneous small groups and pairs of children collaborating often with one another about what they are reading and writing—offers the best potential for growth. Young children are enormously curious about other children, and they want to be like other children they admire. They are constantly scanning and watching others who are about their same age and are likely to be more motivated to read and write well when they have access to peers who do so. This is especially true when good rapport is established among children and adults in the classroom, where there is a feeling of belonging and acceptance for all. Frank Smith (1997) has noted that, with respect to literacy, children feel they are "either in the club or out of the club" by grade 3, and much of this depends on the extent to which they feel the progress they are making is accepted and valued by others in the environment.

Related specifically to literacy, language outcomes are higher in children who participate in DAP programs. They manifest better verbal and listening skills and higher receptive language (Dunn, Beach, & Kontos, 1994; Marcon, 1999). These children demonstrate better comprehension of what is read to them and also of material they have read themselves (Palincsar & Brown, 1989). Studies looking at didactic versus process-oriented and individualized reading programs indicate that preschool and kindergarten children in the didactic settings are better at letter recognition, but children who have been in DAP settings for at least three years have significantly higher scores in reading achievement at the end of second grade than children from the didactic settings (Kostelnik, Soderman, & Whiren, 2004).

Current Approaches to Literacy Practice in the Primary Classroom: How Developmentally Appropriate Are They?

Although there is ongoing scrutiny of developmentally appropriate and academic-intense environments, increasing numbers of professionals are acknowledging the documented cognitive and social-emotional value of the DAP approach to education and emerging literacy. Yet, although teachers surveyed say they favor the constructivist approach and active involvement from children that

is fostered through a DAP perspective, they themselves continue to struggle with applying the principles advocated by such programs.

Studies examining the teaching of reading and writing in the primary grades reveal that the approach to language instruction in observed classrooms varies greatly, not only in terms of time allocation but also in the instructional approach taken by classroom teachers. Widespread differences in teacher preservice and inservice training, teacher autonomy, parent expectations and pressure, and school district and personal philosophies about how young children *should* be learning currently add up to a "crazy quilt" approach to early literacy in the United States.

A tour of a typical elementary school in an urban Midwest setting in October supports this perspective. In one brief conversation, a kindergarten teacher working with mostly high-risk children complains, "The only time they pay attention is when I'm reading to them." When asked how often she does so, she notes, "I try to read to them a couple of times a week, but even that is hard to work in because of all the other content that has to be taught."

The entire class of children can be observed working quietly on worksheets, copying the letter of the week, which is *J*. A few of the children have copied an entire sheet of upside-down *J*s. Others have some facing left and some facing right. When asked, "What is that letter you're copying?" a group of children look at one another expectedly for support. "*G?*" ventures one boy tentatively. The rest of the children pause as if needing confirmation and then receive it from another child who smiles broadly and adds, "Yeah! *G* . . . Guh!" Satisfied, the children continue their copying of "*J*s."

Across the hall, another group of kindergarteners is spending the day in a play-based context. According to their teacher, it is designed to allow literacy to "emerge naturally." Looking more like a typical preschool classroom in which a heavily maturational approach is predominant, the context seems obviously devoid of any teacher-initiated tasks. Although the classroom is stocked with interesting manipulative materials and children's literature, an extended observation indicates only minimal interaction with the teacher about their use; nor is there any definitive assessment by the teacher about what the children are learning in this wholly open-ended classroom. "My program is developmentally appropriate," the teacher says with pride in her voice. "I don't believe in pressuring children this age. When these kids come into kindergarten here, more and more of them have never heard of Humpty Dumpty and Little Miss Muffet. When I get them, they hardly know their colors and shapes, let alone their letters. With respect to their developing literacy skills, I encourage parents to read to them, and I do a couple of times a day in a large group. But phonics and reading groups are not a part of this classroom. They'll learn their letters and how to read when they're ready."

Our next stop is in a first-grade classroom where we ask the teacher to describe her approach to literacy development. She sums it up quickly by pointing to the basal texts and workbooks that are piled beside her and a stack of worksheets that need to be graded. She adds defensively, "It wasn't my decision to stick just with these, but we have to do *something*. Kids today just don't like to read—and it's getting worse." When reading time comes, the children are gathered together in a whole group. Basal texts are passed out, and each child turns to the morning's story on page 57. As the children take turns reading a portion of the text, our eye rests on one boy in the back who is opening and closing his book, which he has pushed up against his face. The teacher frowns and calls his name, and he stops. He stops flapping the book and assumes a posture that suggests he is ready to pay attention. We notice that his book is upside down and that he is also on the wrong page.

In yet another first-grade classroom in the same school, a teacher is reading a familiar book to a small group of first graders. Their eyes move between the teacher's expressive face as she reads Leo Leonni's *Fish Is Fish* and the words in the big-book version of it propped on a nearby easel. Afterwards, they participate actively and enthusiastically as their teacher "milks" Leonni's book, moving through two engaging activities designed to enhance their phonological and print awareness. Later, when questioned about whether she believes her particular approach to literacy is "working," this teacher points to the children. Two of them are at the easel rereading the big book. Another set of children is creating "a new story" about Leonni's fish and toad, with temporary spelling. A couple of others are involved at a white board where they are creating a variety of *ish* words—*fish, wish, dish, swish*. Pairs of other children are experimenting with fish crackers and small fish bowls, writing number strips of all the varying combinations of in-bowl and out-of-bowl fish that are equal to 10. Another two, who have begun writing fairly complete sentences, have taken up the teacher's challenge to write a math story problem about fish and are thoughtfully illustrating their first draft. This ongoing work on the children's part, as well as the work samples they are producing, are carefully observed and documented by this teacher as she consistently gauges each child's progress against expected gains for that child and the desired academic and social-emotional outcomes prescribed by the school district.

The building principal who is acting as our tour guide is unsure about which approach is the most appropriate in these early grades but admits he doesn't mind having quite different learning contexts. "Some parents," he says, "love a no nonsense kindergarten or first grade, particularly if their child has attended a preschool. Others want a softer sell, especially if the child is younger than his classmates. And some just don't care as long as the kids are

Children at work in a best-practice classroom.

happy. We have a lot of complaints by our second- and third-grade teachers, but, by the end of the third grade, most of the kids are reading fairly well."

What the K–1 teachers just described here have in common is that they are all providing a literacy context for young children, and they all firmly believe that their particular approach will yield the best results. You can guess which of these teachers fundamentally believe that the tempo of instruction should be determined by the teacher and that, in order to learn the essentials of reading and writing, the children need activities such as isolated lessons stressing phonics, spelling tests, worksheets, and drill. A quiet and orderly classroom, with children sitting in rows of seats and working on exercises designed by someone who has never met the children, is equated with learning in their classrooms. These teachers have bought into the myth that the developmentally appropriate programs that some of their other colleagues advocate are academically soft and simply work to water down the curriculum.

One has bought into several myths about developmentally appropriate programs—that teachers in such classrooms don't teach, that her classroom should be wholly unstructured, and that any directed "academic" lessons are inappropriate. In essence, she has not only watered down the curriculum, she has dismissed it entirely. Although the materials she provides motivate children's involvement, the children are largely left to learn only what their discovery and exploration can yield. As a result, the social-conventional knowledge (labels, names, tags, vocabulary, facts) and scaffolding of skills that must come from adults to support children's inquiry and construction of knowledge are minimal.

What was seen in the last classroom comes closest to our definition of DAP that best supports literacy acquisition in both early and later primary children. Had we not personally observed these classrooms, it would be tempting to believe that the classrooms just described are exaggerated descriptions. Not so! Currently, only one-fifth to one-third of primary programs studied are based on practices consistent with developmentally appropriate programming perspectives. Even though half of the teachers observed reported having received training in DAP and endorse such an approach, there is still a prevalence of didactic practice. A great deal of time in many classrooms today is still spent on managing behavior, and a scarcity of literacy activities beyond basal readers and workbooks are planned for throughout the day or across the curriculum. Lessons are primarily taught in large groups to all children, with expectations that they must all be on the same level. We believe strongly that if we are to achieve different results with children in our schools—more positive results—the fallacy of such an approach must be challenged.

A heavy reliance on textbooks and workbooks as a primary approach to literacy tends to focus children's attention on isolated skill development or abstract parts of the reading process, rather than on the integration of oral language, writing, and listening with reading. The result is that children often do not associate reading with enjoyment because too little attention is placed on reading for pleasure or to gain information about something in which they are interested.

In such classrooms, where program content does not attend to children's social, emotional, and intellectual development, inappropriate methodologies and narrow perspectives about intended outcomes for literacy work together to *deny* curiosity, critical thinking, and creative expression and to foster negative attitudes toward communication skill building in general (International Reading Association, 1996). What may have been previously fascinating to young children—books and the wonderful stories inside them—becomes instead a task loaded with inherent landmines. Instead of focusing on what is happening to the characters in the story, children's only job is to focus on beginning and ending sounds. The illustrations that were once powerful enough to draw a child mentally right into the text are forgotten in the child's quest to move purposefully from letter to letter, word to word, sentence to sentence—and decode all of them correctly. We owe children more.

APPLICATIONS FOR DEVELOPMENTALLY APPROPRIATE PRACTICE IN THE CLASSROOM

According to the National Association for the Education of Young Children, the organization that has been most active in developing the concept of DAP, there is no single formula for practice. However, there are five basic guidelines that should determine classroom practices on a day-to-day basis:

1. **Create a caring community of learners.** Developmentally appropriate practice supports the development of relationships among adults and children, among children, among teachers, and between families and teachers.

2. **Teach to enhance development and learning.** Strive to achieve a balance between guiding children's learning and following their lead.

3. **Construct appropriate curriculum.** Content includes the subject matter, social or cultural values, families' input, and the age and experience of the children.

4. **Assess children's learning and development.** Assessment of individual children's development and learning is essential for planning and implementing appropriate curriculum.

5. **Establish mutually beneficial relationships with families.** Developmentally appropriate practices evolve from a deep knowledge of individual children and the contexts within which they develop and learn. The younger the child, the more necessary it is for caregivers and teachers to acquire this knowledge through relationships with children and families.

Integrating Learning across the Curriculum

One of the most important principles of DAP is that of integrating learning across the curriculum. It's not a new idea—it was advocated by John Dewey (1902) and others at the turn of the previous century—but it's still one of the best ideas. This approach allows more in-depth, organized coverage of topics that must be included in a curriculum. It also promotes the design of more engaging and diverse activities for children and greater opportunities for child–child and adult–child collaboration. Instead of learning skills for the sake of learning them, children can see reasons for having to develop them. They can also make better connections between the different disciplines. For teachers who work in mixed-age settings or team-teach with others, this approach makes it much easier to design simplification and extension of activities, to find the time necessary for scaffolding, and to facilitate increasingly abstract and complex concepts among a set of learners.

Joanne Brewer (2001) suggests that an integrated curriculum helps a child make sense of the world more easily. It also more closely mirrors the way children learn outside of school, where their experiences are not fractured into subject-matter areas. She writes:

> You probably remember that in elementary school, you had reading first thing in the morning, math right before lunch, and science in the afternoon. Yet when children learn outside of school, they learn in wholes. For example, a child visiting tide pools could learn many things at once: language arts (learning vocabulary for the animals and plants of the tide pools); physical skills (staying on top of the slippery rocks); classification (noticing which animals are related); the environment (noticing pollution or litter); family stories (hearing parents tell about when they visited these tide pools as children); and so on.

A classroom structure that works best for implementing themes is usually one that looks something like a hands-on museum, library, workshop, and laboratory—all rolled into one. It should contain tables on which children can work and basic materials for constructing, measuring, representing, and recording. There should be a well-stocked library, with plenty of narrative and expository books supporting the topic. A dramatic play area large enough to accommodate five or six children at one time and presentation space are also necessary. Wall space needs to be reserved for work samples, photographs, and other representations of project work. Although many classrooms don't come equipped with any kind of storeroom for stocking diverse materials and junk, this is a good thing to include somewhere in a school so that children have lots of "stuff" from which to create theme-related products. Photography equipment (instant and video cameras, film, and VCRs), computers, and tape recorders help children and teachers to capture the unfolding of the theme and presentations.

The Role of Technology in Literacy Development

Today, preschoolers acquainted with cell phones, pagers, and personal computers go into kindergartens where chalkboards and overhead projectors represent the state of the art. (Gates, 1996:209)

How are *you* dealing with the information superhighway? Many educators remain wary about the role of PCs in the classroom, unsure exactly what to do with them. They worry that the current zeal to get all schools on board will result in artificial experience at the cost of good investigative learning. Others see the computer as an excellent tool to manage widening pools of information and provide children with simulations and a multitude of connections they could not otherwise experience.

Sales for popular software programs that appeal to children are soaring. A software distributor (KidSoft, Inc.) begun in 1997 for children 4 to 12 now includes educational videos for infants! A sample of popular software is listed at the end of this chapter under "Suggested Sources for Additional Information."

Programs have been developed that range from simple games to tutoring programs in language, geography, history, mathematics, spelling, and science. Children sometimes don't distinguish the difference between the two, since they work on the same order: They are usually self-paced and are made to be engaging with bright, animated graphics, changing scenes, and sound effects.

To date, some educators have been caught in a ten-second delay with respect to technology. Because of the high cost of hardware and software, schools with limited budgets find themselves continually behind the curve in keeping up to date with state-of-the-art equipment and installation. In addition, there are growing debates about the appropriateness of computer use in the instructional day, limited choice of good software, and costly training that allows educators to become knowledgeable about the technology revolution and remain up to date.

In evaluating the role computers can play in enhancing children's literacy, our first concern is that they be used in developmentally appropriate ways in the classroom. They should not be placed in classrooms where teachers have little or no training in how computers can be integrated successfully into the curriculum. When computers are simply dumped into the classroom with the expectation that teachers will "get kids using them," computer use can be highly inappropriate. Teachers may limit their repertoire of programs to those geared toward remediation, drill, and practice—or use computer time as a leisure-time activity, a reward for getting "real work" completed. Time may be siphoned off from other activities and limit teacher–child and child–child interaction. In one classroom observed, the teacher was spending more time helping children with computer glitches than with

Using computers to enhance literacy.

the literacy skills the program was intended to teach. In another, two children using one program cooperatively had divided the task up so that one child figured out the answer and the other simply pressed the key to move into the next sequence, getting nothing cognitively out of the experience. Teachers may assume that children are learning skills simply because they are spending time with programs designed to teach those skills—when nothing much is happening at all.

Oppenheimer (1997:52) describes one teacher's experience with a bilingual special education class of second, third, and fourth graders. Despite the children's enthusiasm for computer time, the teacher felt the computer lab time diluted the children's attention to language skill building, which they all sorely needed. On the other hand, she felt that the children needed to become "computer-literate" along with their more able peers. Another teacher in the school that Oppenheimer observed felt that computerized programs encouraged children to practice their writing skills because editing was so much easier. Those students who were less diligent became more caught up in the "electronic opportunities to make a school paper look snazzy" than they did in learning process writing skills. Additional studies looking at reading programs concluded that children frequently involved in computerized programs such as *Reader Rabbit* (now used in more than 100,000 schools) had suffered a 50 percent drop in creativity, were less able to answer open-ended questions, and showed a "markedly diminished ability to brainstorm with fluency and originality."

Informative teacher training may produce different results. Haugland and Wright (1997:10–17) have done an excellent job of assessing developmentally appropriate computer experiences. They point out a number of reasons that computer technology in the classroom can be beneficial for young children:

1. Developmental computer experiences fit young children's style of learning because they provide children participatory learning experiences, are intrinsically motivating, and tend to be holistic experiences.
2. The microworld offers participatory learning. In a child-oriented computer experience, children are in control, acting on software to make events happen rather than reacting to predetermined questions and closed-ended problems. For example, when using a software program such as *Wiggleworks* by Scholastic New Media, children learn the relationship between words and objects, letter identification, and how to read words in the process of creating scenes, changing situations, and creating stories.
3. Learning is holistic and integrated, and intrinsic motivation is high. Learning is not divided into separate or distinct subjects such as language, spelling, math, or science. Interacting with the large variety of software available, children can experience a host of simulations that present challenge, appeal to their curiosity, love of fantasy, and desire to be in control—four characteristics of microworlds that maximize their intrinsic motivation to learn. Children are able to create "spectacular visual effects" to illustrate their concepts and stories. In developing reports or stories that may result from a theme they are studying, their writing is "more fluid, they write more, their stories are more complex,

they make fewer mechanical errors, worry less about mistakes, and are more willing to make revisions."

4. Talking word processors and well-selected software provide scaffolding experiences through "assistance, support, and guidance" as children develop increasingly sophisticated cognitive competence. For example, interactive stories enable nonreaders to enjoy stories, to begin to associate words and objects, and to discover cause-and-effect relationships as they interact with programs that allow them to change story outcomes.

5. Computers connect children to the world and provide quick, universal access to information. Through the Internet and CD-ROMs, they provide teachers and children unique opportunities to access people and resources throughout the world, connecting them to endless resources including libraries, museums, data banks, and resource forums. Computers can open up possibilities for children to develop pen pals in other parts of the world, connect with authors they are studying, work on joint projects with others outside the classroom, and build global understanding as they "connect with individuals from diverse backgrounds and cultures," expanding their view of the world.

Many of the studies looking at the effectiveness of computer use in classrooms are of short duration, making it difficult to weigh conclusively the benefits and costs of technology use. One that was more comprehensive was that commissioned by Apple Computer, Inc. Researchers concluded that children did not become social isolates as everyone worried they would. Instead, they engaged in more spontaneous cooperative learning than in traditional classes. Nor did they become "brain dead" or bored; rather their "desire to use it for their own purposes increased with use." Second and third graders developed adept keyboard skills, learning to type 25 to 30 words per minute with 95 percent accuracy, "more than twice as fast as children of that age can usually write." Standardized test scores indicated that these children were performing academically as well as children in traditional classes, and some were doing better.

As we become more comfortable with technology, the debates that divide us about the appropriateness of computers in classrooms will disappear. Better research will be available to look at their effectiveness in preprimary and primary classrooms. Until then, thoughtful teacher judgment about how they currently fit into the overall framework for developing literacy will be required.

Outcomes: Measuring Literacy Growth in a Developmentally Appropriate Context

Our capacity to continually assess children's growth is an important part of being an effective teacher. Assessment and evaluation are usually centered on what children know or don't know following involvement with curricular content. First, however, we must evaluate how well *we* are prepared to understand and deal with the differences children present on entering our classrooms. This requires self-appraisal on our part to examine whether or not a personal philosophy based on grounded research has been developed. Then we must pay attention to the integrity with which it is being played out in the classroom each day. This requires concerted diligence. It means taking time to reflect on what has occurred in the classroom and asking ourselves how well minimal criteria for structuring successful learning experiences for children have been met. This occurs only when children are actively engaged in experiences carefully designed to encourage intellectual independence and pursuit. There must be frequent interaction with others, discussion and organization of ideas, production of increasingly sophisticated work products and concepts, and genuine self-appraisal of their own efforts. Discussed in Part Three of this book will be a variety of methods and strategies to measure whether children are truly growing in all developmental domains as well as in the domain targeted in this text—the language domain.

The authentic assessment and evaluation of young children has taken on new importance. It is not meant to take the place of standardized and normed tests, which can yield critical information for research, diagnosis, and comparisons to other groups of children. However, this information has not been helpful to classroom teachers who need more detailed data to plan well for the children they are teaching. When relied on as the primary source of assessment in schools, standardized testing often narrows the curriculum, ignores higher level thinking processes, puts undue stress on young children and teachers, and drains resources in terms of time and funds. High-stakes tests whose published results might negatively affect school funding and reputation may be sensitive to special coaching and frequently emphasize the one "right" answer.

Potentially, all formal testing of children can have serious consequences, and its inclusion in the educational structure should be carefully considered. Because there are few instruments developed that are truly culture free or highly reliable and valid for the populations of children with whom they are used, the results can often be used inappropriately. In the worst scenario, test anxiety may be created that can last a lifetime. Wortham (2001) suggests that children from minority backgrounds are most negatively affected by standardized test results because their performances influence teachers' perceptions of what they can achieve; as a result of low test scores, children from minority backgrounds are more often placed in low-ability programs, transitional classrooms, and special education classes.

For all these reasons standardized achievement tests have been used fairly judiciously in the early years. However, because of the No Child Left Behind legislation, they are assuming unprecedented importance in all government-supported preprimary programs and many public schools receiving Reading First dollars. When such tests are used with children in grade 2 or below, we recommend that the tests must meet particular criteria in order to minimize their limitations. These guidelines are discussed further in Chapter 7, "Documenting Skills and Concepts."

On the other hand, one of the most damaging myths operating in the area of primary education is that all assessment and evaluation is inappropriate for our youngest children. This is not true. Assessment is a critical and necessary component in early education. *How* it is done is the issue. We need to craft our assessment and evaluation for preprimary and elementary classrooms every bit as carefully as we do the activities for children. Unlike the conventional methods used in the past, authentic assessments help us recognize the individuality of the learner and respect variation in styles and rates of learning. Authentic assessment, in its true form, yields many data points over a period of time, rather than the single snapshot in time provided by standardized assessment. Authentic assessment works best when it is teacher-constructed and teacher-

selected so that it is valid for the children involved. Data collection should be periodic and ongoing, based on children's classroom performance, and should be useful to both the teacher and the child for instructional purposes (Soderman, 2002). Also highly important is the involvement of children in the process in terms of self-appraisal and sharing of information between home and school. It should exclude assessment that is useless for improving instruction or is unduly stressful for children.

The goal of appropriate assessment and evaluation is to provide information on children's individual progress in moving toward specified outcomes that will best ensure a literate future for them. We need to know not only where a child needs additional support in attaining language skills, processes, and concepts, but also where we may be falling short or being particularly successful in structuring an effective program for the children in our classrooms. Shifts away from an emphasis on teaching isolated skills toward literacy taught in an integrated context requires that we become better acquainted with and put into practice the more useful methods we have at our fingertips. Part Three of this book will look more closely at a variety of strategies for measuring and reporting on literacy growth.

Final Thoughts

From a developmental perspective, there is reason to be concerned about children's literacy experiences in many U.S. classrooms where children increasingly present classroom teachers with a variety of challenges. Not all are ready to learn grade-level material or even eager to please. Wide variations in development due to chronological age differences, brain organization, gender, primary-language, and sociocultural experiences complicate the situation even further. When developmental and experiential lags are misunderstood or ignored, they set a trajectory for children that often leads to future literacy problems.

Some of the most promising strategies for transforming knowledge in the formal classroom setting have evolved from a growing interest in social-constructivist theory and developmentally appropriate practices. These are not only profoundly responsive to the wide developmental and experiential variations we see in children but are also effective guides for the day-to-day transactions that go on in the school and home contexts. These include integrating literacy activities across the entire curriculum so that children can make sense of what they are learning, using technology as effectively as possible in the classroom, involving parents more actively in the process, and expanding our ability to evaluate children's

learning and apply that knowledge to improve classroom instruction

We *can* offer all children a solid literacy package. We have the ability to encircle even the most reluctant reader and writer in order to share with them the riches to be had in a literate future. Our task as educators is multidimensional. To reach *all* children, we must organize the literacy-learning environment as effectively as possible, internalize our knowledge of how children come to be literate, design rigorous and engaging activities, and, finally, become truly expert in what to expect and watch for, documenting and evaluating the growth that is sure to occur.

In the chapters to follow, we offer you ideas about organizing the best possible early childhood context for literacy acquisition and for evaluating, nurturing, supporting, and sustaining children's developing skills and concepts. In addition to relevant research and theory, a variety of tried and true activities are described, ranging from those for the emerging reader and writer to those for the more skilled child who is becoming fluent in literacy. We hope you'll adapt these ideas to the needs of the children in your classroom, value their responses, and always keep in mind the underlying tenet of this book—that children's differences must be recognized and respected in order to optimize their literacy acquisition.

Enhancing both literacy and social development.

Challenge Yourself

1. Take the time to do a half-day or day-long observation in a preprimary or elementary classroom. What is the teacher's approach to literacy acquisition? How does that teacher respond to the questions that begin this chapter? Do the answers and what you observed in the classroom match?

2. Identify one point in the chapter that made you most comfortable or most uncomfortable with respect to your own teaching. Explain your reasons. What will you do about this?

3. Take advantage of training sessions offered in your school district or through community education to learn creative ways to use the Internet with children in your classroom. Find out about curriculum modules and web sites that are available to support your teaching and the children's learning.

4. If someone were to ask you to articulate your personal philosophy about literacy education, how would you answer?

5. Find out if there is a written school philosophy where you work. How well does your philosophy of literacy education match the overall philosophy of your district?

Suggested Sources for Additional Information

Berk, L. E., & Winsler, A. (1995). *Scaffolding children's learning: Vygotsky and early childhood education.* Washington, DC: National Association for the Education of Young Children.

Bredekamp, S., & Copple, C. (Eds.). (1997). *Developmentally appropriate practice in early childhood programs,* rev. ed. Washington, DC: National Association for the Education of Young Children.

Haugland, S. W., & Wright, J. L. (1997). *Young children and technology.* Boston: Allyn and Bacon.

Kostelnik, M. J., Soderman, A. K., & Whiren, A. P. (2004). *Developmentally appropriate curriculum: Best practices in early childhood education.* Upper Saddle River, NJ: Prentice Hall.

NAEYC Position Statement: Technology and Young Children (Ages 3–8).

Popular Literacy-Promoting Software for Children

Some popular software for children includes the following:

Bailey's Book House, Edmark.

Creative Writer, Fine Artist, Dinosaurs, Dangerous Creatures, Microsoft.

First Class HyperStudio, Robert Wagner.

Jump Start English, Knowledge Adventures.

Kid's Studio, Storm Software.

Let's Go Read 1: An Island Adventure, Edmark.
Let's Go Read 2: An Ocean Adventure, Edmark.
Mario Teaches Typing, Interplay.
Myst, The Playroom, Living Books Series, Kid Pix Studio, Where in the World Is Carmen Sandiego? series, Broderbund.
Stanley's Sticker Stories, Edmark.

Student Writing Center, Learning Company, Inc.
Tenth Planet Explores Literacy, Sunburst.
The Oregon Trail, The Amazon Trail, Storybook Weaver, Number Crunchers, MECC.
Putt-Putt, Fatty Bear series, Humongous Entertainment.
Tetris Classic, Spectrum Holobyte.

Literacy Links and Processes

"Well, see," said Sasha, "it just happened one day and suddenly it felt like 'Yippee, I CAN READ,' " and he threw up his arms and laughed, "and it made me feel different inside my tummy. I felt kind of powerful." (Polakow, 1986:37).

Wouldn't it be great if all children "instantly" learned how to read as Sasha reports that he did? To have that kind of power—and to see it as power—is a terrific thing for any young child to possess. Sasha believes he can read, and he sees the value in reading. This is the essence of what we want to teach children about literacy. We want all children with whom we come into contact to feel success with reading, writing, speaking, listening, and viewing, and the power that being literate yields.

Left to their own devices, children may quite possibly become literate. They may, as Sasha reports, develop reading and writing skills without specific adult intervention. However, they may not. Years of research show us that there are some very specific things that parents and teachers can do to guide and facilitate the process of literacy learning for all children.

As you read, ask yourself these questions:

- What is meant by *literacy?*
- How does oral language affect literacy?
- What is the link between oral language and written language?
- Are there specific ways to teach literacy?
- What are the core components I must be sure to include in my work with children?
- How do these components develop?

In this chapter, we will provide answers to these questions as we discuss the evolutionary process of literacy and its core components. This chapter is divided into two parts. The first part introduces the concept of literacy and its meaning, followed by an overview of the unique roles and functions of oral language and written language in the literacy process and the important role that adults play. In the second portion of the chapter, we look at the core components for literacy, outline their developmental progressions, and suggest classroom applications to support them.

A Look at Literacy

A Glimpse of Literacy: Philosophies and Definitions

Once upon a time, not too long ago, it was believed that reading consisted of discrete, isolated skills that had to be taught in a prescribed fashion. It was thought that only when a child was "ready" to learn could he or she actually begin learning how to read. Another theory was that the brain had to reach the specific mental age of 6.5 years before it could absorb and understand the reading process. Thus, instruction in reading and writing was delayed until first grade, leaving the preschool and kindergarten years to be spent in "readiness" preparation. This approach was typically referred to as **reading readiness** (Crawford, 1995).

The reading readiness view sees children as ready for formal instruction at a specific age as a result of maturation. This implies that there is a discrete time when children are not readers and an equally separate time when they are (Whitehurst & Lonigan, 2001).

Using much research and many practical observations of children engaged in acts of literacy, we know that the readiness concept is just not true. Children do not reach a magical age at which adults can open up their heads and pour knowledge inside. Rather, we now recognize that from the time that adults start talking, singing, chanting, and reading stories to babies, children begin a lifelong journey down the path of literacy. From their earliest moments of life, young children begin to unravel the mysteries of making meaning in our world of spoken and written language.

This second approach to reading views children as being in the *process* of developing literacy behaviors. It is commonly referred to as **emergent literacy** and, in its most general sense, refers to the process of becoming literate (Teale & Sulzby, 1989). In contrast to the readiness approach, there is no definite starting point, nor is there a definite ending point in the emergent literacy continuum.

Emergent literacy fully supports the social-constructivist theory and developmentally appropriate philosophy introduced in Chapter 1 of this book. In keeping with these philosophies, it is also important to point out here that we are not strictly advocating a whole language philosophy, nor are we advocating a pure phonics approach. Instead, we are advocating a blended, middle-of-the-road approach that draws on the strengths of both whole language and phonics in a manner that serves the needs of the child. This approach is consistent with the findings of the National Research Council's Committee on the Prevention of Reading Difficulties in Young Children, which directs that ". . . reading instruction integrate attention to the alphabetic principle with attention to the construction of meaning and opportunities to develop fluency" (Snow, 1998, vii).

Literacy has been defined in a variety of ways over the past few decades. Let's begin with the definition of literacy that we will be using in this book. **Literacy** comprises reading, writing, speaking, listening, and viewing. We will focus on all five aspects of literacy. First, we'll look at the individual definitions for each process. We will use the definitions published in *Standards for the English Language Arts*, a joint project of the International Reading Association and the National Council of Teachers of English (1996).

> **Reading** is the complex, recursive process through which we make meaning from texts using semantics; syntax; visual, aural and tactile clues; context; and prior knowledge. (p. 75)
>
> **Writing** is the use of a writing system or orthography by people in the conduct of their daily lives to communicate over time and space. It is also the process or result of recording language graphically by hand or other means, as by the use of computers or braillers. (p. 77)
>
> **Speaking** is the act of communicating through such means as vocalization, signing, or using communication aids such as voice synthesizers. (p. 75)

> **Listening** is attending to communication by any means; includes listening to vocal speech, watching signing, or using communication aids. (p. 73)
>
> **Viewing** is attending to communication conveyed by visually representing. (p. 76)

Although many have noted the importance of viewing and include it as a component in their literacy curriculums, it is the least developed aspect of literacy. For this reason, it seems to need further explanation. In this book, we regard viewing as a necessary literacy component in our vast multimedia society. We interpret viewing to be related to helping children learn to take in information visually and be able to analyze it, synthesize it with other information, and use it in a meaningful way.

The word *meaningful* is the key to successful literacy development. In striving to make things meaningful for children, we must keep in mind that everything children learn about literacy occurs within their social environments. Yetta Goodman (1992) describes literacy as a sociotransactional event. Children become literate as they interact with society and its members. Therefore, we must keep foremost in our minds the need to teach literacy as a sociotransactional event, not a bunch of isolated, disjointed skills. If we use the principles of developmentally appropriate practice, explained in Chapter 1, to design and implement a meaningful literacy environment, the social interaction dimension will be taken into account. Let's begin our discussion of literacy with a look at the use of language within literacy.

Language and Literacy

We use both oral language and written language in the complex process of literacy. Oral language is used as a mediator between written language and forming an understanding of what print means (Kamberelis & Perry, 1994). To emphasize the roles that language plays, we will discuss both oral and written language.

Oral Language

Starting with a newborn baby's reflexive cries for assistance, humans begin the process of becoming more and more intentional and purposeful in their use of language to communicate. Initially, as in the case of a baby, communication serves the purpose of eliciting help for basic needs. Gradually, as the higher thinking processes take over and intentional action occurs, children learn to use language for a much larger variety of needs. Children all over the world can be found using language for a variety of reasons: for informational purposes ("why" questions are an infamous example among young children), for entertainment or recreation (songs and stories), and for socialization purposes, to name just a few. By preschool age, children throughout the world have learned the major components of their native languages (Gleason, 2001).

Where do children learn about these varied uses? How do they learn these major components of language? These are questions that continue to cause debate among scholars specializing in language acquisition (Stewig & Jett-Simpson, 1995). What is known, however, is that there are some very specific strategies that adults use both knowingly and unknowingly to help children become proficient oral language users (Weaver, 1990).

Children are influenced greatly by their environment—specifically by the people in their environment. According to language stimulation research, in order for children to develop intellectual oral language competence, they must interact with grown-ups (Bruner, 1983). This talk between children and adults is very important to literacy development (Hart & Risley, 2000). Parents and other significant adults in children's lives, especially teachers, serve both as models of oral language and as "practice grounds" for children to try out their emerging language skills. There is a documented relationship between children's abilities to: talk about words, to recognize the differences between the words used and the meanings children intend in their conversations, and in children's developing abilities to talk about their thinking; and children's progressing literacy abilities (Torrance & Olson, 1985).

Let's consider some of the things children observe and experience pertaining to oral language in both the home and the school. From adults, children often witness the following:

- **Adults model language structure.**
    "You get one and I get one," Mom says to Jennie as she divides the grapes. We may simplify our sentences to suit our audiences, but we usually do not dramatically restructure our sentences when speaking with younger children (except in the case of parents talking to babies).
- **Adults use language for a variety of purposes with children.**
    "What is that?" [to seek information], *"Please hand the book to me"* [to get], *"The red peg goes here"* [to give information]. We give directions, play word games, sing songs, and talk with others. We talk to children, with them, and around them. We model for the children that language is an everyday, normal occurrence.
- **Adults expect children to learn to talk.**
    "Tell me which cup you'd like—yellow or blue." *"Tell me about your day."* We do not look to some children and think that they will talk only at a 2-year-old level forever. We know that they eventually will become proficient users of language for life. We give them time to learn the language, and we expect incremental progress. From birth through adolescence and beyond, we expect children to gradually develop

a larger vocabulary and to structure more complex and complete thoughts as they grow and change.

- **Adults respond to children's attempts at language.**
    "Her taked me tup," Carly cries. Her teacher responds, *"She took your cup? Let's go talk to her."*
    We accept approximations for words and try eagerly to gain meaning from children's incomplete or inaccurate use of language. We correct inaccurate interpretations (*doggie* for *bear*) but are likely to overlook beginning grammatical and phonological errors such as *"Him goed dere."* We recognize these as normal. Often, adults will restate a child's intention, *"Yes, he did go there,"* but they do not tell the child how his or her sentence was wrong, choosing instead to model the correct form.
- **Adults respond eagerly to children's uses of language.**
    After a trip to the museum, Charlie happily tells his dad, "An I saw a steg, a stegla, a stegosaurus!" "You did?" asks his father. "Tell me about that."
    We reward children's attempts at language with smiles and attention. Children generally receive positive attention for what they can do with the language rather than negative attention for what they cannot do.

Note that in all of these examples, language is learned through modeling and purposeful use, not through practice on how to use it (Harste, 1990). Can you imagine saying to a child: "This is a cup. Say *cup*. C-u-p. Here is the juice. Say *juice*. J-ui-ce"?

Written language is also acquired through modeling and purposeful use. Oral language and written language go hand in hand. Oral language is communication in action. Meaning is communicated through spoken words and gestures. Oral language incorporates the verbal and nonverbal components of speaking and listening. Literacy combines these components with written language in reading, writing, and viewing. Just as oral language develops in an emerging fashion in the young child, so does written language. Both are filled with exciting discoveries and developmental processes.

Written Language

All of the behaviors discussed here apply not only to the acquisition of oral language, but also to written language and its bigger component, literacy. Let's look at the roles that adults play for children in written language.

- **Adults model the structure of reading and writing.**
    "Let's make a list of the groceries we will get today at the store." We read and write in front of children as part of our daily living. We show them how to form letters in their names and how to address an envelope. These behaviors encourage children to become literate. They see the value we place on read-

ing and writing and they want to possess these skills too.

- **Adults use literacy for a variety of purposes with children.**

    "Grandma's letter said she was missing you very much. Why don't you write her back and tell her about our camping trip?" From this exchange, the child learns that print can be informational, that it can convey communication over time and space—that print holds meaning. Literacy's uses are seemingly never-ending!

- **Adults expect children to become literate.**

    "Write your name here, Leon. Yes, you made an L!" We expect children to learn to write their names and to read books. Herein lies a difference between oral language expectations and literacy expectations. With oral language, we *know* the child will speak. We are certain that this will happen. Often, we have the *hope* that children will become literacy-fluent, but not the certainty. This difference in attitude is dangerous. It can lead to self-fulfilling prophecies, especially when children are moving at differing speeds down the literacy path. Children in the "slower" lane often are perceived as having difficulty with literacy, and adult expectations for these children are often diminished, which may lead to less diligence in helping these children succeed with literacy.

- **Adults respond to children's attempts at literacy and their uses of literacy.**

    "Look at Maggie's writing!" [a row of scribble marks on the paper] *"She wrote a story! She's our little author."* Those who understand the progression of literacy are quick to accept children's written attempts at meaning making or at retelling a favorite story. Those who do not understand its growth, however, may squelch children's attempts by telling them the "facts": *"You don't really know how to read. You are just memorizing the book."* Or they may not provide times and materials for children to engage in these literacy attempts. Both of these situations send messages to children about our adult expectation for their literacy behaviors and can influence the children's images of themselves as readers and writers. That is why it is so important for the adults to have a good understanding of the ways that we can support and acknowledge literacy development.

Specifically, it is the adults in a child's world who play a very important role in helping children to become literate. We can model the various uses of literacy in day-to-day living, expect children to gradually become literate beings, and respond enthusiastically to children's progressive steps toward fluent literacy. It is what we say and do, and how we do it, that sends messages to the children with whom we work on how we value their literacy attempts. The message is also sent through the types of ac-

tivities and learning situations that we structure for children. If we react in negative ways to children's literacy attempts, children are more likely to dislike reading and writing and to spend less time doing it. Examples of things the children may consider negative include: giving them work that is too easy for them, assigning work that turns them off to literacy (such as sheets and sheets of meaningless activities), or harshly correcting each incorrect attempt at literacy.

If, however, we respond to the children in positive ways by structuring their instruction around interesting practice, with concepts and skills that are just beyond their comfort zone (i.e., in their zone of proximal development), and if we help the students to master these, we are likely to encourage them to develop positive dispositions toward literacy. Children who have experienced positive adult responses to their literacy attempts are more likely to spend time reading and writing, to improve with this time and practice, and to continue to become lifelong literate members of society.

Functions of Oral and Written Language

The behaviors in oral and written language that adults model and foster are quite similar. In many ways, so too are the functions of oral and written language. Within the functions, however, there are some differences. Let's look at the functions of oral language first.

Oral Language Functions

Halliday (1975, 2002) lists the following functions of spoken language, which represent the variety of ways that children and adults use language to communicate (Stewig & Jett-Simpson, 1995:26):

- **Instrumental**—to satisfy needs and wants: *"Can I have a glass of water?"*
- **Regulatory**—to control others: *"You may get a drink from the water fountain."*
- **Interactional**—to create interactions with others: *"Hi, I'm Sheila, want to play?"*
- **Personal**—to express personal thoughts and opinions: *"I think we should take a vote on this."*
- **Imaginative**—to create imaginary worlds: *"Let's pretend that you are the Mom and I am the baby."*
- **Heuristic**—to seek information: *"When is our homework due?"*
- **Informative**—to communicate information: *"The book report is due in two weeks."*

Written Language Functions

In addition to the seven functions of oral language, *written* language includes six more functions. To become successful at reading and writing written language, children must learn these well (McGee & Richgels, 2000). The additional six functions include:

- **Reminding oneself of information/remembering information:** *"The school carnival is on June 1."*
- **Sending information over time and distances:** *To: akm@pilot.msu.edu. "Hello."*
- **Communicating with people to whom we are unfamiliar:** *"Dear Mr. Bridwell, I think Clifford is lonely . . . "*
- **Establishing identity:** *"My name is Tim. My favorite sport is sailing."*
- **Recording information:** *"There are 22 children present today—10 girls and 12 boys. No one is absent."*
- **Increasing knowledge:** *"Let's look on the Internet for more information on the Mars probe."*

Children can be observed frequently engaging in these functions as they experiment and discover the capacities of written language. In any early childhood classroom on any given day, one might find children engaged in any or all of the following: making lists of people they will invite to their birthday party (recording information); writing these invitations at the writing center and mailing them in the classroom mailbox (sending information over distance); signing their names to the cards and inserting a map to their house with the landmarks labeled (establishing identity); and thinking of new people to invite as they write (generating new information).

Concepts of Written Language

There are three concepts within the functions of written language: **content, form,** and **use** (McGee & Richgels, 2000). Like the functions of language, these concepts develop over time. When they are completely developed, children have a good understanding of print. To illustrate these concepts, let's use the picture written by Jiwhan, age 3-6 (3 years, 6 months), shown in Figure 2.1.

Figure 2.1 Jiwhan's writing.

Jiwhan wrote this one summer morning at the writing table and eagerly brought it over to his head teacher, Mrs. Reynolds. "Look, Mrs. Reynolds! I wrote a story for you today!"

As she squatted down to listen, he took his finger, put it under the letters and began to tell the story: "Once upon a time there were three bears. Their mommy made some oatmeal. It was too hot, so they went on a picnic instead. They walked and they walked and they walked. OOOH!"

Jiwhan stopped and covered his mouth. He had been diligently pointing to the letters on the paper, but he had suddenly run out of "words." "I'll be right back. Stay here!" he directed his teacher. He went back to the writing table and wrote more letters until there was no more room on the paper. He then came back and resumed his story.

Jiwhan's story and writing can tell us a lot about his understanding of the three concepts of written language. Let's look at each concept separately.

Content refers to the idea that print holds meaningful ideas. Children learn that there is a language we use to discuss written language and that print contains unchanging messages. What the book said yesterday will be exactly what it says today. Children also come to see print as independent of its surroundings. *McDonald's* says "McDonald's" even when it is not written in yellow on a red background.

Jiwhan's story, a new version of the old favorite, "The Three Bears," was told in a way that shows us that he understands that there is a certain language we use in writing. However, he did not yet understand the second part of content: that it holds unchanging messages. This was evident when he took this very same story to another teacher and told her that it said she was the best teacher in the world and he was going to miss her!

Form refers to the conventions of print—how print is structured on the page (left to right, top to bottom) or in a book (front to back, left page to right page), punctuation, and spacing. It also indicates the formal relationship between print and speech as evidenced in the child's writings, and the awareness of the language segments in print (sentences, words, syllables, onsets, rimes, and letters). Finally, form refers to the variety of formats of print used for organizing language—story print as opposed to expository-informational print.

Jiwhan knows a lot about form. He started writing at the top left-hand corner and went to the right, using this pattern for the entire story. Although his work does not show evidence of punctuation and spacing, he did demonstrate the concept that there is a rela-

tionship between print and language when he stopped reading and covered his mouth because he had no letters left!

Use deals with the functions of print in the world and in children's play. Rules for interaction with print are also housed within this category. Children learn quite early on that books are to read, not to throw. They learn that the pictures in the books are not real things and that the events happening in the book are not necessarily real life, nor are they really happening at this moment as the book is read.

Jiwhan, at his preschool age, already has some understanding of the use of print. When asked the day after he wrote his story how the bears were doing, he looked at Mrs. Reynolds and said, "It's just pretend, silly!"

While Jiwhan's full understanding of the uses of print will continue to develop over time, he already has a good start. Where did he get this start? From many people and places.

Children acquire information about portions of each of these concepts as they encounter print and literate behaviors in the world and people around them. They also discover these subtleties as they play with both oral and written language and explore their varied uses. The exploration and discovery processes are not simply intuitive, chance occurrences. Optimally, they occur with nurturing and support by adults in the children's lives.

Methods of Organizing Literacy Instruction

There are a variety of ways that we as educators can support children's literacy development. Specifically, three types of methods are successful in literacy development: discovery learning, guided learning, and direct instruction. The methods vary in the degree to which the teacher actively interacts with the child and in the person who provides the information and instruction. All three types of methods are relevant in a developing literacy classroom.

Discovery learning is described well by its name. The teacher purposefully prepares the environment to allow children to pursue activities of interest independently, or in small groups. The child chooses the primary direction of the learning, although the teacher facilitates this process through the careful preparation of the environment—by what is added and what is absent. The teacher is nearby to step in with questions and suggestions to keep the children moving along in their activities, as well as to assess the children's progress to plan for future purposeful activities adjusted to the learning levels demonstrated by the children in the class. In discovery learning, the child is the main focus and source of the learning, with the teacher nearby to lend support.

Guided learning describes more of a balance between teacher and child interaction. The teacher or a skilled peer acts as the leader, helping the less skilled child to move to new levels of learning while allowing the child to do as much of the task or activity as possible. The direction the lesson takes depends to a great degree on the child or children involved in the task. The teacher takes cues from the situation at hand, while also paying attention to instructional objectives. Guided learning may be carried out in a teacher–child interaction, in small groups, or in a large group. The context of the situation depends on the children's needs and the objectives of the given learning segment. Vygotsky's technique of scaffolding falls into this category.

Direct instruction is the most teacher directed–teacher controlled method. The main difference between direct instruction and the other two methods is that in direct instruction, the teacher directs the learning. Often, it is the adult who tells the child how to do something or who provides the information. Some believe that direct instruction has no place in a developmentally appropriate setting. This is not true. Certain things must be taught by direct instruction; for others, it only makes sense to use discovery learning, and for still others, guided learning is the best choice.

Any one of these, when used as the *primary* mode of instruction, can leave many children feeling unsuccessful. Some will feel lost, confused, or overwhelmed. Others may be unchallenged and may become bored. However, when they are used together in a purposefully planned concert, all children can feel success and can hum their own literacy tune. It is important to recognize that all three processes should be used to meet instructional objectives and that these should be adjusted to the levels of individual children. The methodology you choose to implement your objectives should best fit the needs of the situation. Look for use of these three methods in the discussions and applications in the rest of this chapter as well as in Chapters 4, 5, and 6.

To determine where and when to use which type of methodology to teach literacy, it is important that you possess a full understanding of the process of literacy and its core components.

Critical Core Components of Literacy

The literacy process lies on a developmental continuum. Because each child lives in a slightly different contextual world, it is not possible (nor would it be desirable) to lay out an age-and-stage recipe for the development of literacy. Therefore, literacy's core components are best explained as stages in an evolutionary process. Please keep in mind that literacy development is not necessarily a smooth progression (Clay, 1991; Sulzby, Teale, & Kamberelis, 1989). Children may make progress in one area while virtually standing still in another. In this book, the process of literacy learning is sometimes chunked into three phases: the emerging phase, the early phase, and the fluent phase. This may sound confusing, because earlier

in the chapter we described the entire process as *emergent literacy,* but now we are labeling the first phase as the *emerging phase.* This does not mean that the other phases are not part of the entire process of emergent literacy. The label *emerging* is also typically used to describe the beginning developing level of literacy. The labels are used only for the purpose of clarifying the progression so that parents and teachers are better able to plan instruction accordingly for individual children. They are *not* intended as a classification of children.

The Role of Oral Language

We are all familiar with oral language. We've been using it for years. Thanks to Halliday (1975, 2002) and our previous discussion of oral language, we are well aware of the seven specific functions of language (instrumental, regulatory, interactional, personal, imaginative, heuristic, and informative) and of the link between oral language and the home environment. As discussed in the previous section, oral language is linked with literacy. It mediates early literacy learning (Thomas & Rinehart, 1990). In fact, the ability of children to *reflect* on language and to communicate new information has been linked to their future literacy abilities (Snow, Cancino, Gonzalez, & Shriberg, 1989). Children's abilities to use language that is **decontextualized,** or not part of the current situation, are also strongly linked to literacy ability (Dickinson & Tabors, 2001).

Halliday (1975, 2002) hypothesizes that the seven functions of oral language appear in a developmental progression as children grow. These emerge as the individual child sees the need for making meaning through a different avenue. Thus, as oral language is developing, children are adding to their concepts of functions of language. In the children that they studied, Thomas and Rinehart (1990) found a direct connection between the functions of language used orally and those represented in writing. For individual children, they also linked the functions the children used with the functions reportedly used primarily in the home.

Thus, in homes where the adult focus was on instrumental and regulatory interactions, the children primarily used just these. Although only a small number of children were studied, it was interesting to note that the children who interacted more with siblings at home and whose parents reported interactions of lower functional levels used lower functions of language orally and in writing than did their counterparts who had no siblings at home and whose parents reported interacting at higher language function levels. Apparently, adults do serve as an important role model for learning the seven functions of language.

If this is true for adults in homes, it must also be true in classrooms. "Implicit in school success is the teacher's own model of the language" (Thomas & Rinehart, 1990:22). In addition to being a model for children, adults can use oral language as a tool to help children take on more complex tasks (Cazden, 1988). Dickinson and

Tabors (2001) found that when preschool teachers used rare words in discussions with children, the children's vocabulary was expanded. The adults' use of rare words was positively related to later literacy development. In addition, when teachers engaged children in cognitively challenging conversations, the children also benefited. Next to the role of the adult as a tool for oral language development in school to support literacy, there are also two other key components: friendship and play.

In addition to modeling language and its use as a mediating tool, Pelligrini and Galda (1996) suggest that friendships serve to strengthen oral language and to enhance literacy development through the cognitive problems that friendships can stimulate. In friendships, children disagree and work to solve their conflicts. This process involves the cognitive manipulation of thoughts and the careful use of language. While trying hard to think about how to solve the friendship problems and say the right thing, children are directly involved in metacognitive and metalinguistic awareness skills that are directly used in literacy learning (Pelligrini, Galda, Stahl, & Shockley, 1995). "Close relationships, like friendship, support synchronous and cognitively complex interactions. The emotional tenor of these relationships afford children opportunities to reflect upon cognitive and linguistic processes which constitute early literacy" (Pelligrini & Galda, 1996:13).

There also has been much research about the link between play and literacy, emphasizing the role of oral language. It is believed that throughout children's interactions with peers in play, both oral language and the mental processes for literacy are supported. In play, children's uses of linguistic verbs, such as *tell, read, talk,* and *listen,* are a good predictor of their future reading abilities (Pellegrini et al., 1991). Children playing together talk about what *is,* what *was,* and what *can be.* They suspend reality and play with concepts, thoughts, and language. Research supports the belief that talk about language and literacy, such as the talk that occurs during play, as well as play with language (e.g., rhyming), is a reliable predictor of literacy (Pelligrini & Galda, 1996; Bradley & Bryant, 1983). This talk about language and rhyming is also an indicator of phonemic awareness (Pellegrini et al., 1995), which is one of the two major predictors at the beginning of first grade for success with reading (Adams, 1990).

Perhaps the most important contribution that play makes to oral language and literacy development is that in play children engage in symbolic thought, the same type of thinking that children must use when reading and writing. To read and write with fluency, children must be able to see one thing (e.g., the letters *c-a-t*) symbolically stand for another thing (the animal *cat*).

Dickinson and Tabors (2001) found that the language that occurs between mothers and children during play was related to later literacy success in kindergarten. During play with mothers, children used language to communicate beyond the here and now, in a decontextualized manner. When adults, including teachers, support sociodramatic play, they are able to enhance language development (McGee, 2003).

Through **book acting** (creative storytelling and acting out books heard), children play with the language of books and stories at a very personal level (McGee, 2003). They meet the characters of books "face to face" and gain deeper comprehension of the text. Compared to children who simply draw pictures and talk about stories heard, children who act out the stories develop better vocabularies, use more complex language, and have better story comprehension (Pelligrini & Galda, 1982). Further, when children use **metalanguage** (language in which the talk is about the actions and dialogue which are going to take place), they develop more emergent literacy concepts than those who use less metalanguage (Galda, Pelligrini, & Cox, 1989).

Ironically, as children mature, it is often the practice that more emphasis is placed on reading and writing and less time and energy is spent during the school day engaged in oral language. Typically, as children progress through the grades, reduced amounts of time are spent in children engaging in meaningful conversation with peers and expressing ideas. Often, quiet work time is the rule. Unfortunately, this does not encourage children to share ideas or talk through difficult problems. Also reduced and often absent is practice with symbolic thought through activities such as block building, dramatic play, and free-form art.

From this discussion, it appears that adults can do six things to support children's oral language development and, consequently, their literacy development. These are addressed in "Applications for Oral Language Development."

APPLICATIONS FOR ORAL LANGUAGE DEVELOPMENT

1. Engage in conversation directly with every child in your care in a meaningful way. These interactions should foster the development of Halliday's seven functions of language.
2. Organize for communication between parents and teachers about the importance of using these seven functions of language with children on a daily basis.

3. Communicate with parents and other teachers about the role friendships can play in cognitive development and their direct link with literacy. Share information on how to focus specifically on friendship skills and coaching.

4. Organize the children's schedule to support their active engagement in meaningful activities. Be sure that this schedule specifically allows for children to work with peers and develop friendships.

5. Allow for children to engage in activities daily to support the development of symbolic thought. Possible activities include block building, free-form art activities with a variety of materials, and dramatic play. What dramatic play looks like for 3-year-olds is not what it will look like with 8-year-olds. The dynamics of the dramatic play situations will depend on the children involved.

6. Support many types of children's play: free play, sociodramatic play, replay of stories, retelling of stories, and acting out stories heard.

The Role of Phonological Awareness

There is a strong back to basics movement in the educational and political arena, which includes an emphasis on a strong phonics approach. To a degree, the call for phonics is not unfounded. Phonics *is* an important tool in the literacy process. It is not, however, the only tool. The power of phonological awareness is also staunchly recognized as a very powerful apparatus for literacy development.

"Great," you say, "we've been this route before. Phonics, phonological awareness—what's the difference? The pendulum of education keeps swinging from whole language to phonics and back again."

This actually is not the case here. Phonological awareness is not the same as phonics. It is a separate, yet complementary, component of literacy. Although both phonics and phonological awareness are important in reading, the emphasis in this section is on **phonological awareness**—the ability to hear the sounds in language and to comprehend them in spoken language (Griffith & Olson, 1992). **Phonics,** on the other hand, is the relationship between sounds and letters in written language (Stahl, 1992). (This will be addressed when we discuss print awareness.) Before phonics instruction can be fully useful to a child, the children seem to need to hear the sounds in language on some level before they can manipulate them in a symbolic form (Busink, 1997).

It is important to note that phonological awareness does not refer to one specific skill. It refers to a number of skills that work together to help the individual hear the discrete sounds—the **phonemes**—in language (Treiman & Zukowski, 1996). While the debate continues over whether phonological awareness is a precursor to reading or a byproduct of reading, there is solid agreement that it is an important element in literacy development (Busink, 1997; Goswami, 2001; McGee & Richgels, 2003; Treiman

& Zukowski, 1996). There is also research indicating that children can benefit from instruction in phonological awareness (Ayres, 1994; Bus & Van Ijzendoorn, 1999). This beneficial instruction can occur both before *and* during reading and writing instruction (Busink, 1997).

Phonological awareness—knowledge of the sounds in speech—is a necessary skill that must be addressed with young children. It has been correlated with many aspects of literacy in a variety of studies. Bradley and Bryant (1985) found that the phonological awareness that young children acquire before learning to read has a powerful influence on their eventual success in learning to read and to spell. Children without any phonological awareness before elementary school begin at a disadvantage. They may spend much time playing catch-up and falling further behind (Bradley & Bryant, 1991). A classic study by Juel, Griffith, and Gough (1986) followed children from first grade through fourth and found that children who were at the bottom of their class in phonemic awareness in first grade remained at the bottom in reading through fourth grade.

Stahl and Murray (1994) reached two conclusions pertaining to phonological awareness and reading. First, the ability to manipulate **onsets** and **rimes** (the beginning and ending parts of words) within syllables relates most strongly to reading, given that the child has a basic level of letter recognition. Second, the child's ability to isolate a phoneme from the beginning or ending of a word appears to be "crucial to reading" (p. 231). Many other studies have shown a strong correlation between the ability to decode words and phonological awareness (Busink, 1997; Bradley & Bryant, 1983). There is too much evidence supporting the importance of phonological awareness to overlook it in the literacy recipe. Phonological awareness is an important ingredient in learning to read and to write. In fact, phonological awareness has been cited as a critical factor in learning to read (Snow et al., 1998; Goswami, 2001).

Like many other aspects of development, phonological awareness proceeds in a set progression. Fowler (1991) contends that the growth of phonological awareness begins with infancy and gradually develops from whole to part. Initially, children hear all of language as one big piece of "blah blah blah." Over time, they begin to discriminate more of the pieces and eventually become able to hear the individual sounds in language. This process evolves *through* age 8, meaning that children through third grade benefit from practice with phonological awareness.

One subcategory of phonological awareness, **phonemic awareness,** does not begin until about age 4. Phonemic awareness is the ability to hear the phonemes—the individual sounds in spoken words. Although this begins to appear at age 4, we can prepare children for it from infancy by using some fairly common, simple language-literacy techniques such as reading and telling familiar stories, reciting nursery rhymes, and singing songs.

Treiman and Zukowski (1991) have documented the specific progression of phonological awareness (see Figure 2.2). First, one begins by hearing the individual words in sentences. For some children, this is an inner event; for others, it is quite public. Have you ever seen a young child begin talking like a robot, one word at a time, and break into laughter from the sheer joy of the activity? This child is demonstrating an understanding that sentences can be broken into words.

After the discovery of words as separate entities, a child will begin to recognize that words are made up of syllables. Children often demonstrate this by roaming around the classroom or the home clapping and saying words at the same time. It also is evident when children are choosing the leader with a poem such as "Bubble Gum, Bubble Gum" and separate the last few words into syllables so they can declare themselves the winner. *"Bubble Gum, Bubble Gum-in-a-dish. How ma-ny pie-ces do you wish?"*

Onsets follow syllables in the progression of phonological awareness. **Onsets** are the beginning sound of any word—for example, **B**-ox, **Ch**-air, **S**-esame **Str**-eet. Note that these are not the first letters, but the first *sounds* appearing before the initial vowel.

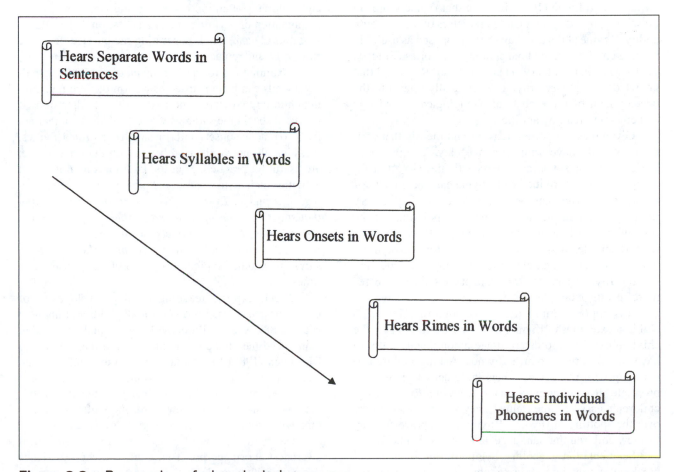

Figure 2.2   Progression of phonological awareness.

Source: Adapted from Treiman and Zukowski (1991).

Rimes (not to be confused with *rhymes,* a different concept altogether) are the portions of the word that follow the onset. In the preceding example, the rimes would be **ox, air, esame,** and **eet.** Children often demonstrate their understanding of onsets and rimes when they write words: **Kt** (*c-at*), **Bd** (*B-ird*).

Phonemes are the final piece of the phonological code that young children develop in the progression. Children with phonemic awareness can take a word like **call** and break it into its components of *c-a-ll.* These intricate pieces of spoken language are the tools children use to decode and to spell words. Through language play, the sounds of language—the phonemes—become more apparent to young children (Maclean, Bryant, & Bradley, 1987). Direct instruction in phonological skills also can play a big role in making these "quiet," camouflaged pieces of language "loud" and apparent.

Within the set of skills called phonological awareness, there appear to be two major sets of skills: general awareness of sounds in language and awareness of the parts of language—the phonemes. To help children become aware of sounds in language, playing with language is recommended. One of the best activities for playing with the language to help the sounds come alive seems to be rhyme.

Ellis and Large (1987) indicate that rhyme scores in preschool proved to be reliable predictors of later reading ability. Rhyme skills also have been proposed as useful in helping children learn about spelling categories (Bradley, 1988). Maclean et al. (1987) and Ayres (1994) found that knowledge of nursery rhymes specifically relates to the development of more abstract phonological knowledge and emergent reading abilities.

Given these important reasons and the fun that children naturally have with language play, it only makes sense to include sound-awareness activities as part of literacy planning. Activities with rhyme can take on a variety of forms. They can be as simple as reciting nursery rhymes or singing nonsense songs and pointing out the rhyming words in each. Other rhyming activities include reading simple rhyme books, listening for the rhyming words in the story and clapping when a pair is said, and playing rhyming games. See Chapters 4 through 6 for more specific examples.

It is important, initially, for the adult to point out to children examples of rhyme, then for the adult to give the children examples to discriminate among, and finally to have the children produce rhymes. Asking children to come up with rhymes as a beginning activity is not appropriate. It is an activity that will *eventually* occur. As children's ears become trained, they will eventually take over the spotting of rhymes. Rhyming is a powerful way to show children that language and literacy can be fun!

Segmentation is another. **Segmentation** is the act of breaking words into discrete phonemes. For example, *Buddy* would be segmented *B-U-D-Y.* Segmentation has been determined by Mueter, Hulme, Snowling, and Taylor

(1997) to be strongly correlated with reading and spelling achievement at the end of the first year of school. Stanovich (1991) suggests also that it is the segmentation ability that facilitates reading development. The act of segmenting directly relates to phonemic awareness. The reason that segmenting appears to be so important in literacy is that in order for children to be able to figure out how to read and write new words, they must be able to segment the sounds of language.

The ability to segment words seems to occur in a progressive fashion. At first children can segment the first sound, then the first and last sounds. Typically, it is not until the end of first grade or sometime in second grade that the other consonants are segmented (Vandervelden & Siegel, 1995). To teach awareness of these discrete sounds of language, segmentation activities work well.

A combination of segmentation and rhyming can occur with onsets and rimes, which are important concepts in the literacy acquisition process. Onsets and rimes are the ways that language users organize syllables (Treiman & Zukowski, 1991). Stahl and Murray (1994) found that after children learned to recognize letters, the ability to manipulate onsets and rimes within syllables related most strongly to reading. One way in which you can focus children's attention on onsets and rimes is to use a combination of rhyming and segmentation. When Philip says *"sand/hand,"* he is separating the onset, *s,* from the rime, *and,* and replacing it with the onset *h* to form *hand.* The separation is a form of segmentation. Matching ending sounds can be construed as a form of rhyming. Giving children two words and asking them to determine if the words begin the same way or end alike is another activity to practice onsets and rimes. **Alliteration** activities, in which all the words used begin with the same sound, are useful for practicing onsets. Examples of alliteration activities include the traditional picnic game. *"We're going on a picnic. Everyone will bring or eat something that starts with the same sound as their name. Alice ate apples. Ben brought bagels, Cameron carted carrots. . . ."* Word families (e.g., *ay: day, play, say, may, stay*) are another typical way to highlight onsets and rimes.

Direct, explicit teaching in the development of phonemic awareness is *crucial* for all children (Lundberg et al., 1988). A few children will learn it on their own, but many need the phonemes pointed out to them. Ball and Blachman (1988) found that kindergarten children who were trained in phonological awareness and letters and sound knowledge had higher phoneme segmentation abilities and could figure out new words more often than children without training in phonological awareness.

The ramifications of not developing phonological awareness are staggering. Young readers who experience difficulty with phonological awareness will be exposed to less print. They probably will practice less. They ultimately will fail to develop automatic word recognition.

Instead, they will spend all of their time trying to decode words rather than reading for meaning. This leaves little time, energy, or interest to spend on comprehension (Stanovich, 1986). It is likely that children who struggle to decode will be turned off to reading, choose to do it less, spend less time reading, and never develop an appreciation for the wonders of reading. Adding to this dismal picture, it only follows that if a child is not reading with comprehension, general knowledge and vocabulary growth also will be affected negatively.

Phonological awareness not only has an impact on the beginning reader, but also greatly affects readers in all other stages. Children who have a strong foundation in phonological awareness are better able to sound out new words or even nonsense words. They also develop greater automaticity—they learn to recognize familiar rime patterns, and reading becomes much more fluent (Stanovich, West, & Cunningham, 1991). Children with good phono-

logical awareness spend more time on gaining meaning from print.

Given the impact phonological awareness has on reading and spelling abilities, it is unfair to wait for it to happen naturally. All children deserve an equal opportunity to become readers. Specifically planning for instruction in phonological awareness helps to ensure success for all children as future readers. Ayres (1994) found that direct instruction in phonological awareness was more effective in increasing children's phonological awareness than indirect methods.

Without a doubt, phonological awareness training belongs in every classroom, preschool through third grade. It could even be included in fourth and fifth grades, just to keep the children playing with language. Of course, the form it takes will depend on the needs of children in the class. The following shows applications for everyday events for classrooms.

APPLICATIONS FOR PHONOLOGICAL AWARENESS

1. Include activities in your day in which children hear, say, and see language simultaneously. This can help children at all stages of literacy development to see some of the connections between oral and written language. **Example:** *At group time, choose big books to read that have rhyme in them. Point to the words as you read. Invite children to clap or snap each time they hear the rhyming, and to tell you the rhyming pair. Make the pair of words with magnetic letters for all to see.*

2. Encourage **word play.** Plan for rhyming activities using stories, games, and songs so that children can hear the sounds of language and manipulate them orally. **Example:** *Take favorite rhyming songs and change the rhyming words. Sing the refrain and first phrase: "We'll catch a snake and . . . " Let your voice drop off, and allow the children to brainstorm new endings that rhyme.*

3. Design **segmentation activities.** With very young children, practice segmenting sentences into words. For older children, segment the entire word into its discrete letters and sounds. **Example:** *To segment sentences into words, count the words in a sentence.*

4. Use **alliteration.** Structure alliteration activities weekly. **Example:** *Write silly poems, read alliteration books, invite students to help create alliterative messages.*

5. Encourage children to use **temporary spelling** (that is, writing the sounds they hear, which may or may not include all of the letters in the standard spelling of the word). As they progress in their understanding, they will revise their temporary spelling into book spelling. **Example:** *Invite children to write in their journals each day.*

Training in phonological awareness alone is not enough for children to develop literacy skills. The training must be directly connected with a working knowledge of

the alphabet as well as an accurate understanding of the correspondence between **graphemes** (the letter symbols) and **phonemes** (McGuinness, McGuinness, & Donohue,

Using phonological awareness for temporary spelling.

1995). This connection is known as the **alphabetic principle.** It has been cited as another major predictor for future literacy success (Snow et al., 1998; McGee & Richgels, 2003). "If this connection (between phonemes and graphemes) is not made clearly and concretely, a child's phonological processing skill may not become engaged in decoding, because visual strategies take precedence" (McGuinness, Olson, & Chaplin, 1990).

Let's continue our discussion with a look at some of the ways that children can learn about print and the connection between phonemes and graphemes.

The Role of Print

Along with hearing the individual words and sounds in spoken language, children need to develop an awareness of words and letters in written language. Children must learn that print symbolizes language and holds information (Adams, 1990). This is called **print awareness.**

According to Adams (1990), print awareness includes five important pieces:

1. Print is categorically different from other kinds of visual patterns in the environment.
2. Print is print across any of a variety of physical media.
3. Print seems to be everywhere.
4. Print is used in many different ways and occurs in many different forms.
5. Anyone can produce print.

In addition to Adams's five concepts of general print awareness, Marie Clay (1991) explains that there are more specific concepts about print which children must learn.

She calls these **concepts *about* print.** These include basic print concepts such as recognizing a letter and a word; understanding that words are made up of letters and sentences are made up of words; knowledge that words are the part that we read; knowing where to begin reading a book and how the text progresses (left to right, front to back). There are 24 concepts about print in all. For more on this, see the assessment for concepts about print (CAPs) in Chapter 7.

The Role of Word Awareness

Just as children must be taught that spoken language is made up of words, so too, do they need training in written word awareness. Following the same progression as auditory training, children also need to become aware that sentences consist of words, and words are made up of letters, which, in turn, stand for sounds. (This is where phonics comes in.) When discussing knowledge about words, two separate concepts arise: **knowledge about words** and **concepts about words.**

Knowledge about Words

Frith (1985) suggests that children go through three stages as they learn about words (see Figure 2.3). The first stage is **logographic.** During this stage, the children give meaning to the logos and pictures found in familiar sights. As early as 18 months, children can begin to associate McDonald's golden arches with french fries. Later, they will refer to the sign as "McDonald's." This is not because the children are necessarily blossoming geniuses (although they *are* blossoming readers), it is because they are relating the sign to the context (hamburgers and french fries). If the McDon-

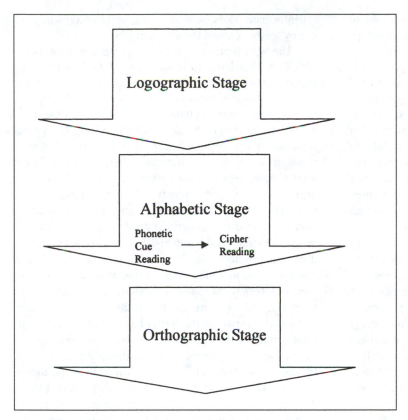

Figure 2.3 Progression of knowledge about words.

Source: Adapted from Frith (1985).

ald's sign were to appear in blue and green on a sheet of pa-per, the children probably would not recognize it.

Logographic reading is commonly seen in young children with a best loved story book. They have heard the favorite book so many times that they know it by heart. By looking at what is on the pages (the context), they are able to associate the illustrations with the words heard be-fore they can read the words. This is not meant to demean this early stage. Indeed, when children engage in logo-graphic reading, it is an event to be celebrated. They are on the path to literacy!

The second stage in the development of word knowl-edge is **alphabetic.** As this concept develops, children who know at least some of the alphabet letters begin to recognize that the letters are associated with sounds. Ini-tially, children at this stage may engage in **phonetic cue reading,** in which they read printed words by remember-ing some sound–letter associations (Ehri & Sweet, 1991). This is evident in early childhood classrooms in which children's names are displayed daily. Children who are using phonetic cue reading will look at the names *Jason* and *Jimmy* and read them both as "Jason" because they begin with *J* and they know that Jason's name begins with a *J*. They are not yet able to separate each letter, *J-I-M-M-Y,* and pair it with a single sound. They cannot sound words out one phoneme at a time, nor can they blend them

back together to form the word *Jimmy.* Later in this stage, however, children can do these things. This stage is called **cipher reading** (Juel, 1991). Cipher readers can read and figure out nonsense words. They figure out what words say by associating sounds with individual letters.

It is not until children reach the **orthographic stage** that they are able to associate familiar letter patterns (rimes) with sound segments. Children at this stage strive to recall automatically or notice these familiar patterns. When this occurs, the event of reading changes for the child. At the orthographic stage, children spend more time reading for comprehension and less time decoding words.

Children in the emerging phase of literacy are in the logographic stage and developing toward or beginning the alphabetic stage. Accordingly, children in the early phase are likely to be found focusing mostly on the alphabetic stage, moving into the orthographic stage. Children to-ward the fluent end of the continuum will be primarily or-thographic readers.

Concepts about Words

The second important topic here is **concepts *about* words.** Orally, we do not typically break our speech into separate words. Doing so would sound like robot talk. Instead, we convey our messages in streams, which are often quite long. Even so, children learn to speak in words and to combine these words into sentences. Just as this develops over time, so do children's concepts of written words. At first, children write in streams, ignoring the spacing between words. As they grow in their understanding of the concept of *word*, they eventually begin to signify their knowledge of words by putting dots or large spaces between words. Roberts (1992) traced the development of the concept of *word* in children and found that as children become aware of words in oral language, they also become aware of words in written language at an intuitive level. Later, they develop a true understanding of written words and, finally, they develop a complete understanding of spoken words. Full understanding of the connection between spoken words and their written counterparts doesn't typically happen until after formalized reading instruction has begun (Ferrerio & Teberosky, 1982).

If you know where children are in their understanding of word concepts, you can more appropriately plan experiences to help them progress. One reason that this concept of word is so critical to help children develop is that it has been found that children's levels of word concept at first grade are a significant predictor of their reading achievements (Estrin & Chaney, 1988). Another significant predictor of reading achievement is knowledge of letters and sounds at the beginning of first grade (Adams, 1990).

The Role of Alphabet Knowledge

As they move from reading familiar signs and pictures to focusing more on letters and words, and then to reading for information and understanding, children typically begin by learning about the alphabet.

The typical progression for learning about letters begins with knowledge of letter names. Children often are introduced to this through a variety of activities at home and in preschools, child care centers, and kindergartens. Once children have the letter name in memory, other concepts such as the grapheme (symbol) and sound–symbol relationship can be attached to it. It is more efficient in terms of both learning and memory to introduce different aspects about letters in a progression. Adams (1990) suggests introducing letter names A–Z, then symbols for all, then their symbol–sound correspondence (the phonics aspect). She also recommends introducing uppercase letters in preschool and lowercase letters in first grade. She does not promote blending them together, which can cause confusion. Once letter–sound instruction has begun, it is beneficial to use a combination of the letter, a keyword, and a picture display in the form of the letter: *S—snake*—a snake in the form of an *S*. Note that even instruction in letters should be done in a way that is meaningful and directly involves the children's participation. Of greatest importance is the specific role of the alphabetic principle. It is hypothesized that through children's development of the alphabetic principle, their understanding of individual phonemes increases (Goswami, 2001).

The roles of print, word, and alphabet knowledge are all important in the literacy process. Here are some things that can be done in the classroom to support their development.

APPLICATIONS FOR PRINT, WORD, AND LETTER AWARENESS

1. Structure daily experiences in which children are actively involved with meaningful text that they hear, see, and say to help them make connections between speech and writing.

2. Pay close attention to your children's individual understandings of print awareness, concepts about print, knowledge of word, concept of word, and knowledge of letters and sounds. Plan ways to move them specifically toward the next level of understanding.

3. Use texts of varying lengths. With the children, take the text apart and discuss its component parts. Segment written sentences into words, first orally, then together with the words. Segment words into chunks and individual letters.

4. Plan activities that teach and reinforce children's knowledge about letters and sounds that are meaningful to the children.

5. Involve children in planning activities to reinforce their knowledge of letters and sounds. For example, invite children to make games about letters they know well to share with one another. Develop riddles about blends and share these with other classes.

The Role of Writing

Although children demonstrate their understanding of the alphabetic principle in their writing, you actually do not see this right away. Instead, you first notice other symbols. One of the most relevant forms of print for children is their own writing. As part of literacy, the same rules apply to writing as to reading. There is no readiness standard that must be met before children begin to write. Therefore, it is a myth that children must learn their letters before they begin writing or vice versa. Writing and reading develop simultaneously. The development is a long, involved process. Sulzby, Teale, and Kamberelis (1989) state that most destructive to children and their creativity (and their disposition toward writing) is the assumption that they cannot write until they have mastered the mechanics of writing and can use conventional spelling.

Children begin the writing process from the time they can hold a writing utensil. Initially, children's drawing and writing may look like the same thing. Over time, however, as the children are surrounded by print, they come to see drawing and writing as two different symbol systems and will differentiate between the two (Dyson, 2001). By age 6, children are able to move freely between writing and drawing systems in producing written communication (Harste, 1990). In addition, through writing, children learn that the purpose of text is to be understood. They learn that written language is not exactly the same as spoken language and that it can be used for a variety of purposes. Children communicate this understanding through the differentiation they make between various types of writing they use in lists, letters, and stories (McGee & Richgels, 2000).

Children's initial concepts about alphabet letters are not the same as adults'. Often, children in the emerging phase do not think of letters as units of language that are part of words and related to sounds. Instead, they may think of individual letters as symbols of things that are meaningful to them (McGee & Richgels, 2000). Imagine reading a book with a young child named Jackie when, from nowhere, she gets very excited, points to the *J*, and says, "Hey! That says *Jackie!*" The child has not yet figured out that her *J* is shared with many others!

A distinction must be made here between writing as a graphic–symbol system and writing as a companion to reading. Those who have looked at writing in preschool and early elementary school have found that at this early point in schooling, developmentally, there is a weak relationship between writing and reading (Pellegrini, Galda, Dresden, & Cox, 1991). As children progress in their understanding of writing, the relationship becomes much stronger. It appears that the distinguishing difference between early writing and later writing is in the way the child is representing language. Initially, children represent language graphically. They use pictures and letters that sound like the word (e.g., *U* for *you*) to stand for

Modeling the role of writing.

things. Only as children learn more about written language and become more proficient at symbolic thought do they make the transition from graphical representation to symbolic representation ("you" means *you*) (Dyson, 2001). Only then does the relationship between writing and reading strengthen.

Children's signatures are good ways to discover children's understanding of print (McGee & Richgels, 2003). A child who has not yet differentiated pictures from letters may draw a blob or a face and say, "That says *Jackie*. That's me." As the children experience print, they will begin to make a scribble to stand for themselves, then a single shape or two, then the first letter of their name, and finally their complete first name. A progression of children's name writing was developed in 1936 by Hildreth (see Figure 2.4).

If they are given time and support in writing the sounds they hear in language, children's everyday writing will reflect their growing understanding of the phonemic structure of words (Adams, 1990). Thus, temporary

spelling (also referred to as *invented spelling*) can positively affect children's phonological awareness. It also has been shown to have a positive effect on word recognition (Baron & Treiman, 1980). Temporary spelling is not acceptable forever. There is a time and a place to be concerned about "book" or conventional spelling. It is important to use conventional spelling in published work by children. This can be implemented quite naturally within the writing process. For more on the writing process, see work by Donald Graves, Lucy Calkins, or Dorothy Strickland.

Production of Print

There are various names for the general stages children progress through in producing print (see Figure 2.5). The beginning, of course, comes when children first hold writing utensils. After initial exploration, they typically begin to make marks on pages. At first these marks are *only* marks, but they begin to take on a variety of forms. This

Figure 2.4   Name writing progression.

Source: Adapted from Hildreth (1936).

Scribble Stage (Mock Writing)	*Marks*
Prephonemic Stage	*Marks that look like letters: Random letters combined together, copying from environment, repeated letters* LDEH
Semiphonemic Stage	*Using some letters to stand for sounds heard in words—missing letters* JO TE BX "Island treasure box"
Phonemic Stage	*Writes a sound for each phoneme* POIA PIP POIA BEEA BE BX
Transitional Stage	*Combination of writing sound for each phoneme and some standard spelling of words* worms are both the boys and grls. Megan Gifford
Standard Spelling	*Dictionary spelling of words* a cat roaring to a bar AIRPLANES are free TO GO

Figure 2.5   Developmental stages of the production of print (spelling development).

Source: Adapted from Gentry (1982).

is often referred to as the **scribble stage** or **mock writing.** Some children continue to use mock writing even after they have moved into other stages.

It is only when the marks begin looking like letters that children move into the **prephonemic stage.** In this stage, children will combine random letters together, copying from the environment, copying the alphabet, and writing random letters over and over again to fill a space or line: "FTFTFTFTFT." Children at this stage often try to make the written symbol look like the object it is

Writing about what matters.

supposed to stand for. For example, Raymond consistently wrote the letter *O* to stand for *I*. When asked why he wrote an *O*, he explained it looked like "an eye." Another characteristic of the prephonemic stage is experimentation with letters, such as making reversals or writing upside down.

Once children discover the alphabetic principle—that letters represent specific sounds—they are moving into the **semiphonemic stage.** Here, children can relate some of the letters to sounds in words, but some letters in words will likely be missing. Typically, children will write one letter for each syllable in a word. Semiphonemic writing seems to progress from writing initial consonants for words (*K* for *cat*) to writing initial and final consonants (*KT* for *cat*), and, much later, to adding middle sounds. The vowels are the last to appear and seem to be the most difficult to master. A common characteristic of this stage

is writing "memory" words like *MOM* and *DOG* along with the semiphonemic words (often called invented spelling or temporary spelling).

As children continue to grow as writers, they will begin to write a sound for each phoneme, thus signaling their arrival at the **phonemic stage.** The focus here is on a letter for each sound, so onset patterns like *th* and *ch* are often written as *f* and *h*. With more reading and print exposure, children will become aware of the variety of spellings for the English language (Stewig & Jett-Simpson, 1995).

There are two more stages of writing: **transitional,** a combination of phonemic and standard spelling, and **standard spelling** (conventional spelling). It is during these last two stages that a focus on spelling is most appropriate for published works.

Besides attention to the marks and letters in writing, emerging writers must learn how writing and speech re-

"Spongebob and Sandy were talking and Sandy had to go away and Spongebob was sad."

Taking pride in what we write.

late, how form and style depend on the situation of the communication, and how to think of an audience's reaction to their work (Schickedanz, 1999). Children also must learn how to organize their writing on the paper: left to right, top to bottom, letters next to each other, spaces between words, and so on.

Considering that writing is the process of dealing with symbols, it makes perfect sense that children engaged in writing often can be found using many symbol systems to create meaning at the same time. Children may draw, tell stories, and even act them out as they are writing (Dyson, 2001). Have you ever noticed that especially young children seem to tell more about the story than they ever put down on paper, or that they seem more interested in drawing the pictures than writing the words? The talk that occurs while children are writing is crucial to understanding their intended messages (McGee & Richgels, 2000). Drawing also is an integral part of the writing process because it is a way for children to organize and plan their written text (Dyson, 2001; Strickland & Morrow, 1989).

Adults, too, practice a version of talking-while-writing. When we are trying to put our thoughts down on paper but are unsure how exactly to state something, many of us will say it aloud a few times to make sense of it before we write. What does this say about silent writing times? If we think of writing as a form of communication, then it only makes sense that young writers look for instant feedback from their current audience through conversation.

Among the countless other benefits children gain from writing, one of the most noteworthy is the sense of power. Children's writing is often a source of power for them (Dyson, 2001). It is a sign of their developing sense of self. One activity that is both inviting and relevant to children is writing their names. A name may begin as a special scribble but will emerge into conventional print over time (Sulzby et al., 1989). Allowing children to sign their names in their own way rather than signing for them is not only a way of empowering children in the classroom; it is also a way of showing them respect.

APPLICATIONS FOR WRITING DEVELOPMENT

1. Plan for daily writing experiences. Keep a portfolio or sampling of pieces of children's writing to document progress and plan for future instruction.
2. Invite children to discuss writing with peers before, during, and after the process.

3. Schedule a time in the day for children to share writing with one another. This can be done in pairs, small groups, or as a class. **Example:** *Use a special chair (often called an Author's Chair) in which only authors may sit to read their stories to the class.*
4. Write with children as a class, in small groups, and individually to model writing's uses, concepts, and techniques.
5. Pay close attention to individual students' writing levels, and structure ways to scaffold children to the next level.
6. Display children's writing. This shows the value you place on their writing.

The Role of Books in the Classroom

In addition to learning about print from writing, children learn a lot about literacy behaviors from being read to and reading to themselves and others. It has been acknowledged in research, both in homes and in classrooms, that the single most important activity we can use to build knowledge and skills that are eventually required for reading continues to be reading aloud to children (Adams, 1990).

Like the other areas of literacy, behaviors with books have a progression (see Figure 2.6). In the beginning, with the first exploration, infants encounter books as they do anything else—through the mouth. They explore the properties of the book (**exploration**). Gradually, children begin to point to pictures and label them with words and sounds "Doggie—ruff, ruff!" This is called **labeling.** With time and experience with books, children will chime in with favorite parts of the book and add parts that were skipped or

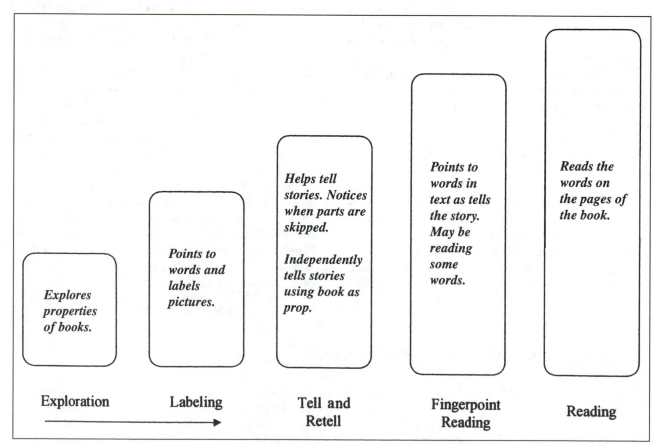

Explores properties of books.

Points to words and labels pictures.

Helps tell stories. Notices when parts are skipped.

Independently tells stories using book as prop.

Points to words in text as tells the story. May be reading some words.

Reads the words on the pages of the book.

Exploration   Labeling   Tell and   Fingerpoint   Reading
                                        Retell   Reading

Figure 2.6   The progression of behaviors with books.

left off, "It says 'He huffed and he puffed,' *not* 'puffed and huffed'!" This is called **tell–retell,** as they tell and retell favorites over and over again. Children eventually "read" books based on picture clues and good memories. Often at this point they will point to words in the book as they read to show their understanding that words that we read come from the words in the book and not the pictures (Ehri & Sweet, 1991). When children get to this point, it is thereby called **fingerpoint reading.** At the end of this progression, children will inevitably begin really **reading.** A child who is given support, guidance, encouragement, and respect as a competent literate person who can learn to read *and* who is expected to make mistakes and corrections can move along this continuum successfully.

Besides the sheer enjoyment of the personal exchange that takes place between adult and child when reading a book, reading aloud has an impact on many areas of language and print development. According to Schickedanz (1986, pp. 39–50; 1999, pp. 50–60), children learn:

- **How books work.** They learn that books go from front to back, left to right. They also learn that it is the words that we are reading.

Finger-point reading.

- **Print should make sense.** Questions are asked and conversations occur as a natural outflow of reading together.
- **Print and speech are related in a specific way.** The words read remain the same day after day. No new ones appear.
- **Book "talk" is different from conversational talk.**
- **Books are enjoyable.** They are sources of both pleasure and information.
- **New vocabulary.** Adults point out the new words within the text and pair these words with known words and experiences relevant to the children's worlds.
- **Sounds of language.** Books can help children pay closer attention to the sounds of language.
- **Things in books are related to things in children's worlds.** Books provide places for children to extend their knowledge. Children can further explore new ideas or be introduced to novel ideas.

In addition to these, there are three more important benefits children gain from adult–child interactions with books. First, they learn patterns of interacting that are characteristic of behaviors expected in a school setting, possibly the culture of school language, which is just being explored as a key contributing factor to children's future literacy success (McGee & Richgels, 2003). Second, they learn the metalanguage of literacy through the discussions that revolve around book reading (Galda & Cullinan, 1990). Children use the metalanguage to mediate and understand literacy. Third, from hearing books read aloud, children's vocabularies increase, and they develop "senses of story" (Jalongo, 1988).

Through book reading, adults communicate different features and messages to children about not only the book at hand, but also about literacy behaviors and skills. Many of these messages are appropriate and intended, but some may be unintended and may present mixed messages (Kirby, 1992). For instance, if the adult is unfamiliar with the book, she may mix up the characters and use the wrong voice intonations for them, which may be confusing to the children or may cause them to lose interest. If, instead, she practices the book ahead of time and is clear about who says what and how they will sound, the children are more likely to understand the story and to remain interested. Therefore, it is very important for teachers to plan carefully and thoughtfully for book-sharing experiences to maximize their instructional potential.

There are some important elements that are effective to include when reading to children. Besides enjoying the book with the children, it is important to reflect on its form and content, develop and support curiosity, examine the print, lead discussions, explore the meanings of words, relate the text to the world of the listeners, and demonstrate the value in reading (Wigfield & Asher, 1984).

Children in control of the big book, too!

One great way to connect group book experiences with direct literacy instruction is to use big books so all students can see the words as they are being read. Big books are ideal for making public, or external, the private or internal process of reading (Harrison, 1996). Using big books helps all students see the process being discussed. The problem with using small books with large groups of young children is that, unable to see the print clearly, they may misinterpret the literacy event and conclude that the part that you read comes from what they can see—the pictures (Goodman, 1992). It is ideal to schedule times in your day when you read large books with the entire class for print exploration purposes and other times with small groups and individuals to focus on specific instruction geared to those children's instructional levels. This is not to say that there is never a time when reading a small book to a large group is appropriate. Rather, it is important to consider carefully what your goals and objectives are for the reading and assess beforehand if the size, print, and story meet those specific instructional needs.

Unfortunately, some teachers are unaware or only slightly aware of the numerous benefits children derive from story times. Uninformed teachers are likely, on busy days, to set story time aside for more "scholastic" work. Their lack of knowledge about the cognitive and social dimensions of story time impedes them from making the most out of this important learning experience. These same teachers often turn to skills-related worksheets and workbooks to meet the ever-increasing demands for formal literacy programs (Strickland & Taylor, 1989). It is ironic that many of the isolated skills on the worksheets can be easily addressed in a holistic and more effective manner through literature and other print-rich activities.

APPLICATIONS FOR LITERACY KNOWLEDGE FROM BOOKS

1. Plan for shared reading experiences daily.
2. Read a variety of books to children, both fiction and nonfiction, for a variety of purposes.
3. Plan questions to discuss with the children *before* reading. Be sure to use questions that refer to the print (if the children can see it) as well as questions that focus on comprehension.

4. Emphasize concepts about print and literacy using big books.
5. Model your enthusiasm for reading with students.
6. Read sometimes "for fun" with children. At other times, model other reasons or functions for reading with children, such as reading notes from the office aloud or sharing thank-you notes from other classes.
7. Invite people who are important to the children to read to them. Help these guest readers prepare and structure their reading time with the children.
8. Select a word to focus on to further vocabulary development. Introduce the word and connect it to children's worlds through primary experiences whenever possible. Use the word often to assist children in incorporating it into their understandings.

The Role of Comprehension

The primary purpose of reading is to understand or gain information, which is the goal of comprehension. Therefore, a discussion of the literacy process is not complete without addressing this component. In a general sense, **comprehension** means finding and making meaning from information. It includes using and modeling comprehension strategies, such as figuring out words from context clues, predicting what comes next, asking questions, thinking about what is being read, making connections between what is read/heard/seen and personal experiences, and summarizing and evaluating. Of course, many more specific strategies are used when trying to comprehend information. How each of these strategies comes into play depends on the specific skill set and level of understanding of individual children. Comprehension should be emphasized throughout the entire literacy evolution, with different emphasis placed on it during differing periods in children's individual literacy development. Comprehension instruction is different at various times depending on the child's needs and skill level. Tunmer (1989) found that decoding skills are critical in the beginning stages of reading, whereas comprehension becomes more important later on, after the children have mastered basic decoding skills.

Comprehension for little people.

In general, with younger children, comprehension practice takes place through oral language. Using stories the students read together, reading to the children aloud, or after viewing a play or video, the teacher is able to introduce comprehension strategies and engage in guided practice with these strategies. For older students, the actual text is used more frequently for comprehension practice. This difference is due in part to the fact that younger students often do not possess all of the core concepts about written language that the older students do, nor do they possess the same level of cognitive ability to deal with abstract thought. Rather than ignoring comprehension until the children can read words, instruction in comprehension begins in an oral language capacity so that the process of finding meaning is always at the forefront of all literacy events.

For instance, with younger children, most of the comprehension activities that are used involve the adult scaffolding the child through the process using modeling and posing questions for the children to think about.

In Ms. Powell's kindergarten classroom, she introduces the concept of the main characters. She reads a story with the children and thinks aloud about who seemed to be the most important actors in the story. The children help her out by suggesting characters. She takes each of their ideas and discusses the characters at hand. By asking questions such as, "Could the story still be told without mentioning the Mom?," she helps the children think further about what the story was all about.

For older children, typically mid–second grade and up, who already possess many of the literacy concepts such as phonological awareness, a good understanding of phonics, and knowledge of story components, planned comprehension activities and lessons take on a more independent air. Rather than the teacher guiding the children through the entire process, the children may work on some comprehension strategies independently, using the teacher as a reference point. However, as the students learn new strategies for comprehension, their teacher will guide them once again. Through this progression of introduction, guidance, and independence, children can become quite successful and proficient at comprehension.

APPLICATIONS FOR COMPREHENSION

1. Take opportunities to use all literacy events as stages for comprehension practice. **Example:** *Use the school assembly, a video shown for science, or reports that students give orally or in written format as springboards for classroom comprehension conversations.*
2. Consistently look for the "meaning behind the words" as you work with children both on their individual writing and reading and on what is done as a class.
3. Work on all of the literacy concepts and skills discussed up to now so that they become "automatic" for the students, who can eventually focus primarily on the comprehension.
4. Use questioning strategies to help mediate children's understanding of literacy events and items.
5. Think aloud strategies with students to model *your* comprehension strategies.
6. Encourage students to explain the thinking behind their answers to encourage metacognitive abilities.

Final Thoughts

Literacy is a very complex process. It involves numerous concepts and skills that you must diligently plan for, implement, and observe in your students to help them on their literacy development journey. Although the portions of literacy have been represented as pieces of a pie for the purpose of this chapter, it is important to remember that all of the literacy behaviors flow into one another, with often indistinguishable boundaries. It is equally necessary to point out that any one phase—emerging, early, or fluent—is not fixed across the board. The categories are not meant to be used as labels or comparisons between children. Rather, they are provided as a guide to help you recognize where individual children have been, where they are going, *and* what the journey ahead will look like so that you can serve as an expert informed guide.

In this chapter, we've discussed the importance of oral language development; phonological awareness; print, word, and letter knowledge; writing development; literacy knowledge from books; and comprehension. We've also explored general ways for you to implement these in your classroom.

Chapters 4, 5, and 6 of this book will give you more specific suggestions for working with children along the continuum of literacy development. Some of the activities for the individual levels may look very similar. This is deliberate. Examine these carefully to distinguish the fine differences between them. All of the activities at any phase—emerging, early, or fluent—can be modified to go up or go down a level. Although some concepts may be more emphasized at one level than at another, all do function to some degree at each phase. For example, whereas oral language is of primary concern in the emerging years, it continues to be emphasized in the fluent years. The classroom applications presented at the ends of these chapters have been used by real teachers with real children and have produced real results. We hope you will take these strategies and activities and adapt them to fit the needs of your children and your community. There is no one right way to do this. It is up to you to take your knowledge and understanding of the children with whom you work and combine it with your knowledge and understanding of the evolution of literacy to devise a plan to fit your needs.

We wish you success as you continue in your classroom quest for literacy. We hope that the activities and strategies provided in Chapters 4, 5, and 6 will be as successful for you as they have been for us.

Challenge Yourself

1. Observe some children writing. Try to figure out what level of writing development they are at based on the descriptions here. Make a chart to hang in your classroom showing the levels so that you can share this information with parents and administrators.

2. Choose one area's applications and write a plan for how you will implement these in your classroom.

3. Choose a book to read to a group of children. Outline a plan for how you will read this to the children. Specify which literacy concepts and skills you will specifically cover.

Suggested Sources
for Additional Information

McGee, L. M., & Richgels, D. J. (2000). *Literacy's beginnings: Supporting young readers and writers* (2nd ed.). Boston: Allyn and Bacon.

Neuman, S. B., & Dickenson, D. K. (Eds.). (2001). *Handbook of early literacy research.* New York: Guilford Press.

Organizations

Association for Childhood Education International. *Phone:* 1-800-423-3563.

International Reading Association. *Phone:* 1-800-336-7323.

National Association for the Education of Young Children. *Phone:* 1-800-424-2460.

3

Organizing for Literacy

Exploring the Literate Environment

Miss Monahan's classroom

As you enter Miss Monahan's classroom, you are stepping into an active world. Here, you see students working together, and independently, in a variety of innovative ways.

The first thing you see is Suzi and Joe playing restaurateurs. She's passing out make-believe menus to real customers seated in her make-believe eatery. Joe is back in the kitchen, cooking up a storm while referring to posters of simulated recipes. "We're starving!" the customers say.

Next, you step through the eatery and find a cozy nook where Kara is lounging on pillows. She hardly notices you because she's intent on scanning a picture book of horses.

You move on, struck by a barrage of labels, displays, signs, and posters. A few steps away, Mr. Hanover—a parent volunteer—is sitting with Kim in the manipulatives area, guiding her in creating patterns of brightly colored blocks.

Wait a minute! Where's the teacher? Oh, there's Miss Monahan. She just finished taking dictation from five youngsters who told her stories of how they spent Halloween. She wrote their masterpieces down in her "Big Book." Later, she'll read each story back to the class, showing them how the words look.

But right now, you've caught her eye. She motions you over and tells you how proud she is of her kindergarten class.

As you explore the literate environment, ask yourself these questions:

- How does any environment foster literacy, while respecting the learning differences evident in the classrooms of today?
- What are the classroom layouts that encourage literacy?
- Are there unique learning materials and unusual classroom schedules that offer advantages in teaching literacy skills?
- How does a teacher's attitude affect reading and writing in the classroom?
- What can teachers do to foster a positive environment for literacy learning in students' homes?

In this chapter, we will describe a classroom environment that fosters literacy. A description of the physical structure of the classroom, detailing suggested areas, along with corresponding materials to enhance the literate environment, is captured here. This is followed by a discussion of time as it pertains to classroom organization. Finally, we offer ways that a teacher can enhance the literate environment by projecting a positive attitude and communicating that attitude to both students and parents. In this chapter, you will see how these links come together to create the literate environment.

The scenario depicting Miss Monahan's classroom captures the essence of an environment that facilitates and supports literacy development for all learners. This scenario exemplifies the leading theories about how children learn best. To create this type of learning environment, teachers must provide instruction sessions and other learning experiences that address and build on what individual children already know. Then, the children must

When the physical environment is supported by a positive social environment, great things can happen.

have opportunities to become actively involved with new information.

Shaklee and her coauthors (1997:11) suggest that four components are necessary to support the literate classroom environment:

- A **flexible layout** accommodates a variety of instructional approaches. For example, a variety of furniture allows the creation of numerous settings for learning in small groups.
- **Interactive materials** motivate the learner to manipulate, construct, and experiment while building on prior experiences.
- An **adaptable time** component allows children to learn at their own pace, expanding for in-depth exploration and shrinking if learners are frustrated or ready to move ahead.
- A **positive attitude** on the part of the teacher reinforces the other components of the literate classroom environment. Being positive means accepting many learning styles, focusing on children's capabilities, and showing enthusiasm for all aspects of literacy.

Just as a building has structural components, these four elements are the structural components of the literate classroom environment. When integrated, they form the optimal environment for teaching the skills of literacy. To create and foster such an environment, teachers must carefully consider how to build these structural components into their classrooms. Above all, it is the teacher who plays the key role in the make up of the environment. Beyond setting up a good physical structure, the teacher is also responsible for creating the social structure to support a network for literacy learning (see Roskos & Neuman, 2001). When the physical environment is supported by a positive social environment, great things can happen. Let's first examine the physical environment.

The Physical Structure: Classroom Design and Layout

Spatial Area Guidelines

Little did you know that educating young children might require a degree in architectural design! Classroom design and layout involve careful evaluation of instructional processes relative to the ways that children learn best. A classroom that nurtures literacy development accepts and encourages the diverse learning styles of young children. Thus, it should include a variety of spatial areas, offering many literacy experiences.

There are some standard rules of thumb to consider when designing the physical space. Above all, it is of great importance to remember that space has a strong influence on the interactions between children and on their learning (Roskos & Neuman, 2001).

1. **Provide adequate space.** It is recommended that at least 25 square feet are available per child. When there is not enough space, children are likely to argue.

2. **Organize the space to include an area for meeting as a large group, areas for small groups of children to work together, and areas for children to work independently.** Remember that large open spaces invite running and rough-housing. Use classroom elements such as furniture and materials to naturally divide the room into inviting niches and nooks, while maintaining safe visual supervision of the entire room. These smaller spaces invite children to work together and engage in conversations (Roskos & Neuman, 2001).

3. **Designate areas not only by space, but also using signs and pictures** (Reutzel & Wolfersberger, 1996). Not only do signs and pictures depicting the use of an area communicate its use, they also are good models for the functional uses of print in the environment.

4. **Create visually appealing areas.** Adding materials such as little lamps, picture frames, and rugs can serve to soften the environment and make it more cozy. As you do this, consider ways you can reflect the culture of the community in which you work (Isbell & Exelby, 2001).

5. **Arrange similar areas near or adjacent to each other.** For example, placing the writing center next to the story reenactment center and the book corner may facilitate more literacy events that move freely between these areas. Children may write stories at the writing center, act them out at the story reenactment center, and then place them in the book corner for others to read.

6. **Involve the children in at least some of the decision making and rule setting for the environment.** This helps them begin to develop a sense of ownership over the room and the materials and leads to a more cooperative clean up crew! It also establishes a sense of community, which is vital for ultimate literacy learning to take place (Routman, 2003).

Figures 3.1 and 3.2 offer examples of a classroom design or layout specified to fit the developmental needs

Sharing classroom responsibilities.

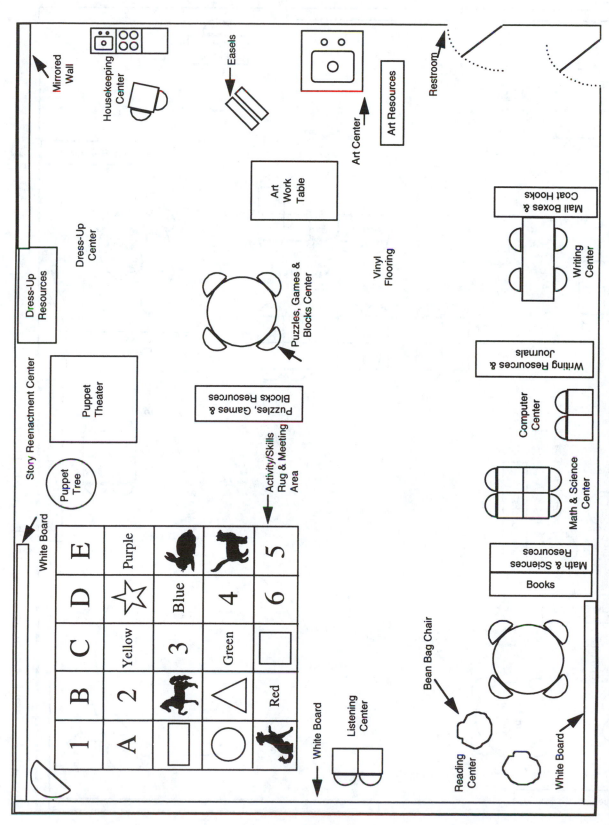

Figure 3.1 Sample classroom design for the emerging-to-early learner.

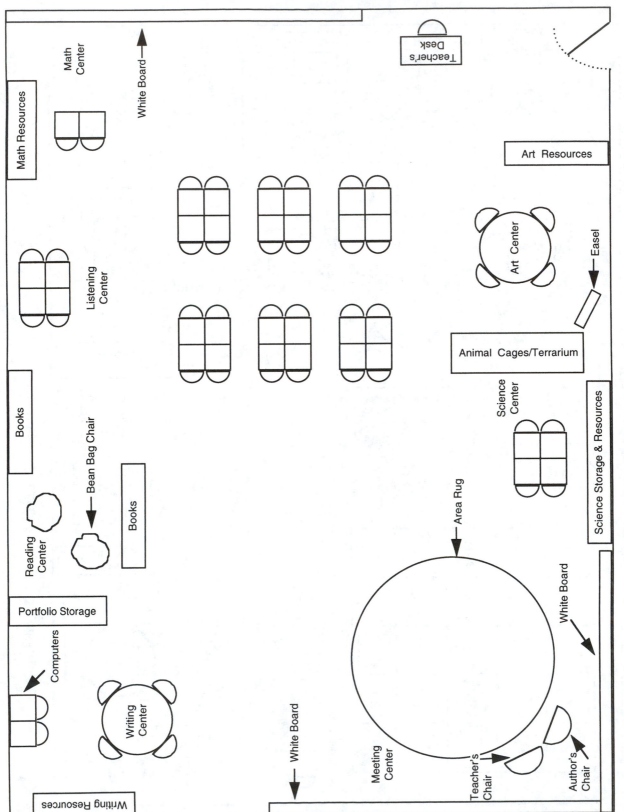

Figure 3.2 Sample classroom design for the early-to-fluent learner.

and styles of learners functioning at the emerging-to-early level, as well as those at the early-to-fluent level.

Of course, these suggested optimal designs may have to be modified to utilize the space, materials, and other resources you have. Note the variation in the types of centers and their placement in the room. Such differences derive from the varying degrees of focus within the literate environment of the emerging-to-early learner and the early-to-fluent learner. At the emerging-to-early level of learning, there is a greater emphasis on oral language, on which symbolic play has a tremendous impact. Therefore, centers such as the dramatic play and story reenactment areas have a more significant role in a classroom designed for the young learner than for one operating at the early-to-fluent level. In both classroom settings, however, the placement of learning centers in the room should allow for a flow of materials in a manner that will encourage the integration of reading and writing across the curriculum. In addition, both classroom designs are meant to foster *active* involvement on the part of the student in a cooperative sense of learning. It's important to remember that real classroom communities are more than just a look. "Real communities flourish when we bring together the voices, hearts, and souls of the people who inhabit them" (Miller, 2002: 17).

Creating Interest Areas

Let's explore in detail the following interest areas:

- The classroom library
- The listening center
- The classroom writing center
- The dramatic play area
- The music center
- The block area
- The sand and water table
- The storytelling area
- The area for puzzles and manipulatives
- The science area
- The meeting area

Teachers who work with older children at the fluent level may be thinking that this section will not apply to the developmental needs and interests of learners in their classrooms. Don't be so sure!

Significant research and experience support the argument that the spatial classroom areas listed here offer compelling learning opportunities to learners at many levels. Certainly, the spatial areas will differ from classroom to classroom and across various developmental groups in their appearance and in the ways they are presented to students. But their unique values for enhancing literacy remain intact.

For example, the spatial area for dramatic play may be *adapted* for older children by staging a "Reader's The-ater," in which students act out favorite stories or poems using literacy props (see Chapter 6).

Likewise, the physical concepts explored with the sand and water table at the emerging-to-early levels may be adapted for the fluent level by incorporating them into science experiments. Perhaps there is no designated block area in your classroom of older children. Still, the involvement and stimulation of hands-on construction is present during art time or at a woodworking table, offering unique opportunities to incorporate literacy props.

These examples reinforce our belief that each of the spatial literacy areas presented here can be adapted to succeed with a wide range of students. Although a given spatial area may not become a permanent part of your classroom, each has a place in a curriculum supportive of literacy development. We hope that you will view our list merely as suggestions. Use only those that you find will enrich your scope of instruction. Then, develop others from your own inspirations or those of your students! After all, what better way is there to teach literacy than to organize learning structures that have special meaning for you and your students?

Places to Learn and Explore

Classroom Library

A well-designed classroom library should be both informative and inviting. Your library's bookshelves should be well-stocked, featuring both fiction and non-fiction books from many genres. Be sure to include a variety of printed materials, such as joke and riddle books, songbooks, big books, comics, magazines, catalogs, newspapers, and reference materials (including highly visual and colorful references such as encyclopedias and atlases). Don't forget to also include student-made books. Periodically check your shelves to be sure your reading materials are representative of the culture of your students.

Reutzel and Wolfersberger (1996) suggest that the number of books needed in a classroom for young children should be no fewer than 90 and as many as 500 books, or approximately 4 to 20 books per child. A well-conceived book corner, typically surrounded on two or three sides by bookshelves, becomes a cozy refuge from the classroom. Both research and experience suggest that the library be large enough to accommodate at least five children at once, thus occupying 15 percent of a classroom's total floor space (Reutzel & Wolfersberger, 1996). You can add touches of comfort and familiarity here by providing pillows; a rug; a comfortable chair, couch, or beanbag recliner; and even a plant or lamp. Displaying stuffed animals or puppets related to available literature also contributes to good reading behaviors.

To attract young readers to your classroom library and to spark their interest in a subject, you can arrange a display of books and objects related to a current unit of

Enjoying an organized reading center.

Sharing a listening center experience.

study or theme. You might choose an "author of the month" or a specific literary genre, such as biographies.

Listening Center

Children of all ages enjoy listening to a good story. Create a place for listening to literature, either within the classroom library or in a designated space nearby. Be sure to include ample copies of the printed version (books, poems, songs) that will be heard. One of the voices that children enjoy most is their teacher's. Consider creating your own recordings or those of children and other significant adults in your learning environment.

Although audiotapes are an enjoyable alternative for all students, they have special benefits for those that struggle with reading or oral language. After hearing spoken words, struggling readers bring extra meaning and excitement to their attempts at reading the same words.

Poems are an alternative genre for the listening center. Highlighting poetry at the listening center helps English language learners get a sense of the sound of English words and phrases through poetry's rhythm and rhyme. Poems on tape provide additional models of effective oral reading, pronunciation, and expression. The short lines of poetry may appear manageable and less intimidating to struggling readers. There is nothing quite like hearing the poets read their own work, and many poets have recorded their poems. Once students become comfortable with reading a favorite poem, they may choose to tape-record themselves reading it aloud, copy it in their best handwriting, include an illustration, and place this version of the poem and text in the listening center for others to enjoy. Another asset to including a poetry collection at the listening center is the inclusion of bilingual poetry. There are many collections of poetry in both English and Spanish. English language learners or their parents may also choose to read poems in their native languages and provide a written version as well. Focusing on other languages in this way can foster a positive learning environment for all (Hadaway, Vardell, & Young, 2001).

Writing Center

The spatial area devoted to writing is typically located near the reading area to promote the connection between reading and writing, allowing literacy ideas to flow between the two. The focus of the writing center may vary depending on the skill development and needs of the learners. For emerging learners, this area becomes an important place for groups of children and the teacher to gather. Here, the process of writing is modeled and practiced as it relates to oral language and reading experiences. For the early-to-fluent learner, this area becomes a place where individuals or small groups meet to revise or edit their written pieces in preparation for publication (see Chapters 5 and 6 for more on the writing process).

The writing area usually includes a table and some type of storage shelf or bin containing a variety of writing implements and tools. These tools might include:

- Markers (both thick and thin lined)
- Colored pencils, pens
- Crayons
- Stamps and stencils
- Highlighters
- Glue sticks
- Three-hole punch
- Paper clips
- Staplers
- Envelopes
- Alphabet/word cards

A well-stocked supply of both lined and unlined paper, index cards, stationery, and newsprint of various sizes should also be on hand in this area. Items for making books may also be found here, such as construction paper, tag board, wrapping paper, contact paper, and yarn. You may wish to have the classroom computer and a printer located in this area, as it can be a key component in publishing.

Dramatic Play Area

It's in the dramatic play area that the actors and actresses of the classroom take the stage. In this area, children love to dress up in the provided props and act out various roles relating to the given theme. Such themes might include a home setting, a restaurant, or hospital. If this area has been designated as a home, one way to develop the literacy component is to add a phone book with paper and pens available for taking messages. Or, perhaps in the kitchen of the home, sample recipes might be provided along with picture cues for students to follow as they use cooking utensils and measuring cups to concoct pretend dishes. Don't forget to supply blank recipe cards, too, as children have been known to invent some amazing recipes! These may not be edible, of course, but credit should always be given for a good imagination. See Table 4.1 in Chapter 4 for other pretend play themes and related literacy props.

Many studies have been conducted on the connection between literacy and dramatic play. Most theorists have come to the conclusion that play truly does encourage children to write. Vygotsky (1978) firmly believed that early writing begins in symbolic play.

> Given the current state of psychological knowledge, our notion that make-believe play, drawing, and writing can be viewed as different moments in an essentially unified process of development of written language will appear to be very much overstated . . . But experiments and psychological analysis lead us to this very conclusion. (p. 116)

As children engage in dramatic play, they practice representing one thing or person as another, which ultimately helps them to represent their ideas with letters and words (Fields & Spangler, 1995:32). The notion of dramatic play can easily be adapted to fit the needs of older students. One such way is referred to here as **Theatre in a Bag.** This simple, quick activity involves first assembling small bags with props or costumes, such as old necklaces, stuffed animals, hats, toys, and so on. Students placed in small groups of three or four then choose a bag and are given 3 minutes to figure out what each one will wear, 5 minutes to discuss the plot and ending, 10 minutes to practice, and 2 minutes to put on the play. **Reader's Theater** is yet another means of applying the literacy skills embedded within dramatic play (see Chapter 6).

Music Area

Learning that takes place in this area is music to your ears. It is here that children may experiment with various instruments, sing along to well-known songs, or simply draw or write to the beat, if they are so inspired. In addition to their repetition, rhythm, and rhyme, choosing songbooks and singing songs instantly engages and motivates children to read the words. With repeated readings, **phonemic awareness** is increased, along with sight word vocabularies (Miller, 2002). Depending on the theme or focus, the literacy props provided here may change regularly. Such props might include an instrument of the week or month, along with musical notes to read and play along with for the older student; songbooks or chants on display, along with a tape or CD version of the songs as a guide; and paper, pencils, markers, and crayons to encourage the visualization of images as inspired by the music heard. In recording such images in either a written or illustrative format, students are making that all-important literacy link.

Block Area

Literacy props in the block area may include paper, index cards, pencils, tape, and a clipboard. Using such materials, children are encouraged to label their block structures or to draw plans for constructing them. Children also may see books on display here. These provide information on various building structures, or how and where people live (Goldhaber, 1996–1997).

Older students may enjoy a woodworking center, providing materials such as hammers, nails, screwdrivers, and lengths of wood. One way to link this area to literacy would be to ask students to design a wood project, list the steps they will follow to make it, and then to build the project using their written procedure. The end results may cause many students to revise their initial list of procedures.

In all of these examples, students attach meaning and purpose to their experiences through the use of literacy props.

Storytelling Area

This is an area of the room equipped with storytelling props such as puppets, stuffed animals, and dress-up clothes. A puppet theater or flannelboard display are nice features to add for helping children to reenact stories they have read or have heard read to them.

Teachers may use such props when telling stories to children, to make stories come alive. Retelling or reenacting stories encourages children's emotional and intellectual involvement with literature. The combination of a book and a prop may "evoke an emotional response that teachers and children can share, discuss and ponder" (Reutzel & Wolfersberger, 1996:276). Storytelling activities such as these offer children a unique and thoroughly involving means to further explore the language and themes of literature, as well as the connections between literature and real-life experiences (McGee & Richgels, 2000). See Chapters 4, 5, and 6 for more related activities.

Puzzles and Manipulatives

This is an area where children use problem-solving techniques and mathematical reasoning. In supporting literacy, young children may be encouraged to recreate a developed pattern of colored blocks when supplied with paper, pencils, and markers or crayons. The teacher may begin with a prompt, such as, "Show me how to make that same pattern of the blocks using your crayons and paper. Trace the block shapes first, and then color them following your pattern that we see here."

This area can easily address the learning levels of all students. Fluent learners may be given a challenging prompt, perhaps asking them to develop their own pattern. Or they might be asked to solve a mathematical story problem, requiring them to manipulate materials in order to complete the given task. Asking students to give a written response demonstrating their thought processes in reaching the solution provides an important link to literacy, while encouraging reflection on their learning.

Science Area

Literacy is supported here with books that are related to a unit of science study or current student interest in science.

For example, when teaching a unit on the oceans, a teacher may display many related books, both fiction and nonfiction, along with real-life objects such as shells, a shark's tooth, sand, and so on. The area might also be equipped with magnifying glasses, scales, measuring tapes, and other scientific items. In addition, students might find a number of blank booklets nearby, along with markers, colored chalk, pencils, and pens, encouraging them to draw scenes of ocean life, then add a dictated or written caption to the picture. These may be bound into individual booklets for children to read (and reread!), or grouped together as a class project. Regardless of the details, the important end result is that students are provided with opportunities to connect science interests to literacy skills in ways that involve them in meaningful, memorable experiences.

Meeting Area

It is in the meeting area that the class comes together as one. In this open designated area of the room, there is ample space meant to invite group participation and foster inclusion. Here the entire class may sit in a circle and meet face-to-face. In many classrooms, this is where the teacher and students gather each morning to begin their day. Some of the ways a class might choose to utilize this space include the following: to share news, go over the schedule for the day, to discuss classroom issues and solve problems, or to play physical games and activities. The whole group meeting area is basically the heart of the learning environment, where the classroom community is built and nourished (Clayton, 2001).

Structural Support: Materials for a Literate Environment

Establishing a classroom environment conducive to literacy development requires the use of innovative learning materials. Your goal in choosing and assembling the appropriate learning materials is to create what we call a **print-rich classroom.** These materials fall into two categories: literacy props and print.

Literacy Props

The use of **literacy props** is an effective means of developing children's literacy skills. Literacy props are the concrete, hands-on materials that offer children personal, creative experiences with the meanings and functions of the printed word. When props are logically arranged to support a common idea or concept, they can support both language development and print awareness (Roskos & Neuman, 2001). For example, in the block area, you could place plans for a house that included simple directions, pencils, and graph paper for recording student constructions.

A meeting area to share ideas.

The types of literacy props and their arrangement in your classroom will change over time, based on the changing interests, experiences, and skills of the children you are teaching (Goldhaber et al., 1996–1997). Changing and rearranging props will be necessary to accommodate a new theme presented in the classroom, to target a new skill, or to entice learners to a new area of the classroom yet to be discovered and enjoyed. Reutzel and Wolfersberger (1996:273) support the need for prop changes. They state:

> Two weeks to one month seem to represent a reasonable time frame for planning changes. Children's written language products should be displayed two weeks or less to encourage increased production rates. At least one new book should be introduced to children daily.

Many of us are familiar with the placement of such traditional literacy props as books, magazines, and poetry in the classroom library, and with the placement of paper and various writing tools in the writing center. We encourage you continually to broaden your perspective on the use and placement of literacy props. They are an excellent way to add a creative and personal touch to your classroom.

Now let's take a peek inside one kindergarten classroom to see how props work:

Brian frequently chooses to explore the block area during "choice time" in Miss Murray's kindergarten classroom. Although he thoroughly enjoys building elaborate constructions, his teacher would like to see him explore other literacy-related materials, to broaden his reading and writing experience. Upon his next visit to the block area, Brian discovers some changes. Miss Murray has added a basket filled with cards, tape, and pencils. She encourages Brian to create a label for his block structure and tape it to his creation.

Later, Miss Murray shows Brian the clipboards and paper in the block area. She suggests that he use them to draw a structure and then construct a similar structure with blocks. As he works, she shows him how his drawing becomes a point of reference during the construction.

As Brian works with his blocks, Miss Murray points out books on display nearby, with pictures of buildings and other structures. These help Brian see a connection between his play and the world outside the classroom.

Miss Murray added literacy props to a spatial area not normally associated with literacy skills. You can do this, too, simply by placing paper and pencils in play settings such as the block area. In fact, the use of paper and pencils as literacy props is limitless. The simple introduction of writing materials in any spatial area within the classroom invites children to represent their play experiences, discoveries, and constructions through writing and drawing. You can also provide books, signs, and posters in a play setting, being mindful of the cultural differences represented. Choose those materials that combine words with pictures to enrich the contextual meaning of print words with images relevant to the children's play and prior experiences. (See Table 3.1 for specific suggestions.)

Reutzel and Wolfersberger (1996) offer the following reasons for using literacy props to help create a literate classroom environment:

- Literacy props *extend and enrich virtually any curriculum area.*
- Literacy props *add interest and involvement in learning,* so that children stay on task for longer periods.
- Literacy props *teach children to learn independently* by providing individual learning situations.
- Literacy props *teach children to learn interdependently* by fostering interactions involving literacy skills.
- Literacy props *typically work in conjunction with classroom areas* to develop skills and interest in literacy.

The Print-Rich Classroom

On entering a literate classroom environment, one should be bombarded with examples of the printed word. These examples should be *everywhere,* used in ways that are both functional and illustrative. Immersing children in literacy not only enhances their general awareness of its importance, but it also encourages the development of cognitive skills necessary for becoming literate. Lipton and Hubble (1997) state that literacy development occurs most readily in an environment that is saturated with examples of the printed word, especially when there are opportunities for children to use the printed language in meaningful ways.

Surround your students with a range of printed materials that draw on their shared experiences and relate to their needs and interests. Such materials include labels, lists, charts, books, dictated stories, songs, displays, and photos with captions. Some of the photos may come from a home visit or trip to a neighborhood where your students live. While there, study the environments and look for possible connections to your curriculum. Taking pictures of the areas that these students are familiar with and posting them for discussion in the classroom would not only be a powerful connection to your students' communities, but may also help English language learners.

Table 3.1   Suggested Props and Tools to Support Literacy around the Classroom

Pretend Play	Paper, pencils, phones, typewriter, books, telephone book, and other props suited to your theme (see Table 4.1)
Blocks	Paper for recording structures, Polaroid camera, writing utensils, craft sticks, tape, small paper for making signs for the block constructions, blueprints of other constructions made for reading
Art	Writing utensils for recording names, paper of all shapes and sizes, directions for making projects, pictures of nature and artists' works
Manipulatives	Paper, markers, and crayons for recording creations; books with relevant pictures in them for constructing; directions on how to make some creations
Computer	Sign-up sheet for those waiting for a turn in line, books to look at while waiting, a menu of games to choose from, directions for turning the computer on and off
Snack	Signs for washing hands, number of snack items to take, label of the snack of the day, poll taking for the next day's snack, thank-you cards for today's snack
Story Center	Books, story props, tape recorder for recording shows, puppets, paper for writing scripts
Writing Center	Markers; stamps; books; blank books; tape recorder to tell story to; paper of all shapes, colors, and sizes; typewriter; computer; pens; pencils; stapler; tape; letters posted; letters to trace; magnetic letters; alphabet cards; word cards; dictionaries
Around the room	Signs of the areas, classroom rules and directions, ideas for upcoming themes, lists for things to buy at the store, lists of songs we know, lists of books we've read, labels of things in the classroom relevant to the children

Environmental Print

The printed material that surrounds us every day on labels, signs, advertisements, and packaging is referred to here as **environmental print.** This is typically the first exposure to recognizable print for children as literacy skills begin to develop. "In studies of early readers, the most frequently mentioned sources of stimulation for literate behaviors are vast displays of environmental print and an adult reading aloud to the early reader" (Reutzel & Wolfersberger, 1996:269). However, environmental print is important for all levels of literacy learners. Consider the following when incorporating print into your environment:

1. Print should be at the children's eye level.
2. It should be both meaningful and useful.
3. Children should observe others using the print (as models) and try out the functions of print for themselves.
4. The print should be always nearby. Children should be able to grab the relevant print material and use it.
5. Culturally relevant print materials should always be present. This helps create the connection between home and school cultures (Neuman & Roskos, 1998; Neuman, 1999).

What does this mean for the use of "environmental print" in our classrooms?

> Bombarded with print in the environment, students see road signs, theater marquees, store fronts and advertisements emblazoned with product slogans every day. This environmental print provides the impetus for students to plaster the classroom with writing generated from their own experiences. (Lipton & Hubble, 1997:34–35)

A simple way to get students involved in designing their literacy classroom is to send home a letter informing parents of the value and importance of environmental print in the development of their child's literacy skills. Encourage parents to work with their child to find samples of environmental print around the home. This activity may continue as a year-long project (see Figure 3.3).

As samples of environmental print are brought into the classroom, including such items as cereal box labels, newspaper and magazine ads, and coupons, you can display the printed materials in a prominent area of the room. Take the time to discuss the collected print with children, reading it together and encouraging its use in their writing experiences.

LABELING   The main purpose of establishing a print-rich environment in the classroom is to convey to students an understanding that print carries meaning. Labeling objects around the classroom helps the learner con-

I Can Read

Environmental print is the print we see around us every day—the print on signs, labels, advertisements, and product packaging. It is usually the first print a child recognizes as literacy skills begin to emerge. Beginning readers find environmental print easy to "read" because of the shapes, colors, and pictures that surround the words.

Have your child bring environmental print samples to school. Coupons, newspapers, and magazines are excellent sources. We will use the samples in a variety of ways. I will post them on a bulletin board for everyone to read. We will use them for buddy reading, whole-group reading, and to help us when we are writing. Please spend about a week doing this activity at home with your child. If you find more words during the year that we can add to our "I Can Read" board, then please send them in at any time.

Happy Reading!
Mrs. Getsinger and Mrs. Kubik

Figure 3.3   Sample newsletter informing parents of environmental print.

nect print with something that is tangible and familiar (Lipton & Hubble, 1997).

Labeling may be conducted in a variety of ways (Lipton & Hubble, 1997):

1. Label things in your classroom. For example, the door, the window, and the desk can have labels.
2. Label students' functions when they work in cooperative groups. Examples include recorder, timekeeper, and maintenance.
3. Label the classroom using adjectives and descriptive phrases—for example, "the *dirty* window" or "the *flowering* plant."
4. Label events or behaviors with characteristics that introduce humor or reinforce expected classroom behavior. For example, on one of those days when you can't find that pen that you "just had in your hand," your students might label you "disorganized!"

Labeling should always involve student participation in the process to establish literacy connections. One kindergarten teacher did this by having her students decide *what* to label as well as by creating the labels themselves. As the labels posted provide models of print for learners, they should appear in conventional spelling. To do this effectively, the teacher may act as a facilitator in the labeling process, working with small groups of children whose job it is to "help" with the true spelling of the word. To accommodate English language learners, you can encourage students to create labels with words in their native languages along with the English label and pictures as needed.

Not only can labels be used for objects in the classroom, but you may also use them to indicate the location of materials, to identify children's cubbies or mailboxes, or to indicate where children sit in the classroom. For children operating at the emerging level of literacy, labels accompanied by picture cues are most helpful in assigning meaning to the printed word.

Regardless of how the labeling process is applied in the classroom, it will only carry significance for the development of literacy skills if these constructed labels are pointed out and utilized. Some creative ways to do this include taking a "label walk" on a regular basis around the room, reading labels as you go, or making a game of it by asking children to hunt for the new labels posted in the room as they arrive. Reutzel and Wolfersberger (1996) maintain that labeling objects, storage containers, shelves, and other areas of the classroom helps students to take responsibility for the maintenance and organization of their environment. For more on using labeling strategies in the classroom, see Chapter 4.

CLASSROOM DISPLAYS   Print also can be displayed in a way that encourages interaction between the learner and the printed message. Interactive learning with print might include solving posted story problems, correcting daily oral language, establishing a message center, composing letters for the classroom mailbox, or sharing the "News of the Day."

For students operating at the early-to-fluent level, it is beneficial to present print in a functionally *challenging* way. For example, language displays might include problem-solving puzzles, independent center activities with the directions and rules provided on display, or even step-by-step procedures for assembling something. For instance, one third-grade teacher in a Michigan school posted a "Problem of the Week" in a corner of the classroom, which displayed a mathematical story problem that the students could choose to try to solve in their free time. At the end of each week, the teacher took the time to discuss the problem with the whole group, identifying developed solutions and presenting the individual thought processes involved.

Lipton and Hubble (1997) discuss the idea of using a message center to facilitate communication among the members of your classroom. The message board was originated by Carolyn Burke of Indiana University. This display fosters interaction through writing and provides a purpose for developing fluency with the written language. Here students may post such messages as reminders, invitations, advertisements, or creative ideas to be shared. Teachers may wish to post directions or provide information for students on the message center.

The task of creating a print-rich classroom requires teachers to assemble and present a wide range of unique learning materials. (See Figure 3.4 for material suggestions.) Teachers can incorporate these materials into their regular classroom activities. They can also use them in specialized learning situations and activities. To finish the task, teachers must extend their efforts to the home, enlisting parents in the effort to saturate a child's environment with samples of printed material and props that are appropriate to the youngster's developmental stage and interests.

Establishing a print-rich classroom is a crucial part of constructing an overall environment conducive to literacy. It may seem challenging because much of the material is teacher-generated. But don't think of it as a chore. Instead, enjoy choosing materials that are playful, topical, or meaningful to children. Print-rich learning materials offer a multitude of ways to build literate connections between young learners and their world.

We conclude this section with applications for providing a flexible classroom layout to support the development of literacy skills in the classroom.

APPLICATIONS: PROVIDING A FLEXIBLE CLASSROOM LAYOUT

1. Organize the space in your classroom to meet the needs of students learning to read, write, listen, speak, and view. Placement of interest areas should allow for literacy experiences to flow into one another. A cooperative, active style of learning is to be encouraged here.

2. Develop and create interest areas to meet the learning needs and interests of your students. Some interest areas may change over time as interests or topics of study change.

3. Make use of literacy props or hands-on materials throughout the interest areas. Such props will offer the children a multitude of experiences with the meanings and functions of the printed word.

4. Create a classroom environment in which print is significantly and prominently displayed, adhering to the guidelines from this chapter. Include judicious labels, charts, songs, books, and various displays. Be sure children's cultures are represented in your print.

5. Involve your students in lessons that convey the relationship between the written word and everyday communication. Activities such as daily language practice, letter writing, and the message board convey a sense of purpose for literacy.

Classroom Collections
(A list of *must-haves* for the literacy-supportive environment)

White boards (large display and slate size)

Classroom tables with slots for belongings
- An alternative option for individual desks is to push the desks together to form groups, and using light sheets of plywood, place these pieces over the grouped desks to form a flat, workable surface for the activity.

Classroom library
- See the section of this chapter on classroom areas.

Writing center
- See earlier section of this chapter for development.

Pocket charts

Song charts

Job charts

Daily schedule

Big books

Language play books (using rhyme and alliteration)

Poetry charts/books

Fiction/nonfiction literature

Literature representing a variety of genres
- Fables, folktales, myths, legends

Newspapers

Magazines

Construction paper, white lined paper, white paper, tag board

Art materials
- Fabric, felt, pipe cleaners, tissue paper, yarn

Dramatic play area props (see Chapter 4)

Storytelling props (puppet theater, flannel board)
- See Chapter 4 for more details.

Wooden stands to hold markers

Glue sticks

Rubber cement

Tape recorder and headphones

Displays of children's work

Fabric pieces used to open and close center areas

Left/righthanded scissors

Writing utensils
- Markers, pens, pencils, highlighters, colored pencils

Labels on objects, areas, personal property

Cards with student names on them for use with name games

Three-ring binders (these make great portfolios!)

Reference materials
- Dictionary, thesaurus, atlas, encyclopedia, visual dictionary, "quick words" book (commonly misspelled words, with space allotted for independent word lists)

Figure 3.4 Suggested list of classroom materials to support literacy.

The Structure of Time

Just as the classroom layout and materials send messages to children about how we value literacy learning, so too does our treatment of time. When we make a decision to spend time doing one thing, we are making a decision (perhaps unconsciously) to not do something else. It is very important to consciously make decisions about the use of our time with children. Time can be thought of in many ways. Here we will focus on the structure of time as it pertains to elements of routine and daily schedule.

Educators everywhere can understand the constant challenge of managing time efficiently throughout the school day. Keeping the basics of the classroom schedule somewhat structured and routine will enable children to take responsibility for their own learning by making decisions about their work (Kostelnik et al., 2004). However, one finds it necessary to remain flexible in the implementation of daily instruction because of the breaks that typically occur throughout, such as time for gym or time for recess. Despite such interruptions, it is vital that the teacher continue to communicate to his or her students the importance and value of literacy. This may be done by designating blocks of *uninterrupted time* (an average of at least 60–90 minutes per block each day), in which the processes of reading and writing are modeled, practiced, and integrated throughout the curricular content areas, providing meaningful literacy experiences for students.

Integrating Subject Matter

Integrating reading and writing into content-area projects has appeared to encourage children to develop their critical thinking skills more fully (Many et al., 1996; Kostelnik et al., 2004). This integration can also help to enhance children's literacy growth while strengthening their content learning (Guthrie et al., 1996; Morrow et al., 1997). Integration of subject matter works best in the classroom in the following ways (Shanahan, 1997:18):

1. When there are specific outcomes that take advantage of the "most rigorous thinking of the disciplinary fields, but that go beyond this base to outcomes that would only be possible from integration"
2. When it encourages children to make the connections from material presented, and when it "focuses their attention to the cultural differences that exist across disciplines and how to translate across these boundaries
3. When children are given continued opportunities for ample instruction, guidance, and practice to allow for successes

One outcome of the integrated instructional approach for which there is convincing evidence is the claim that this approach provides greater motivation (Lehman, 1994). According to Lehman, students were more likely to find meaning in an integrated approach and, therefore, to enjoy learning more and be more committed to the learning process.

Planning Your Day

"Oh, we get to start our spring projects this afternoon!" This exclamation comes from a third grader as she looks over the posted daily schedule in the classroom. Just as adults like to know their plans for the day, children also like to know what's in store for them. In posting a schedule, you are providing a sense of security for the students in your room.

For the emerging learner, post the schedule using both printed words and correlated pictures of the event to provide a visual cue for the given print. For more literacy-accomplished children, displayed words alone are suitable. We have provided sample schedules for both the emerging-to-early learner and the early-to-fluent learner (see Figures 3.5 and 3.6). These schedules offer frameworks of instruction beneficial to the needs and interests of the learners in your classroom and allow for adaptations and modifications to be made as needed. Although each schedule has a different appearance, the underlying philosophy remains intact. Students benefit most when they are actively involved in making discoveries, reflecting on their learning, and engaged in discussing the processes used to get there in a meaningful, cooperative style.

Routines: Guiding and Facilitating Instruction

Certain routines will build on and expand children's opportunities to develop their reading and writing skills in the classroom, regardless of their learning level. In providing and modeling classroom routines, certain work habits are developed, such as working independently or cooperatively to complete a given task. More time can then be allotted for instructional grouping strategies and conferencing. When students gain responsibility for their learning, you have more time to guide all students along the literacy learning continuum.

FLEXIBLE GROUPING   One instructional approach found among literacy-supportive classrooms is the strategy of flexible grouping.

> Literacy learning is a developmental process that the teacher facilitates by providing modeling, authentic experiences, mini-lessons on specific topics and frequent opportunities for students to consult with and learn from each other. Students learn as they create their own meaning and actively take charge of their own learning. (Heuwinkel, 1996:28)

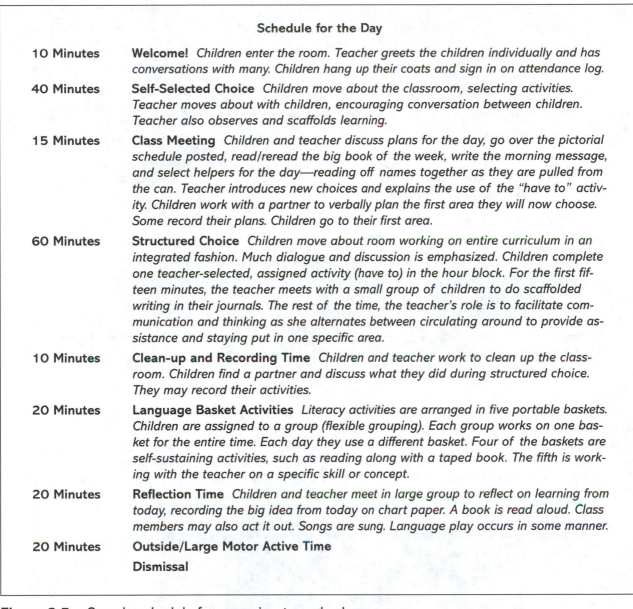

Schedule for the Day

10 Minutes   **Welcome!** *Children enter the room. Teacher greets the children individually and has conversations with many. Children hang up their coats and sign in on attendance log.*

40 Minutes   **Self-Selected Choice** *Children move about the classroom, selecting activities. Teacher moves about with children, encouraging conversation between children. Teacher also observes and scaffolds learning.*

15 Minutes   **Class Meeting** *Children and teacher discuss plans for the day, go over the pictorial schedule posted, read/reread the big book of the week, write the morning message, and select helpers for the day—reading off names together as they are pulled from the can. Teacher introduces new choices and explains the use of the "have to" activity. Children work with a partner to verbally plan the first area they will now choose. Some record their plans. Children go to their first area.*

60 Minutes   **Structured Choice** *Children move about room working on entire curriculum in an integrated fashion. Much dialogue and discussion is emphasized. Children complete one teacher-selected, assigned activity (have to) in the hour block. For the first fifteen minutes, the teacher meets with a small group of children to do scaffolded writing in their journals. The rest of the time, the teacher's role is to facilitate communication and thinking as she alternates between circulating around to provide assistance and staying put in one specific area.*

10 Minutes   **Clean-up and Recording Time** *Children and teacher work to clean up the classroom. Children find a partner and discuss what they did during structured choice. They may record their activities.*

20 Minutes   **Language Basket Activities** *Literacy activities are arranged in five portable baskets. Children are assigned to a group (flexible grouping). Each group works on one basket for the entire time. Each day they use a different basket. Four of the baskets are self-sustaining activities, such as reading along with a taped book. The fifth is working with the teacher on a specific skill or concept.*

20 Minutes   **Reflection Time** *Children and teacher meet in large group to reflect on learning from today, recording the big idea from today on chart paper. A book is read aloud. Class members may also act it out. Songs are sung. Language play occurs in some manner.*

20 Minutes   **Outside/Large Motor Active Time**
                 Dismissal

Figure 3.5   Sample schedule for emerging-to-early classroom.

Flexible grouping is a time when students come together to conference as they consider specific elements of literature, a certain author, or a common theme or interest (Lipton & Hubble, 1997). Flexible groups may be formed based on a variety of factors:

1. Students are grouped who have been reading the same book, books with similar themes, or different books within the same genre.
2. Students are grouped on the basis of identified needs or interests.
3. Students are grouped on the basis of specific skills that the teacher wants to introduce or reinforce. The members of the group may change as students gain mastery or require support.

The role of the teacher during flexible grouping is that of a mediator, structuring time for students to interact with their learning process. Such groupings allow the teacher to monitor student progress while allowing also for flexibility and choice (Lipton & Hubble, 1997). The goal of the group might be to respond to literature, to conduct research on a given topic, or to work on developing particular reading strategies.

Groupings of students are expected to form and disband depending on the specified goal of each group (Fields & Spangler, 1995:234). Shanahan (1997) reminds us that even within an integrated instructional approach, there still remains a need for mini-lessons and guided practice, as are found in this type of educational approach.

What does our day look like?

Morning Message
(5–10 minutes)

Sustained Silent Reading
(20–30 minutes)

Class Meeting
(15 minutes)

Language Arts Block
(90 minutes)

Special Classes: Music, Gym, Art

Lunch

Math
(whole-group instruction with options
for flexible grouping)
(90 minutes)

Recess

Journal Writing
(15–20 minutes)

Thematic Project Study
(integrating language arts across
the curriculum)
(40–45 minutes)

Written/Shared Reflections
(10 minutes)

Story Read-Aloud
(15–20 minutes)

Dismissal Procedures
(10 minutes)

Figure 3.6   Sample schedule for the early-to-fluent learner.

WHOLE-GROUP AND SMALL-GROUP INSTRUCTION   Whenever you engage in a discussion about working with children in small groups, such as with flexible grouping, someone will inevitably ask the question, "What do I do with the other children while I am meeting with the small group?" We admit, it is no easy feat at first to juggle the needs of all the children in the class as you work with four or five. However, given the appropriate structure for your specific group of children, it is possible and can be quite rewarding. There are a few distinct pos-

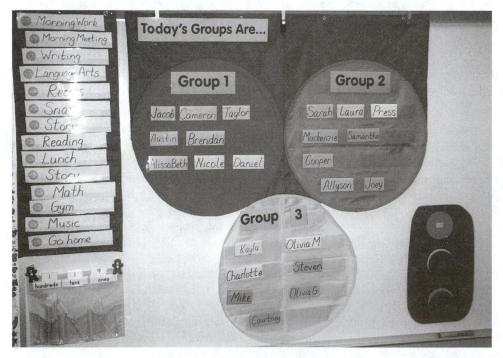

Flexible groupings.

sibilities which you can select to use. The key is that with whatever you select, the children are able to work in a self-sufficient, self-sustaining manner during the period that you are unavailable. Some people use this as a time to have children write in their journals or in their learning logs. Others prefer children reading to themselves or to buddies. Finally, the most popular method is centers or child-choice areas. Note here that seatwork is not listed as a solution to the problem. Children learn when they are engaged—hands on, minds on—typical seatwork is not supportive of this.

You may be wondering if all instruction now must occur in small groups. Is whole-group instruction passé? Not at all. With time at a premium, we must use whole-group instruction, small-group instruction, and independent practice carefully and to their fullest potentials. For that reason, it is important to consider the role that each plays in literacy learning.

Children learn new ideas best when they can actively experience them and when they can discuss their learning (Kostelnik et al., 2004). This makes small groups an ideal

place to introduce new concepts and skills. In small groups, children have more occasions to talk and are more likely to do so, compared to large group time. At large-group meeting times, it is very useful to practice and review skills learned previously. It is also meaningful to engage in group discussions about new ideas and relate them to past learning. Finally, individual time to reflect on, to practice, and to try out learning can be quite useful for consolidating ideas and branching out to consider new ones. To best meet the learning needs of all of the children with whom we work, we must consider structuring all three types of groupings into our daily work with young children. As a rule of thumb, a third of the time should be engaged in whole-group instruction, a third of the time in small-group instruction, and the last third in child-choice or independent work. Therefore, a day with Madison's class may include one hour of whole-group time, one hour of choice time, and one hour of small-group instruction. Of course, the actual day isn't necessarily chunked exactly this way. Instead, these hours are blended into each other and flow quite naturally back and forth.

APPLICATIONS FOR STRUCTURING THE COMPONENT OF TIME

1. Recognize the power of routine and let it work to your advantage.
2. Organize your classroom curriculum into blocks of uninterrupted time (at least 60–90 minutes each day), in which the processes of reading and writing are integrated throughout the content areas. Post these schedules daily.
3. Develop grouping strategies that will encourage students to consult and learn from each other. Flexible groupings and literacy circles serve such purposes.
4. Utilize all three configurations for instruction and practice of concepts and skills: whole-group, small-group, and individual work.

Structuring Connections: Linking Home and School
The Teacher Role

Throughout this chapter, we have discussed the structural components of the literate classroom environment. The components have included the flexible layout of the classroom, the interactive learning materials found there, and the need to adapt time and schedules to learners' needs and interests.

But a truly successful classroom needs much more than inanimate components and guidelines. There must be a caring, competent teacher at the helm to guide the way. You make all of the difference in the world by what you say and what you do. It is truly important to work on

building a positive relationship with each and every student (and their families). This type of relationship establishes a level of trust that communicates your care for the students. It is this type of trust that must be present in order for optimal literacy learning to occur (Routman, 2003).

It is the teacher's attitude which greatly impacts the amount and type of learning which will occur. We want to be sure our attitudes are positive ones. Teachers should have a "You can do anything" way of looking at children's literacy learning. When we believe in the children, they come to believe in themselves.

Care must be taken to plan for the children placed in our classrooms. Planning must be based on their backgrounds, the information they already possess, the goals they hold for themselves, and the developmental goals we hold for them.

Observation plays a key role in this planning as we move in and out of children's play, aware of both their interests and their levels of understanding (Goldhaber et al., 1996–1997). This type of classroom support continues over time, changing as needed, reflecting student needs, all the while expanding and challenging children's developing literacy knowledge.

The Connecting Piece: Strengthening Parental Support

Both the teacher and the parent play equally important roles in developing and strengthening a child's literacy skills. Parents are their children's first teachers. "The foundations of children's literacy are in their home environments. Capitalizing on the language experiences children bring to school is critical to their success as learners" (Lipton & Hubble, 1997).

A longitudinal study exploring the relationship of home factors to literacy development identified certain key factors as instrumental in linking literacy skills between the home and school environment (Weinberger, 1996:17). These factors include the following:

1. Children's development of a love for favorite books at age 3 is linked to the books they actually read in school at age 7, and is significant in children's literacy development.
2. The use of a child's level of reading book at age 7 as an outcome measure has the advantage of revealing the types of literature that children of different abilities actually use.
3. The literacy learning that takes place in the home must be made more apparent to teachers, so that the learning can be enhanced within the school setting.

As educators, we must be supportive of the experiences that parents are already providing for their children to develop literacy learning. Working together and building a solid relationship will provide the best learning environment for children. "When schools cultivate partnerships with parents and reach out to the community as a resource, everyone benefits" (Lipton & Hubble, 1997: 150).

"Why aren't there any worksheets coming home?"
"My child's teacher hasn't corrected her spelling mistakes in the story she wrote."
"Where are the spelling books and the Friday tests?"

Comments such as these are commonly made by parents who have become confused and concerned by the recent media attacks on schools for the growing illiteracy problems in our nation. Parents taught to read through a highly structured phonetic approach are especially disillusioned by the new learner-centered philosophy currently adopted in many of our nation's schools.

How do we relieve and prevent such concern in our own communities? In one word, we *communicate*. Communication is the key to building a solid base of support and understanding between the home and school environments. Because many parents are unfamiliar with current literacy research, it is of great importance that educators effectively convey information about literacy development. This may be done through the use of parent workshops, newsletters, and open invitations to visit the classroom where literacy experiences are taking place. This builds an awareness of the way that the school system supports children's growth, addressing all levels of learning across the curriculum.

Fields and Spangler (1995:250–251) support the value of parents as partners in the educational process:

> The most important thing parents can do is work with their children. It means encouraging library use and buying books, reading aloud to children and having them read to parents, writing notes and participating in home–school journals, and actually stamping and mailing letters to grandparents. Supporting literacy at home means regulating television, talking with children, and paying attention to what they say. It means not criticizing developmental writing, being accepting of invented spelling, and being patient with slow and stumbling reading.

One vehicle for conveying information on the literacy experiences in your classroom and how parents might support these at home is the classroom newsletter. Classroom newsletters should be reader-friendly, free of educational jargon, and written in a caring and supportive tone. Newsletters should be appealing to the eye, making use of pictures and adequate white space.

A classroom newsletter may include a description of the week's events, upcoming classroom studies or field trips, important announcements, and special features such as "Word of the Week." You also may wish to add a personalized touch to the letter by featuring a child's poem, joke, short story, or possibly a drawing or cartoon. Titling that section of the newsletter "Kids Corner," or possibly devoting one newsletter a month to children's work and ideas, reinforces the learner-centered approach you endorse within your classroom. Another related idea is to take dictated reports from children at the end of each day, regarding their favorite activities or something they learned. These might be included as a special section of the newsletter. Newsletters are also a wonderful way to enlist parental help for at-home activities or to thank parents publicly, which, in turn, will encourage more parents to volunteer.

A final component in communicating with parents is to keep them well informed of their child's progress in school and to provide opportunities for parents to be key players in the child's evaluation process. Conferences should be times when everyone participates—the teacher, the parent, and the child. Portfolio conferencing is one format used to carry this style out effectively. More information on portfolio conferencing is provided in Chapter 8.

APPLICATIONS FOR THE DEVELOPMENT OF A POSITIVE ATTITUDE— CREATING STRONG LINKS AMONG TEACHERS, PARENTS, AND STUDENTS

1. Know where your students are developmentally, and plan for their learning accordingly.
2. Cultivate a partnership with the parents of the children in your classroom. Effective communication through newsletters, workshops, and open invitations to visit the classroom is a key component here.

Final Thoughts

Plato once stated, "What is honored in a country will be cultivated there" (Morrow, 1989). This ideal also holds true with regard to fostering a love for literacy among our nation's children. We live in a time in which the teaching of reading and writing not only is more important than ever but also must be done better than ever. With this in mind, it is of vital importance that we, as educators, provide the type of instructional environment captured here, which cultivates the seeds of literacy for our students.

In this chapter, we've discussed the four structural components needed to establish a literate classroom environment: a flexible layout, interactive learning materials, an adaptable learning time, and a positive attitude on the part of the teacher. We recounted many examples for each of these structural components. Now it's time to see how your classroom's new-found look of literacy can be progressively matched to the needs and interests of emerging, early, and fluent learners.

Challenge Yourself

1. Design your classroom environment. Create a diagram of the layout of your classroom (or potential layout of a potential classroom). Label the areas. Check to see if you have included all of the elements discussed in this chapter. Do you have interest areas? Are they logically placed? Does the room allow free flow of movement, yet not invite running or unintended behavior? Where will you place print? How will you involve children in using the print within the environment?
2. Create a schedule for your day. Check whether it has all of the elements discussed in this chapter to support a successful literacy environment. How will you balance the varied needs for all of the children within your environment?

Suggested Sources for Additional Information

Morrow, L. M. (2003). *Organizing and managing the language arts block: A professional development guide.* New York: Guildford Press.

Routman, R. (2003). *Reading essentials: The specifics you need to teach reading well.* Portsmouth, NH: Heinemann.

4

Emerging Literacy
A Nurturing Classroom Context

In the beginning of the school year, Mrs. Peterson is busy assessing the children in her kindergarten classroom on various reading concepts. The following conversation occurs:

MRS. PETERSON: *Can you read any of these words, Ben? [Showing him a word list]*
BEN: *Sure.*
MRS. PETERSON: *O.K., go ahead.*
BEN: *O.K. [Silence]*
MRS. PETERSON: *You can start any time.*
BEN: *I already did.*
MRS. PETERSON: *I am sorry. I guess I didn't hear you. Please do it again.*
BEN: *Well see . . . I can read anything in my head, but nothing out loud! It just works that way!*

Sure it does! But what are we actually talking about? What is *it?* Where does *it* come from? How does *it* develop? All good questions, especially for the earliest of the literacy learners. For us—as good early childhood professionals—to be able to support and scaffold literacy in our preschoolers, kindergartners, and perhaps early first graders, we must recognize the key components of this emerging literacy phase and understand the critical role that we play.

As you read, keep in mind the following questions:

- What is the difference between emerging literacy and emergent literacy?
- Why is there so much attention on this phase?
- What best describes children's behavior during this emerging phase?

- What are the big ideas of literacy that children must learn to be most successful in the future?
- What are the key factors currently linked to children's future success in literacy?
- What is the role of play in literacy learning today?
- What can I do to support children in the emerging phase?

In this chapter, these questions will be addressed as we explore the beginnings of literacy, somewhere around the middle of the second year of life. (Of course, we are well aware that literacy begins a few years prior to this point, but we had to begin somewhere.) The first half of this chapter is theory, discussion, and classroom implications. The second half contains the classroom applications: tried and true activities to increase young children's literacy understandings.

Exploring the Emerging Phase of Literacy

Before we begin our discussion of the emerging phase of literacy, it is important to delineate the differences between the terms *emergent literacy* and *the emerging phase of literacy.* **Emergent literacy,** as discussed in Chapter 2, is a term that describes children's processes of becoming literate (Clay, 1966). It describes a continuum of behaviors involving both oral and written language. Through numerous varied experiences as both a sender and a receiver of oral and written language, children develop an understanding of literacy that evolves over time. Please note that the term *emergent literacy* refers to the entire process of becoming a fluent user of literacy.

In this chapter, we will describe the beginning phase of the "becoming literate" process. Because we are describing the beginnings of literacy, we are talking about the time within the process of emergent literacy when literacy is emerging. Therefore, this phase is called the **emerging phase.** It is during this time that the dispositions for literacy begin to become established. This means that the messages that adults send to children at this time in the support of reading, writing, speaking, listening, and viewing and the types of activities that we provide can significantly shape children's attitudes toward literacy.

Learning about literacy is not a natural process. As discussed in Chapter 2, some children, a very small number, teach themselves to write and to read independently. However, most children need some support along the way. One of the most important things to remember about literacy is that it is an *active* process. In fact, it is really an *inter*active process. Both the child and the adult take an active role in helping the child become literate. Both parties are engaged in the process continuously. The adult's continual support can take numerous forms. It may take the form of observing, assessing, planning, modeling, setting up a supportive environment, facilitating discovery learning, taking the lead role in guided learning, or directly instructing.

You may wonder, "Just when do I begin teaching my children or students about literacy?" The answer is, "Yesterday." Children are never too young to start. Does this mean we are advocating reading lessons for babies? Well, in a sense . . . yes, but not the way that you would typically think of lessons. In this interactive process for adults and children, it is the adult's responsibility to make sure that the learning for the child is designed to support each child individually, using what we know about both child development and literacy development, as well as developmentally and culturally appropriate practice. This means that direct, purposeful activities and experiences must be planned to best meet the needs of the children with whom you work. As we discussed in Chapter 2, both direct and indirect methods of instruction are useful in teaching children literacy concepts.

There is currently a lot of attention being paid to children's literacy learning prior to first grade. This is due largely to the research that is bubbling forth demonstrating the immense importance these early years play with respect to children's future literacy and lifelong successes. Study after study documents that the level of children's literacy abilities prior to formal schooling sets the stage for their future potential success (Dickinson & Tabors, 2001; Hart & Risley, 2000; McGee & Richgels, 2003). Therefore, now more than ever, there is a cry for increased literacy instruction for young children. The International Reading Association (IRA) and the National Association for the Education of Young Children (NAEYC) have responded to that cry with a joint statement about early literacy that includes a continuum of expected literacy development (see www.NAEYC.org for a copy of the statement). Their continuum provides the basis for the discussion in this chapter. This chapter captures what NAEYC and IRA refer to as the Awareness and Exploration phase and the Experimenting phase (Neuman, Copple, & Bredekamp, 1998).

No two children are typically at the same point in the emergent literacy journey. Nor are any two children within the emerging phase progressing at the same rate or doing the same things at any given time. The range and pace of the development of literacy behaviors is vast. During the emerging years, children are becoming aware of and trying to sort out the meanings behind the various components and uses of literacy.

Children's Emerging Literacy Behaviors

Children in this emerging phase can be found anywhere along the beginning end of the continuum for any one facet of literacy learning (reading, writing, speaking, listening, and viewing) and at the opposite end in another area. While Sofia grapples with the new vocabulary being introduced in her environment, she may become quite focused on the letter *S* while writing her name and think that every *S* she sees on signs belongs to her. This wonderful mix of understandings within each individual child is what makes this phase so exciting. It is so important that we are careful in how we observe, plan, and implement plans for young children's learning. Let's further examine children's literacy behaviors in the emerging phase.

There are some big ideas surrounding each aspect of literacy, which are essential for children to understand. Many children may intuitively come to understand these important concepts; however, to ensure that all children are successful in their literacy endeavors, we must keep these ideas as the focus of our observations and instruction.

EMERGING READING BEHAVIORS   The big ideas for reading are:

- Words have meaning.
- Words tell the story.
- Pictures can tell the story, too.

Children explore these ideas at this phase primarily through experiences with books and other forms of print (such as posters, pocket charts, and writing produced by themselves and others).

Children in the emerging phase can be found doing a vast number of things associated with reading. Behaviors range from telling stories to listening to stories to retelling favorite stories.

LISTENING TO AND RETELLING STORIES   Children at this stage generally enjoy listening to books. They are eager to "help" read the books, chiming in as predictable or repetitive phrases are read and reminding you

Supporting emerging reading behaviors through repetitive and predictable text.

when you've "SKIPPED A PAGE!" in a favorite book or "said it WRONG!" after paraphrasing something you've read for the hundredth time. They also may pretend to read books by making up words to go along with the pictures, or they may know the book so well that they can say it from memory, word for word.

While reading, children in the later part of the emerging phase often will point to words in the text as they tell the text they've memorized. This is called **finger-point reading** and really is recognized as a form of reading. In order to get to this finger-point stage and beyond, the children must have some knowledge of print; an ability to break some phonemes into segments; and knowledge of letters (Ehri & Sweet, 1991). By using a familiar text to help practice these reading behaviors, children can further their reading development through this type of reading.

UNCOVERING CONCEPTS ABOUT PRINT While listening to books read and looking at them on their own, emerging readers pay close attention to the pictures. Depending on where they are on the emerging continuum, they may also look for familiar letters and words in the print. However, they may or may not associate specific meaning with these recognized pieces of text. Although their interest in pictures can be used to help children follow and think about the meaning behind stories, it is also important to point out to children that the letters on the pages make up words that tell the story. This is part of what Marie Clay (1975) called "concepts about print." Through experiences such as being read with (i.e., as active participants in the process) and other meaningful literacy events, children learn that books work in a special way:

- Books go from front to back.
- Print is organized from left to right and from top to bottom.
- Words are the things that we read.
- Letters stand for sounds we say.

These and other concepts about print all help children learn the connection between oral and written language. Children in the emerging times are just making this connection.

One of the first big connections young children make is between their spoken name and the way it is written. Their own names may be the first thing that children learn to read. Names have such a deep personal connection with children that they should not be taken lightly. Using children's names for instruction in emergent literacy concepts can be a powerful tool.

Often it is the letters in one's name that are learned first, along with a few favorite words such as *Mom, dog, cat,* and *stop.* These often lead children to become aware of and interested in other letters surrounding them. Children in the emerging phase can be busy learning about letters and sounds and figuring out their purpose in language. They often become interested in what signs say and take a great interest in letters everywhere ("Mommy, what does that say? What about that?"). They come to recognize logos and take great pride in reading them as the bus zooms by: "McDonald's! Kmart! The Dollar Store!" Each new discovery about print can be amazing to the emerging reader.

Emerging Writing Behaviors

Children continue to explore print as they engage in writing. The big ideas in writing are:

- Anything that is said can be written down.
- Print says the same thing today as it will tomorrow.
- Print can be organized in a specific way.

Children explore these ideas as they play with print. Many people have described reading and writing as parallel supporting activities (i.e., reading supports writing and writing supports reading). At the early stages of writing, however, this is not the case. Initially, children engage in symbolic writing with pictures. This is similar to what they are doing in their play. In both play and early writing, children practice manipulating symbols (Pelligrini & Galda, 1994). It isn't until later, when the children make the switch from writing to represent symbols to writing to represent language, that the two processes of reading and writing are finally parallel and more supportive of each other (Juel, 1988; Pellegrini et al., 1991). Children in the emerging phase can be found writing both ways. It is as children move through the later part of the emerging phase

toward the early phase that they begin to write to document language.

EXPERIMENTING WITH SYMBOLS Emergent writers move from drawing to scribbling to using letters in play to using them purposefully in the context of the real world (see Figure 4.1). They move from calling everything they make "writing" or "drawing" to distinguishing specifically between the two. As their names are a fascination for young children, they may spend much time writing and rewriting their names. Just as in reading, where they can be found wanting to read or hear the same book over and over again, the same is true in writing. In writing, children at this phase like to write the same letter or word or signifier for a word over and over again. As they are trying to distinguish the difference between letters and numbers, their purposes and uses, children do lots of experimenting with them. Their writing may take on a variety of forms. In the beginning, they may scribble, then they may mix letterlike forms with scribbles, then use letters. Drawings may accompany any of these stages. Finally, they may use letters separately from drawings. As might be expected, the experimenting and learning about what letters and sounds are all about and their connection will leave children's early attempts at writing words looking nonwordlike. Early "words" may contain one letter or a mix of letters. Emerging writers often use unconventional spelling (temporary spelling) to represent the sounds they hear in words. As their understanding increases, they include more sounds. All of these forms of writing are an excellent way for children to put into practice their emerging understanding of literacy.

Children's writing is an equally great opportunity for adults to observe and document their students' progressive literacy understanding and to plan for future instruction. Children's writing is typically accompanied by talk. Writing is a social activity, as well as a personal task of recording symbols and thoughts. Both what is written and what is said are important to take into consideration when observing, assessing, and planning for children's literacy development.

Emerging Oral Language Behaviors

You'll recall from Chapter 2 that oral language is the foundation for all work in early literacy (Dickinson & Tabors, 2001; Hart & Risley, 2000; McGee & Richgels, 2003). Oral language includes speaking and listening. Examining one at a time, let's first look at the big ideas and then explore common behaviors in children according to the four focus areas for oral language: sounds, rules, meanings, and social interactions.

EMERGING SPEAKING BEHAVIORS Some children speak continuously. Others seem to never speak.

Figure 4.1   Samples of children's writing in the emerging phase.

How children communicate with adults, with other children, and even with themselves is extremely important to monitor and support. The big ideas surrounding speaking as a literacy act are:

- Language is made up of words.
- Words are powerful.
- Language shapes our world.

Children in the emerging phase are busy playing with the **sounds of language.** This is often evident in the rhymes they try: "fee fee, wee, wee!" They try out the power of words to see the adult reaction: "pee, pee!"

They are also involved in figuring out the rules, or **syntax,** of oral language. They may mix up the tense in sentences, saying "goed" instead of "went," or they may try to formulate a question that actually ends up sounding like a statement, "We are going to the park today?" instead of "Are we going to the park today?"

As their vocabulary grows from experiences with those around them and through stories they have shared with more knowing "others" (peers, parents, teachers, etc.), children work to try to figure out how the words have meaning in their own world. They grapple with the **semantics** of language. When Sofia practiced the words *kingdom* and *cooperation* in her play, she was demonstrating how children personalize new words.

Finally, children at this phase truly enjoy trying to figure out the **social pragmatics** of oral language—where they can and cannot use certain language. This is ever evident as they begin to try out jokes as a form of their language play:

> **KENNEDY:** Knock, knock.
> **CHRIS:** Yeah.
> **KENNEDY:** No, you say, "Who's there?" Okay? Knock, knock!
> **CHRIS:** Okay . . . Who's there?
> **KENNEDY:** Chicken.
> **CHRIS:** Chicken who?
> **KENNEDY:** Chicken poo!

The children then burst into a round of pure satisfied belly laughter and tell the joke again and again.

Children also play with the power of language as they talk with friends. For instance, "If you let me have the swing, you can come to my birthday party!" Children in the emerging phase often retell stories or versions of stories they have heard before. They also make up their own stories. These stories may have a beginning, a middle, or an end or even all three parts. They may be extremely simple or complex with characters, problems, and a series of events. Often, these stories are based on personal experiences.

Children learn the behaviors of oral language from the adults in their world (Hart & Risley, 2000). Depending on the environment and adult modeling, some children at this point in emerging literacy are quite proficient at expressing their needs, desires, and ideas. Others, who have not been encouraged to do this, are not quite at the same point.

It is important to recognize here that children for whom English is a second language may not demonstrate their true oral language capabilities *while speaking English.* As with other children, the language level used depends on the prior experiences outside of the formal environment. English learners' language level must be understood so that their literacy development may be supported. In cases where English is not the primary language, every attempt to evaluate and further support the child's level of home language should be made (Tabors & Snow, 2001). This is also essential when it comes to the other half of oral language— listening.

EMERGING LISTENING BEHAVIORS The big ideas we want children to understand about listening are:

- Words are made up of sounds.
- Words carry a message.
- Listen for the message.
- Think about the message.

Children in the emerging phase are typically evolving in their ability to hear the sounds in language (see Chapter 2 for the development of phonological ability). As children play with the sounds of language, they are demonstrating their understanding of the sounds they hear in spoken language. They demonstrate their emerging understanding of the rules (syntax) of language when they alter their language after you have restated their words. Jimmy said, "I goed there." You say, "Oh, you went to the store." He responds, "Yep, I went there." When children reenact stories or respond to questions, they may be demonstrating their evolving understanding of the meaning (semantics) of the language they encountered. This is evident when playing listening games such as Simon Says. Finally, the pragmatics or social interaction component of listening is quite visible during daily informal as well as formal conversations with the children. For many children at this level, it is difficult to listen to a message they consider not important or interesting, which makes the case once again for personally relevant instruction.

CRITICAL VIEWING Finally, the big ideas behind viewing for the emerging phase are:

- Things we view send a message.
- Listen and watch for the message.
- Think about the message.

The last skill, to view or watch critically, is one that is currently receiving more attention than in the past because of the state of modern technologies. Children spend much time viewing and taking in information. They watch television for large amounts of time. In fact, in the years before first grade, children often spend more time watching television than they do in school or playing with others (Levin & Carlsson-Paige, 1994). This makes the skill of viewing critically an important one to focus on in the emerging years.

Often, children in this phase have difficulty separating fact from fiction. Part of this is due to cognitive abilities. Rather than waiting for children to "grow out of this," however, we can pose problems or questions for them to think about to help them begin to distinguish what is real from what is pretend. Whether or not children master this differentiation at this time is not as important as it is to give them the opportunity to work on becoming more critical viewers.

Emerging Literacy Resources

Numerous resources to support children in the emerging literacy process are well within each educator's reach. The role of the adult cannot be minimized. Adults are children's primary literacy resources. We serve as the guides, interpreters, and mediators. However, just being present is not enough. Adults have specific roles to play in this phase of literacy learning. Beyond designing a nurturing environment, as discussed in Chapter 3, we have the responsibility to teach children important concepts and skills using as many primary, real-life experiences as possible so that we can help children see the connection between their world and literacy. Using this constructivist style for literacy instruction has been recommended for achieving success with all learners, regardless of skin color or income level (Xu, 2003).

Factors Linked to Future Literacy Success

All children greatly benefit from numerous experiences in each of the areas of literacy. Although we adapt our instruction depending on children's individual developmental needs and background experiences, it is imperative that the opportunities offered are authentic, fun, and purposeful. This means that our plans for children's learning must be made carefully. Clearly within the five areas of literacy (reading, writing, speaking, listening, and viewing) there are multiple concepts on which to focus. Where do we begin? Luckily, there has been an explosion in research at the emerging level of literacy and the experts have been able to link four factors to children's future literacy success. These areas include: children's *language ability*; their understanding of the *alphabetic principle*; their *experiences with print*; and their *ability to "do school."* Let's briefly discuss each one.

LANGUAGE ABILITY Children's overall language ability is being targeted as a crucial aspect for future literacy success (McGee & Richgels, 2003; Snow et al., 1998). Although improving children's overall language abilities should be the goal for early childhood professionals, a few specific areas have been highlighted by the research to be of great importance.

Number of Words Simply the sheer *number of words* children are exposed to in direct one-on-one communication seems to correlate with future literacy success (Dickinson & Tabors, 2001; Hart & Risley, 2000).

Vocabulary The number of *vocabulary words* a child is able to use and understand is an indicator of future success in reading (Dickinson & Tabors, 2001; Hart & Risley, 2000). When adults purposefully use new or rare words in relevant situations such as snack time, group time, or face-to-face conversations, children can acquire these words. Apparently, the more words a child knows, the easier it is to learn new words and the faster the child can decode and understand new words. Also, the more words children have at their disposal, the better they are at truly communicating their ideas.

Decontextualized Language Children's ability to use **decontextualized language,** language that does not refer to the current situation, has been strongly linked to future literacy success (Dickinson & Smith, 1994). Decontextualized language often occurs during explanations and discussions. Two types of talk have been shown to be quite powerful in this area: narrative talk and explanatory talk (Dickinson & Beals, 1994). **Narrative talk** is used to tell stories about events or ideas at another place and another time (decontextualized). **Explanatory talk** is used when giving explanations or descriptions of causes and intentions. As a bonus, both narrative talk and explanatory talk can also be powerful vocabulary builders.

Phonological Awareness Finally, phonological awareness has been shown in numerous studies to be highly related to future literacy success (Goswami, 2001).

You'll recall that **phonological awareness** is the ability to hear the sounds in language and to comprehend them in spoken language, and **phonemic awareness** is the ability to hear the individual, discrete sounds in language. One of the best ways to develop phonological awareness is through experiences with rhyme and segmentation (Bradley & Bryant, 1983; Mueter et al., 1997). Nursery rhymes have been documented as a good vehicle for emphasizing these concepts with young children (Ayres, 1994). In nursery rhymes, such as "Humpty Dumpty," children can recite the rhyme. They can play with the rhyming words, listening for words that sound alike and stomping their feet when the hear them. They can try putting in new rhyming words to see if they can make a new nursery rhyme. They can verbally cut rhyming words into parts (*H-umpty, D-umpty*) to find the part that rhymes. They can sing rhyming words and chant rhyming words, all the while experiencing the sounds of language on a personal level through enjoyable language play. See Chapter 2 for more examples of these as well as ideas for everyday classroom phonological awareness activities. Remember that phonological awareness is a concept, which means it develops over time through many purposeful experiences. It is not a skill to be drilled (Adams, 2001).

ALPHABETIC PRINCIPLE   Phonological awareness activities and training have been reported as an important avenue for uncovering the **alphabetic principle,** which is the idea that individual letters and letter combinations match specific sounds in oral language (National Research Council, 1998). When children understand the relationship between letters and sounds, they are more likely to do well accomplishing literacy tasks. Knowledge about the alphabetic principle comes about through various sources. The best way for the alphabet letters and sounds to be taught is through meaningful interactions with print (Adams, 1990). This can occur as you help a child form a letter in her name or find the sounds in a word that she wants to write. It can occur through direct instruction (*"Here's how you make a B, the first letter in your name"*) or through indirect instruction (*"Let's read*

the 'Napping House' today. At the beginning of 'Napping House' is the same sound as in Nancy's name.").

EXPERIENCES WITH PRINT   Children who have multiple experiences with print prior to formal schooling seem to do better than those who do not. Clay (2000) reports that as children are purposefully exposed to print, they develop specific concepts about print, described earlier in the chapter, which are linked to future success with reading and writing.

Concepts about Print   To develop concepts about print, one of the best activities to use is reading with children (Jalongo, 1988). In shared reading, you can model "how to's" and thought processes involved in reading by thinking these processes aloud. It is important to be sure that children can see the print as it is being read. Children's understanding of concepts of print also can be increased whenever an adult writes with the children or in front of them. This helps the children see the rules for working with print. Again, modeling the thinking that accompanies this activity by telling the children how you are making decisions for what to write is just as important in the modeling process as the writing itself. Sulzby (1985) found that the more that children were read to and the more they participated in the reading process (reading to themselves, to others, to toys), the better they understood

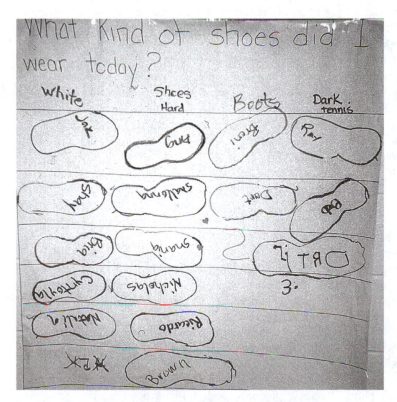

Integrating the curriculum: writing for real purposes.

the way books work, which is another predictor of reading success. As children progress from listening to stories, to telling stories, to retelling stories, to finally reading words, word awareness is developing.

Word Awareness   **Word awareness** is discovering that the words in print are the words we say. These words are made up of the letters in the alphabet. Word awareness can come about through writing with children, cutting the sentences into separate words and recombining them to make the same sentence or to re-create new ones. It can also be enhanced through matching words in known stories, fingerplays, or nursery rhymes with word cards that the children can manipulate. The more hands-on the activities for word awareness can be, the better the children will come to understand this concept. Knowledge about words, concepts of print, the alphabetic principle, and phonological awareness are what Beach and Young (1997) have determined to be the four crucial concepts for emerging literacy.

ABILITY TO "DO SCHOOL"   A relatively new factor being linked to young children's future literacy success is their ability to **"do school"** (McGee & Richgels, 2003). This term refers to the culture and language that is specific to school and school behavior. Schools expect children to conform to a certain level of language—to both use and understand this level, which is primarily reflected in middle class homes. Children coming to school who do not operate at this level are at a disadvantage and have been found to be perceived as possessing a lower degree of readiness, unrelated to the children's actual level of readiness (McMillon & Edwards, 2000). Although not a complete panacea for this problem, one thing adults can do to help is to read books to children. Storybook reading to young children has been found to increase their understanding of the language of school (see Chapter 2). Another way to help children learn how to "do school" is simply to play school with them and invite them to play it on their own. Let's take a look at some of the advantages that play can offer in our quest for "literacy for all."

Play and Emerging Literacy

One of the best places for children to explore real and pretend and for them to try out all of the literacy behaviors in a "safe" environment is in play. There is strong support in the research for the use of play in the emergent years to support the development of literacy concepts, skills, and behaviors (Musthafa, 1995).

LITERACY PROPS AND TOOLS   Children who are surrounded by numerous literacy props and tools in a print-rich environment often will take their literacy concepts and knowledge and combine them into their play themes (Neuman & Roskos, 1991; Roskos, 1988). In play,

Exploring the alphabet with paint.

children are likely to use the props to read for information: *"I'll look in the phone book,"* says Jason, as he takes it off the shelf in the play kitchen.

They are also likely to write for a purpose: *"Your appointment will be at 3:00. Please sign your name by this X, Mr. Pink,"* Jamey says as he performs his receptionist role in the pretend hospital. Thus, it is important to provide literacy-rich play experiences in the classroom. These play experiences need not be limited to the dramatic play corner.

Adding literacy materials, including environmental print, to all classroom areas can influence children's ability to read this environmental print. However, it is truly useful only if certain criteria are met:

- They know what to do with these props.
- The children notice the print.
- The print introduced into the area holds meaning for the children.

One significant way to help children see this print and to see the situationally relevant uses for the props in play is for an adult to interact with the children with these materials in the play setting. This combination of exposure to literacy materials, with functional experiences involving adults within the context of play settings, can help children

Princesses making guest list and party invitations for the ball.

Sample of party list.

Reading with a prop.

associate meaning with print (Christie & Enz, 1992; Vuke-lich, 1994). Neuman and Roskos (1991) report the follow-ing observation: "Teachers demonstrating literacy practices (in play) helped to extend and give meaning to children's reading and writing behaviors" (p. 221).

Rowe (1998) also found in her work with preschool-ers that adding props to the storybook reading sessions in the reading corner greatly enhanced children's under-standing of stories. She found the children would play out the stories in other areas of the room later in the day. There were also many more conversations connecting personal experiences with the stories when the props were added. Table 4.1 lists some props and tools for various play themes.

The Adult's Role in Emerging Literacy

The adult's role in facilitating emerging literacy is multi-faceted. True support for emerging literacy includes main-taining a subtle yet conscious balance between indirect opportunities for literacy development and more direct teaching.

As part of indirect instruction, it is important to pro-vide the setting and time for children to explore literacy behaviors independently. This allows for children to prac-tice and try to make personal meaning of their emerging literacy concepts and skills. In a discussion of writing, Dyson (1990:56) states that "self-expression, the shaping of inner worlds through outer forms, seems to be nurtured by the tensions between the need for social connection and for personal voice." This seems to capture the needs of the child in an emerging classroom. The child has to have time to be social and to share work and ideas with others, as well as time to think privately on his or her own. The indirect aspect of the adult's role nurtures this need.

The other half, direct teaching, is an equally impor-tant component. Children don't have all the answers and may waste precious time stumbling along to find them independently. They must have some direction and in-struction to guide them along the path. To conduct this push-me, pull-you type of program, integrating child ex-ploration and independence with direct guidance and in-struction, we offer the following guidelines (also known as the ten commandments for emerging literacy).

Guidelines to Support Emerging Literacy

1. Talk! Talk! Talk! Create meaningful conversa-tions with children and between children each day. Re-member the power of words and help children and families understand the powerful role that oral language plays in literacy learning.

2. Listen! Listen! Listen! Invite conversation and then be quiet and actively listen. Ask open ended ques-tions such as, "What do you think?" or "How does it work?" Use paralinguistics such as *umm* and *ohh* and *hmm* to invite further talk. Show each child in your envi-ronment that you are interested in what he or she has to say.

3. Play! Play! Play! Use the power of play to fa-cilitate conversation and instances for playful practice of literacy learning. Trust the power of play as a time for children to practice and explore their new understandings. Observe children's play. Show your acceptance with gen-uine smiles and useful props. Help the play along with coaching from the sidelines (*"Maybe a menu would help your customer order"*). Step into the play when it is stalled or when the play is at a low level (such as contin-uous dog or cat play). Be careful to leave the children's play as soon as you are not needed. Pursue the children's ideas within the play and allow them to be the true authors of the scenes. Your role is that of director, to help the au-thor's intentions come through.

4. Model! Model! Model! Children take into their play and everyday interactions much of what adults in their environments do. Deliberately model literacy behav-

Table 4.1   Literacy Props and Tools for Various Pretend Play Themes

Pretend Play	Possible Literacy Props and Theme Tools
Hospital	Prescription tablets, medical reference book, pads of paper for taking notes, clipboards with paper and attached pencils, charts of the human body, labeled medicine cabinet, intercom, telephone, sign "The Doctor is IN/OUT," magazines, books, calendar for scheduling appointments
Restaurant	Menus, restaurant's name on a sign, pads for taking orders, pens, credit card machine and slips, keyboard for entering orders, board for writing specials of the day, wheel or clothespins on a line for displaying orders to be made, OPEN/CLOSED sign, phone book, phone, awards for the restaurant
Entomology lab	Microscopes, phone book, computer, calculator, books with bugs in them, posters of insects with the parts labeled, paper for writing orders and observations on, chart of upcoming experiments, graph of insects spotted around room
Office	Computer, typewriter, paper, books, pencils and pens, slogan for company on the wall, NO SMOKING sign, phones, directions for using the phones, calendar on wall, to-do lists, phone message pads, file folders with the alphabet for organizing
Publishing company	Books, paper of all shapes and sizes, book-making materials, markers, pens, pencils, typewriter, name of company, letters to authors, IN box and OUT box, computer, phones, fax machine, materials for binding books
Grocery store	Paper for making lists, pens, signs for sales, name of store, OPEN/CLOSED, P.A. (to announce lost babies and sales), rolled paper for sales slips, paper for writing checks, credit card machine, scanner, boxes and cans with clear labels, coupons

Parking lots: using play to support literacy.

iors each day. Tell the children what you are doing and why you are doing it. Discuss your thought and decision-making processes as you model.

5. Experience! Experience! Experience! Provide as many primary experiences for children as possible on a daily basis. When children are able to see, smell, taste, and touch, they create more of a connection with the event at hand and are thus better able to incorporate it into their knowledge base. Use these primary experiences to teach children new vocabulary and strengthen existing vocabulary and concepts. Reflect on the experience together. Write about it. Read what you wrote. Read related books. Reenact the experience in play and group time. Enjoy it time and time again. Children benefit from multiple experiences with the same thing.

6. Read! Read! Read! Model reading each day. Read with the children. Read books for pure pleasure. Read books for facts (nonfiction) to seek information. Read fiction to experience the power of words and imagination. Read to support a concept. Read to explore the rhythm of language and to increase phonological awareness. Remember the power of reading aloud to the children and with the children each day. Also provide time for children to read alone or with peers daily.

7. Write! Write! Write! Model writing each day. Write to the children. Write with the children. Write to send a note of thanks. Write to remember an event. Write to clarify understanding of a topic. Write to explore your imagination. Write just to write. Model this each day and be sure children have time to write too.

8. Act! Act! Act! Act out stories. Provide props for children to act out stories. Scaffold children's reenactments of stories by acting as the narrator. Act out events. Reenact the roles you witness from field trips, classroom visitors, and other primary experiences.

9. Plan! Plan! Plan! Plan for each child to work at his or her own level. Plan time for children to be ac-

tive as well as time for children to relax and reflect on literacy learning. Assess children through various means. Use these assessments to further plan fun meaningful learning.

10. Enjoy! Enjoy! Enjoy! (also known as Laugh! Laugh! Laugh!) Enjoy time with children each day as you emphasize literacy learning. Your enjoyment of a grand story or a long relaxed conversation with a small group of children sets the tone and acts as a model for a positive disposition toward current and future literacy endeavors.

LANGUAGE EXPERIENCE APPROACH (LEA)

One of the tried and true methods, this oldie but goodie continues to provide for children crucial experiences with print that can help them increase their understanding about the concepts of print. Traditionally this is used as a group dictation of a common experience. The children learn from each other as they participate in the process as well as from the modeling and direct instruction the teacher does during the lesson. In a traditional Language Experience Approach, the teacher does the writing.

Main Purpose To increase children's understanding of the concepts of print, letter recognition, and sound–symbol relationships

Materials Chart paper
Markers
Interesting experience

Procedure This is a two-part lesson. It can all happen on one day or on separate days.

First Provide children with an experience. Any experience they find interesting will work.

> *Before the experience:* Tell the children you will be writing a story about this later and to think about things they want to put into their story.
>
> *During the experience:* Emphasize vocabulary specific to this experience: *"Yes, the bees* **pollinate** *the flowers."* Encourage children's active participation in the experience, give explanations, ask leading questions, and make analogies between children's prior experience and this current experience.

Second Begin the dictation process.

1. Tell the children you are going to write a story about the experience.
2. Discuss the title, where it will go, and leave room for it. (You can tape a note card with the word TITLE on it to the space you are reserving for the title.)
3. Ask the children for ways to start the story. Refer to stories that have been read in the classroom and ways that they started. Vote on a beginning. Repeat the beginning phrase.
4. Ask the children where to start writing. Begin with a capital letter, and point it out to the children with a reason for using it. Ask children to help you with the sounds in the word. Say each letter as you write it. Go back and reread the word when it is complete. Go back and reread the sentence, using your hand to track the print.
5. Invite children to add parts to the story. When the children give an incomplete sentence or one with poor grammar, help the child or class to think of another way to say it, in "book form," because this will be a published piece, which will hang in the classroom.
6. As each part is added, invite the children to help "find the sounds" in the words. Say the sentence. State each word. Think aloud the sounds,

and invite children to contribute. State the individual letters as they are written. Reread the sentence, and periodically go back and read the entire work while tracking the print.

7. Point out conventions of print when appropriate. For example, when you get to the end of a line, ask children where you should finish. Talk about leaving spaces between words, and using letters to make words, words to make sentences, and sentences to tell our stories. Keep a dictionary handy to model looking up words.

8. At the end of the story, read the story together. Decide on a title that tells about the story. Add it. Read it one more time as a finished product.

9. Go back at other times and read it. Send a copy of it home in the weekly newsletter for children to share with their parents (make it an enlarged copy). Hang the story in the classroom at a level that the children can physically touch the words and practice reading the story.

Classroom Application

Mrs. Beezley's class went on a nature walk around the school. Before they left, she told them to pay close attention to everything they saw so that they could help write a story about it when they came back to the classroom. She said, "Use your eyes, ears, and noses as we walk to see what you can find."

On the walk, the children were quite enthusiastic, shouting out "spottings." "Hey," cried Daniel, "I see some feathers on the ground!"

"I see a big bird," said Jessica.

"Yes," Mrs. Beezley said, "that big bird is a hawk. Look at his wing span—how far it is from the tip of one wing to the tip of another." And so the walk continued.

Back in the classroom, Mrs. Beezley calls the class up to the group time area and uncaps her big black marker.

Singing and reading along.

"Now it is time to write our story about what we saw. I'll be the word writer, and you can be the word thinkers. Remember I said that we were going to use our eyes, ears, and noses on the walk? Let's write about that."

Moving to the white chart paper hung on the big book easel, she begins: "Well, every story needs a title. We'll have to leave room for that. Where should we put the title?

"Yes, Kysha, it goes at the beginning. Right up here at the top. Let's leave a space for writing it. I'll mark our space by taping this card on top that says 'TITLE' so we remember what that space is for.

"Now, let's start the body of the story. How could we begin?"

The children make suggestions. "How about 'once upon a time'?" asks Mel.

"Yes," Mrs. Beezley responds, "sometimes stories do start with 'once upon a time,' but usually those are about pretend things. Was our walk real or pretend—did we really go on a walk or did we make it up? Yes, we really went. Let's think of a beginning for something that really happened. . . ."

Three possible beginnings are suggested. The class votes on them and selects "Today we went on a walk." Mrs. Beezley writes, *"Today, tttt."* Timmy shouts out, "T!"

"Yes, there is a *t. O, Dddd D AAAA Y.* This says *today* (running her hand across the word). "Today we . . . Okay, we have to write *we. WWW* is *w. EEEE* is . . . ?" The children all say, "E!" And so the story proceeds, with Mrs. Beezley prompting the children for the next parts of the story while providing factual literacy information as the need arises (as with the beginning of the story), along with connection between letters and their sounds.

After the story has been written and read and reread a few times by the entire class, with Mrs. Beezley pointing to each word, it is moved to a wall space *while the children are present*. Mrs. Beezley invites the children to go over during choices to read their new class story. She tells them they will all have a copy of it to take home, too, to share with their parents.

Variations

1. Use pictures with the words you are writing in the language experience to help the children to the next level. For example, when writing about "what we smelled," you could put a little nose above the word *smell* to help children remember what it says.

2. Put the story on sentence strips and put them into the pocket chart for children to play with.

3. Separate the story into sentences and put them on separate large sheets of paper. Have children working in groups illustrate the sentence. These can then be hung as a class mural or put into a class big book.

Hints for Success

- As the experience you will be writing about is happening, help children remember events and objects. Use prompts such as, "Oh, this is something we may want to put in our story later," or "Hmmm, I wonder what part of this ride [segment of the experience] you will be wanting to remember for our story."

- The first few times you compose with the children, you may have to do lots of prompting and thinking aloud about what to put in the story. It may be that you do most of the thinking and writing. However, as the children see the process, they can be counted on to chime in with suggestions and ideas more and more in future language experiences.

- Be sure all children present can see the writing as it is done on the paper.

SCAFFOLDED WRITING

This is a fairly "new" technique that has come directly out of Lev Vygotsky's theory of the way children learn. Elena Bodrova and Deborah Leong of the Metropolitan State College of Denver developed it and have used it successfully with children.

When asked to tell a story, a child has no problem going on and on and on. However, when asked to write it, the child often writes very little or doesn't even know where to begin and thus writes nothing. It is theorized that the reason for this vast difference is that the child doesn't have the focused attention and deliberate memory strategies to hold the story in mind long enough to write it down. Thus, while involved in the process of writing the first word, the child often forgets what comes next. This is a strategy to help the child learn to regulate his or her own learning through a gradual scaffolded process. Children writing with this technique can be found writing at a more sophisticated level than if left unassisted.

Scaffolded writing begins with much teacher guidance. Gradually, the child begins to use the strategy with some teacher help and then progresses to using it completely on his or her own. The child continues to use it until it just "drops off" and the child no longer chooses to use it. At this final point, the child has developed internal strategies to use in place of these external strategies.

Main Purpose

To increase children's ability to write on their own
To increase children's understanding of the conventions of print
To increase children's understanding of the connection between spoken language and print

Materials

Highlighter
Paper
Writing utensils

Procedure

1. Ask the child to dictate a story. Instead of writing words, make a highlighted line for each word that the child says. End with the proper punctuation. Explain that the lines will help the child remember what he or she said. If it is a long story, stop after the first sentence or two. Tell the child that you'll write the story in parts. This is the first part.
2. Go back and "say" the lines. Point to each line and say the word that goes in that space. Have the child help you "say" it again.
3. The first time through, model for the child what to do with the lines. Start with the first line: "Okay, this story started with the word *today*, so I write that here. Hmm, I hear a *ttt-T* . . ."
4. As each word is written, go back and reread the entire line while pointing to each and say the word that comes next.
5. After the technique has been modeled for the child, take the dictation again, making the lines (and punctuation) with the highlighter and reminding the child what the lines are for.
6. Together, say the words that will go on the lines, while pointing to each. Have the child do this independently.
7. The child then begins to write in the spaces, one word at a time. Help the child reread what has been written and say what will be in the upcoming spaces.
8. At the end of the writing, the child reads the work in its entirety.

Eventually, in upcoming sessions, the child will take over the highlighter and make his or her own spaces and punctuation.

Classroom Application
Leona wants to write a story about birds. She drew her picture and now wants to add words. She is not yet writing independently. Ms. Jenna, her preschool teacher, decides to use scaffolded writing to help her get started. "Okay, Leona, you tell me the story and I will make a line where we will put each word when we write the story. These lines will help us remember what you wanted to say."

Leona dictates: "One day the baby bird got hungry and wanted to eat. The mama bird got him some food." As Leona talks, Ms. Jenna is using her highlighter to make a space for each word she says. She makes the spaces longer for long words and adds the periods at the end of each sentence. "Okay, Leona, let's go back and remember what you wanted to say. I'm going to point to the spaces and say the words that will go in those places." Ms. Jenna points to each blank as she tells the story back. "This time, you help me say the words." They say the words and point together.

"Now let's put the words in the spaces. Your story started with *One*. That word goes here, in the first space. *One* . . . hmm, do you hear any sounds you know in that word?" She hears an *N*. "Yes, there is an *n*. It has o*Ne*. This says *one*. Let's see what comes next." Ms. Jenna reads *one* and points to the next space.

"*Day,* what sounds do you hear in *day?*" Together, they figure out the sounds they hear in each word, each time going back and reading what is there and what comes next in the story.

In this example, Leona was being very much directed and guided by the teacher, Ms. Jenna. As Leona grows in her confidence of writing, she will move to using Ms. Jenna only to write the blanks, and Leona will fill them in with the sounds she hears. Eventually, she will progress to using the highlighter to make her own spaces without help and fill in her own words. Finally, she will stop using the highlighter and just write the words. Please note this is a child-specific process that evolves gradually.

Hints for Success
- Use unlined paper.
- Accept invented or temporary spelling.

PLANNING PLAY "SETS" *WITH* CHILDREN

Children inherently love to play. In play, children create and contribute in ways that we don't always see in the classroom. While in the play situation, children can be found thinking in a complex manner, far beyond the level we observe in "typical" classroom activities.

Allowing play in the classroom is only one piece of the role of the early childhood professional. We must also facilitate it. This activity capitalizes on children's interest in play.

Since play is an activity that children are naturally drawn to, and in play children spend much of their time planning out what they will do, a perfect way to include meaningful literacy events in your program is to invite children to help you plan the upcoming changes in the play area in your classroom and then to carry out the plan. In its most basic form, the planning consists of lists.

The activity of planning for the play "set" may be a few days' group-time event, or it may be an ongoing literacy activity. Either way, it is likely to bring about eager participation and enthusiasm by all of the children in your class. It can also be a terrific bridge between school, home, and community.

Main Purpose	To increase children's understanding of the integration of speaking, writing, reading, listening, and viewing in their literacy learning through personally meaningful participation
Materials	Chart paper Marker Ideas
Procedure	Depending on the amount of time you have to make the change and the level of control over what is chosen, you may decide to start at #7 rather than from #1. The first few times you do this, you may start at #7 to help limit the possibilities. However, as your time with children progresses, it is important to allow for the children to be involved in the entire process so that they can see it through from start to finish.

1. Tell the children you are going to be changing the pretend play area, but you need some help with it.
2. Ask children to tell you new some things it could be "changed" into. Tell them that you will make a list of their ideas so that everyone can remember what was said. Before you begin, tell them that you will all vote on the new "area" together.
3. Title the list "Ideas for Play." Take suggestions from the children. State their idea, then write it down, saying each letter as you make it. (You could also invite children to write their ideas, but this may take longer, so consider your time constraints and the children's energy.)
4. Read the list as you make it. Invite the children to help you read it.
5. Vote on the new theme. (You may end here for the day or continue.)
6. Post the list somewhere in the classroom where you and the children can refer to it next time it is time to change pretend play. (When it is time to revisit it, read through the list and ask for any additions before voting, then proceed with #7.)
7. On a new piece of chart paper, write the theme name down. (Note that the theme of pretend play does not have to be the same as your curriculum theme.)
8. Ask children to tell you things that this "theme place" would need to work. The children will eagerly add ideas. Write these down as they arise. Caution children to listen carefully to see if someone else thinks of their idea. If someone does, the child can put his or her thumb up so that others know he or she had that idea too. (This will invite active listening.) If children get stuck, refer back to things needed from other themes. (Of course, you have saved these lists.)
9. Ask children how you will get these supplies. Note the source next to the items on the list (school, store, Ethan's house, etc.). In another session, write letters to the sources asking for the given materials. If they are community establishments, send these letters.
10. As the supplies come in, check them off the list. This can be done quickly during group times. The thank-you committee can compose thank yous, or the class can do this together.
11. On yet another day, ask the children: "What are the characters for this theme? What parts could be played?"
12. List the characters for the theme on another sheet of paper with a "job" description for each (e.g., Wait staff: Takes orders, delivers food, tells the cook what to make).

13. With the children's help during a choices/activity time, set up the center *or* tell the students you will be setting it up and to look for it the next day.

14. As the theme is "running," ask literacy questions like, "How do I know the store is open?" to encourage children to see the "need" for signs, books, writing materials, and other related literacy props.

15. Periodically, check in with the children at group time to get their assessment of how the play set is working and if any changes should be made.

Classroom Application

"So we decided that our theme will soon be a computer store. Today we are going to make a list of all the things we might put into our store. When you think of an idea, raise your hand.

"Reba, do you have an idea?"

"Yep, I think we should have computers!"

Mr. Holmes smiles, repeats *computers* and begins to write it on the list, "*Cccc* (the children help with C) *omPPPP* (P) *uteRRR* (R)."

He reads back, "Computers," then asks, "Real computers? How many do you think we need?"

"At least 10," Johnathan contributes.

"That may be hard to get; could we use something for pretend?" Mr. Holmes guides.

"Sure," pipes in Yuval, "We can use boxes to pretend they are the computers. We can draw on them to make them look real."

"Okay, so should I add boxes and markers to our list?"

The children agree. The list grows.

After the list is complete, the children and Mr. Holmes reread it. He asks: "Now, where will we get all these things? Before you volunteer to bring them from home, go home tonight and talk with your families about what we need. When you come back tomorrow, you can write your name next to the things are able to bring. We'll read the list and who signed up for what tomorrow and brainstorm where we can get whatever is left." The list is then read one more time and hung on the wall where all can see it and touch it.

Variations

1. Choose one aspect of the theme planning to do. You may just make a list of supplies needed, or just the characters, or just possible new themes. With each different theme, plan a different portion together saving the entire planning for the end of the school year.

2. Form committees to "manage" the supplies. These can be as simple or complex as you choose. For instance, one group writes reminder notes (which can be pictures, copied words, dictation, etc.); another group writes thank-you notes; a third keeps track of which supplies are still needed.

Hints for Success

- Provide the children with hands-on experiences and field trips to increase their awareness and understanding of the world around them. This will lead to richer planning of the play areas than without their experiences.

- Model the process you use each time it is done. Discuss your thinking aloud as you lead them through. They'll probably join in, so be prepared to write!

- You may choose to write a language experience story about a favorite play set after it is all done.

Labeling the characters in *Goldilocks and the Three Bears*.

SHARED READING

Reading with children has been documented in many articles and studies as a solid way to facilitate literacy. Countless sources tell early childhood educators about the benefits of reading with children. However, few actually spell out the process. What follows is a good beginning on which to base your book interactions with children. It contains the "meat and potatoes" of book interactions. You obviously will adapt it to make it your own and to emphasize different concepts and skills depending on your group of children and your objectives.

Shared reading begins with much teacher modeling and direction. Gradually, as the child grows in his or her awareness and understanding of literacy, the interaction will become more shared. It may be that, in the end, it is the child who is doing the leading and the adult who is doing the following. However, in order for the child to get to this step, the modeling must come first.

Main Purpose To model literacy behaviors and skills for children

Materials A book large enough for all involved to see both the text and the pictures

Procedure You can share storybooks for a variety of purposes. The things you do to support oral language may not be the same things you do to support print awareness. The following are steps that foster both:

1. Show the children the cover of the book.
2. Ask them to predict what the book will be about.

3. Read the title. Ask if there are any more predictions.

4. Tell the children that first you are going to take a "picture walk" through the book. Look at each page and, with the children, discuss what is happening in the pictures. (This is excellent for oral language development!)

5. Go back to the beginning of the book. Tell the children that this time you are going to read the words.

6. Read the title, pointing to the words as you read. Read the names of the author and the illustrator, reminding or asking the children what these two people do ("The author writes the words and the illustrator makes the pictures").

7. Read each page with appropriate emphasis. (Change your voice as the characters speak to help the children start to differentiate between characters.)

8. Point to the words as they are read. Be sure your finger or pointer is well below or above the words so the children's view of the word and pictures is not blocked.

9. Accept and invite conversation as the book is being read. It is a balancing act to invite conversation while trying to stick to the story, but the oral language and the active involvement of the children during the story is crucial to children developing skills in thinking about text and images (metacognition).

10. When the book is finished, invite general comments from the children. Follow this up with a pointed conversation about some dimension of the story. You may choose to focus on the problem, the characters, the rhyme, or making connections between the children and the events in the story. Whatever you choose, prepare specific plans for doing this ahead of time. You may choose to use a sticky note to mark specific spots in the text that are important to your discussion or to record your questions.

11. You may choose to reread the book before or after the discussion. If it is a predictable book, invite the children to read with you.

12. You may choose to act out the story or make a class book that is patterned after the book just read.

13. You may choose to point out specific print awareness concepts within the text after the first reading. Or you may point out specific focus words that occur often in the book, such as *in,* and look on the pages of the book for more *in*s.

14. Whatever options you choose, be sure to leave the book out for the students to have ready access to it during their activity or choice time. A taped version of this book with your voice on it is a perfect complement to enhance children's rereading of the book.

15. Go back and reread books to the children. This rereading is as important as the first reading. You can use the rereading sessions to review concepts and skills learned previously as well as to teach new concepts and skills.

Classroom Application   "Here's the book we are reading today," Mrs. Kessler says as she holds up *The Napping House* for all to see. "Look at the cover and think about what this could be about. When you have an idea to share, raise your hand."

"It's about a house!" says Jared.

"No, it's about a haunted house!" squeals Phil.

"I think it is about a house, too," says Jennie.

"You are all thinking about the same thing . . . you think it has something to do with a house. That is what the title says, *The Napping House* [points to title and words as they are read]. Do you have any more ideas about this book now that you know the title?" The children tell her it is about a house that sleeps! "Okay, now let's take a picture walk through the book to see if we can get a better clue about the story. You help me talk about what is happening in the pictures. Let's open the book and go past the title page to the first reading page. What do you see in this picture?" (They discuss things in the pictures and add to their concept of what this story may be about.)

"Now, let's go back and this time we will read the words because together the words and the pictures tell the story. The title is. . . . [the children "read" it]. The author, the person who thought of the words in the story, is Audrey Wood. The illustrator, the person who drew the pictures to help tell the story, is Don Wood [pointing to where the names are as she says them]. Let's turn the page. Oh, look, here is the title page. It says the same kinds of things that the cover said. Here is the title . . . here is the author and the illustrator."

Mrs. Kessler turns to the beginning and starts to read, "There is a house. A napping house. Where everyone is sleeping." As she reads, she points carefully to the words.

"Hey, she looks funny! Like a grandma!" shares Penelope.

Mrs. Kessler smiles and reflects, "She reminds you of an older lady," and continues reading. The children begin to chime in on "In the napping house where everyone is sleeping."

At the end of the book, Mrs. Kessler asks, "So why did everyone get up?" The children begin a lively discussion of retelling who and when each character woke up. "What about you, how do you wake up? Do you use a flea too?" More discussion ensues. The children are eager to share their thoughts and experiences.

"Tomorrow we are going to read this book again. You may want to look at this or listen to it in the listening area during choices today so that you can help read it tomorrow."

Variations   Take the picture walk one day, then read it the next day and discuss, then do rereadings the third day.

Hints for Success
- Prepare ahead of time for the concepts and skills you will teach from the book.
- Carefully select quality literature to read.
- Select literature that is both in "story form" (narrative text) and in "fact form" (expository text).
- Be sure to not overfocus on teaching skills and concepts to the point that reading is not an enjoyable activity. Read sometimes just to enjoy the reading. The children learn much from these times, too!

JOURNAL WRITING

Writing in journals can be a wonderful activity to use with emerging writers as well as writers at any stage. We've discussed the power that children can experience through writing. In the journaling process, children can come to feel like writers. They can safely practice the concepts and skills they are acquiring. It can serve to document their growth in writing over time. It is a powerful strategy that can be used with even very young children on a daily or weekly basis.

Main Purpose	To allow children to practice their evolving understanding of the connection between oral and written language
Materials	Writing utensils (pencils, markers, crayons, pens) Paper stapled together or bound into "book" form
Procedure	To introduce children to writing in journals, you may consider the following strategy:

1. Show children your journal.
2. Tell them it is your special place where you can write anything.
3. Tell them sometimes you like to share what you write by reading it to others, sometimes you don't.
4. Tell them they can have a special journal of their very own to write in too where they will be authors and illustrators.
5. Show them their journals.
6. Tell them that in the journals, they can write pictures and words and stories. Tell them that they can write using the sounds they hear so their words may or may not look like those in books.
7. Show the children the special place where the journals will be kept and tell them when they can access them. It is useful to make them accessible at all times.
8. Show the children where they can share their writing in their journals with the class and when in the day this will occur. Use a picture to add this to your schedule.
9. Tell them when they will be able to take their journals home. (A good rule is once they are filled, the teacher looks at it overnight—to assess and record children's progress and write a note on it to the family— then it may go home the next day.)
10. Have the children decorate their journals and write their names on the cover (because real authors and illustrators always have their names on the front of the book).

Now you are ready to begin!

To support the journal writing once it is started:

1. It is useful to set aside a special time each day for everyone to write in his or her journal. If this seems overwhelming, have one small group at a time work on journals, but be sure to provide this opportunity as often as possible (daily is ideal). Move about the room observing and working with individual children on their journals, helping them at their individual levels. Some children may be at the scribble stage, and others may be writing sentences. You will be able to work with them individually to help each child progress. You may take dictation for some children and help others learn to leave spaces between their words. It all depends on the child.
2. Set some tangible method for children to know how long the journal writing will last. A timer works well. For children who finish early, give them other literacy options such as reading favorite books or telling the flannel board stories. If time is not an issue, don't worry about timing the writing. The ideal situation is for the children to determine when they are finished writing for the day.
3. Allow children to talk during journal time. Writing and talking go hand in hand, especially for emerging writers.

4. Allow children to choose their own topics for writing. Some children will write the words they know. Others will copy from the environmental print or favorite books. Some will draw only pictures at first. Keep the faith. With this opportunity for writing and your support, the children will all progress along the writing continuum.

5. When the children ask you what their writing says, ask them what they want it to say. If they ask you if it *really* says that, be honest with the children and tell them that they are practicing writing so they can become great writers. Agree that their writing is not in book spelling but in "practice" spelling. This usually appeases most children. You can also have picture dictionaries handy for children intent on book spelling. At this stage, however, it is more important for the children to use practice (also known as temporary or invented) spelling so that they can get thorough practice with the connection between phonemes and letters. This practice is strongly linked with future reading ability and success.

6. Be respectful of the children's writing. Ask before you write on their pages. If you are really concerned that neither you nor the child will recall what the story said, use a sticky note on the back of the page.

7. Set aside time each day for the children to share their writing with the class. A special author's chair or stool for the child sharing to sit in is not only treasured by the children, but also shows your support and respect for the children's writing and reading accomplishments.

Hints for Success

- In the beginning, make the number of pages in journals small. You may start with three pages. The children are eager to take home their journals and have not yet grasped the concept of working on something over time. Gradually, add a page at a time to the journals.

- Keep the journals where the children can get them when they are ready to write. "Journal time" does not have to be the only time in the day children have access to these.

PREDICTABLE CHARTS

Repetition in the early literacy stages is an essential teaching strategy, and predictable charts (Cunningham, 1997) are a mechanism to not only model writing for children but also to provide products that they love to read over and over, simply because they can. Hall and Williams (2001:3) offer a number of ideas about this approach that help all children become successful readers and writers. "What the children say, the teacher writes; and what the teacher writes, the children can read back later." Because the charts use children's language and ideas, they enhance self concept. As children listen to how other children finish a sentence, watch the teacher writing it down, and hear it read back, their reading and writing skills are developed simultaneously. They also develop an appreciation of what other children know and can contribute.

Main Purpose   To acquaint children with phoneme–grapheme connections and to model conventional spelling and sentence structure

Materials   Easel
Paper
Markers

Procedure

1. Choose a topic that is familiar to every child. Ideas can come from the events and classroom activities and from narrative and information texts that are read to the children.
2. Give the children a model sentence to follow (e.g., My favorite color is _____).
3. Complete the sentence with your own contribution and put your name in parentheses at the end.
4. Point to the words and have the children read the sentence.
5. Create a new sentence beginning and have a child dictate the ending of the sentence to you. Write exactly what the child says and place his or her name in parentheses at the end.
6. After each dictation, go back and have the child read the sentence he or she contributed.
7. When every child has contributed, go back and have the children read all of the sentences together.
8. Display the chart in the reading area so that children can reread the chart independently.

Classroom Application

"We had a good time visiting Mr. Meijer's store, didn't we," asks Mrs. Timmons as the children gather in the large group area. "He sells a lot of items. I'm thinking that each of you could name something special that we might buy if we could. Let's make a list of what each of us might like to buy. Personally, I would like to buy flowers," Mrs. Timmons notes as she writes:

I would like to buy flowers. (Mrs. Timmons)

"Let's read what I wrote here, children" (the children read the sentence). "What do you think, Kaitlin? What would you like to buy?"

"I would buy a stuffed animal," says Kaitlin thoughtfully.

"Ah, a stuffed animal," says Mrs. Timmons, as she adds Kaitlin's choice to the predictable chart:

I would like to buy a stuffed animal. (Kaitlin).

"Kaitlin, read the sentence you contributed back to us." (Kaitlin reads her sentence).

"Who else has something he or she would like me to write down?" asks Mrs. Timmons.

Once all of the children have contributed something, and their ideas have been recorded and read, Mrs. Timmons says, "Okay, we have a lot of different items we would purchase if we could. Let's go through our list and read all of the sentences together." The children do so and then Mrs. Timmons suggests, "I'm going to put this great list over in the reading corner because it might be fun to go over again later this morning. I'll bet you won't have much trouble reading them, either. See the clues? Each of your names comes right after the sentence you contributed, and you all know how to read one another's names by now, right? Remember to use your skills in sounding out a word if you forgot what someone dictated to me. Okay, authors, let's listen to a special story by _____."

Hints for Success

- Always relate the predictable chart to a familiar topic.
- Encourage children to reread the chart when placed in the reading center, inviting one or two individual children to do so.
- Extend the activity by cutting the sentences into strips. Have children paste their own sentence on paper and illustrate it. Make a class book.

READING AROUND THE ROOM

This is a popular activity for preschoolers through second grade. It is simple to do and is a powerful motivator for meaningful reading.

Main Purpose To increase children's print awareness through environmental print

Materials Big glasses with no lenses (perhaps clown glasses) (two or three)
or a magnifying lense (two or three)
A pointer: ruler, paint stick, magic wand, glitter stick, fly swatter, etc.

Procedure
1. Children don glasses and pick up pointer.
2. Children move about the classroom, reading the print of the environment.

Classroom Application During literacy centers, one group is assigned the task of "reading the room." James is thrilled as his group begins with this task. He eagerly rushes over to the RTR (read the room) basket and puts on a pair of glasses and selects the fly swatter to point or swat at words. He begins moving around the room with his pal, Mickey. They rush from one point to another trying to beat the other to the words. When they spot a new word, they squeal with delight. They rush up to the word, slap their swatter on the word and explode with, "GOATS." Their goal from Mr. Carney is to find and read ten words. Mr. Carney gives them a sheet to record their ten words. When they have filled all ten slots, they must take the words to two friends to read, have them initialed, and then turn in the "proof" that learning took place.

Variations
1. Writing around the room. Children take clipboards around the room and copy down words. The teacher may structure this with a blank numbered paper indicating the number of words expected. As with RTR, children should read the list to two people before signing off.
2. Read the hallway instead of the room. Use parent volunteers to assist with this.
3. Read the neighborhood. Take a walking field trip to see the words in the world.

Hints for Success
- Give the children structure in this activity. Tell them how many words are a minimum for reading.
- Show them how long they will have to accomplish their work.
- Be sure there are enough supplies for reading the room, but beware of too many. Just as too many cooks aren't good, neither is an entire classroom of reading the room.

AUTHOR! AUTHOR! (AUTHOR STUDY)

There are many ways to help children become enthusiastic about reading and writing. One successful oldie, but goodie, is to engage in an author study.

Main Purpose To increase children's understanding about various authors and types of writing

Materials A group of books by one author

Procedure
1. Introduce the author as a person. Tell things the author did as a child, then as an adult.

2. Show children some of the books the author wrote. Discuss the grouping. Is there a theme? How do the books reflect what you learned about this author? Does this remind you of any other books or authors?
3. Select one book and enjoy it together.
4. Discuss the book. You may choose to do an activity with the book such as make a class book following the pattern in which each child contributes one page, or create a parallel book as an entire group, or create a different ending, or imagine a different character—perhaps one from another of this author's books.
5. The next day or week, read another book from this same author.
6. Discussions with comparisons between the books the author writes and other authors will increase over time.

Classroom Application "Today we are going to meet one of my favorite authors, Frank Asch. I was looking for some information about him today and do you know what I found? When he was little, he liked to . . . What do you think of that? I wonder how things he liked to do as a kid influenced his writing. These are some of his books. Perhaps we can begin with *Sand Cake*. Did you notice anything special about the book? What did you think of it? Does this remind you of anything? If you were going to write about the beach, what would you describe? We are going to set this aside. You can come read it during choices if you'd like, or listen to it at the listening center."

Hints for Success
- Use this activity sparingly. Remember to enjoy the books above everything else. If you try to overdiscuss or overcreate, you may lose your crew.
- One author a month is a good pace.
- Send home copies of the author's books to share with families. Be sure to include a tape recorder with batteries and a recording of the class reading the story. Invite families to add their reading or retelling of the story to the tape.

POCKET CHART SONGS AND CHANTS

Songs, poems, and chants are typical fare in early childhood classrooms. These seem to have a magical quality that captivates children. This medium is a very good place to help children develop their literacy concepts and skills. As the children are actively engaged in singing or chanting, they can be learning behaviors that will contribute to their overall literacy development.

Main Purpose To develop oral language, phonological awareness, and print awareness

Materials Songs
Pocket chart
Sentence strips
Markers
Pointer or hand
Scissors

Procedure The following is a sequence that takes place over time, not on one day.

1. Choose a song or chant.
2. Sing the song or chant the chant with the children.

   To teach it: Instruct the children to listen to the song or chant as you sing or chant it through. Then tell them that you'll sing or say a phrase and then they'll repeat it back to you. Sing or chant through the song or poem this way once, then combine phrases and sing or chant through parts of the song. Finally sing or chant through the song or poem completely. Adding actions to the song or poem will help children remember the words.

3. Write the words on sentence strips in front of the children. Reread each sentence as it is written. Sing or chant that part of the song or poem. Place it in the pocket chart.

4. When the entire song is in the chart, sing it through in its entirety while pointing to the words.

5. Have the children close their eyes and mix up the sentences. After the children open their eyes, have them help you put it back into order.

6. After the children can do this well, then bring out a second set of strips that matches the first set (master set). Have the children match the strips to the master set.

7. Sing or chant using one set and then the other while pointing to words. Compare to be sure they are the same.

8. Take the scissors and cut one sentence into separate words. Take all of the sentences out of the pocket chart except the one sentence in the master set that matches the sentence you just cut. Leave this one strip in the chart.

9. Give the cut-up words to different children. Ask the children to predict what word they each have from the song or chant.

10. Sing or chant the phrase. Ask them to tell you the thinking behind their guesses. Then have them go to the pocket chart to find the matching word in their sentence.

11. Sing the sentence or phrase through as each word is added. Emphasize the word that was just added. ("Five LITTLE snowmen fat." *Little* was the added word.)

12. Each day, cut apart another sentence and play this game until all the words are cut up.

13. Practice moving the words around and singing what they say. Ask children if it is right and if it makes sense.

14. Look at the words and see if there are repeat words such as *the,* words that end the same such as *fat* and *cat,* or words that begin the same such as *snowman* and *sunny.* Use these things to direct children's attention to the connection between what we say and sing and what appears in print.

Hints for Success
- Cut the strips into words in front of the children.
- Use black for the master set of words. These will not be cut apart.
- Use blue for the cut set. The different colors will help the children focus on the formation of the letters and tell which set is which.
- Make the charts and cut-up words available for children to use independently. Include a tape recorder and the song or chant for the children to follow along with.

DAILY MESSAGE—DAILY NEWS

Children see many uses of print each day. Some types have more meaning for them than others. One common favorite type of print for children is mail. Children love receiving mail. You can capitalize on this in your classroom by "sending" daily letters to your class each day. Of course, you are not mailing these; you are just writing them before the children come to school and either posting them for the children to see when they walk in the door, or sealing them into real envelopes to be opened at group time. The messages, while simple in format, are of high interest to the children because they are pieces of mail for them! These messages are a wonderful purposeful daily activity, which is full of meaning for children and presents numerous opportunities for teaching literacy.

Main Purpose
To show children that print carries meaning
To communicate with the children through writing

Materials
Chart paper
Black marker for message
Another color such as red or orange for noting parts of text
An envelope if you intend to have it in official letter form

Procedure
1. Compose a message to the children. *Hint:* Start off with a very short message, such as: "Dear Class, Today is Monday. Mandy is the leader. Love, Mr. Barnes."
2. Either post it at your group time area at the children's level so they can interact with it *or* seal it in an envelope and put it at the group area (with a space reserved for hanging it as it is read).
3. When the children first see the letter, allow them to explore it. Don't read it right away. They will try to figure out what it says. Listen to their strategies and use them as part of your discussion or teaching later.
4. Read the letter "together." Point to the words as you read each one. Emphasize the punctuation. Say aloud the techniques you are using to read so the children can "see" the process. (Obviously, you aren't going to say each technique, but pick one or two to emphasize each week during the readings.)
5. Reread the letter one more time, still pointing to the words. Over time, the children can take on the role of pointing (with your help) and later pointing independently.
6. Take a moment and emphasize one skill in literacy and relate it to the letter. *For instance, you may say, "Well, Mandy is our leader, and Mandy and Monday start the same way. We can hear that they have the same sound. Can you see anything in these words that is the same (pointing to the words)? Oh, well, look at that! Mandy and Monday both begin with the same sound and the same letter. Anyone know what letter that is?"*
7. Use the nonblack marker to underline or trace the concept you are working on. This takes only a few minutes each day, but the children will be interested in it.
8. Keep the letter posted for the day. Put old letters into a book or folder or hanging clip for children to revisit.

Classroom Application
The letter is written before school and sealed in an envelope, which is put on the big book easel. The children come into the classroom and make their way to the group area. They discuss what might be in the letter today. Alicia guesses, "I think it will say 'Dear Class. . . .'" Marcus chimes in, "Yeah, and 'Love, Mrs. Gregory,' too."

When group time begins, Mrs. Gregory opens up the letter and hangs it on the big book easel. All of the children can see the print. She tells them to think about what it might say. The children offer suggestions. She then says, "Let's read it now." Taking the pointer, she tracks the print as she reads. The children help her with the beginning, "Dear Class, Today is Monday."

Mrs. Gregory stops reading and looks at the children. "Oh, see this? It's called a period, and it tells me to stop reading for a minute and take a breath. Okay, let's continue. Jake is the leader. He is bringing his snake to share! Love, Mrs. Gregory."

She pauses for a minute. "Okay, let's read it one more time together," and they do. "Hmmm," she says, "sounds like we have a visitor today!" The children start discussing the snake.

After a few minutes, Mrs. Gregory brings their attention back to the letter. "Notice any words today that sound alike at the end? Listen as I say the last two sentences. *Jake* is the leader. He is bringing his *snake* to share." She emphasizes *Jake* and *snake,* and so the rhyming lesson begins. This entire process takes less than 10 minutes and is literacy packed!

Variations	1. Ask the children questions in the letter that they can answer verbally or by voting—for example, "We will be making soup next week. Would you like potato soup or vegetable soup?" The children sign their name under the potato column or the vegetable column during choices time.
	2. Use this technique at the end of the day by writing what happened as a message to the afternoon class or to be included in the newsletter for families. Instead of the teacher generating all of the ideas and content, the children participate in telling what happened that day. Both the daily message (first thing) and the daily news (last thing) can be used in a complementary fashion.
Hints for Success	• Use the same salutation and similar bodies in each letter. This will help the children be able to predict the words.
	• Write large so that all children can comfortably see the print and the spaces between the words.
	• Start with just a short sentence. Work up to a few, but not so many that it takes too long to read and review.
	• Use high-frequency words in the letters. If they are used daily, the children will come to be able to read these words.
	• Use the children's names in the message. Not only will the children learn to read each others' names, they will have interest in what you say because they see what you are talking about in real life.

USING NURSERY RHYMES

Nursery rhymes, a favorite in many homes, are a wonderful way to stimulate oral language concepts and skills in the classroom. They have been used successfully many times in successful research training programs to help develop phonological awareness in young children (Ayres, 1994). They have long been a typical activity in nursery schools and are recently beginning to break through to the elementary schools. Their benefits are numerous in the realm of literacy and are a must-do for any emerging literacy program.

Main Purpose	To develop oral language concepts and skills, particularly rhyming and segmentation
Materials	Nursery rhymes

Props to support the nursery rhyme
Posters of nursery rhymes
Books of nursery rhymes

Procedure
1. Choose a nursery rhyme to focus on. One at a time works best.
2. Say the rhyme. Chant the rhyme. Clap the rhyme.
3. Find the rhyme in a book. Hang up a poster of the rhyme. Track the print as you read it.
4. Talk about what is happening in the rhyme. Act it out with props.
5. Have the children act it out for each other.
6. After children are familiar with the rhyme, break it into pieces. Take the first few lines and emphasize the rhyming words. "Jack and *Jill* went up the *hill*." Stop there and ask children if they heard anything funny there.
7. Repeat the phrase again. Point out to them that *Jill* and *hill* sound alike: "We call this rhyming!"
8. Using the same method, have the children listen for more.
9. Go to other rhymes you've learned and see if you can find rhyming words.

Classroom Application

When he begins using nursery rhymes, Mr. Noble's preschool class votes that they want to do "Hey Diddle Diddle" first. The next day, Mr. Noble recites the rhyme "Hey Diddle Diddle." The children say it with him. He pulls out his *Mother Goose Big Book* and finds the rhyme. Together they all say the rhyme as he points to the print on the page. The next day, he brings out a poster of it and they read it on the poster. They read it with quiet voices, with loud voices, with angry voices, and with excited voices. Then he produces props for the rhyme and gets volunteers from the class to be the characters. The class acts it out a few times, and the props are put in the story area for use by the children at choices time.

The next day, he begins: "You know, I was telling my dog that rhyme we've been doing, 'Hey Diddle Diddle,' and it suddenly sounded kind of funny. I heard some words that sounded like each other. Listen to this, and see if you hear any words that sound alike: 'Hey diddle diddle, the cat and the fiddle.' There, did you hear it? Yes, diddle and diddle are the same, and there is another word that sounds like it is almost the same. . . . Yes, fiddle! Let's see if we can find more." He finishes the rhyme, telling the boys and girls, "In this nursery rhyme, the words that sound alike at the end part are also called rhymes! Tomorrow we'll look for rhymes in 'Jack and Jill.' You think about it tonight and see if you think there are any rhymes."

Variations
1. Illustrate the rhymes and make classroom books or murals of favorite rhymes.
2. Provide props for children to act out the rhymes during choices time.
3. Make a tape of the class telling the rhyme to go along with a class book. Send this home for families to share.
4. Make up new versions of old rhymes.
5. Find new rhyming words that fit into the old rhymes.

Hints for Success
- Start with familiar rhymes.
- Be sure the children are familiar with the rhyme before looking for the rhyming words.
- Do the rhymes many times so that the children who don't catch on the first time to rhyming can eventually get it.

SURPRISE BOX

Learning to think about what is said and to ask questions are two things that are difficult for many children at the emerging level. One great way to practice this on a daily basis is to use a technique such as surprise box. The enthusiasm for guessing what might be in the box makes practicing these skills fun for all.

Main Purpose To practice active listening, formulating questions, and metacognition skills

Materials Tin or lunchbox that you cannot see through
An object
Three clues written on a slip of paper inside the tin

Procedure In the beginning, the teacher may spend one week putting the surprises in the box and writing the clues for the class. After this has been modeled, it can start going home each night with a different child, who will place an object inside along with three clues to help the other children guess what it is (the child will work with an adult or older child to think of good clues and to write them down).

1. Select an object and place it into the surprise box.
2. Write three clues that would help someone guess what the object is.
3. Put the clues in the box, too.
4. At group time, pull the clues out carefully so that no children see them.
5. Explain to the children that there is something in this box that is a surprise. Their job is to listen to the clues, think about the clues, and then raise their hand if they want to guess what it could be.
6. Have the children tell you back the steps: "Listen, think, raise hand to guess."
7. Read the first clue. You can make the clues on a large sheet of paper so all can see them, or on smaller paper for just you to see. (It depends on what literacy goals you'd like to work on here.)
8. Wait at least 10 seconds for children to think.
9. Call on children to make a guess. As they guess, help them formulate their guess into a question. You may choose to help them say, "Is it a _____?"
10. Tie the children's guesses into the clue given. If the guess doesn't fit the clue, gently redirect other guesses to think about the clue.
11. Take three guesses, then read the next clue, then take three more before the last clue.
12. If the children guess it, pull it out. If not, at the end of the three clues and guessing, pull it out anyway.
13. Send the box home with another person for a new object (or put your own object in).

Classroom Application "Today I put something new into the box. You are going to guess what is inside. Remember, you are going to listen to the clues. Think in your brain about what it could be that fits that clue. Then, if you know the answer, close your mouth and raise your hand high to wait for a turn to guess. Okay, let's start. The first clue says [reading from the clue paper], 'It has four legs.'" Pause. "You are thinking in your head right now about something that has four legs."

Ten seconds go by. "Jenna, you have your hand up. That tells me that you have a guess. What do you guess?"

"Dog."

"Okay, Jenna, you want to ask us, 'Is it a dog?' "

Jenna repeats this.

"You were thinking that dogs have four legs so maybe this is a dog. Good guess, but it is not a dog this time. Philip, you have your hand up. What is your guess?" "A bird," he replies. "Oh, you are asking, is it a bird?" "Yep," he says. "Well, a bird is living and you were probably thinking that something with four legs is alive, but birds don't have four legs. Think some more. Think about something that has four legs."

The guessing and clue giving continue. It was an elephant!

Hints for Success

- Use simple, obvious clues.
- Send a letter home with children explaining the surprise box, and tape the directions for "how-to" inside the box for handy family reference.
- Use a durable container.
- Keep a record of who had the box and what they brought. This running list can show children one of the functions of print.

LABELING THE CLASSROOM

Every early childhood professional wants the children in his or her care to become literate. We know that increasing the environmental print in the classroom can help with this process. Providing things for children to read in the classroom that are meaningful to them is an important part of this. One kind of print that children find especially interesting is labels. By labeling the classroom with the children, you can help them increase their understanding of the concept that print carries meaning.

Main Purpose

To increase children's print awareness through meaningful print in the classroom

Materials

Index cards
Black marker
Tape or sticky tack to attach paper to items labeled

Procedure

1. Tell the children that you are going to put labels on things in the classroom so that you and the visitors that come into your classroom can practice reading words and know what the things in the classroom are.
2. Choose a thing to label. Walk over to it. Take a card and work together to write the word. Since this will be for public view purposes, book spelling is necessary. If the children are writing the words, you may follow up, helping them edit the writing.
3. Say the word. Look for familiar sounds in the word. Say each letter as it is formed.
4. When it is completed, read the word and tape it to the object. (It is great when the child reads it back to you and does the posting independently.)
5. Continue this process as long as interest remains. You may choose to label three words a day for a month.
6. Each time you go back to make more new labels, take a tour of the room, reading the old labels.
7. Refer back to the labels often throughout the day to help the children make the connection and see their significance.

Classroom Application
"Today we are going to start labeling our class so that we can all read things in our room and so that visitors know what everything is. Do you see anything that we could put a label on so that it says what it is?"

"How about the sink?" suggests Darrin.

"Fine, let's go over to the sink. What sounds do you hear in *sink*? Listen carefully: *SSIINNKKK.*"

"Yes, Juanita, there is an *S*. Then it says *ink*. *Ink* starts with *I*. What do you hear after that? *Nnnnn*. Yes, *N!* Then *KKKK*. *C* is close; this time it is a *K*. So, what does our word say? Yes, *SINK!* [running hand under it]. Darrin, come up here. What does this say?"

"Sink," he answers.

"Okay, then hang it on or near the sink! Let's find something else to label."

Variations
1. The child may do the writing while you give support and help revise into correct spelling.
2. Instead of having the entire group go to the place being labeled, one person could go over and point to it.
3. In the future, post a picture on a large sheet of paper and label it as a class.
4. Create and label murals or displays of books or events together.

Hints for Success
- Use black markers to write the print.
- Whenever possible, post the word where children can touch it.
- Take frequent tours of the labels and point out their significant uses (e.g., while children are writing in journals or stories).

ENJOYING ENVIRONMENTAL PRINT!

We live in a world of print. Often we are so busy leading our lives, we take the signs and labels in our world for granted and do not make a big deal about them. For young children, however, who are just beginning to recognize print, specifically letters in their environment, these everyday signs and labels can be powerful indicators to the children themselves that they are becoming true readers and writers. Nancy and Martha Navarro of Port Huron have found a way to capture the energy emitted from these environmental icons. They make them into books!

Main Purpose
To increase children's print awareness using meaningful print from their everyday world
To increase children's enthusiasm and pride in literacy endeavors

Materials
Some type of book with a cover and pages—a binder with clear overhead protector sheets works well if you want to be able to change the print from time to time. However if you want permanency, simply using a glue stick with paper works well. Also include pictures of labels from children's everyday environment that are meaningful to the child.

Procedure
You can make these books ahead of time or give them to children ready to be made. The bonus of making them together is the oral language—the rich conversation that can occur as you discuss the various labels to include.

1. Select spots to photograph for inclusion in the book. Be sure the words and logos on the signs are clear. You may want to brainstorm this list as a class.
2. Photograph the sites.
3. Develop the pictures (print them, pick them up, etc.)
4. On a table with books with blank pages, spread out the pictures. Be sure to have at least three copies of each picture.
5. Invite children to work with you at the table to select some pictures to include in their books.
6. Secure the pictures in the book.
7. Take turns reading the books that have been made.

Classroom Application

"Today we are going to start a project about words in our world. Can you think of any words you see as you come to school? Let's list those words on our chart paper." Children provide words. "This weekend, I will go photograph these sites, and next week we will use the pictures I take to make your own personal world word book!"

The next week: "When you come to this center, you will make your world word book. Remember the list from last week? I now have the pictures. You get to be in charge of your book. Pick words that you see when you come to school, are on the bus, or when you are riding in a car. Everyone will have their own book. While they may be similar, there is only one you and your book will be unique, special to just you!" Children select pictures individually and glue them into the book. They then read the books to each other at the book corner, smiling with the satisfaction of knowing they are actually reading words.

Variations

1. You may make the books ahead of time and they may all be the same. You can practice reading them together and send them home for families to enjoy together.
2. You can have a box of alternate words and logos for children to select from periodically, if you are using the overhead projectors.
3. Instead of making books, invite families to take pictures of words in their world and send them in for a bulletin board. Be sure this board is at the children's eye level and that they can reach much of it when pointing to words and logos.
4. Instead of using environmental print, use snack print—on a bulletin board or in a class book, hang or staple the labels from daily snacks.

Hints for Success

- Start with five words in each book. Increase the number as children show success with these.
- If you are using books, create the book pages ahead of time so that the focus can be on the words, not the stapling.
- Be sure to have at least three copies of each picture; to determine the exact number of copies needed, consider the number of children represented in the picture and the quality of the task and picture being represented.

NAME GAMES

Children are most interested when something pertains directly to them, and nothing gets closer to a child than his or her name. Using name games with children to help them learn about language and literacy is a successful way to teach these concepts and skills. Name games take on a variety of formats. A few favorites are suggested here.

Main Purpose To increase children's phonological awareness while having fun

Materials Children's names
Optional: Names on cards

Procedure There is a vast variety of name games that can be played with children.

Names go up!

1. Sit in a circle so all children can see one another.
2. Go around the circle and say each person's name. Demonstrate clapping the syllables in each name. Have the children repeat it after you.
3. Teach them this chant: "Names go up, names go down, tell me how your name sounds!"
4. Start with the first person next to you in the circle. Say the chant. When she tells you how her name sounds, clap the syllables (*"Mar-y"*). Have all the children clap after you.
5. Go around the circle saying the chant and having the child whose turn it is say and clap his or her name with everyone else repeating.
6. When you've gone all the way around, tell the children you are going to clap a name. If the child thinks it is his or her name, the child should stand up.
7. Clap XX. Children with two syllables stand. Check to see if they all are XX by saying and clapping their names. *"Let's see, Lis-a, Ja-mal, Pe-ter, A-lys-sa! Whoops, that is three claps. We'll do that one soon. Listen carefully for it!"*
8. Repeat at different times with a variety of syllables. Use this as a way to transition to new activities.

Leader Language

1. Take the child's name who is the leader of the day (or who brought snack, or whose Mom is in _____).
2. Use the first sound in his or her name to change everyone else's name into that beginning sound for the day. *"Lilly is our leader today. Lilly's name starts like LLLLL, so now Manuel, you are 'Lanuel' today. Jessica, you are 'Lessica'! Louise, you are 'Louise'! What will we call Charlie today? Yes, that is right . . . Larlie!"*

Rhyme Time Nime

1. Use picture cards. Find a card to rhyme with each child's name (first, middle, or last, or even a part of his or her name if it is a tough one to rhyme).
2. Tell the children that you are going to practice rhyming with their names. When you hold up a card, they have to say the card and think aloud about whose name rhymes.
3. Before you hold up the card, tell them if it rhymes with a first name, middle, last or partial name: *"This is a last name."*
4. Hold up the card. The children say picture name and person's name. The talking aloud is important. This way you can hear who understands rhyming and who is using other strategies and discuss these: *"Ring . . . King!"*

Hints for Success	• Use each child's name.
	• If a child does not want his or her name used, respect that. That child will still learn from classmates' names.
	• Enjoy these teaching moments as games. If you are playful, they will be too.
	• Tell parents about your name games at school, and invite them to play along at home.

Final Thoughts

In this chapter, we have explored reading, writing, speaking, listening, and viewing at the emerging phase of literacy. Each of these also has developmental progressions that are included in Chapter 2. We discussed general behaviors that children in this phase often display. We explored the literacy resources that are necessary tools for children to develop at this phase and gave general suggestions for supporting literacy in your early childhood classroom.

If you think of emerging literacy as supporting the start of reading, then the recipe for beginning reading is really quite straightforward. Of the many studies of reading that have been conducted, findings indicate that there are two significant predictors of early reading achievement for prereaders: letter name knowledge and the ability to discriminate phonemes auditorily (Adams, 1990; Chall, 1967). These are developed both through experiences of exploration and through purposeful direct instruction. Either approach used alone is less likely to bring about the results that can occur when they are used together. Especially for these emergent years, children must have a balanced approach to literacy, with time for exploration and practice and time for purposeful instruction.

Challenge Yourself

1. Choose three centers in your classroom. List the things you will add to these centers to make them more literacy-centered. Explain how you will introduce these to the children in your class.
2. Implement one of the strategies or activities from the chapter. Discuss the students' response. What worked well? What would you change for the next time you do this with children?
3. Select one of the strategies discussed and design an application to fit your students' interests and their needs.
4. Implement the application you designed and evaluate it. How effective was it? How efficient in teaching the concepts and skills was it? How did the students respond?

Suggested Sources for Additional Information

McGee, C. M., & Richgels, D. J. (2003). *Designing early literacy programs.* New York: Guilford Press.

Neuman, S. B., & Dickinson, D. K. (Eds.). (2001). *Handbook of early literacy research.* New York: Guilford Press.

www.IRA.org
www.NAEYC.org

Early Literacy
A Supportive Classroom Context

When I am working with children—whether it's the whole class, a small group, or one at a time—I look for ways for students to shine. I am especially alert for the quiet child, the withdrawn one, the one whose hand never goes up, the disruptive child. I have learned from years of teaching that if a child experiences immediate and early success as a reader and writer, that child willingly engages in reading and writing with a spirit of "I can do this." If, on the other hand, the child experiences years, or even months of frustration and failure, it is unlikely he will become a successful reader and writer. Success breeds more success; repeated failure leads to the feeling, "I can't do this." Often, students just give up. (Routman, 2003:14)

What are *your* earliest memories about learning to read and write? Were they positive? How much of your leisure time is spent in reading today? Would you call yourself a skilled and confident writer? Are you a skilled and confident speaker in front of groups and an interesting conversationalist on a one-to-one basis? Would people who know you well classify you as a good or poor listener?

This next phase of literacy is a critical one for young children. As they move into the primary grades, their emergent literacy takes a distinctive turn. The naturalistic experiences that have been so much a part of their literacy development—songs, fingerplays, rhymes, and storybooks—will now be supplemented by more formal, teacher-structured experiences specifically designed to expand their inside-out information system described in Chapter 1. The internal structures of words, decoding strategies, and sentence grammar will now take center stage. However, this should all take place in a highly social, interactive learning context.

As you read, keep in mind the following questions:

- Why does verbal communication continue to be one of the most important learning avenues for the young child? What happens to children who spend time in learning contexts that ignore this?
- What biological and psychosocial changes take place in primary children that prepare them for these new directions in literacy development?
- What key experiences should be shared with children on a daily basis in order to promote strong development of literacy skills and concepts?
- What strategies can teachers use to maintain children's high interest in learning to read and write in the early years?

In this chapter, these questions will be addressed as we focus on the developmental changes in children who are making the transition from emerging literacy toward the higher level skills and concepts we see in early readers and writers. We'll look closely at the kinds of activities and experiences that can support each child's journey and maintain each child's powerful desire to read and write.

Children in the Early Primary Grades: Primed for Developing the "Tools of the Tribe"

It's important to remember that in the early grades, children still need plenty of opportunities to talk informally with one another about what is personally meaningful to them and simply to have fun with language. This is particularly true because cognition and literacy continually develop in close concert with a child's oral language experiences (Hohmann & Weikart, 1997). Vygotsky believed that thoughts not only were expressed in words but also actually came into existence while a person articulated them aloud to others. Children's informal communication with one another and with adults is so much more than just talking about their ideas and desires; it is a primary mode of regulating conceptual development (Tishman & Perkins, 1997). The obvious implication is that the teaching of literacy must be considered more broadly than reading and writing activities.

Children at this age have already learned a lot about literacy. They have a range of understanding about letter–sound associations, know about print conventions, and handle books with a great deal more confidence. Most can retell a story in sequence. Now they are eager for activities that will help them acquire more sophisticated literacy capabilities. We see this in their growing fascination with such activities as playing school and pretending to read and write. It's also apparent in the numerous questions they ask about what something says and their delight in constructing a message that is "real writing."

As pointed out in earlier chapters, children have innate capacities that allow them to develop the abstract rules and principles to make sense of spoken language and convey their thoughts to others (Gardner, Kornhaber, & Wade, 1997). However, this is *not* true of the social-conventional understandings they will need in order to read and write well. Here, scaffolding will become essential, as children construct and learn these concepts and skills with the help of knowledgeable others through an interactive process. Each child's teachers, parents, and peers will be the most important protagonists in the transformation that will take place.

How do children become independent readers and writers? Because the human brain is a pattern-seeking organ, literacy will be the result of their *wanting to learn* something they perceive as useful, *exposure* to the knowledge they seek on a daily basis, and a great deal of *practice in engaging in activities with others* skilled in helping them to be successful. Children in this early phase of literacy development are primed in every way to learn strategies for interpreting what they read and what is read to them. In these years, they will work hard at linking letters in familiar print to the sounds those letters represent; once they have made these initial phonemic links, they will move to "chunking" as they recognize patterns or letter clusters that appear again and again in their reading. Increasingly, they will pick up on the value of using visual cues and can be observed "cross-checking"—drawing on their visual memory as they search text for familiar words that *look* like one they're having trouble decoding (Stewig & Jett-Simpson, 1995).

As children hear the flow of language from others who tell and read them fascinating stories, and have plenty of opportunities themselves to read books they like, they build additional phonemic awareness and gain strength in utilizing structure and grammar clues. To the extent that children accumulate these strategies and can apply them, they grow in their ability to self-correct their own miscues and begin

Becoming independent readers.

to tackle more difficult literacy tasks. Those who continue to practice and internalize these strategies within literacy-rich contexts—at home and at school—dramatically enlarge their receptive and expressive vocabularies, abilities to recognize increasing numbers of words by sight, and abilities to decode and encode print.

Children in the early primary years often become enamored of print and pay close attention to how others "write down talk." Figuring out ways to write increasingly sophisticated printed messages, they move quickly from unconventional to conventional forms. We begin to see punctuation in their stories, and they can more quickly identify topics they want to write about. In the second grade, they use reference materials more easily and begin to proofread their work and that of their peers. If they are given opportunities to use a variety of language skills to solve problems in which they are interested, expand their comprehension and fluency skills, and observe the many connections between spoken and written language, they often stride with visible confidence into the next stages of literacy development. Examples of how specific patterns in reading behaviors move from emerging skills to more fluent skills can be seen in Figure 5.1.

Emerging Reader	Transitional Reader	Beginning Reader	Advanced Beginning Reader	Consolidating Reader	Accomplished Reader
• Focuses on pictures • Develops directionality • Begins phonemic awareness • Develops understanding of conventions of print • Does "pretend reading" • Begins to write and name letters	• Begins to recognize some sight words • Uses pictures and some initial consonants to figure out words • Still relies on memorization of story • Predicts from pictures • Begins to spell semiphonemically	• Focuses on meaning cues • Focuses on letter–sound cues • Begins to use several cues at a time • Expands sight-word knowledge • Begins to use cues to self-correct • Develops phonemic awareness • Spelling includes some semiphonemic and phonic spelling; standard spelling is increasing	• Develops chunking strategies • Develops cross-checking strategies • Refines self-monitoring and self-correction • Uses transitional and standard spelling	• Works to become automatic with strategies • Increases sight words • Handles more and more complex text	• Controls cross-checking strategies • Self-monitors • Develops more word meaning vocabulary • Develops strategies for complex text structures
Indicators of Advancement	**Indicators of Advancement**	**Indicators of Advancement**	**Indicators of Advancement**	**Indicators of Advancement**	**Indicators of Advancement**
• Attention shifts to print • Memorized story rereading	• Voice–print match • Begins to try to use most letters to figure out words	• Cross-checking cues • Begins to see spelling patterns	• Effective chunking • Consistent use of cross-checking • Consistent self-monitoring and self-correction	• Becomes strategic • Silent reading speech exceeds oral	• Ability to be flexible in multiple reading settings • Moves from novice to more expert reading behaviors with familiar topics

Figure 5.1 Patterns of literacy development.

Source: Jett-Simpson and Leslie (1994).

All of the gains during this period are made possible by significant changes in neurophysiology that allow early primary children to make huge leaps in language, logical-mathematical connections, and social-conventional knowledge. It is during the early primary years that brain connections are in the greatest growth spurt since infancy, developing pathways that lead to greater knowing as well as greater *capacity* for knowing. Significant brain growth, neural connection, and increased myelinization result in greater verbal and visual memory, better integration of the right and left hemispheres of the brain, more sophisticated eye development, and more solidified auditory discrimination. How the child will behave cognitively in the future will be a function of what happens in this period of neural development, for, at about 10 years of age, a "ruthless" destruction of the weakest synapses in the brain (those that have not been reinforced by activity) takes place, leaving the child with strongest connections in areas of the brain that have been "magically transformed by experience" (Nash, 1997:56). These developments then set the stage for how each child tackles academic tasks ahead.

The Adult's Role in Early Literacy: Strategies for Providing Needed Support

Children in these early grades are moving into a psychosocial stage whose major theme is mastery of life skills, one in which they consciously apply themselves to learning the skills and tasks necessary for functioning well in society. Erikson (1963) referred to this period as one in which children are ready to receive systematic instruction in the culture for handling "the tools of the tribe." Gordon and Williams-Browne (1996) note that the abilities to read books and to write are two such tools, and that the danger for children lies in their coming to feel inferior during the process of working toward mastery. Adults can help children negotiate this tightrope between preserving self-esteem and challenging themselves sufficiently to take learning risks by paying attention to the children's mastery of non-literacy skills as well: How are they doing in problem solving and initiative taking? Do they see mistakes as learning opportunities? Are they consistently making good learning choices? Are they building the metacognitive skills to take advantage of the many key experiences provided daily to support literacy?

Certain key experiences on a daily basis will provide children with the connections and practice needed for literacy development. We will want to work actively on forming an authentic reciprocal relationship in which we and the children in our care take turns leading and following, speaking and listening. This forces children to become more autonomous, take initiative, and be responsible. It also instills in children a sense of their own power and limits. They don't always have to wait for cues from an adult before they can move ahead in their own learning.

Following are the guidelines we believe are absolutely essential in structuring the best literacy practices possible in primary classrooms.

Oral language and communication experiences should take center stage in the primary classroom. Children need to talk with one another and with us, and plenty of that can be built into the activities that form the child's daily work in the classroom. In addition, we will be central players in demonstrating aspects of oral language and standard English, including how to structure complete and complex sentences (syntax and morphology) and develop word meanings (semantics). Through us and through the good literature that we read aloud every day, children also develop their vocabularies and gain an understanding of the various social conventions of language or pragmatics (see Figure 5.2 for a reminder of the various basic components of language). When interacting with children, remember to pick up and record some language samples at several junctures throughout the year.

Rather than correcting children's approximations—their incorrect grammar and pronunciations—it is best

---

Antonyms: Words with opposite meanings (*good/bad*)

Blends: Two or three consonants in immediate sequence blended together (*str* in *strength*)

Digraphs: Letter combinations that represent single sounds (*ch, sh, th, wh, ph*)

Diphthong: Two vowel letters in immediate sequence representing a single sound (*oi* in *noise*)

Grapheme: Written representation of a phoneme

Homographs: Words spelled the same but pronounced differently (*tear/tear*)

Homonym: Words with sound and spelling similarities

Homophones: Words that sound alike but are spelled differently (*there/their*)

Morpheme: Smallest meaningful unit of language

Phoneme: Smallest unit of sound

Phonics: Teaching sound–symbol correspondence and spelling rules

Phonological awareness: Ability to manipulate sounds

Pragmatics: Social and cultural aspects of language use (dialects, nonstandard English)

Synonyms: Words with the same or similar meanings

Syntax: Structure or grammar of a sentence

Figure 5.2   Defining some basic components of the English language.

simply to model and then elaborate on the syntactic, semantic, and pragmatic features of language that we want them to develop. For example, six-year-old Lamanzer told his teacher excitedly, "I be seein' my grandma tonight!"

"Ah," smiled his teacher. "You'll be seeing your grandma. That's something special to look forward to!" Since Lamanzer's teacher knows that outright corrections only diminish children's attempts to communicate with others, she responds warmly with a complete and more complex sentence. Without directly pointing out errors and shutting Lamanzer down, she converts his dialect into standard English and models the morphology and syntax she wants him to use pragmatically.

Frequent read-alouds of stories that use both familiar and unfamiliar vocabulary and illustrations to help children connect newly gained vocabulary with context are invaluable. When stories are particularly engaging and meaningful to children, they stimulate conversation and discussion. Children pick up concepts of effective speaking by listening to the modeling of pitch, stress, juncture (pause), imaginative qualities of print, and dialects when we broaden the scope of their reading and listening. This might be a good place to comment on the value of promoting active listening skills in children. Despite the fact that listening is included as a major component in literacy, it receives very little attention in the curriculum and in directed teaching. Yet we know that a child who has poorly developed listening skills will be penalized in terms of following directions, ability to complete assignments or tasks, interactive skills with others, phonological awareness, and vocabulary building. Something that essential should not be left to chance, and simply telling children to "be good listeners" is not enough. Some activities that help children develop effective and differentiated listening skills include:

- Using rhythm sticks or hands to tap or clap out the syllable patterns in their names
- Going on a sound walk to discover sounds in the environment
- Playing games such as Simon Says and also games such as charades to emphasize nonverbal "listening"
- Playing tapes of sounds they can identify, or making their own tapes
- Asking questions prior to the reading of a story, pointing out vocabulary words or concepts they need to listen for
- Playing sound discrimination games
- Playing games such as "Guess What's in the Bag?" (Guess What's in My Hand, Guess What I'm Thinking About), in which they have to listen to clues until they guess correctly
- Having them respond to multistep directions or repeat in correct sequence and detail messages they hear
- Rhyming activities and writing
- Modeling good listening behaviors and discussing useful listening strategies such as looking directly at someone who is speaking, sitting relatively still, and waiting for one's turn to speak

Structure numerous daily activities to develop independent reading and writing skills, using the applications that are described in this chapter and your own creativity in varying them to maintain children's interest. For children who are struggling with early skills, it will be important to step back and provide the kinds of activities described for the emerging learner in Chapter 4. For children in your classroom who have moved considerably ahead of others and seem to have early literacy skills well in hand, you will want to take advantage of the activities offered in Chapter 6 for the more fluent child. This would also be the time to teach revising, editing, and proofreading as appropriate to children who seem ready for these steps.

Extend children's knowledge of phonics in context as much as possible. Routman (1996:199–200) presents the following documented facts about the teaching of phonics:

- Research demonstrates that in classrooms where phonics is taught in the context of rereading favorite stories, songs, and poems, children develop and use phonics knowledge better than in classrooms where skills are taught in isolation.
- Effective phonics instruction focuses children's attention on noticing the letter–sound patterns in initial consonants and consonant clusters and in rimes (the vowel of a syllable plus any consonants that might follow, such as -ake, -ent, -ing, -ure). Focusing on rimes rather than on vowels alone is particularly important in helping children learn to decode words.
- Teachers and parents can help children gain phonics knowledge by: (1) reading favorite poems, songs, and stories and discussing alliteration and rhyme within them; (2) reading alphabet books to and with children and making alphabet books together; (3) making lists, word banks, or books of such words that share interesting spelling or sound patterns; (4) discussing similar sounds and letter sound patterns in children's names; (5) emphasizing selected letter–sound relationships while printing something that children are dictating; (6) helping children write the sounds they hear in words, once the children have begun to hear some separate sounds; (7) encouraging children to predict and confirm words that are unfamiliar, using prior knowledge and context along with the initial consonants and then looking at the rest of the word to confirm or correct their predictions.

The teaching of phonemic awareness can be pretty deadly when not attached to anything meaningful or engaging—in essence, killing children's interest. O'Donnell and Wood (1992:47) report that the problem in using a phonics-only approach with beginning readers is that there is not a perfect one-to-one correspondence between

Daily activities to develop independent reading and writing skills.

letters and sounds in English. If there were, children could simply "decode words by mastering spelling to sound correspondence rules."

The latest research looking at the war between a phonics-only approach and alternative approaches such as whole language conclude that it isn't one or the other but must be both if children are to have the best chance in developing useful literacy skills and concepts (Snow, Burns, & Griffin, 1998). Having seen the best teachers stress phonological awareness instruction in the context of good literature, we agree. They weave in the element of surprise, challenge, and gaming to help children make the necessary connections.

Use heterogeneous, dynamic, small groupings as a primary teaching mode for general skill and concept development, with the addition of homogeneous groups for mini-workshops and targeted teaching. Children learn a great deal from one another and are pushed at this age to notice what their peers are doing well and to copy those behaviors. Much as we would like to believe that the major part of their learning comes from what we structure and present in the classroom, the skills they see demonstrated by other children about their own age are what really capture their attention. Mrs. Steinmetz takes advantage of this by structuring daily *literacy rotations* in her classroom. During a two-hour literacy block each morning, the children spend 20–25 minutes in large group with Mrs. Steinmetz while she explains to them the activities that will occur in three 30-minute, rotated heterogeneous groups (the makeup of these groups changes from week to week). During this time, she also demonstrates procedures and strategies for the activities they will be carrying out independently. This approach is especially useful in multiage classrooms to take advantage of the varying skill levels in children. It is also effective for breaking a class down into smaller groups so that the teacher can work intensively with a smaller group while other children gain independence in reading and writing activities. Mrs. Steinmetz maintains that these small groups allow her to make closer eye contact and communication with each child on a daily basis and to gauge the amount of understanding each child is gaining relative to new skills and concepts she is introducing. In addition, she is building self-regulation and problem-solving skills in the children, allowing them to independently practice what she teaches them during each day's skill-based mini-workshops. Today, Mrs. Steinmetz calls the entire class together for a short period of time, with a group starter that immediately engages their interest. For example, today's activity is a secret message (see Figure 5.3) she has structured for them to figure out, something they love to do! Another day, she might do the daily message described in Chapter 4. She takes time to have them read with her a familiar poem they have read at the start of each day's session, and then she does a brief activity with some enjoyable phonics work connected to the poem. She reminds them about ways they can take responsibility for their own independent learning and designates a person in each group who will act as a "traveler"—the child who will bring any questions to her that someone in the small working group cannot answer. She explains carefully what the red group will be doing as they start in the independent writing center and demonstrates the process to them. They will be using the materials provided on the table to form as many contractions as they can and to write them in their reading journals, listing the two separate words and then the contraction that can be made. They may work with a partner or independently, and if they have additional time, they are to make up some other contractions they can think of.

The blue group will begin with silent or buddy reading work, choosing from a selection of books the teacher has gathered. After reading one of the books independently or with a partner, they are then to go back, look for all the contractions they can find, and list them in their reading journals.

The green group will begin their rotations with Mrs. Steinmetz. For them, she begins a shared reading experience with a book they have already enjoyed, Dr. Seuss's *Oh, The Places You'll Go!*, and challenges them to hold up their index fingers silently any time they spot a contraction during the reading. Following the reading, she asks the travelers in the other small groups if they have any questions that someone in the group cannot answer. She then returns to the group of children with whom she is working and does some additional work with the text for phonological and print awareness, with a follow-up activity for comprehension of the material. Today, she provides the children with copied pages of the text and invites them to discuss the

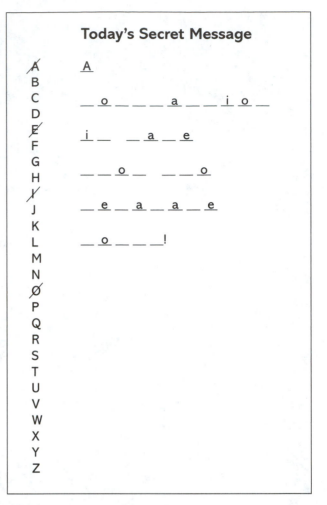

Figure 5.3 Secret message: "A contraction is made from two separate words!" (Teacher has provided vowels as clues.)

order in which they appeared in the book, to hang them on a clothesline in that order, and then to see how well they remembered the sequence by using the book as a check.

Mrs. Steinmetz observes the transmission of learning that goes on as children answer questions she has about the text and also pose their own. She likes the fact that the children have learned to be fairly autonomous about the independent work they have been given to do, so that they do not interrupt her focus with the shared reading group. She remembers that it wasn't always this way and that it was necessary in the beginning to take time to teach the children how to handle independent work. Her patience and careful structuring have paid off. Because she is able to work daily with the children on a small-group basis, she is able to assess differences in the understanding, skills, and concepts of the children; then addresses their needs more intensively during the day by working with children on an individual basis or in small, homogeneous groups of two or three as needed. As she enthusiastically describes the process, "I win and they win!"

Share your goals about literacy with the children and have them set their own. Explain to children why particular strategies you use are important and meant to be helpful. For example, to encourage children to rely more on their own invented spellings and develop their skills in writing conventions, Mr. Lillard told his first-grade class that he would *not* be taking individual dictation from each child but that he would write dictation in large or small groups every day in order to model conventional writing. He told them that it might be frustrating to them at first, because they had been used to having their teacher help in this way during kindergarten. He also reminded them they would have lots of resources to rely on in terms of theme and concept charts they had been producing in a large group, word wall, and word study. They could also rely on one another and on many other materials when they really got stuck. "Just try it and see how much you will grow once you put your own brain into high gear," he challenged. "Right now, anything goes, and all I ask is that you do your best!"

Shirley Hodgins, who teaches second graders at Gundry Elementary in Flint, Michigan, helps children develop a set of 10 skills they want to accomplish in literacy. She reinforces the children in their efforts to master these and then conferences with them once a month to go over the list and see what progress they've made. When appropriate, she encourages the children to provide samples of their work from their portfolios to support their self-evaluation.

Accept children's work, letting them know that you expect they will do their best. Be careful about exercising a red-pencil mentality with early primary children. For example, early in the school year, a first-grade teacher implemented journal writing with her class, which was made up primarily of African American children. Many of the children were not using standard English on a day-to-day basis. Inviting them to write about a school assembly they had just attended where a puppet show had been featured, she watched as they wrote down their excited versions of what they had just seen. Circulating about the room, she asked them to read their versions back to her and then proceeded to cross out their nonstandard wording and replace it with a corrected version. In her zeal to "teach" them to use standard English, she forgot that her primary goal was to get them to put their ideas down on paper and keep them both excited and comfortable about writing. She also forgot that she would have many opportunities to model and teach correct usage during writer's workshop. Donald Graves, who has provided us with so much wisdom about how children learn to write reminds us that most of what children write in the early years should *not* be revised—seldom in kindergarten or first grade—so that they will write extensively and experience the flow of writing, concentrating on only one skill at a time. He suggests that boys particularly find this tedious and a turn-off to learning the writing process.

Don't forget to partner with parents. Remind parents that this is an especially important time in their child's development to reinforce at home the classroom focus on literacy. Ask them to:

- Read daily to their children and partner-read with them. Chapter books are especially good for second graders.
- Serve as reading and writing models for their children.
- Limit TV time to no more than one or two hours a day (acknowledging that this will call for a sacrifice on their part if they want to be effective models).
- Take their children on a regular basis to a public library to browse and check out books.
- Continue to play word games with their children such as Boggle (Parker Brothers) and Scrabble Junior (Milton Bradley).
- Keep reading and writing enjoyable. Don't force children to read or write at home or use it as a punishment. When reading interactively, be careful about *requiring* them to sound out words. Don't correct their spelling.
- Have high expectations about literacy, and communicate those to their children.
- Give books as gifts to show how much they value them.
- Provide a variety of reading materials, including comic books they see as appropriate and children's magazines (e.g., *National Geographic Kids, Highlights for Children, Sports Illustrated for Kids*).
- Take their children to storytelling sessions at libraries and local bookstores.

Finally, *continually work to build positive attitudes toward literacy activities.* Calkins (1997:33) notes the importance of this philosophy in setting the tone for the way children view literacy learning. For example, instead of saying "You've got 15 minutes for reading. Let's get started now," say "We've only got 15 precious minutes for reading. I know we would all like more time, so let's not waste a single second of the time we do have!"

Children Who Experience Literacy Problems

These early primary years are ones in which skill levels in literacy become more similar among children. Given plenty of daily opportunities to experience the kinds of activities we have described so far in Chapters 4 and 5, 85 percent of children will learn beginning reading and writing skills. Although boys, as a group, will be significantly behind their female counterparts in transitioning to beginning reading during first grade, gender differences will generally disappear by second grade (Soderman et al., 1999). But what if they don't? When should cautious concern move to formal intervention and, possibly, to special instruction?

Taking time to practice and enjoy reading.

McCormick (2003) has identified the **disabled reader** as anyone reading significantly below his or her own potential. Thus, the first step in determining whether a child needs corrective, remedial, or clinical reading services is to assess potential or reading expectancy. In the past, this was usually determined by considering whether the child had average intelligence and was free of neurological difficulty and sensory deficits (hearing or visual impairment). However, because of the growing concern about the appropriateness of standardized tests with young children, a preferred method is to read a series of graded passages in informal reading inventories (IRIs, described in Chapter 7) to a child, beginning with very easy ones. The child listens to the passages and answers a series of questions to determine his or her comprehension of what was read. The child's frustration level based on that comprehension is then determined and matched to a particular grade level. Another method is to assess the child's listening comprehension using one of the published tests that include listening comprehension subtests.

Following determination of potential, the child's present reading achievement is assessed with a well-constructed standardized reading survey test. Tests that are simply lists of grade-level words are *not* appropriate. Finally, the gap between a child's *potential* and *actual ability* is determined.

Here, we are concerned with the kinds of classroom applications that must be made to ensure the most effective learning possible for children who are experiencing significant difficulty. Once assessment has been conducted, there are a number of mechanisms that can be considered that will scaffold children forward to higher-level skills. These include:

● Personalizing instruction in the classroom. Here the teacher meets with an individual child or small group of children to work on a targeted literacy problem, scaffolding instruction.

● Structuring collaborative learning among same-age and cross-age peers, pairing more knowledgeable and less knowledgeable children together.

● Assigning independent work during which children carry out specific, individualized assignments directly following teacher-directed instruction for short periods of time and under direct supervision of the teacher.

● Expanding the child's time on task in conjunction with one-to-one tutoring.

● Letting children actually read more and giving them additional time to practice their skills with highly meaningful material.

● Encouraging more outside reading.

● Providing demonstrations of effective reading behaviors through interactive reading and role playing the thought process of useful strategies to use when comprehension has broken down.

● Providing ongoing, timely feedback on the spot to correct children's ineffective strategies.

● Stimulating motivation by helping children to expect they will be successful. Be sure they know that achievement is not a matter of luck but rather a matter of taking charge of their own successes and failures and working harder to achieve the success they want.

● Establishing a close working relationship with others who are tutoring the child or providing special services so that insights about the child, professional knowledge, and intervention plans can be shared.

• Enlisting parent involvement by encouraging them to read aloud to their children every day and also have their child read orally to someone every day.

• Researching the child's literacy problem. Although reading disabilities continue to be complex, we have learned a great deal in the past two decades. You will have the best chance possible of addressing specific problems if you take the time to investigate what is known and expand your understanding rather than relying totally on a specialist to help the child. This will allow you to provide the highest quality literacy instruction possible to that particular child (McCormick, 1995; 2003).

• Using one-to-one tutoring programs, such as Reading Recovery (Clay, 1993b) and Success for All (Slavin, Madden, & Dolan, 1996).

Today, a number of one-on-one tutoring programs can be found in almost every school district. Perhaps the most universal is Reading Recovery, which was designed as a *preventive* rather than remedial measure to address significant lags in the lowest 20 percent of first graders in any particular school. First graders are selected as early as possible in the fall based on informal assessments administered by the first-grade teacher and also on each child's responses to the following six measures of a diagnostic survey:

1. Letter identification (upper- and lowercase)
2. Word test (the Dolch list that is used can be seen in the Appendix)
3. Concepts about print (Clay's assessment of child's knowledge of print and book handling)
4. Writing (exhaustive list of child's known words, ability to write high-frequency words, writing samples from class)
5. Dictation test (assessing knowledge of 37 phonemes presented in a sentence)
6. Text reading (running record for purposes of determining the nature of the reader's errors and highest level at which 90 percent accuracy is attained)

For the next 12 to 16 weeks, one-on-one instruction is provided for 30 minutes a day with a trained Reading Recovery teacher. During the first 10 days the teacher and child simply get acquainted with one another and explore reading and writing in a nonthreatening way. In subsequent days, a specific format is followed in the 30-minute session that is designed to help each child develop a self-improving system and return eventually to the regular classroom with the skills to be an independent reader. Each session would look much like this:

Six-year old Shawn, who has been in Reading Recovery for a month now, knows the routine. During today's meeting with Ms. Kardos, he will read two or more familiar books (ones at which he has a 90 percent accuracy rate). Ms. Kardos will take a running record (see Chapter 7) on the new book from the day before. After allowing him a short period to work with magnetic letters, she will have him write one or more sentences, providing phonic segmentation procedures and helping him to analyze the word into isolated sounds when he experiences problems. Afterwards, he cuts his sentence apart and then reassembles it. When he first started to do this, he began with whole phrases and then moved to cutting his sentence apart into separate words. In the future, Ms. Kardos will challenge him to divide the contents of the sentence even more finely, dividing the words into structural segments, clusters of letters, and even single letters. Before he leaves to go back to the classroom, she introduces him to a new book he hasn't read before, orienting him to the text by discussing some of the vocabulary which might be unfamiliar. He reads the book a first time with Ms. Kardos's help and then a second time to gain fluency. When he is finished, Ms. Kardos places the book in a box with others he has read and says, "We'll look at this one again tomorrow, Shawn. You're piling up a fair number of books." As Shawn makes his way to the door, he grins and says, "See you tomorrow, Ms. Kardos."

Children who are learning English also need added support in this early phase of literacy development, but the question of how to provide the most effective context for young English learners remains controversial. Freeman and Freeman (2003) warn that the approach many schools have adopted based solely on word recognition; teaching subskills in a rigid, sequential manner; and the solitary use of decodable text is *not* supported by second-language acquisition research. Instead, teachers must be given latitude to use a *sociopsycholinguistic approach*. This means providing children with extensive exposure to less controlled texts (trade books) as well as decodable texts, structuring repeated opportunities for them to see reading modeled and to read themselves, and setting up collaborative activities with English-proficient peers to compare words, notice common features of words, explore relationships among words, discover patterns, and then debrief with the teacher about their findings (Cummins, 2003; Freeman & Freeman, 2003).

As English language learners read and reread familiar stories and participate in explicit phonemic awareness and phonics instruction related to these stories, they do what all children in this phase do: internalize alphabetic principles and develop effective strategies for both decoding and comprehending text. English learners should also be encouraged to read as much as possible in their primary language, and they should have access to engaging stories in that language in the classroom or in the school's media center. They should be encouraged to check out these books so that parents can read to them in their primary language. This is particularly true for children from high poverty areas where there may not be much in the way of children's literature in the home in either the child's primary language or English (Krashen, 2003).

Tips for scaffolding language and literacy development in the multilingual classroom include the following (Graves & Fitzgerald, 2003a; Crawford, 2003; Cummins, 2003):

● Do picture walks through texts and, initially, focus the child's attention on a particular word below the picture that describes something in the picture. Later, as the child moves toward some sight recognition of words that are becoming more automatic, and an ability to decode other words, provide direct instruction of vocabulary words and key concepts that will be included in a selection.

● Have someone introduce a selection in the child's primary language, including key vocabulary and concepts, and then read through the story in English.

● Help children conceptualize new information through the use of concrete materials and illustrations. Have them do a lot of drawing to illustrate the ideas they want to express, and connect their writing to familiar stories they are reading in English.

● Be accessible to them. Watch for signs of stress and frustration.

● Correct oral language errors only when they interfere with communication.

● Speak slowly and use gestures to enhance comprehension. Allow children to use nonverbal responses (pointing, shaking head yes or no) until they are comfortable enough to use one- or two-word responses, which will give way to longer, more complex narratives. Provide sufficient wait time for responses. Be patient with children who are in a preproductive stage of second-language development in which they are building receptive understanding and may only respond with gestures before moving on to speech-emergent stages.

● Immerse children in a predictable, literate environment in which there are consistent routines and rich communication is used. Involve children in shared reading activities using big books.

● Focus on the use of a word wall and encourage children to develop their own rebus dictionaries for use in reading and writing activities.

The many intervention programs available for helping young children move toward literacy must be evaluated objectively in light of developmentally appropriate practices. Do they take developmental and experiential factors into consideration? Are instructional approaches based on the best research we have about how children learn and acquire literacy skills? How effective are they in building and maintaining children's skills and developing attitudes toward literacy? Are they structured to provide the safety nets needed *throughout* the preprimary and primary years? When they don't meet DAP criteria, can they be adapted in some way to do so and still provide the support they are designed to deliver? The answers to these questions will be important ones to consider as we continue to develop the very best support programs possible for early learners.

Although developing literacy is very serious business, we may have become *so serious* about it that we've removed much of the joy that can be experienced in these early years—by children and teachers. Probably one of the most critical factors in making sure children are moving toward fluency is to provide them with heavy daily doses of enjoyable "languaging." This means we must allow lots of informal communication to take place in the classroom in addition to the formal instruction that is planned or the intervention that becomes necessary for some children. We need to take greater advantage of serendipitous teaching and learning events and to structure activities each day that not only predict good skill and concept building but also provide opportunities for children to exercise them with one another and with us in a very natural way. It's good to keep in the backs of our minds why children learn so easily when they are *not* in the classroom. Following are some key activities that we think will be useful as you continue to build positive attitudes in your classrooms toward literacy activities.

INTERACTIVE READING/WRITING ACTIVITIES

Judy Nyberg (1996) has developed a collection of activities for use following the telling of selected, familiar stories and rhymes. These focus on creating charts or visual displays in the classroom that provide reading, writing, and thinking opportunities for young children, extending familiar stories into other curriculum areas. The activities can take any form. For example, a letter might be written to a character in a story. Children might take a poll for which they develop individual questions related to some aspect of the story. They might create and label a graph, develop a new ending for a story, or list the ways a character solved a problem and how that might be different in real life. They may select the first letter in the name of a character and think of a number of objects that begin with the same letter, drawing the objects beside the word. They can create maps, do a KWL (What do we know? What do we want to know? What did we learn?) activity related to the story to begin a spin-off investigation, write a related poem, or create a game. Through the various activities they and the teacher develop, children see reading and writing modeled and better understand the relationship between various literacy components.

Main Purpose To extend children's perspectives about the many purposes for and uses of writing and reading

Materials Easel
Chart paper or easel paper
Markers

Procedure
1. Choose a familiar text that the children love (e.g., *Little Red Riding Hood*).
2. Read it again and also read variations of it by other authors.
3. Discuss with the children the differences in illustrations between the two or more texts and any differences in the viewpoints of the authors.
4. Discuss the story with the children, helping them to see the ways in which its concepts are related to their own lives.
5. Make a web of topics or ideas related to the story. For example, in this case, children are familiar with woods, grandparents, being safe, animals.
6. Think creatively with the children about an activity that involves writing that relates to some aspect of the familiar text.
7. Work with the children to set up the activity and follow through to completion.

Classroom Application Mr. Bingham's first graders troop back into the classroom. They are still excited about the snowmen they have worked together to make out on the playground. After they've settled down for a story, he reads them Roy McKie and P.D. Eastman's book *Snow*. They listen intently, having just shared many of the experiences written about by the author.

When finished, Mr. Bingham says: "You know, it might be good to write a letter to Mr. McKie and Mr. Eastman to tell them about the three snowmen we've just built. I think they'd like that. Let's get some of our thoughts down on paper before we forget how it went!"

He begins to write at the easel, involving the children as much as possible in sounding out the words and in the actual writing as they list the steps they took in constructing the snowmen. Afterwards, Mr. Bingham and the children look at their finished product. He has them read with him the list of steps again. "Yes," says Mr. Bingham. "I think this is a good list to send to Mr. McKie and Mr. Eastman. They'll enjoy it as much as we did reading their book."

Mr. Bingham folds the easel paper and places it in a large envelope. In front of the children, he prints the authors' full names on the envelope— Mr. Roy McKie and Mr. Phillip D. Eastman—and says: "Our next job is to find out where to send our letter. How can we do that?"

When the children suggest that they ask Ms. Villareal, the media specialist who knows everything about books, Mr. Bingham suggests that they walk down to the library to get the information. Mrs. Villareal shows the children how the publisher of the book is listed inside the front cover and then gets on her computer to find Random House. "Here it is," she says." "Random House Publicity, 201 East 50th Street, 22nd floor, New York, NY 10022. Someone write it down!"

Hints for Success

- Familiarize children with new vocabulary and concepts before reading or telling them a story.
- Engage the children as much as possible in the writing. For very young children who have not yet developed strong letter–sound relationships, the teacher will do most of the writing. Still, ask them to help you identify the letter the word begins with, and allow them to take over as much as possible.
- Have activities that allow children to collaborate with each other. For example, in taking a poll, children can construct the question and illustrate the page. Other children can then be asked to respond with a simple check mark, a yes or no, or a longer written response in answer to a question.
- Stretch your imagination for story-related activities. Nyberg (1996) suggests that teachers ask the following questions:
    —What would the children enjoy doing?
    —What is relevant to their experience?
    —How can I expand their thinking and imagining?
    —What activities will help them focus on print?
    —What activities reflect authentic reading and writing?
- Involve children in conversations following the reading of stories to expand their thinking about the story's meanings and connections for them. Don't move immediately into activities.

WORD WALL

Developed by Cunningham, Moore, Cunningham, and Moore (2000), a word wall has become a universal practice in many elementary schools. In effect, a portion of one wall in the classroom becomes a giant alphabetic listing of familiar, high-frequency words that children need for their everyday writing. The words usually are chosen from familiar reading, with five to ten words per week chosen for study and posting. They are also chosen on the basis of containing spelling patterns that can be transferred to the spelling of many other words not posted.

A word wall is most advantageous when placed adjacent to the writing center.

Main Purpose	To increase children's understanding of the concepts of print, letter recognition, and sound–symbol relationships
Materials	Various colored cards or paper on which to write the words Markers
Procedures	1. Choose 5 new words each week that are high-frequency power words or words with discernible patterns. For second graders, you may want to choose up to 10 words if you believe the group can handle that number. 2. Talk about each of the words, looking at the individual letters, patterns within the word or matching other known words, configuration of the word, and meaning of the word. 3. Have children offer sentences in which the word is used in a meaningful way. 4. Write the words on different colored cards with dark marker. 5. Post the words under the relevant alphabetic letter. 6. Daily, have children participate in activities during which they say, chant, snap, or march to the letters in each of the words.
Classroom Application	The children in Julie Carpenter's room at Grand River school in Lansing, Michigan, actively use their word wall. In large group, Miss Carpenter tells the children that they'll be glad to see the new word that will be going up on their word wall this week: "It's one that a lot of you are using in your writing and one that we see over and over in our reading. The word is *where*. Let's take a closer look at it."

Miss Carpenter writes the word at the easel and points out how easy it is to mix it up with another one they use frequently, *were*. "One of the ways we can tell the difference," she says "is the *h*—the second letter—sticking up right here."

She has them spell the word several times and then says, "I think I noticed this word *where*—w, h, e, r, e—several times in the big book we read this morning. Let's read through it and when we come to the word *where*, let's shout it out. The rest of the words, we'll just read the way we always read them, with indoor voices."

After reading through the story and finding the word over and over, Miss Carpenter challenges the children to think up some sentences in which they would use the word.

"*Where* is my dog?" offers Ronda. "I know *where* you live!" laughs Chico. "*Where* are you going?" asks Tyler, enunciating the word with a lot of force. "Mmm, I guess we need to put *where* on our special green paper so that we don't mix it up with *were* when we need to write it," says Miss Carpenter as she prints the word with her thick black marker on the small square of green construction paper. "Who wants to place it on our word wall?"

Hints for Success

- Begin the year by posting some of last year's words that were hard to spell.
- Place words as close to children's eye level as possible.
- Choose examples from:
    —Each initial consonant—*b, c, d, f, g, h, j, k, l, m, n, p, r, s, t, v, w, y, z* (including both common sounds for *c* and *g*)
    —The most common blends—*bl, br, cl, cr, dr, fl, fr, gr, pl, pr, sk, sl, sm, sn, sp, st, str*, and *tr*
    —The most common digraphs—*ch, sh, th*, and *wh*
    —The two-letter combinations—*ph, wr, kn*, and *qu*
    —The most common vowel spelling patterns—*at, make, rain, day, car, saw, caught, went, eat, see, her, new, in, like, night, girl, thing, not, those, coat, go, for, how, slow, out, boy, look, school, us, use, hurt, my, very*
    —The highest utility phonograms—*ack, ail, ain, ake, ale, ame, an, ank, ap, ash, at, ate, aw, ay, eat, ell, est, ice, ick, ide, ight, ill, in, ine, ing, ink, ip, it, ock, oke, op, ore, ot, uck, ug, ump, unk*
    —The most common contractions—*can't, didn't, don't, it's, won't*
    —The most common homophones—*to, too, two; their, they're, there; right, write; no, know; one, won; your, you're*
    —Frequently used words such as *favorite, teacher, school, family, sister*
- Write words that could be confused (*our, are; their, there*) on different colored cards.
- Place your writing center in close proximity to the word wall for easy reference by the children.
- Plan daily activities, and encourage children to check the words for use in their independent writing.
- Expect children to spell the words correctly once they have been posted on the wall.
- Ideally, have no more than 120 words at the end of the school year.

GUIDED READING/SUPPORTED READING

This is a highly interactive process between children and teachers that involves the whole or a large group to think about, talk about, and read a narrative or expository section of text together for a specific purpose. It sets the stage for self-selected, independent reading at higher levels.

Main Purpose To extend children's strategies for decoding and making sense of print

Materials Selected text

Procedure
1. Lay the groundwork for a successful reading experience by discussing with children the concepts of the selection and scaffolding information, including language structure, vocabulary, and key words.
2. Read text with children, discussing reading strategies during the guided reading, helping them learn a variety of methods to solve problems with text.
3. When the reading is completed, follow up with retellings or elicit responses to the selection.

Classroom Application "Look what I found over the weekend at Schuler's Bookstore," says Miss Azzari to a small group of children in the book corner. "It's a new book of poems written by A. Nonny Mouse (Jack Prelutsky, 1993). You know how much fun they are. Come on over and we'll take turns reading them."

Miss Azzari plumps down on the floor with the four children in a tight circle around her. "Remember that these are poems, so some of the words might rhyme or sound the same as words that came just before. Sometimes, though, there may not be any rhymes. Brian, you choose one and start." Brian begins: "I had a little pup, his name was Spot, Wuh...wuh..." "Remember that chunk that's made out of *wh,* Brian?" says Miss Azzari. "And it looks like two words together to make up a long one. See—*when* and ...(she slides her hand to cover *when*). "Whenever?" Brian offers and, seeing Miss Azzari smile and shake her head affirmatively, he continues: "Whenever we cooked, he licked the pot...Whenever we ate, he never forgot...to lick the dishes as well as the pot." The children and Miss Azzari laugh, and she quickly reads the entire poem once more. "Who sees any rhyming words in Brian's poem?" asks Miss Azzari. Baylee's hand shoots up. "Go ahead and name them for us, Baylee, and then choose one you'd like to read."

Hints for Success
- Select challenging text that is at an appropriate instructional level for your group. That means that children should be able to read 90 to 95 percent of the words independently.
- Provide follow-up activities that include content areas or various modes of creative expression.
- Provide follow-up activities that solidify the meaning of the story/ selection.
- Use books for early readers that have rhyme, rhythm, and repetition so children can use all three reading cue systems.
- Use selections that contain a high percentage of known words so they can use more than one reading strategy to figure out unknown words.
- As children gain independence, gradually withdraw support in the guided reading process.

READ-ALOUDS

Combs (1997) says that read-alouds are absolute musts. Different than shared reading, they allow children to simply sit back and hear the flow and rhythm and magic of good literature without having to struggle with the text themselves.

Main Purpose	To extend children's concepts of the rhythm, tone, flow, syntax, and semantics of print
	To extend their knowledge of effective oral reading behaviors, both nonverbal and verbal
Materials	Books that can help children build a background knowledge about the world, mirroring life and allowing children to learn more about themselves and about others
Procedure	1. Invite children to gather on the floor around you.
	2. Tell the children you have found a special book to share with them.
	3. Share any interesting information about the author and illustrator.
	4. Encourage children to make predictions about the story.
	5. Watch children during the read-aloud to notice when particular responses take place and how they seem to be connecting to and receiving what is being read.
	6. Connect the illustrations as you read, pointing out the cues they provide for the reader and how they connect with the text.
	7. Follow with discussion, helping children to articulate where they felt connected to the story and what meaning it has for them.
Classroom Application	Lunchtime is over, and the children are finding their way to the large-group area. A couple who choose not to sit on the carpet bring chairs along. When it is quiet, Mr. Schleusner begins.

"This is my favorite part of the day—to just pick out a book I think you'll all like. This is a special one that someone gave me when I graduated from college. It's called *Oh, the Places You'll Go!,* and it's written by one of your favorite authors, Dr. Seuss. He opens the front cover, and they see a boy start-

Reading to children to model fluency and prosody.

ing out in what looks like a maze. "Which way do you think he should go? Which way would you go, Tanisha?" Mr. Schleusner asks. She points to the left. "Ahh, you'd go left. What do you think he's going to run into? Let's see."

Mr. Schleusner reads the text, stopping at particular places to allow them more time to look at the creative pictures and make comments. In other places, he asks them what they think some of the phrases mean. "Don't worry . . . don't stew. Just go right along . . . what do you think Dr. Seuss means when he writes 'Don't stew?' " he asks. When no one offers anything, he suggests: "Maybe it means the same thing as don't worry . . . don't worry, don't stew. Hmmmm."

When he finishes the entire book, he asks, "Did any of you ever do something that didn't turn out exactly the way you thought it would?" After eliciting some of their thoughts, Mr. Schleusner says, "Lots of things—fun things and things that aren't so fun happen to us, don't they? Well, just as Dr. Seuss says, just go right along—and use your brains and do your best. I could tell you really liked the pictures in this book and the way lots of the words rhyme. I'll leave it over in the book corner for you to look at later on."

Hints for Success	• Pick books that you really enjoy yourself.
	• Preview and practice before sharing with the children.
	• Allow ample time, and adjust your pace as you read.
	• Make sure children can see the text and illustrations as you read.
	• Connect with the children frequently, with good eye contact.
	• Read with expression, but in your own style.
	• If the book turns out to be a poor selection for the group, feel free to abandon it.
	• Make the book available to the children for rereading independently.

BOOK MAKING AND OTHER CREATIVE WRITING

This is meant to keep us out of writing ruts and to stretch children's imaginations about what writing can convey and its many, various purposes.

A variety of individual books can be produced: flip books, shape books, pop-up books, peek-a-boo books, accordion books (see Scholastic's *Making Books across the Curriculum*). Children can also create and illustrate individual pages that can be put together to produce class books. These can be placed in the reading center where children select favorites to read alone or to each other. They can also check out these much-loved resources and take them home to read to their families.

Main Purpose	To extend children's writing skills, processes, and concepts
	To encourage creative literacy experiences
Materials	Paper of different colors, weights, and sizes
	Markers, colored pens, paint, and brushes for illustrations
	Glue
	Stapler
	Scissors
	Scraps of decorating materials: glue, yarn, and so on
	Computer and word-processing program (optional)
Procedure	1. Invite children to create a book of their own (flip book, shape book, pop-up book, peek-a-boo book, big book, accordion book, etc.).

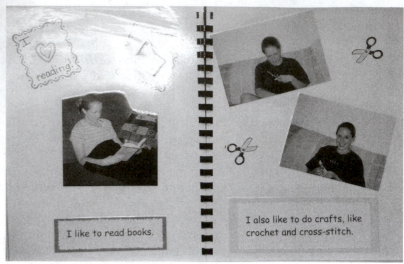

A teacher-made book to introduce herself to her class at the beginning of the year.

2. Share techniques for producing each of the different formats. For younger children, use only one at a time.
3. Have children compose the text for their books on separate sheets of paper and edit as is developmentally appropriate.
4. Provide time and materials to construct the book cover and pages.
5. Have the children plan and transfer their text to the book pages.
6. Encourage the children to share their books with others or to display their books.

Classroom Application   "I've been intrigued with the kinds of books you've made so far this year," Miss Tetchie tells her second graders. "It's a good thing you've kept them

Class books promote reading success because of their familiar content.

Include class-made books as a choice in the reading center.

in your portfolios because I have a real challenge for you this month. Let's see how it would be to publish one of your books on the computer. To help you do that, I have a new software program called *Make-a-Book*. This week and next, during our center time, Brian Judge's mother will be in the writing center to show you how this works and to help you put your book into still another form."

"This is a pretty good software program. It can help us make books of different sizes and even has colored fonts, which will be fun. Let me show you a few examples from a little book I just wrote about my cat Ebenezer."

Miss Tetchie shows the class several different examples of sizes, styles, and fonts she has printed off. "One thing I also think you'll enjoy is that when you are finished, the text will be spoken. It'll sound as if someone is reading your book." Kendall waves her hand excitedly and says, "Miss Tetchie, when we have our celebration evening to show our Mom and Dad our portfolios, we could show them our book on the computer . . . and have it talk and everything . . . just like TV, right?" Several of the children indicate their excitement about that possibility.

"A *very* good idea, Kendall," says Miss Tetchie. "Let's plan on that. Something that I think they could improve are the illustrations available in the program. They are not as good as the ones we can make ourselves. See . . . this cat doesn't look much like Ebenezer, so I'd rather make my own picture of him. So . . . you may want to reproduce your original illustrations for your second book or dabble around a bit with theirs just to find out how they work. I'll let you decide."

Mrs. Judge says: "Well, we may be able to solve that problem, too. I can bring in my scanner and see if we can get some of our own pictures and artwork in. I think we can."

"Well, this is exciting," says Miss Tetchie. "Mrs. Judge thinks she can work with about 10 of you this week and another 10 next week. Since she showed me how to work it, and Brian also knows how, we can also help when Mrs. Judge isn't here. There will be a sign-up sheet in the writing center, and if you think you're ready to go this week, please sign up so that Mrs. Judge can call you when she's ready to work with you."

Hints for Success

- Supply models for techniques (e.g., how to cut, fold) but not for content (illustrations, text).
- Have children observe how published authors illustrate and format books.
- Provide children with a variety of other creative experiences and challenges. For example, they can:
    —Write letters to the editor or to advice columnists.
    —Provide the answer to their own letter or have another child actually write an answer.
    —They can write and illustrate their own greeting cards, puppet shows, scripts, and sketches for Reader's Theater, newscasts, ads, fact files, cartoons, and posters.

POWERPOINT PRESENTATIONS

PowerPoint for first and second graders? "Absolutely!" says Jessy Belue, who teaches first grade at Riverview Elementary in Fort Mill, South Carolina. She writes, "Every year, I have children who come to school who have a computer at home and feel very comfortable with computers. I also have children who have never used a computer. At the beginning of the year, I try to just get my class comfortable with the computer. We go to the lab and type in Word or draw in the paint program just to expose them to how the computer works. I introduce PowerPoint about a month after we have been in school. I start by showing them a very simple PowerPoint presentation I have made and explain that it is a program that is used to present and share information to an audience. When they see mine, they can't wait to make their own!"

Main Purpose To acquaint children with the computer as a writing tool

Materials Computers and PowerPoint software

Procedure and Classroom Application Ms. Belue continues: "The first thing that we create on PowerPoint is an autobiography. We work on one slide every few days, doing each step together. I always do things in the same order: type the text, add clip-art, add animation, and then save. The children respond to the routine and soon memorize the steps in making a slide. After they make their biography, we invite their parents to watch. Each child stands up and presents his or her slide show. My children are fascinated by the computer and excited when they see a final product [see Figure 5.4].

"After this, the focus becomes using PowerPoint to enhance literacy. The children read an information book together in small groups, each group with a different nonfiction book. The children then think of questions they

Meet Ben, creator of his own PowerPoint biography.

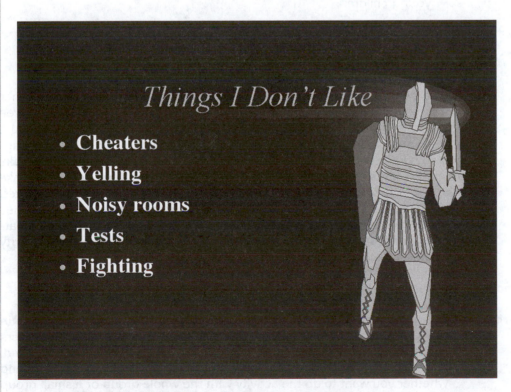

Figure 5.4   Ben's slide about things he doesn't like.

have about their topic that are not answered in the book. We then make a trip to the school library and find all the books we can on their topics. As we read the books, children look for the answers to their questions. After we finish research, which may take several weeks, the groups work together to make a PowerPoint presentation to share some of the information they learned through their research. The groups then share with one another what they learned via their PowerPoint creations.

"Using PowerPoint is a wonderful way to integrate reading, research, technology, and speaking. It helps children organize information they have learned and also fosters cooperation and communication among the children working together in small groups. Finally, it helps children take what they have learned through books and share it with others in an exciting and current format.

"Many teachers are hesitant to use PowerPoint because they are unfamiliar with the program, but it is actually a simple program. I have learned more about computers and technology by using it in the classroom, making mistakes, and observing my students. For those who would like to visit our class web page, you can find us at the following: www.fort-mill. k12.sc.us/RVES/msbelue.html. Visit us and see what else we're doing!"

Hints for Success

- Practice putting together a very simple presentation before diving into the activity with the children.
- Start first with what is most meaningful to children, their autobiography.
- Structure more knowledgeable children to work with those who have only limited experience. Monitor to see that a good scaffolding experience is going on, rather than the more experienced child taking over.
- Allow children plenty of time to practice and make mistakes; watch to ward off frustration. Celebrate with children who make breakthroughs in their understanding and competence levels.
- Bring in knowledgeable adults to work with children. Discuss with adult helpers what makes an appropriate scaffolding experience with young children.

MAKING WORDS

You've seen the word *literacy* many times in this book. How many other words could be made using the eight letters, five consonants, and three vowels that make up that word? *Race, try, tray, lay, crate,* and *tear* are just a few. Can you spot at least 10 others? Pat Cunningham (2000) has suggested a winner. Children are given some sets of letters and asked to make as many words as they can and to try to use all the letters, finally, to make just one "big" word. Children are eager to do this and are always amazed at the number of words they can make by switching letters around. They come to see the quickest way to develop the most words is to spot a pattern or word family, and then they really go to town. This is a good activity to develop decoding skills.

Main Purpose To extend children's phonological and print awareness

Materials A set of laminated movable letters, with vowels in red and consonants in black, uppercase on one side and lowercase on the other side. The letters can be made using a computer and then copied back to back, laminated, and cut into small squares. Depending on the number of children and whether you want to do the activity with the whole group or a small group of children, make up multiple sets of the letters, at least 15 or 20 of each

Creating and recording words from movable letters.

letter. You also may want to make up squares with punctuation and quotation marks if you want to extend the exercise into making sentences.
Paper or index cards or writing journals and pencils
Ziploc plastic bags in which to store the sets of letters (You may want to construct a sturdy box with 30 separate sections, one to hold each set of letters and four extra spaces for sets of question marks, periods, quotation marks, and exclamation marks that can be used in sentence making.)

Procedure
1. Before asking children to do this activity, demonstrate it in large group.
2. Begin with a "big" word you want to end with, usually choosing it from the children's favorite or current stories.
3. Start with simple two-letter words and then show the children how three-letter words can be made by simply adding letters to the beginning or end or changing a beginning letter. Talk about the value of finding patterns of words or word families.
4. When children understand how the process works, provide them sets of the letters in the word you have chosen. Provide a set for each child or for each pair of children.
5. In a 15-minute period, have children make all the words they can think of. Tell them to remember there is one "big" word that can be made from all the letters and to see if they can discover it.
6. Have the children list the words they make in their writing journals.
7. Debrief with the children. Ask:
   —Did they discover the "big" word?
   —Did they see any word families or patterns?
   —Did they have any words (e.g., *cold/clod*) that used exactly the same letters but in a different order?
   —Did they make any proper nouns? If so, did they remember to use the uppercase?

Classroom Application "Today, when we go into our literacy rotation centers," says Ms. Arbanas, "we'll have a chance to work with our movable letters again. That's always a lot of fun, isn't it? As you go to the writing center, you'll find three sets of letters on the table. There will be eight of the same letters in each set, three vowels—*i, e,* and *a*—and five consonants. I'll keep those a secret for right now and just let you discover what they are. I'd like to have you work with your literacy buddy for this activity. For example, Darian and Spencer will be working together. Take your writing journals with you and, as you think of the words, list them in your journals. You may be able to get a whole page full—maybe even two pages. See if you can think of some four- and five-letter words today. If your brain is really in high gear, you might be able to discover the one word that all eight letters make. Red group will start in the writing center, blue group will be in the shared reading center, and purple group will begin with me this morning. Okay, let's get started! We have a lot of work to do."

Hints for Success
- Start with simple two-letter words, then move to three, and so on.
- Eliminate unnecessary competition by not centering on who had the most words unless you are having children work in teams.
- The "big" word should be one that children have seen recently in the books they are reading.
- To extend, have children categorize by beginning letters and write the words into their journals. Have them enter the words into their journals with the smallest words first and the longest words last. Have the children try to make sentences out of some of the words.

CHALLENGE WORDS

Janiel Wagstaff (1995), a second-grade teacher in Salt Lake City and author of *Phonics That Work,* brings us this great idea. Children are able to offer a "challenge" word that they don't know how to spell, and ask the group if they can figure it out. It can be a simple one-syllable word or a very difficult polysyllabic word. The group then works together with the teacher to see what spelling strategies they can use to spell the word correctly before looking it up in a dictionary. Much review of spelling strategies takes place as children move through the process, becoming more aware of how others try to spell a difficult word.

Main Purpose To build phonemic awareness and demonstrate what real writers do in determining a spelling

Materials White board
Markers
Dictionary

Procedure
1. Have a small group of children gather together with their writing workshop folders.
2. Ask for a word a child is interested in learning to spell. Ask if the child can use it in a sentence.
3. Have the children say the word several times and think of any other words they know that sound like that word.
4. Then tell them to give it a go, using their memories, the word wall, patterns from other words that sound like that word, chunking it into syllables, and any other strategies they can think of.

5. Write all their final suggested spellings on the white board.
6. Have them decide which one looks correct to them.
7. Circle their choice.
8. Look the word up in the dictionary, or have a child do so if able.
9. If correct, recircle the word, and have children say the word and chant the letters in the word. Congratulate them for "turning their brains on high!"
10. If incorrect, write the correct version and then have the children say it and chant the letters. Congratulate them for "turning their brains on high" and using the many strategies they know, including using the dictionary when all else fails.

Classroom Application

It's Friday morning at the Sheridans School, and six of the second graders in Mr. Kostanza's room are gathered around a table with him. A dry-erase board is nearby on an easel. The children are leafing through the week's journal entries for words they found difficult to spell each day and are using red markers to underline the words.

After giving them time to do this assessment, Mr. Kostanza asks if anyone wants to pose a challenge word, one that he or she found particularly hard. "I've got a good one," says Rashad. "Remember when we were writing about our favorite foods? I wanted to spell *avocados*." Rashad holds up his journal to show the group his sentence: I love pizza with ovucdles. "I know it isn't right. It's really hard."

"All right," says Mr Kostanza to the group, "What do you think? That's one I think I'd have to look up in the dictionary myself. Let's say it out loud . . . ah-vo-ca-dos; ah-vo-ca-dos; ah-vo-ca-dos. Let's give it a go. Any suggestions?"

Several of the children make suggestions—"ovokoddos," "avakoddoes," "avocottles." Mr. Kostanza writes each of their suggestions on the board. "I'm curious, Trainor. Why did you suggest starting the word with an *a* rather than an *o*?"

"Because it sounds like *a* . . . like when you're just saying *a* boat . . . *a* cat . . . *a* knife . . . if you say *a* really slowly or go *ah* . . . " Mr. Kostanza asks if there are other suggestions and then asks the children to decide on one of the three they think is probably the correct one or comes closest to the correct spelling. They decide on *"avakoddoes,"* with *"ovokoddos"* as their second choice. "This is a case for the dictionary if there ever was one," says Mr. Kostanza. "Rashad, because it's your word, let's have you do the looking today. What do you think . . . does it start with an *a* or an *o*?" When Rashad decides he's going to go with the *a*, Mr. Kostanza asks the group to name the next sound. They decide on a *v* but can't decide whether the next letter is an *a* or an *o*. Rashad looks up the *a* first and, when it isn't there, moves to *avo*. After some searching and lots of suggestions from the group about the *k* probably being a *c*, "like *could* on the word wall," he finds the correct word. He says, "Right here! It's *a - v - o - c - a - d - o . . . s! Avocados!*" Mr. Kostanza prints the correct spelling slowly on the white board, saying each letter distinctly and then asking the children to chant the letters and say the word. "Hey, you're all in business," he tells the group. "Next time, you can not only order avocados on your pizza, you can spell it, too. Who else has a word? We'll take a couple more."

Hints for Success
- Allow at least 10 minutes for the activity. If a first word is solved quickly, move to another word that is offered.
- If children do not have a word, have one of your own ready to offer.
- After children have spelled the word correctly, see if they can suggest a couple of sentences for its use.

- Point out to children when their analogies were logical but didn't work because the spelling of the challenge word was irregular.
- Keep a list of challenge words in the classroom so that children can refer back to them.
- Add challenge words to the classroom dictionary.

RETELLINGS

These are postreading or postlistening recalls that are either oral or written. Said to be powerful in their genuine ability to assess what children understand about their reading, they can provide the following information:

- What the child thinks is important to remember
- What the child thinks is important to retell
- If the child's retelling fits the purposes set for reading
- How the child structured and sequenced the retelling and if the structure and sequence matched that of the text
- To what degree the child's responses are text-based or reader-based
- The importance of the information that was retold
- The closeness of match between the text and the retelling

Main Purpose To assess the child's comprehension of printed text

Materials Selected text, narrative or expository
Tape recorder and tape
Pencil and paper

Procedure
1. Select a text to read that is within 95 to 100 percent of what a child can read independently.
2. Have the child read the text.
3. After the child has finished, ask him or her to put the book aside and retell everything he or she can remember.
4. When the child appears to be finished, ask if there is anything more he or she would like to add.
5. Analyze the retelling and make notes for the child's folder relative to these criteria.

Classroom Application "Rossie," says Ms. Ortiz, "I haven't had you read to me for a while. Because you enjoy drawing so much, this is one I think you'll like. It's a story that reminds me of you whenever I see this book. It's Vera B. Williams' *Cherries and Cherry Pits*. Come read it for me, and then we'll do a retelling. Remember, that's when you just tell me about the story after you finish—without using the book. I'm going to tape your reading so that you can listen to it later if you want to. You may even feel like putting it into your portfolio for your Mom and Dad to listen to when they come in for our celebration evening."

Rossie and Ms. Ortiz settle down in the reading corner and Rossie reads through the story, commenting on the way the story unfolds along with the drawings. Afterwards, Ms. Ortiz takes the book, returns it to the shelf in back of them, and says, "Rossie, if you were going to tell that story to your little brother when you get home this afternoon, what would you tell him?" She notes that Rossie leaves out the first part of the story about the first character but completes a pretty good retelling of the last two events. "Tell me why you think the little girl planted the cherry pits instead of just

Sharing a retelling with Ms. Ortiz.

throwing them away, Rossie," says Ms. Ortiz. "Because then *everyone* would have all the cherries they wanted . . . forever and ever . . . and every year the trees would have blossoms and make cherries," answers Rossie. Later, Ms. Ortiz makes a record of the text level, some of the words Rossie had trouble with, and some of the strategies she needed additional help with when trying to decode them. She also makes a brief note about Rossie's ability to interpret the author's purpose and the problem the story was centered around. She places the record in her teacher's portfolio of Rossie's work.

Hints for Success
- Before the child reads the text, let him or her know that you will request a retelling after the reading.
- Tape record the retelling for later reference.
- If useful, follow the free retelling with a guided retelling or the following questions:

  —Can you tell me more about _____?

  —Why do you think _____ happened?

  —What problem was the story concerned with?

  —Describe _____ at the beginning of the story, and describe _____ at the end of the story.

  —What happened after _____?

  —What do you think the author was trying to teach or tell you?

  —Why do you think _____ did that?

STORY MAPPING

Some children complain that they just don't know how to get started writing a story. Others get lost in the process. Still others never seem to bring their work to a conclusion. Story mapping or webbing is a process that helps more advanced young authors focus on developing their story characters, setting, plot, and conclusions by asking the following questions: (1) Who do I want my story to be about? (2) Who else do I want in my story? (3) Where do I want them to be? (4) What do I want to have happen? (5) How will my story end? (O'Brien-Palmer, 1992:23–24). It builds into the child's mind the important aspects that make up any story and helps as much in reading comprehension as in writing skills.

Main Purpose To develop children's strategies for writing and ability to plan and organize their ideas in a logical sequence

Materials A story map formatting sheet
Pencils, pens, or markers
Easel and chart paper

Procedure
1. Before implementing this activity, develop your own story map format sheet (see Figure 5.5, "Story Map Format Example").
2. Prior to having children write a story, ask them to help you list some of the important components of stories they read (main characters, supporting characters, setting, events that make up the plot, and conclusion or how everything turns out).
3. Tell them you have a tool that is used by authors to make sure they don't forget any important aspects of a story.
4. On the easel, draw a larger version of the story map depicted on their formatting sheets.
5. Use the form to develop an example of story mapping with a familiar story they already know, demonstrating how to fill in each piece.
6. After the pieces are filled in, make a one- or two-sentence statement of the main idea of the story, based on the component parts. For example, "The main idea of this story is . . . "

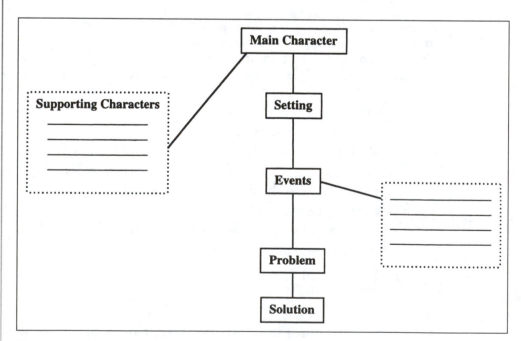

Figure 5.5   Story map format example.

7. Pass out the story map forms, noting that the parts are exactly the same as the one just developed and that different stories can be mapped.
8. Ask the children to work together in pairs to develop a simple story to share with the larger group. Remind them to fill in the space for the main idea.
9. Have the children share their component parts and main idea summary statement.
10. Have children independently compose a story web or map of their own.

Hints for Success

- Remind children that authors often write about real events from their own lives, sometimes stating exactly the facts as they happened to produce a nonfiction story and sometimes changing events, persons, or facts to produce a fictional story.
- Complete the above procedure over several days, rather than at one sitting.

THEME/CONCEPT CHARTS

Theme and concept charts are a wonderful spinoff on the word wall concept. The activity takes place early in the implementation of a theme as a prewriting activity in which children brainstorm all the words they can think of that they may use in their writing over the course of the theme. The words usually come from their reading before and during implementation of a theme. For example, in a unit on shadow after reading several books focusing on light and shadow, children brainstormed the following words in large group while their teacher wrote them on chart paper: *sunny, cloudy, shadow, groundhog, project, shape, source, block, length, position, shortest,* and *longest*. As their investigations about shadows progressed, they added additional words they hadn't thought about during the initial brainstorming session: *flashlight, translucent, transparent, opaque*. Theme charts may center around common content areas that are frequently the target of a young author's writing: family words, sports words, weather words, transportation words, friendship words.

Concept charts usually center around a specific writing principle (for example, words that end with a silent *e*, words that end with a *y*, words with a long vowel, words that end in *lly*, words that end in *ee*). They are maintained over the course of several months or the entire year and are posted near the writing center for easy reference by the children.

Main Purpose

To extend children's vocabularies and the varieties of words used in their writing

To move children toward conventional spelling by extending their knowledge of phoneme/grapheme production and patterns in word construction

Materials

Colored chart paper or posterboard
Markers
Narrative and informational books on the topic
Dictionary

Procedure

1. On a sheet of chart paper and in front of the children, write the title of the theme or concept across the top (e.g., Shadow Words).
2. Have children generate words they remember from readings about the topic and record them on the sheet, involving children in the correct spelling of the words.

3. Ask, "If you were writing a story or report about this topic, what other words that are *related* do you think you would need for your writing?" Record these, again involving children as much as possible in the process.
4. Post the chart in a place where children are likely to access it for use in their writing.

Hints for Success

- Restrict the posting of words on the chart to those that are related to the theme or concept.
- Encourage children to add words to the chart as they discover them in their reading.
- Write the words large enough and with dark marker so that they can be seen from a vantage point where much of children's writing is done.
- Use poster board or easel paper that is of a different color for each concept chart to encourage easy access.
- Prior to writing activities about a theme, review with children the words that are available on the theme chart and ask if they have others they need to add.
- On the concept charts, encourage children to bring exceptions to the attention of the group and add them under a subtitle of exceptions.

INTERACTIVE JOURNALS

Interactive writing between teacher and student has quickly established itself as a highly worthwhile practice to promote literacy (Hall, Crawford, & Robinson, 1997). There is usually a greater spirit of mutuality than is afforded through other activities in which the teacher is scaffolding, grading, or guiding a student's writing. Here, the teacher becomes a writing partner with each child in the classroom in order to provide motivation for daily reading and writing.

Main Purpose To provide children with real purposes for writing on a day-to-day basis and to model correct conventions of written language for the child

Materials Students' journals
Pencils and pens

Procedure

1. Because this is an activity to enhance children's writing skills, processes, and concepts, introduce it as such. Share the positive aspects of an ongoing exchange—getting to know one another better beyond just being teacher and student, and the excitement of seeing what someone has written each day and how he or she has answered a question or comment.
2. With the class's help, structure some guidelines about the process: How much should be written at a minimum? How often? When? When are the teacher's responses expected to be completed? The student's responses?
3. Follow through to provide time for the activity on a consistent basis.

Classroom Application One well-known children's author has captivated conference audiences with his account of how one of his elementary school teachers began writing interactively with the children in her class about the books they were reading. He joined in reluctantly, not considering himself a very good reader or writer. His minimal, two-sentence responses to her soon grew into two paragraphs and, eventually, two pages by the end of the school year. About this time, his teacher asked him to go with her down to the school library. He remembers that as they walked quietly down the hallway, he worried that she was going to ask him about all the books he had reported on. But he could never have imagined what happened next. His teacher asked him to look on a shelf where all the authors' names began with the same last initial as his. Unexpectedly, all of the books were missing from the shelf, and when he told the teacher there were no books, she said, "We've left room for all the books you will write in the future." She had discovered a special talent in this child who had previously been unmotivated in literacy. Was she possibly the catalyst in setting the trajectory for his future? Could a child's interaction with one teacher for one year be that important?

Hints for Success
- Respond to children's writing thoughtfully and seriously, rather than in a typically "teacherly" way.
- Teach by modeling correct usage, rather than correcting the child's mechanics, organization, spelling, or grammar. For example, if a child misspells a word, include the correct version of the word in your response.
- Keep your responses sensitive to the child's current level of understanding and functioning—very brief for kindergartners and first graders, and then expanded as children's abilities expand.
- Vary the use of punctuation and words.
- Respond with complete sentences and correct usage rather than informal phrases, which might have the tendency to teach or support incorrect usage. At the same time, promote an interactive exchange that is more like a conversation between friends or pen pals than teacher and student.
- If children talk about personal problems within their families, respond seriously and thoughtfully with a possible strategy that can be used by the child, but do not take over the problem or try to manage it.
- Keep the focus on the student's agenda, not on yours, in order to keep "teacherness" out of the exchange. You want to get children writing about their interests.

PROCESS WRITING

Once children have developed a good sense of phoneme/grapheme association, have begun to develop words into sentences, and have a rudimentary idea of capitalization and punctuation, it's time to scaffold them toward evaluating their work and editing some of their pieces for publication. This is a fragile process and very dependent on carefully observing children's readiness for the next step. Some first graders may be ready for a scaled-down version of this during the second half of the year, and most second graders are ready for beginning process-writing strategies at the beginning of the year. Although what is known as process writing may vary slightly from classroom to classroom, it usually involves a five-step process, including prewriting activities, drafting, revising, proofreading, and publishing. The revising and proofreading steps may be repeated over time until the writer is satisfied that the piece is his or her best possible work and is ready to be published.

Main Purpose
To develop children's abilities to plan, organize, evaluate, and revise their writing
To provide children with opportunities to talk with peers and the teacher about the goals and challenges in writing

Materials   Writing paper, construction paper, or other materials for making book covers
Pencils, pens, markers
Computer
Stapler or binding materials

Procedure
1. Introduce the exercise by discussing with children that good writing is usually a process that involves several steps:
   a. Prewriting activity that may include mapping or webbing; talking with a peer or the teacher about a writing idea; and writing out questions that need to be answered about the content or format.
   b. Producing a draft in pencil, leaving a line between each line of writing and adequate margins for purposes of editing; reading the initial draft(s) aloud to catch any errors or omissions; sharing the piece with a friend who reads it out loud so that the writer can hear the flow of what has been written.
   c. Revising, taking special care that each sentence is complete; looking for a main idea in each paragraph and seeing that there are sufficient supporting details; adding descriptors (adjectives and adverbs) where appropriate; eliminating run-on sentences or too many "ands"; and replacing a poor choice of words with better ones.
   d. Proofreading to catch capitalization and punctuation errors, to look at subject–verb agreement, correct tense, indented paragraphs, and legible writing. This step should involve a peer doing a second read-through, pointing out any difficulties in understanding what is written and making suggestions for additional revision.
   e. The last step, publishing, takes place after all revisions are finished, with the final version or draft written in ink or on the computer. The title is centered or placed on a title sheet or book cover, and all former drafts are attached to the final draft so that the process that took place in developing the piece can be seen easily by interested others.
2. Show children a published, simple piece of your own work (not necessarily a formally published piece), bound in some way and containing the corrected versions leading up to the final draft. Talk about persons who read the drafts and some of their suggestions for editing or revising.
3. Invite children to take the first step and, when finished with it, to proceed to the second, working their way through the process and checking with you after completing each step in the process and before beginning the next.
4. When a piece of work has been completed, the author confers with the teacher about possibilities for sharing the completed work (e.g., Author's Chair, Author's Evening, Student-Led Conference).
5. The process is reimplemented, so that the child is always working on a piece of writing in one stage or another.

Hints for Success
- When implementing this for the first time with a group of young children, go through each step thoroughly, covering no more than one step on any given day.
- Use the overhead projector to work through some examples at particular stages.

- Encourage children to write about what interests them, to connect their writing with what they are interested in learning more about and reading more about.
- Provide scaffolded help and practice as needed for moving the child through the process.
- Encourage children to work with one another in the drafting, revising, and proofreading steps of developing their work.
- Be sensitive about inappropriate expectations (beyond the child's zone of proximal development or abilities) or demanding that a piece must be perfect before it is ready for publication; maintain a supportive and encouraging context, guiding the child to do his or her very best.
- Evaluate the richness of the classroom setting with respect to print, communication opportunities, and activities to enhance skill building in young writers.

SELF-SELECTED READING

There are lots of different names for this activity. Some of our favorites are: Silent Sustained Reading (SSR), Drop Everything and Read (DEAR), Sustained Quiet Uninterrupted Independent Reading Time (SQUIRT), Read a Book because It's Time (RABBIT), Zip Your Lips and Read (ZYLAR), and Go Read a Book (GRAB). You can make up your own acronym (or, better yet, have the children do it), but be sure that you provide these opportunities for children every day if possible. We recommend a period no shorter than 10 minutes for preprimary and kindergarten children and no shorter than 15 to 20 minutes for primary children.

Main Purpose   To have children practice the skill of reading, increase their fluency, and experience and enjoy a variety of reading material

Materials   Lots of reading material of all kinds, supplied by both the teacher and children

Procedure
1. Announce ahead of time that an opportunity for self-selected reading will be taking place shortly and that children should make their selections and get settled. Trips to the bathroom and for drinks should be taken care of ahead of time.
2. Until they have internalized the rules (children should be involved in structuring these, by the way), remind them that it needs to be quiet during the period, with no interruptions until you announce that it is time for another activity.
3. Tell them you will be participating and share what you will be reading that morning (e.g., a letter from your mother, a cook book, a novel, a health pamphlet).
4. Help children find their materials and settle down in a comfortable space.
5. Remember to monitor time and observation of the rules.
6. Enjoy the release from stress that self-selected silent reading can bring to a busy day!

Classroom Application   Cassie loves the last half hour of the day in her multiage classroom. That's when Mrs. Rodriquez and the class do DEAR (Drop Everything and Read). Cassie considers that *her* time of the day because she can read anything she wants. Right now, she's deeply involved in Lois Lowry's *Anastasia Crupnik* and can't wait for 2:30 to come so that she can find out what will be on Anastasia's list at the end of today's chapter. She thinks about asking Mrs. Rodriquez if she can check in the library for more of the Anastasia books.

Last Thursday, she didn't have anything special she was reading, but she remembers that it was a good time because she chose a number of the picture books she especially loved a couple of years ago and read through them again. Cassie likes this time because it's especially quiet. As she tells it: "No one's talking at you. No one's asking you to do anything. No one's expecting anything to get finished. It's just plain reading!"

Mrs. Rodriquez has noted the variety of material the class chooses to read and how they swap books they have especially enjoyed with one another. Although some of her colleagues report that they have begun having children complete book reports on the texts they are reading, Mrs. Rodriquez is adamant about keeping the activity stress-free and as enjoyable as she can make it. She says, "It's a time when I get to catch up on my *Newsweek* magazines . . . or just a novel, and I wouldn't want to have to do a book report on either one. That would ruin it for me."

Hints for Success
- Model the process by participating fully yourself.
- Establish guidelines about time allocation, quiet participation, no book sharing during the appointed time, and so on.
- Provide a wide variety and selection of reading materials, including joke books, magazines, expository and narrative books, and sports trading cards.
- Encourage children to bring materials from home if they wish or to read books they have checked out from libraries or media centers.
- Follow up by having children make brief notes about their reading in a journal or log, making a story map or web, providing a summary of what they have read, sharing one idea they remember, or other activities.
- Provide comfortable places other than desks and hard chairs for reading if possible.
- Encourage parents to simulate this experience at home in the evening.
- Be enthusiastic about the opportunity to spend uninterrupted time with print.
- Occasionally introduce new reading material that becomes part of the silent reading selections by reading just the first paragraph and telling children it will be available for selection.

ONSETS AND RIMES/WORD FAMILIES

Word families consist of words that share the same vowel and ending letters and rhyme. Once children discover that many words can be made by simply changing the beginning letter(s) of words, they quickly increase the number of words they can write and decode. As you know, *rhymes* and *rimes* are not the same. *Rhymes* are words whose endings *sound* the same (e.g., *cow* and *bough*). *Rimes* are words whose endings *are* the same (e.g., *top* and *mop*). *Onsets* are the beginning phonemic sounds in words that can be interchanged to make new words, and *rimes* are the remaining part of the word following the initial phoneme.

Main Purpose To increase children's phonological awareness, writing skills, and decoding abilities.

Materials	A large white board (may substitute easel and chart paper) Small white boards, one for each child (may substitute paper) Markers

Procedures

1. At the top left of your white board, write the word *can,* saying each letter as you print it. At the top right of the board, write the word *will.* Separate the words by drawing a vertical column down the center of the board.
2. Have children repeat the process on their white boards.
3. Under the word *can,* print the word *man.*
4. Say the words, *can . . . man.*
5. Ask the children what they notice about the words (spelled almost the same, the words rhyme).
6. Write the word *fill* under the word *will.*
7. Ask again what they notice.
8. Tell them, "This is how we make word families. The words in word families have different onsets or beginning letters, but they end with the very same vowels and letters and rhyme." Have the children chant the words on your white board.
9. Ask if anyone can tell you another word to put in the *an* word family or the *ill* family. Have them add the words to their lists.
10. Then tell them you will give them some additional words (e.g., *fan, gill, pill, pan, tan, hill*) one at a time and they are to write the word under the word family in which it belongs.
11. After they have written the word, ask which word family it belongs to and then write the word on your white board.

Hints for Success

- Use words for the beginning activity that sound very different from one another.
- Enunciate the words clearly.
- If children write the word in the wrong category, allow them time to place it in the correct one.
- Point out words that can also be names. Ask if they remembered to write these words with an uppercase initial letter.
- Allow adequate thinking and writing time.
- Encourage children to write silently rather than blurting out the answer, so that everyone has a chance to think and learn.
- When time for the activity is up, have children chant the words in each word family. Ask if they can think of other words that belong in the family and add them to the list.
- As you complete a word family listing, ask for a volunteer to transfer the list to chart paper. Display it and have children add to it during the week.
- Add a word from those completed word families to the word wall for the week.
- Remind children in their decoding to check the ending of a word to see if it is like another word they already know.

AUTHOR'S CHAIR AND AUTHOR'S NIGHT

Providing a forum such as Author's Chair and Author's Night for children to share their writing with others inside and outside of the classroom conveys to children the idea that writing is a social act and that we write to affect the lives of others (Graves, 1994). Author's Chair is a classroom sharing session in which children are given opportunities to share their writing with others and to hear and respond to what others have written. Receiving feedback from others helps children know when a piece lacks clarity, detail, or interest.

Once children feel their written piece is ready for sharing with the group, they let the teacher know they'd like to participate in Author's Chair. It is scheduled several times a month or once a week. Children sit in front of the group, share their written work, and then lead and control a brief response time for comments and questions.

Graves discusses the problems inherent in shared writing. The most common is dull, pro forma questioning (e.g., "What's your favorite part?" "How did you happen to choose the topic?"), trivial and meaningless responses ("I liked . . . "), and ritualistic behavior such as having children clap at the end of the sharing, no matter what the quality of the presentation (we think just getting up in front of an audience is worthy of clapping). These are issues that teachers can discuss with children after they have had some experience in the process. With very young children, such responses might be expected; we can modify less helpful responses by simply modeling thoughtful questions and comments. This should not be an experience, however, that is dominated by the teacher.

Author's Night is an extension of the classroom activity. It can be held in the classroom, in the school media center, or somewhere in the community. For example, a community library or local bookstore might allow children to present to parents and others who might not visit the school. Published pieces of the children's work, complete with binding, book covers, and illustrations, can be made available for viewing by those who attend. Advance publicity about the event, decorations, and refreshments can become a part of the literacy activities carried out by the teacher and children, parents, and others in the community interested in sponsoring such events. During Author's Night, children who wish to do so take several minutes to tell their name (or are introduced by another child or by the teacher), the title of their work, and a reflective comment or two about it before reading it to the audience and then yielding the chair to a classmate.

Both Author's Chair and Author's Night involve all aspects of developing literacy concepts and skills: oral language, writing, and reading. When one evaluates the richness of the activity in terms of the breadth of concepts and skills that are enhanced, its value in the primary classroom cannot be overemphasized.

Main Purpose To provide opportunities for children to share their writing with others and respond to the writing of others, building a sense of the purpose of writing and also skill in writing clearly and interestingly for others

Materials A chair that is designated as Author's Chair
Children's work that is ready for sharing (readiness for sharing will vary significantly from that produced by very young children to that which is edited by older primary children)

Procedure 1. The class gathers in the large group space, with the young author coming to the front and sitting in the Author's Chair.
2. The author shares an aspect of his or her work that children can watch for—for example, "This week, a really wonderful thing happened in my family. I'm going to share that with you." "This story is about how we named our new puppy. Listen for what we called him!"
3. The author reads the piece, holding the book so that others can see the text and pictures if possible.

4. When finished, kindergartners can open up the discussion for questions or comments. For children in first or second grade, Graves (1994) suggests that they tell the class, "Okay, remembers, reminders, then questions . . . and only two reminders!" The "remembers" part of this is that children in the audience have a chance to tell what details of the reading they remember. This is an important comprehension strategy and ensures that they are listening to the reader. The author, on the other hand, must pay careful attention to whether or not the members of the audience are remembering the most important details and remind them of any they miss. The "reminders" are personal stories or thoughts that members of the audience were reminded of as they were listening to the author's story. Usually, so that this doesn't get out of hand, the author controls the number by setting it out in advance when opening up for questions. Finally, either the teacher or the author (preferably the child) can ask for any comments about the piece.

Hints for Success

- Before implementing the activity, model it with a piece that you have produced. Tell the children you are going to read a piece that you have written and that you will be asking them afterwards how many things they can remember and that they will also have a chance to ask you any question they wish about the piece. Talk about some guidelines for Author's Chair, basing them on the developmental levels of your children. Also review with them some active listening behaviors for members of an audience.
- Before children read their piece, encourage them to reflect on what they want to highlight.
- Limit a reading to no more than 5 minutes and the response period to no more than 10 minutes.
- Don't always wait for children to offer to participate. Although sharing from the Author's Chair should be a voluntary experience for a child, some children will participate only when encouraged to do so. During large-group sessions, you may want to ask children to go around the circle and tell what they are working on, and you can suggest that pieces near a finished state might be shared in Author's Chair.

Final Thoughts

Sometimes, because we know these previous strategies work so well with young children, we run the risk of oversimplifying the process of teaching them how to read and write, making it sound as if it's simple if you'll just do what is suggested. In reality, because we also work in school settings on a regular basis, we know that good teaching is rewarding but also the most challenging and difficult work there is. Occasionally, our best-planned lessons absolutely bomb, and we suffer the disappointment that comes when children don't catch on to a concept or enjoy the activity as much as we thought they would. Other times, quite wonderful and new spin-offs develop naturally out of children's excitement with a learning activity, and we feel as if we're cutting off a good thing when we finally have to move them on.

Your school year will probably be much like this. We're hopeful that the ideas and activities we have suggested here will contribute to the best of times—and also to best practices as you work to support children being literate and continually excited about what can be learned and expressed through words. Regie Routman is an author we admire greatly for the stand she takes in protecting children from inappropriate practices and for the treasure of ideas she has given to classroom teachers to keep children enthusiastic about literacy. She writes, "If we want our students to be excited about learning, they need to have teachers who relish learning, who are passionate about reading and other interests, and who find the classroom an inspiring and thrilling place to be" (Routman, 2003:22). We wish that for you.

Challenge Yourself

Organize your thoughts about your teaching this year by completing the following self appraisal:

1. Have I developed a good sense of the major outcomes I want for children during this school year?
2. Is there anything in my approach to teaching that should be eliminated or altered in order to create more excitement about reading and writing (and learning in general)?
3. How effectively do I use scaffolding techniques to teach new concepts to children?
4. Do I allow adequate practice time to cement certain literacy concepts and skills in each of my students?
5. How well do I model the concepts and skills I want children to learn, and how well do I monitor the gains children are making?

Suggested Sources for Additional Information

Clay, M. M. (1993). *Reading recovery: A guidebook for teachers in training.* Portsmouth, NH: Heinemann.

Lyons, C. A. (2003). *Teaching struggling readers.* Portsmouth, NH: Heinemann.

McCarrier, A., Pinnell, G. S., & Fountas, I. C. (1999). *Interactive writing: How language and literacy come together, k–2.* Portsmouth, NH: Heinemann.

Pinnell, G. S., & Fountas, I. C. (1998). *Word matters.* Portsmouth, NH: Heinemann.

Schickendanz, J. A. (1999). *Much more than the ABCs.* Washington, DC: National Association for the Education of Young Children.

Strickland, D. S., & Morrow, L. M. (2000). *Beginning reading and writing.* New York: Teachers College Press.

Children's Technology

Reader Rabbit's Interactive Reading Journey 1, ages 4–7, The Learning Company.

Reader Rabbit's Interactive Reading Journey 2, ages 5–8, The Learning Company.

Reader Rabbit's Reading Development Library, ages 5–7, The Learning Company.

Reading Blaster Jr., ages 4–7, Davidson & Associates, Inc.

The Amazing Writing Machine, ages 6–12, Broderbund Software, Inc.

Arthur's Birthday, Arthur's Teacher Troubles, The Berenstain Bears Get in a Fight (available in Spanish), ages 6–10, Living Books.

Early Learning (reading, writing, filling in letters), ages 5–7, Josten's Home Learning.

Explore a Story Series, ages 5–11, William K. Bradford.

First Connections: The Golden Book Encyclopedia, ages 5–9, Jostens Home Learning.

Imagination Express: Castle, Imagination Express: Neighborhood, Imagination Express: Ocean, Imagination Express: Pyramids, Imagination Express: Rainforest, Imagination Express: Time Trip U.S.A., ages 5–12, Edmark Corporation.

Make-a-Book, ages 4–12, Teacher Support Software.

Stickybear's Reading Room, ages 4–8, Optimum Resources, Inc.

Wiggins in Storyland, ages 6–10, Virgin Sound and Vision.

Moving toward Fluency

Developing Greater Self-Efficacy in Literacy

Michael Jordan with 5 Legs!!!

Alien Barneys: Their Song "I Love You" Drove Us Crazy!! We Were Hypnotized . . .

Real Dino Eggs Bought at Roadside Stand!

Sound like the *National Enquirer?* It's not! These imaginative headlines appeared in *The Liar's Bench,* a student publication put out by fifth graders at Leggett Elementary School in Waterford, Michigan. Complete with creative illustrations and reporter by-lines, the paper is a favorite of children, parents, and staff. Children work hard to produce an engaging, wildly *inaccurate* story (remember, this is called *The Liar's Bench*) that includes the customary journalistic *who, what, when, where,* and *how* components. These children pay close attention to the writing conventions they are learning in the classroom and take their stories through the writing process, conferring with their peers and teacher about style, word choice, dialogue usage, and strategies to write in a convincing and entertaining manner. They consult information books about their topic and page through reference books, carefully editing their work in a literacy-alive classroom that exudes good practice. Children in this classroom are not developing skills as a means to an end; they are developing skills they believe they *need* to complete a task—one they find intensely enjoyable.

What we are describing here is a group of students immersed in the final phase of literacy. It is a period that will stretch itself out over a lifetime, but the essential building blocks they must have will be gained or lost in these later primary years. Throughout this phase, children must develop the kinds of skills needed to exercise greater independence in applying the conventions that govern literacy. How such skills are honed and polished during these years will be the focus of this chapter.

As you read, keep in mind the following questions:

- What does "fluency" look like? Where is the later primary child in the overall literacy process?
- What can and *should* we be doing about children who are lagging behind seriously?
- What are the developmental needs of children in the later primary grades? In what ways are these children changing?
- What kind of learning context best promotes the acquisition of competencies and concepts of children in the transitional years of middle childhood? What role do adults play?
- What types of activities are most likely to get children involved in social interchange about language, motivate their curiosity, and provide emotional satisfaction as they move toward greater self-efficacy?

In this chapter, you will read about the characteristics of children who are moving toward fluency, the role of professionals in shaping that pathway, and the activities that are most likely to result in high levels of literacy following the middle childhood years.

Almost There: Children on Their Way to Fluency

As would be expected, *most* children in the later primary grades are dramatically different from younger children in the early stages of literacy. Their language development has become more sophisticated, and that competence can be seen in their ability to communicate what they are thinking, the expansion of their personal reading interests, and their written work. As a group, they will become more *strategic* in their approach to literacy, more *in control,* and more *automatic in skill and concept application.* In fact, this is what fluency and functional literacy are all about—a smoother, easier flow in connection to every aspect of receiving and expressing communication.

Fluent Readers

Colin is a story reader! He can't wait to get at his latest book. Now in the third grade, he finds himself spending more of his free time devouring the gold mine of books he has discovered—and all for free! He is now allowed to ride his bike down to the library, which is only six blocks from his house. He feels he'll never be able to read all the good books they have, especially the new chapter books by Dav Pilkey (Captain Underpants) *and Tony Abbott* (Secrets of Droon). *These have become his favorite authors.*

Children in this stage definitely have a new relationship with print. Because most have developed a fairly solid understanding about its basic functions, they can enjoy a wider variety of material, including information text. Automaticity has set in and so they now read without worrying about the *sound* a particular letter combination makes. Instead of just decoding accurately and reading the words quickly, most children at this stage now read with more expression, employing prosodic features "that account for tonal and rhythmic aspects of language." These two important elements, automaticity and prosody, contribute significantly to children's understanding of what they are reading as they more effortlessly group phrases together in meaningful ways (Morrow, Gambrell, & Pressley, 2003:131). When they do have problems with decoding, they are experiencing greater independence in using the strategies they have learned about the schematic systems of print. Tompkins (2001) has identified a number of strategies that children pick and choose from in trying to make sense out of print. These are summarized here.

TAPPING PRIOR KNOWLEDGE   Children who have developed fairly extensive vocabularies, have a wide range of life experiences, and are familiar with many kinds of literary genres are able to make swifter connections to what they are reading. This ability to get meaning out of what they are reading allows them to extend their existing information stores and strengthens all their subsequent contacts with print. It is perhaps the *most* critical strategy influencing children's comprehension and ability to remember what they have read.

PREDICTING   Children find this strategy useful for predicting what a story might be about and guessing what's going to happen prior to reading at certain junctures in a story. These are then weighed against what actually happens, helping children to maintain their interest in and focus in what they are reading. Children also learn to use previewing techniques (e.g., looking at headings and subheadings) prior to reading informational text and to raise questions that guide their reading.

ORGANIZING IDEAS   Early on, children become acquainted with the fact that all stories are organized into a beginning, middle, and end. Later, they learn to use a variety of graphic organizers to categorize story elements and to sequence events within stories.

FIGURING OUT UNKNOWN WORDS   Children develop a variety of methods, such as knowing when to skip over an unfamiliar word and then using context later to pick it up; they also use strategies such as word identification skills, using reference materials, or simply asking someone else.

VISUALIZING   As children develop the technique of visualizing, they learn to create mental pictures while reading, perhaps placing themselves in the role of one of the characters or thinking about how they might solve such a dilemma.

MAKING CONNECTIONS   Children relate what they are reading to their own lives by recalling similarities between experiences they have had or between characters in a story and people in their own world. Also, they make intertext connections with other works of a particular author, with other versions of a story, or with other texts they have read.

APPLYING FIX-UP STRATEGIES AND REVISING MEANING   Realizing that they are not comprehending what they're reading, children will resort to a number of different strategies to try to catch up. These include continuing to read but with greater conscious focus, rereading an entire section, gaining additional meaning from the pictures, skipping ahead, and stopping and discussing the material with a peer or the teacher.

MONITORING   Children may apply this strategy unconsciously, becoming aware of it only when they realize they are not comprehending what they are reading.

PLAYING WITH LANGUAGE   Children pay attention to figurative and novel uses of language in the material they are reading, including idioms, jokes, riddles, metaphors, similes, personification, sensory language, rhyme, alliteration, and invented words.

GENERALIZING   Children draw general conclusions about the "big picture" by remembering ideas and information and mentally putting these together. They are more likely to remember these than details when describing the theme of a story or registering their opinions about it.

EVALUATING While children are reading, they are simultaneously making judgments about the content and value of the material; afterwards, they reflect on what they have read and also on their own reading behaviors.

All of these comprehension strategies are designed to increase children's meaning-making skills and strategies to understand and appreciate text. Typically, teachers will want to teach these skills one at a time and should always model them, one process at a time, before expecting children to employ them. Prediction is a good one to start with, and that might be followed by any of the others. It may take an entire year for a teacher to highlight each of these, and as new strategies are added to a child's repertoire, the teacher should continue to encourage the student to demonstrate the previously taught skills until he or she begins to do it without prompting (Block & Pressley, 2003).

Visualizing is an especially rich strategy to get children mentally involved in what they are reading. Debbie Miller (2002:80–85) makes ten or so copies of three or four short poems she knows children will love, reads each poem aloud several times, asking children to "listen carefully to think about which poem creates the most vivid mental images for you." She then has the children take a copy of the poem they've chosen, gives them about 10 minutes to depict the image that was in their head and then to share their work. She then clusters together the children who have chosen the same poem to share their images and talk about what they noticed. A final component of this visualizing lesson is to have the small groups report back to the large group about the different schemas and words elicited among the children by the poem. The imaging that children do in Miller's room also includes dramatizing a selection, rereading a poem after the children have shared their images with a peer, and having them pay attention to both sets of images on the reread. These opportunities to verbalize the mental pictures that print produces in their heads—to invent phrases such as "the stream squiggles down the mountain" and "the golden sun sets behind the purple mountains in flashes of pink and red"—begin to appear in another literacy component, their writing.

When children are able to apply many of these strategies and also to recognize thousands of words on sight, they shift their attention toward making sense of what is embedded in story structure: character development, main ideas, setting, events, problem, and solution.

This new emphasis on comprehension has implications for classroom instruction. For children to connect with what they are reading, teachers must help them appreciate the important connections between prior knowledge and new information. This requires taking as much time to introduce material and talk about what children already know (and *almost* know) as for moving through the information itself. It also requires a solid debriefing period after reading to see how well children have understood and organized relevant pieces of information and how that translates to their ability to apply it.

Children in a fluency stage continue to read for pleasure, but they are choosier about what they *want* to read. They have come to know more about their favorite authors and the illustrators who make the books more exciting. They are more apt to choose materials that range farther away from their background knowledge and personal experiences, and their repertoire of selections is widening.

Their growing cognition is reflected in their ability and desire to wade through much longer books, deal with more complex characters and plots, and retain and apply the ideas for writing activities. It can also be seen in their tendency to be more reflective and critical about what they read. Because they are developing their own opinions, they no longer always agree with an author and are more articulate in expressing their perspectives. In addition, a much more sophisticated use of front and end matter in books is apparent; they more frequently use tables of contents and indexes to gain information they need about text.

The good readers have become active and strategic about their reading. Block and Pressley (2003:114) describe these intentional readers:

- They generally read from the beginning to the end of a text, although they sometimes jump around, looking ahead in anticipation of information, or looking back to clarify an idea not understood on the first pass.
- They encounter information especially relevant to their goal in reading the text (e.g., to find out the president's perspective on educational vouchers).
- They anticipate what might be in the text based on their prior knowledge about the topic of the text.
- They monitor as they read; that is, while reading, they are very aware of which parts of a text are important, and which ideas are vague or confusing. Such self-monitoring guides decision making during reading (e.g., deciding to slow up, read faster, or skip sections of text).
- They reflect on what they read, for example, thinking about how they might use the ideas in the text. Such reflections can be interpretive, often affected by prior knowledge and present opinions.

This remarkable transformation in children at the fluent stage is not confined to their reading. We see it reflected in all areas of their literacy development and especially in an almost spontaneous increase in the quality and quantity of their writing.

The Fluent Writer

Gail is serving on her school district's literacy committee. She has been teaching in the same district for 18 years, and when interviewed about the way the writing curriculum has changed, she says there has been a "180 degree transformation," particularly in the late elementary grades.

"It used to amount to teaching them handwriting. Now, we talk in terms of journaling, writing across the curriculum, a writing process program, and writing workshop. I don't let a day go by without modeling writing with my third graders. I've learned a tremendous amount about writing myself, and I know my kids are learning, too."

And so they are. In Gail's classroom and in others throughout her school, the effects of a carefully crafted writing program are clearly evident. The children coming into the later primary program have been immersed in meaningful writing activities on a daily basis and surrounded by writing demonstrations by knowledgeable teachers who:

- Expect children to take responsibility for their writing and use it in a variety of contexts
- Provide feedback that is appropriate to children's writing development
- Recognize approximations and temporary spelling as natural steps in learning
- Collaborate with children in working through new learning (Stewig & Jett-Simpson, 1995:249).

The result of this approach to writing in the emerging and early stages of children's development in this school has paid off and can be seen in Gail's third graders. For the most part, they have good phonemic awareness, take pride in their ability to spell conventionally (although their first drafts still contain some interesting inventions), and are fairly skillful in using reference materials to support their writing. They are able to think about topics for their writing without always needing a prompt, and they know something about many different types of writing. When they have to call on their writing skills to complete assignments in other areas of the curriculum, they do so with increasing confidence.

At least once weekly, Gail confers with each of them about the writing they are doing. During these mini-conferences, she notices that their approximations are far less frequent. They are increasingly placing punctuation where it belongs, writing more legibly, and expressing complete thoughts. Their paragraphs are more confined to one topic, and they seem to be getting the idea about leading off with a topic sentence. Lately, she finds that, overall, their writing is more interesting, since many of the children have begun to be a bit more creative about their sentence beginnings and plot development. She knows the children need as much practice as possible in working with the word-processing programs on the computer, and they are finding it easier to use the technology available to publish and illustrate their work.

Perhaps the thing Gail likes best about how these children are developing is the independence they are demonstrating in editing, proofreading their own work, and providing feedback to their peers. She believes that the time she has provided for this has let them develop the ability to be more analytical about the writing process and to sequence their ideas in a more logical way. When she thinks about the transformations that have taken place in the approach to writing in her school, she feels good about the fact that she has been a part of it and that almost every child in her classroom is well on the way to becoming an effective reader and writer.

Those Who Are Not "Getting It": Children with Learning Problems and Disabilities

You'll notice that as we describe children in this stage, we say that *many* of them are *almost* there. We add those qualifiers for two reasons. Almost all of the children in the later primary grades have emerging and early literacy skills well in hand, but a small percentage clearly do not. These children need continued instruction and practice in prerequisite skills. They are at the tail end of a natural distribution of learners at this age—a tail end that we are out to diminish. Although they have average abilities, they may have moved around frequently or had spotty experiences in previous classrooms relative to skill teaching in the early years. Some are struggling with chaotic family situations or have behavioral patterns that are at odds with learning. Others have developmental histories that suggest they take somewhat longer to achieve concepts and skills than do other children but have few problems once they are provided with additional time.

Also included in this group is an even smaller percentage of children who aren't "getting it." Some are children who can decode beautifully—but simply can't understand what they are reading. When, despite good instruction, comprehension breaks down frequently in a child, there are two categories of factors that have to be considered in determining what's not working (O'Donnell & Wood, 1998).

Factors in the Reader

1. Lack of experience (world experience, language experience, cultural experience, or literacy experience) or adequate prior knowledge
2. Lack of interest in the material that is provided, resulting in a lack of motivation to concentrate on it
3. Lack of fluency

4. Lack of metacognitive awareness—that is, awareness about one's own thinking and how to solve a problem at hand

Factors in the Text

1. Concept density—material that contains too many concepts in a short amount of text, especially if the concepts are outside of the reader's own experience.
2. Text that is not reader-friendly because it is organized in ways that make it difficult for the reader to see a relationship among the ideas that are presented. This includes text that has a faulty layout or visual presentation—lacking an adequate introduction, relevant visual aids, boldface topics, and summary statements.
3. The author's style may be unfamiliar and confusing to students, particularly if it contains complicated syntax, vocabulary, or technical terms.
4. Poor readability, in terms of length of sentences and difficulty of vocabulary, can lead to comprehension difficulties.

Obviously, the material we select for the children in our classrooms has a great deal to do with how engaged they can be with it. We have a better chance of helping them to be successful if we make available a wide variety of content they find appealing and personally and culturally relevant. We also enable them when we choose reading material that is well written, age-appropriate, and highly readable.

In addition to the children described here, there are children who exhibit a more comprehensive and debilitating set of problems that make literacy learning a desperately trying experience for both them and their teachers. They may demonstrate average reasoning abilities in other content areas, have good vocabularies, and even be exceptionally "bright" in the way they attack nonliteracy tasks. Lyon (1998:12) notes that many are "children with robust oral language experience, average to above average intelligence, and frequent interactions with literacy activities," but they still have difficulty learning to read and write. These children are likely to be diagnosed as "learning disabled," a special education category that has tripled since the late 1970s. That ballooning may be the result of better diagnostic procedures in school districts, but it also reflects the increasing number of children coming into the classroom from less-than-supportive environments. However, for parents who have provided nurturing beginnings and whose children are obviously bright but unable to learn, the oft-cited "epidemic" is both real and heartbreaking (Wingert & Kantrowitz, 1997:58) .

As was pointed out in Chapter 1, when these learning disabilities are the result of different brain organization, we must collaborate with specialists who have expertise in alternative approaches to teaching and learn-ing. With the advances we are seeing in brain-imaging technology, we expect we will have answers in the near future to help us pin down a more exact picture of any one child's disabilities. Until then—and *even* then—we must be creative in helping these children strategize ways to build strength in literacy and preserve their motivation to keep trying. Most important, we need to keep a close watch on every child's progress so that no child is floundering without support. Teachers will want to assess skill levels often and carefully. In addition, a literacy curriculum must consist of what children *need for literacy* rather than "grade-level" material. Some children who are having difficulty will still require regular instruction and practice with some of the same phonological awareness activities described in Chapters 4 and 5. Unless we stay within each child's ability to learn and to use developmentally appropriate approaches and materials, we waste our time and theirs. We also frustrate them, actually contributing to the meltdown we see in many children who find reading and writing laborious, uninteresting, and something that must be done only when forced to do so.

The Role of the Teacher in Developing Learning Contexts That Promote Continued Skill and Concept Attainment

Even at this stage, when most children become increasingly independent and able to use the strategies taught to them in the early phases, we need to maintain our intensive focus on literacy skill and concept building. The tendency to be content with already developed competencies and to shift major amounts of attention to other parts of the curriculum would be a mistake. However, because of developmental changes in the child, we may want to alter our instructional approach somewhat to fit better the learning characteristics of the later primary child.

The middle childhood years have been described as transitional years. Children are going through major cognitive changes that allow them to become "true readers and writers" (Wortham, 1998:342). This is an age at which children experience a shift toward more logical thinking and ability to think abstractly about ideas and possibilities. There is significant growth in their focusing abilities, information-gathering skills, and long-term memory storage and retrieval. Their organizing skills are more efficient. In addition to their increased ability to analyze and clarify information, they are becoming more capable of inference and combining facts to produce new information.

In addition to cognitive reorganization, these children are experiencing significant interpersonal and intrapersonal growth. Adults are becoming less important in their world, while their peer group and achieving personal independence are becoming all-important. Even as they are

Having fun with literacy: "The one and only game show!"

Reader's theater group.

enjoying more confidence in many areas of their lives, they are worrying more about not knowing the right answer and not fitting into the group at school. Children want and need to fit in, and it is important that they do so; it is in the peer group that children achieve a sense of belonging, learn new skills, and feel valued beyond their own family (Kostelnik, Whiren, Soderman, Gregory, & Stein, 2004). Teachers not only will want to provide plenty of opportunities for cooperative and collaborative learning but also will want to observe closely for children who are experiencing peer rejection. Some children will need coaching in negotiating conflict and developing friendship skills. For this reason, many later primary teachers use friends and friendship building as topics for

thematic study, thereby promoting skill and concept building in both the language and social domains.

Many children in this age group become increasingly vocal about what they would define as a "good learning experience." They are more inclined than early primary children to attend selectively to classroom activities they feel are useful and interesting—and to opt out mentally of those they perceive as less personally relevant.

As children move through these in-between years, their basic needs can best be met in classrooms responsive to their psychological needs for *belonging, power, freedom,* and *fun* (Glasser, 1992). We've seen such schools. These are learning environments where teachers actively teach, but they are more inclined to do so with fewer

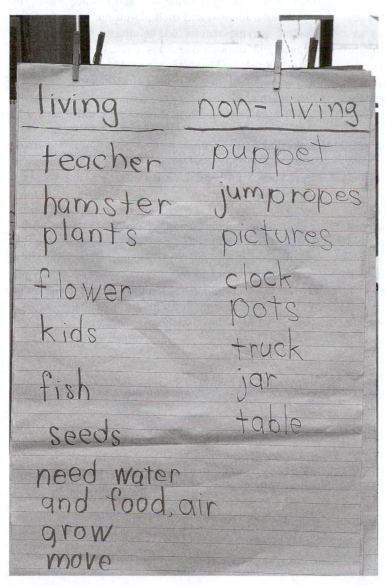

Tapping prereading knowledge.

large-group presentations. Instead, their predominant mode of interaction with children is one of conferencing on an individual basis and with small groups of children in mini-workshops centering on particular concepts. Children are encouraged to use their prior knowledge, life experiences, and current interests as the basis of what they speak about, read, and write. Because of this, such children are often able to interpret for themselves what they have to do to improve their own literacy-learning agenda (Koeller & Mitchell, 1997). In addition to continuing an active teaching approach to close the gaps in skills and concepts, effective teachers at this level spend a great deal *more* of their time observing, encouraging, conferencing with children, facilitating, scaffolding, and assessing. In short, they continue with all of the roles they would have played with younger children, but appropriately place less emphasis on directed teaching and more on building independent learners.

Children in middle childhood are avid learners. They should be encouraged to explore as many literacy avenues as possible. They should critique and produce pamphlets, monographs, song lyrics, commercials, and other forms of ads. Classroom activities should integrate the examination and production of instructional manuals, memos, e-mail, spreadsheets, databases, booklets, plays and melodramas, employment and other "form" applications, resumes, surveys, petitions, and assessment measures. The list is endless. The Internet, web sites, and CD-ROMs should become common resources for accessing information. Our goal should be to expose children to as many varied forms of literacy as possible and to provide the kinds of classroom experiences that will hold them in good stead for twenty-first-century careers and satisfying leisure pursuits.

For the English learners in your classroom, you will want to encourage them to continue reading in their native language, which will strengthen their automaticity and prosody in both languages. If they've spent time reading print they enjoy, phonics instruction probably isn't necessary. However, word study can be highly beneficial. For example, a Hispanic child can be given a list of 5–10 key vocabulary words and a Spanish/English dictionary with the task to define the words first in Spanish and then in English. The next task involves writing definitions, both in Spanish and English, and looking for any similarities in word roots or derivations (Krashen, 2003).

Graves and Fitzgerald (2003b:102) recommend the frequent use of a scaffolded reading experience (SRE). This consists of an initial planning phase during which the teacher assists the child in relating to the material by tying it to prior knowledge and background experiences. This is also the time to remind the child about helpful strategies such as summarizing, paraphrasing, and imaging. The next phase, implementation, includes such prereading activities as previewing the text or chapter, going over major concepts strategies, and talking about key vocabulary, idioms, and multiple-meaning words. Postreading activities can include helping the student to build connections through questions and discussion, writing, drama (Reader's Theater is especially valuable), and art activities. Children can benefit from creating their own dictionaries, Venn diagrams, and graphic organizers. Reteaching material may be necessary, and it would be better to use fewer selections and to delve more deeply and completely in them than to have English learners move at a surface level through the "normal" amount of text. This is probably true for some English-speaking children as well.

The activities that follow are designed to sustain the earlier phonemic awareness of children moving toward greater fluency and also to provide exercises in meaning making as they evaluate text and construct their own. The activities can be adapted to the various levels of capability that can be found in any middle childhood classroom. We hope you find them useful and that the children in your classrooms will find them meaningful.

SPELLING PATTERN RECOGNITION TEAMS

This simple rhyming game can be done one or more times a week, and takes only about 15 minutes to complete. It is fun and adaptable to all learning levels. It not only reinforces phonemic awareness as children develop rhyming words, but also builds a knowledge base of spelling pattern words and reinforces vocabulary in contextual use.

The basic objective of this game is that children will learn to recognize different spelling patterns through the application of rhyming words. Although we are suggesting teams for this activity, teachers who are opposed to competitive activities may want to use it as a whole-group or small-group activity without making comparisons between the groups. We have found that children in grades 3 through 5 are motivated by competing in groups and find such activities fun; however, the competitive aspect of the game should not be overemphasized, nor should individual competition be encouraged for any classroom games.

Main Purpose To extend children's phonological awareness and conventional spelling ability

Materials Whiteboard or chart paper
Marker
Paper and pencils for children
Dictionaries

Procedure
1. Write a word on the board or chart paper.
2. Divide the class up into teams containing three to five children each. Have the groups select a team name, and list these on the board for a competitive game.
3. Give the teams two minutes to come up with as many words as they can think of that rhyme with the word that you have displayed on the board. The team must be able to define the word if asked to do so, and it must also be spelled correctly if it is to be counted.
4. Ask the children to put down their pencils at the end of the two-minute period. If engaging in a competitive game, choose one team to go first. Have the individual members of the team give you all the rhyming words they wrote on their lists. Delete the words that are repeated more than once. Do the same with the next team.
5. Request a definition from children for those words that sound alike but are spelled differently and have different meanings. Write the correct spelling on the board as you go along. For example, if the team offers the word *read* to rhyme with *bead*, ask for clarification by saying, "What kind of *read* (*reed*) do you mean? The kind you do with books or the kind used with a clarinet?"
6. The team that generates the most rhyming words is the winner. Teams could be maintained for a week or two, graphing the results, and then changed so that all children have an opportunity to interact with one another.
7. As a final instructional step, you might have the children sort the listed words into groups. The preceding example might have the *-ead, -eed, -eid, -ede* patterns emerge as part of this lesson. These might be posted on chart paper for a wall reminder.

157

"We need teamwork today," says Mr. Metzko, beginning the class's morning group gathering. "Let's count off for a spelling activity I have for you."

After the children count off and get into their respective groups, he has each team create a name for itself and then records the names of the groups at the top of three columns on a nearby whiteboard: Spin-Masters, Dynamic Dynos, Night Stalkers.

"All right," he says. "I have a challenge for you, and you will have only two minutes to do this initial task. I will write a word on the board and give you a definition. Then, in the time allotted—remember, only two minutes [he grins at the exaggerated groans from the children], each of you will individually write as many words as you can that rhyme with my word. You must know a correct definition of the word if you use it for your list. Otherwise, someone from another team can challenge and you will not be given credit for it. Of course, if someone from another team challenges and you are able to *meet* that challenge, a point will be deducted from his or her team's score. Also, you must spell the word correctly in order to have it count. At the end of the two minutes, I'll give your team another two minutes to discuss and consolidate your lists. We'll see who can generate the most rhyming words. Here we go. The word is *cowl*, c - o - w - l. It actually has two meanings: a monk's cloak with a hood, or a large tub for holding water . C - o - w - l, *cowl*. Go for it!"

The children work hard for two minutes and then confer with one another in their teams for an additional two minutes. Coming back together, the teams list words such as *yowl, growl, crawl, trowel, howl, prowl, bowel, dowel, towel, vowel, jowl,* and *foul.* They determine which team has generated the most words, and then Mr. Metzko asks if there are words they thought of that seemed close at first but were rejected after more thought. Some of the children offer words such as *follow, pillow, yellow.* He then has them suggest ways that the words can be categorized and has individual children come up to the whiteboard to circle with a colored marker all the words that fit together under the categories they have identified. "Ready for one more?" he asks? "Ready!" the children retort.

- Use words that correlate either with a unit of study or possibly a story being read together in class.
- Follow up the game by asking children to choose a certain number of their "favorite" rhyming words and use them correctly in a sentence format. Depending on the level of ability in the class, ask children to create a poem using several of the rhyming words. Children can share their poetry if they wish, and a class book of rhymes can be compiled.

BUDDY BIOGRAPHIES

Buddy Biographies uses an interviewing technique as an initial step in outlining a descriptive written piece about another child in the classroom. The activity offers a fun, interactive way for students to develop both writing and speaking skills. Although what we describe here centers around a study of friendship, the strategy could be adapted in a variety of ways by having children modify it for other areas of study that might involve interviewing members of their family or people in the community. To add choice for students, encourage them to think of creative forms in which to present their biographies. These can include poetry, a short story or essay, audiovisual presentations, artwork, or even an obituary! It's a great way for children to find out some interesting details about others and to develop skills they will need later in life.

Main Purpose For children to write for a variety of purposes, including gaining information and presenting information
To enhance children's effective oral language skills and ability to formulate and answer questions

Materials Interview form
Paper
Writing tools
Tape recorder (optional)
Video camera (optional)

Procedure 1. Lead a discussion with children about the kinds of situations in real life in which people have to interview another person to gain information (e.g., on television when a tragedy has occurred or someone has accomplished something special; when people are talk show hosts; when someone has to introduce another person who is speaking at a conference, dinner, or other social event). Extend the discussion to times when a person might interview another person for a book he or she is writing about that person—a biography (here is a good opportunity to focus on the differences between an autobiography and a biography). Show children an example of some biographies that are at their level, and note that these will be in the reading center for their use during the next couple of weeks.

2. Tell the children that you will be pairing them up for the activity, which has three parts:
   a. They will be interviewing one another to find out more about what the other person is like and likes to do, using a question–answer form that will be provided to record the answers. This form is made up ahead of the activity and could be titled, "Finding Out about Friends." It could include such questions as the following:

   What is your full name?
   What is your age? Birth date?
   Who are the people in your family?
   What is your favorite color? Favorite food?
   What might we find you doing when you are alone?
   What do you like to do the most with others?
   What is your most valued treasure?
   What was one of the happiest times in your life? The saddest time?
   What is your favorite subject in school?
   What was a memorable experience for you?
   What do you see yourself doing in 20 years?

   The form could include a space for additional questions that the interviewer could add prior to doing the interview.
   b. Interviewers will use that information to "introduce" the person they have interviewed to the rest of the class, giving a brief summary of the person's life and other interesting information. Here, discuss with them strategies and styles that talk show hosts and reporters use to make their introductions personal and interesting, rather than simply listing the answers to their questions.

    c. They will develop a written buddy biography from the recorded facts and their discussion with the other person during the interviewing process.

    3. Allow blocks of writing time for the children to develop their pieces through the formal writing process.

Classroom Application   "This week, during our writing time, Brian's mother, Mrs. Judge, will be in the writing area to demonstrate a new software package called *Timeliner,*" says Ms. Seaman. "There is a sign-up sheet there, and I'd appreciate your putting your name in a slot that's convenient for you. The package is something that I'd like to have each one of you learn to use. It allows you to create a timeline of historical, present, and future events over a segment of time. Let me show you a sample of what it can do."

She shares a printout depicting her own computerized timeline, showing some events in her life prior to teaching at Challenger Elementary, some events that have occurred during the time she has been teaching in the building, and still another section on the continuum listing a few things she is hoping to accomplish in the future. Each event has a date attached to it. "I thought this software might be especially useful for the buddy biographies you're involved in writing right now, a nice graphic to include in your finished product. Some of you may elect not to use it that way, but I'd like to have you at least try it out. It will call for taking some of the information you've gained about your buddy in the interviews you've done, attaching a date to those events, and then setting it up on a continuum just as I've done here. Pretty neat, huh? I believe we can even color code these three sections and print with the color printer. Mrs. Judge has shown me how to work it, and Brian also knows how to run it, so if you need some help when Mrs. Judge isn't here, we'll be glad to get you on track."

Hints for Success

- Talk about biographies and read some short examples prior to initiating the activity. Point out that biographies are written in a variety of styles that range from dry and formal to highly entertaining and engaging.
- On video, bring in short clips of different television personalities so that students can watch them and then discuss similarities and differences in presentation styles and strategies to promote audience interest.
- Tape record or videotape the interview sessions. Encourage children to speak with expression and to bring in props that mirror the special qualities they each have (a favorite hat, stuffed animal, food, piece of sports equipment, etc.). Videotapes of individual performances can be a neat addition to the student portfolios (see Chapter 8).
- Bind the individually developed pieces into a Biography Book that is placed in the school library and can be checked out by children and their families.

LANGUAGE DETECTIVES

This activity is a spin-off on the morning message activity used with younger children. Here, older primary children get to exercise their ability to detect problems in written language: errors in punctuation, capitalization, indenting, grammatical usage, spelling, sentence structure, and clarity. Instead of the teacher or a peer acting as a proofreader of what they produce, the tables are turned, and they get to correct the teacher's (intentional) errors. There are many forms that this activity may take, as well as a variety of strategies to focus on during implementation. It is typically done on an individual basis initially and then discussed and corrected as a whole group as a follow-up.

Once children are well acquainted with the activity, the teacher can assign pairs of children to become responsible for developing the next day's sample to be used. In purposefully constructing a sample to challenge others, they will have to think carefully about the correct forms of whatever they are producing—always a powerful learning experience. The activity can be made more or less challenging, depending on the skill levels of the children. With later primary children, the teacher can even structure competitive teams and keep a graph of how many errors each team can spot and correct on a daily basis. Children can also be asked to work individually on discovering and correcting the errors, with the teacher using this from time to time as an assessment strategy to get at individual conceptualization of writing conventions (see Figure 6.1 on becoming a language detective).

Main Purpose To have children learn more about conventions used in written language
To have children become independent in their ability to correct errors in their own work and assist others in doing so

Materials Spiral-bound notebook in which to record corrected versions of daily sample
Whiteboard or chart and easel to display the written language sample
Markers
Pencils

Procedure 1. Establish a set procedure for the process in your classroom on a daily basis. For example, the teacher can post the sample in a designated area of the room each morning and establish the job of correcting it

---

Halloween Language Detective

October _____, 2005

dear count dracula

halloween is lurking just around the corner the holiday wood not be complete without the party held at the home of mr and mrs b brave

we will bob for bats play musical brooms and pin the tail on the goblin you will hav a chance to visit frank n stein and c a ghost, to

the fun begins at the stroke of midnight on saturday october 31 were just dying two see you their

eerily yours

brave

Figure 6.1 Becoming a language detective.

as part of the morning routine or as children enter the room to begin their day.

2. Prior to the children coming into the room, produce a writing sample and display it in the designated place. The sample may consist of a sentence or two containing errors in capitalization, punctuation, spelling, or run-on sentences, depending on the ability level of your students. You may wish to write a personalized message pertaining to upcoming events for the day (including students' names) or you may want to reinforce vocabulary and facts the children are studying by including them in the piece.

3. Following the independent completion of the exercise, work in large group to correct the piece by having students volunteer to come up and make a correction. Have other children follow along with their notebooks to make any additional corrections they did not discover independently.

4. As students' ability levels increase, continue to challenge them by extending the difficulty level of the mistakes and kinds of errors.

Hints for Success

- At the beginning, keep it simple. Include mistakes that are easily identifiable by your group of students.
- Demonstrate the process in large group before asking them to do it individually. All of the errors can be corrected in large group with either the teacher or the children coming up to make the corrections. The teacher can then move to having the children tell where there is an error and having the teacher circle the place but not make the correction. The children then have a hint about how many errors there are but must make judgments themselves about how to correct them. Once they have had sufficient practice in doing this, the teacher can move to having children work completely independently in making their corrections in their journals.
- Vary the format. For example, use it to write a letter to have the children think about the component parts. Thus, you are able to reinforce indentation of paragraphs and paragraph development, as well as their general editing skills.
- Periodically assess progress in identifying mechanical writing errors by using this as an assessment of individual capabilities.
- Be sure to ask children to rewrite the sentence in the **correct** form. Having them rewrite the incorrect sentence first, followed by the correct way, will only reinforce bad writing habits. The only exception to this rule is when children are working in a team to think up a piece of writing containing purposeful errors in order to catch their classmates.

WRITER'S WORKSHOP WITH PEER CONFERENCING

This activity carries children through the writing process and is made up of the components of prewriting and drafting, drafting/revising, rewriting/editing, and publishing/sharing (for more information about this process, see Galda, Cullinan, & Strickland, 1993, at the end of this chapter under "Suggested Resources for Further Reading"). Writer's Workshop occurs daily at a regularly scheduled time each day for 50 to 75 minutes (remember, if we want to produce children who can write well, they must have opportunities to write every day). While there are a number of variations, the general format usually consists of a 10- to 15-minute initial mini-lesson focusing on a particular writing skill or strategy, writing for 30 to 45 minutes, and 10 to 15 minutes at the end of the session for sharing. During the mini-lesson, the teacher may share a skill such as use of the comma, use of quotation marks, form of a business letter, or some other skill that is needed in the type of writing being done. Students are reminded of the rules for Writer's Workshop. During the actual writing period, children work at their own pace, moving through all the writing stages. At this time, the teacher moves about the room conferencing with individual children for anywhere from one to five minutes, questioning, listening to plans, and helping with revisions and editing. Some teachers prefer to meet with one-fifth of their students on a given day so that each child receives individual attention sometime during the week.

At sharing time, children are encouraged to share drafts of their work or finished publications. Classmates are encouraged to comment, ask questions, ask for clarification, or even offer suggestions. This phase of the workshop is meant primarily to encourage the writer with positive comments about what listeners found especially enjoyable.

During Writer's Workshop, children are encouraged to be "real authors" as they write about things that are meaningful to them, developing their own sense of voice and style. The activity is easily adaptable to fit the needs of learners at the emerging and early stages of literacy, but it is at the near-fluency stage that the writing process gains growing significance as children work to convey meaning through the written word. It is also at this level that children can begin to act as editors for other children's work and to gain additional skill from conferencing with their peers.

Typically, Writer's Workshop begins with the teacher modeling some aspect of the writing process and talking out loud about the decisions he or she has to make about print while actually writing something that is personally meaningful. For example, Mr. Garrison tells children that today he has brought in five or six ghost stories, all written and illustrated by the same author, who is a favorite of his. He chooses one of them to read, then stops reading after a certain point when the story is at a critical stage, temporarily disappointing the children, who are eager to have him finish it so they can find out what happens. He tells them: "Anything is possible. In fact, I'm going to create the ending myself! What do you think might be a possible ending?"

After they have generated some ideas and he has written them down on the easel beside him, he proceeds to model how he would end the piece, thinking out loud about what is possible given the events that have already happened and the nature of the characters that has already been established in the first part of the story. He attempts to use the word *ghoul,* writing it as *goul, goal, ghoal*—and then finally says, "Arrmin, would you hand me the dictionary?" and looks it up. He finishes the piece with a satisfied look on his face and says, "Of course, there were lots of ways I could have ended it, but this was a good one!" He invites anyone who is interested to write their own ending to the story, create an entirely new ghost story, or continue working on a piece of their own that is already in progress. The choice is theirs, since this is Writer's Workshop and the most important thing is for them to be writing about something that interests them.

During the period that the children are writing, Mr. Garrison moves about the classroom, acting as a facilitator, working with students individually or in small groups, and focusing on any areas of difficulty or teaching a brief on-the-spot lesson. Writer's Workshop ends by having four or five children share what they have written that day, including any works in progress.

To extend this process another step further, the teacher can integrate peer counseling into the process, adding another dimension and helping children to become less reliant on the teacher as the only person in the classroom who can be helpful in learning something new.

Main Purpose	For the children to develop an understanding of the writing process: brainstorming, composing, revising, editing, publishing, and sharing
Materials	Stories to generate ideas (story starters) Chart paper and easel Overhead projector Paper and pencils
Procedure	

1. Begin by sharing a story with the class, allowing much discussion and connecting of children's own experience with the book.

2. Explain the purpose for writing relative to the shared story. This may be an extension of the story, such as changing the ending or creating a sequel—or creating a character similar to the one found in the story but with an entirely different story line involved.

3. Generate ideas together, creating imagery for the children and listing all their suggestions about what might be done.

4. Have students begin drafting their story, allowing enough time that they can produce something to share with a small group of peers at a follow-up session. The follow-up session could be scheduled for the next day or the next week, depending on the ability of the children to produce an almost-finished piece of work that can be shared. It should not be scheduled so far in the future that children have lost interest in the piece they are writing.

5. At the follow-up session, explain that children will be meeting in groups of five to share what they have composed so far. Be specific about what should go on in the group and what you expect to have happen. For example, Mr. Garrison expects the following:
   - The "audience" will list three things they liked about the story.
   - The writer will have an opportunity to ask the "audience" questions about problems encountered in writing the piece.
   - Audience members will make one suggestion for the writing and will write this suggestion down on a slip of paper. The author will save these and attach them to his or her final copy.

6. Again, allow sufficient time for children to make changes in their work and publicize the next scheduled peer conferencing follow-up meeting.

7. Have children exchange papers with a peer who will use a Peer Conferencing Checklist to respond to the writer's work (see Figure 6.2). Peer conferencing can also be conducted in small groups. Patricia Kostell, an educational consultant working with school districts in South Carolina has found that teaching children to use the "talk of writers" is an empowering experience for them. She advocates helping children not only use story-writing rubrics such as those in Figure 6.3 and editing checklists (see Chapter 7) to improve their own writing, but to teach them how to provide more helpful feedback to one another. For example, 8-year-old Romas is sitting at the table with his teacher and two of his peers. After having listened to what Mrs. Sternquist always calls "writer talk" with them a number of times about their own work, the children get to practice it with each other today. They're excited about playing this more grown-up role. Romas is confident enough to go first and after he has shared his writing, one of the children suggests, "You need to extend your writing, Romas. There aren't enough details." Mrs. Sternquist smiles and nods in agreement.

   "Yeah," adds another child, " go back to the original prompt about losing a tooth. I was wondering if you had to help it fall out and did your mouth bleed? Did you wash the tooth off before you put it under

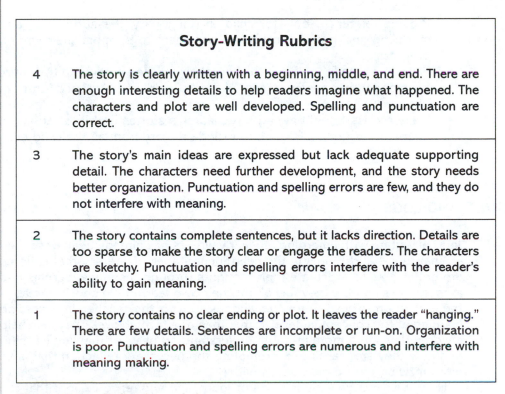

My Peer Conferencing Checklist

Name of student writer: _____

Name of peer evaluator: _____

Date: _____

YES	NO	1. I listened to my conferencing partner read his/her text aloud.
YES	NO	2. I told the writer about a part that I thought was the most exciting, interesting, or clear.
YES	NO	3. I pointed out a place that could be improved.
YES	NO	4. I gave a specific reason about why I thought it could be improved.
YES	NO	5. My conferencing partner and I discussed a way the improvement could be made.

Figure 6.2   Peer conferencing checklist.

Story-Writing Rubrics

4	The story is clearly written with a beginning, middle, and end. There are enough interesting details to help readers imagine what happened. The characters and plot are well developed. Spelling and punctuation are correct.
3	The story's main ideas are expressed but lack adequate supporting detail. The characters need further development, and the story needs better organization. Punctuation and spelling errors are few, and they do not interfere with meaning.
2	The story contains complete sentences, but it lacks direction. Details are too sparse to make the story clear or engage the readers. The characters are sketchy. Punctuation and spelling errors interfere with the reader's ability to gain meaning.
1	The story contains no clear ending or plot. It leaves the reader "hanging." There are few details. Sentences are incomplete or run-on. Organization is poor. Punctuation and spelling errors are numerous and interfere with meaning making.

Figure 6.3   Reflection rubric.

your pillow?" Romas decides he can easily add several additional details that were "in his head" but not included in his story.

The children in Mrs. Sternquist's room are taking pride in their ability to "talk like writers" and their ability to provide genuinely helpful feedback beyond just complimenting one another. Using this approach, they are building strong, internal concepts about what good stories should include to make them interesting to others, clear, mechanically correct, and fully developed. There is good evidence that the feedback they are learning to provide to others is clearly making them more reflective about their own work.

8. Allow children time to complete their stories, encouraging them to use the reference tools in addition to the comments they have received from their peers. Let them know they will be sharing the stories with the class and compiling them to make a class book.

9. Assess each child's finished work, using a developed writing rubric that has been previously shared with the class (see Figure 6.3, "Story-Writing Rubrics," for example). This promotes an awareness of appropriate writing expectations.

Hints for Success

- Encourage students to write about what is personally meaningful to them.
- Allow time every day for children to work independently and large enough time blocks so they can concentrate and get involved in what they are doing.
- Provide guidance for children in how to structure peer conferencing suggestions so that they are as positive as possible while still supplying honest feedback to a peer. Stress the building of community in the classroom.
- Let children know that you are available for a conference if they have additional questions that are not resolved in the peer conferencing sessions.
- Provide reference tools for children (dictionary, thesaurus, etc.) and modeling and training in how to use them to support their writing progress.
- Provide a time for children to share their finished work with the entire class or another audience (see "Author's Chair" and "Author's Night" in Chapter 5).
- Make a class book, binding the children's stories and illustrations of their work together. Be sure to include a story from all the children.

RESPONSE JOURNALS AND LOGS

Journal writing with emerging and early writers has already been described in Chapters 4 and 5. It is in the near-fluent stages of literacy that children are better able to articulate their thoughts through response journals and logs, expressing how they feel about their own learning in specific areas of the curriculum. These are a tremendous tool to the teacher in assessing learning at the conceptual level, rather than at a factual level. They also help children develop a more in-depth understanding of what they are learning and how they are learning it, promoting the necessary reflection that is so often missing after classroom activities.

Here, we describe various forms of journaling and response logs that can be used to assess conceptual growth over the curriculum and to integrate literacy naturally into other curricular areas. Best of all, it's a good strategy to get children moving that pencil across the page every single day. Figure 6.4 shows a sample entry from a child's response journal.

Main Purpose To have children writing for a variety of purposes
To allow opportunities for children to reflect on their learning (metacognition)

Materials Paper and pencil
Journal binder with dividers (optional)
Three-hole punch

Procedures The first step is to provide children with some type of prompt to get them writing. Prompts will vary depending on the purpose for the writing. Variations include:

- **Personal journals:** These have already been described. They use a diary format in which students write about their life experiences, ideas that interest them, events happening in their family, and so on. We think children who write regularly have little problem finding something to write about, but some teachers prefer to occasionally provide

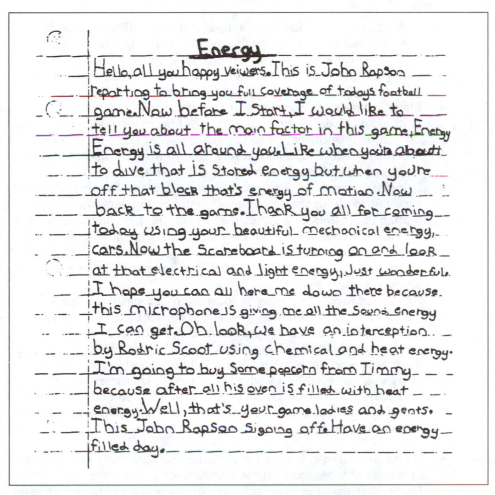

Figure 6.4 Sample entry from child's response journal.

topics for children to explore. Some suggestions for appropriate and interesting topics would include the following:

What is the best job in the whole world?

What bothers you the most? Why?

If you could go anywhere in the world, where would it be? Why there?

Other than lunch and recess, what is your favorite subject? Why?

What would you do with a million dollars?

Why are there laws and rules? What would happen if there were no laws and rules?

How do you decide who your friends will be?

What is your favorite day of the week? What makes it so special?

If you could become a cartoon character, which one would you be?

If I gave you ten dollars today, what would you do with it?

What is the meanest thing anyone ever said to you? How did it make you feel? What did you do?

Who is the greatest person or persons you have ever learned about? What makes that person great in your eyes?

What is the funniest thing that you have ever seen?

What is the kindest thing you have ever seen anyone do for someone?

If you could fix up your room any way you wanted, what would it look like?

Which do you like more, being alone or being with other people? Why?

If you could change one thing about yourself, what would it be?

If you had three magic wishes, what would they be? Could there be any bad effects if all of them came true?

If you were president of the United States, what would be the first thing you would do? What difference would that make?

- **Math journals:** Children may respond in these to questions regarding mathematical terms or concepts, offering prior knowledge about a skill to be introduced, or to summarize what has been learned about a concept following a lesson (e.g., "In your math journal, tell what is the same and different about a square and a triangle").

- **Science journals:** These are the perfect place for children to make predictions about the outcome of an upcoming experiment or to summarize the results of a conducted experiment, including their reasoning for the outcome. You may also wish to have children define vocabulary for a scientific study here (what they think it means at this point in time), and then go back and redefine the words once the study is underway.

- **Response logs:** This type of journaling can easily be applied to any subject area or experience. This is the student's opportunity to reflect on an experience, story, or lesson, and the teacher's opportunity to assess what the student has gained from it. Response logs can take the form of a reading response log ("Tell why you liked or didn't like the story you just read." "Tell who your favorite character was in the story and why." "Tell which character is most like someone in your family and why.") or a response to a film shown, a field trip taken recently, or a resource person's presentation in the classroom.

Hints for Success
- When providing prompts for children, be sure they are open ended and require more than simple answers for a response.
- Remember that the main purpose of journaling is to get children to write and to simply express their thoughts, ideas, and opinions. This

is not the type of writing that needs to be taken through the writing process with major revisions made. Instead of correcting their work, respond to it with further questions or comments to extend their thinking processes. The return dialogue method in journaling is a wonderful way not only to reinforce the idea that writing conveys a message but also to promote higher level thinking skills. Simply asking students to clarify their written message for the reader or to expand on their idea does precisely that.

KWHLH

The acronym KWHLH stands for what is *known* (K), what we *want* (W) to know about something, *how* (H) we think we could find it out, what we *learned* (L) after investigating and, finally, *how* (H) we learned about it. This is a spin-off on the traditional KWL strategy (Ogle, 1986) that has long been used. It's particularly effective when used along with expository text for assessing, first of all, what children know prior to reading, eliciting what they might want to find out, and then reviewing what was learned. We've added the additional parts in which children ask themselves how they could find an answer to their questions and then later review how something was learned to reinforce metacognitive capability. Implementation of this strategy provides teachers with useful information about the kind of knowledge children bring into a learning situation, how much they are learning, and the approaches they take to access information.

Main Purpose To develop metacognitive skills, including making connections between personal experiences and the text read or images viewed

Materials Chart paper
Writing utensils
Reference books

Procedure
1. Brainstorm as a class what is already known about a selected topic, concentrating on the key concepts most central to the expository text. List some ideas on chart paper. Categories related to the topic of study may be constructed for the listed ideas.
2. Both children and teacher generate what they want to know or learn about the topic. Children can also write down the questions they want to have answered through reading the selection or studying the topic.
3. Go over each of the proposed questions and ask, "How do you think we can find out this information besides reading about it in the expository text piece I have here?" List their ideas.
4. Children read the article to see how many of the questions they had can be answered in the article. They also note whether the facts they brought as prior knowledge are, in fact, true—according to the article. They note which of the facts brought as prior knowledge could not be corroborated by the article.
5. After reading the text, a discussion is held during which children and teacher review the K column for accuracy or to address misconceptions discovered in the reading. The W column is also checked to see which questions were answered and which still require an answer.
6. The teacher highlights information that is still needed and provides time for children to access additional resources (e.g., a person who has expertise, other available text). Children may volunteer to take a particular

point to research, and a time period for getting information back to the class is set. The teacher can also volunteer to take one.

7. At a set time, an additional discussion is held, with children volunteering to share information they gained about the unanswered questions still on the chart.

8. The K and W columns are reassessed. A final listing of what was learned, the L list, is made.

9. A final discussion is held relative to whether or not all the original knowledge was corroborated in the reading and additional study and whether all the questions were answered. A debriefing about how each fact was corroborated or each question was answered is held.

Classroom Application   Ms. Lieberman's class is just beginning their study of the moon. She has done an assessment of prior knowledge by using the initial three components of the KWHLH process. "Friday afternoon, we finished generating some facts that we knew about the moon and also some of the questions we have," she says and points to their list of questions:

Is the moon a planet? Is it a star?
How were the moon's craters made?
Why does the same side of the moon always face Earth?
How far away from Earth is the moon?
Does the moon change its shape each night?
Is the moon smaller or larger than Earth?
Where does "moonlight" come from?
What color is the moon really? Does it change color?
What is the moon made of?
Why would we weigh less on the moon?
What are the "seas" on the moon? Where did they come from?
How long does it take for the moon to revolve around the Earth?
Why can we still see the astronauts' footprints on the moon?
Does the moon have a day and a night?
What is an eclipse of the moon? What happens?
What do astronauts have to take to the moon for survival?
Does the moon only shine at night?
What are the phases of the moon?
Who was the first man on the moon?

She continues: "When I asked you how we could get the answers to some of our questions, the first thing you suggested was that we could get some information books about the moon. Well, over the weekend, I took a trip to the public library and found a number of them that have not only wonderful pictures but also a lot of information. I've taken your questions (and added seven more of my own) and cut them into individual strips. The strips are in the basket you see here. I'd like to have each of you pick out one of these questions from the basket and then use the information texts and other sources you can think of to see if you can find the answer to your question. This is something that we'll take the rest of the week to work on individually, and then we'll compile what we find out into a class book. Chris, you can be the first to select a question and then pass the basket."

The children are excited to see which question they get, and there are exclamations of, "Oh, no . . . look at the one I got!" But the children get right to work searching for an answer. Ms. Lieberman then guides them through a series of activities. Once they have found the information they need, the children write an answer to the question in paragraph form, making sure to include the reasons for their answer and how they found it out. After this, they take the paragraph through the writing process, conferencing with Ms. Lieberman as needed and sharing their finished report with others in the group.

Culminating the process is their production of the book titled, "What We Knew, Wanted to Know, and Learned about the Moon . . . and How We Found It Out!"

Hints for Success
- Be sure to supply a variety of informational text, including easy-to-read science books that are easily understandable for children.
- Try to pull out those questions that reveal common misconceptions about the topic.
- Use the researched answers as a continued learning experience throughout the unit of study. For example, when discussing a particular topic, ask, "Who researched that question?"
- Don't leave any of their questions unanswered. Try to find some resource that will provide a reasonable answer if such information is known.
- Be sure to have children use the Web to search for information about their questions. Encourage them to think of multiple sources to access information.

SORT, SEARCH, AND DISCOVER (SSD)

Given all the controversy about teaching spelling and the need for individualized instruction, Mary Jo Fresch and Aileen Wheaton (1997) set out to identify the best practices they could find relative to developing proficient spellers. They concluded that simply taking words out of children's study or writing was too random and was not getting the job done. Still, they did not want to go back to the traditional speller and have children memorize a list of words, which children then often failed to translate to their everyday writing.

SSD is a process whereby the teacher chooses a list of spelling words to be studied during at least a five-day period (including the weekend). The words on a particular list all have something in common and are chosen to reinforce a particular understanding about certain patterns or rules, based on the weaknesses the teacher is seeing in the children's written work. For example, they may be having trouble with the rule about making plurals by changing the *y* to an *i* and adding *es*, or understanding when to add an *s* versus *es* to words to form the plural.

The strategy involves children in open (i.e., the child experiments and devises self-designated categories) and closed (the child uses key words to guide the categorization) word sorts, which have proved to be a viable method to promote children's understandings of the patterns and rules of conventional spelling. These word sorts motivate children to form generalizations about the properties of all the members of a particular category and to use those generalizations to form hypotheses about new challenges in conventional spelling. Thus, by manipulating language, children are moved away from simple memorization, which often is not translated into their everyday writing, and toward greater differentiation and integration of phonemic relationships.

Main Purpose
For children to develop strategies to use in moving beyond invented spelling and into predicting correct, conventional spelling

For children to become active in making sense of and drawing relationships about the English language

Materials
Teacher-constructed pretest and word bank sheet
Paper and pencil
Sticky notes, cards, or small slips of paper
Scissors

Procedure   1. Pretest/word selection:

    a. The teacher chooses specific words that have a common pattern or rule for application, including words that are below, at, and above grade level.

    b. Children receive a Pretest and Word Bank Sheet (see Figure 6.5).

    c. Children take the pretest and self-correct it. They then select additional words to study from the self-selected list on the same page (children may also add other words they prefer to study that maintain the common pattern or rule being focused on for the week).

    d. Children copy the list three times: one list to post at home, one to cut and staple into their writing folders, and one list to cut into individual words for word sorting.

2. Word sort and word hunt:

    a. Have children cut their third list of words up into individual words and either rewrite or paste them onto separate cards or slips of paper for categorization by pattern or rule. They can work alone or with a partner.

    b. Once they have sorted the words, they are to write a generalization about the pattern they've discovered. These can be shared in a small group or whole-class situation to reinforce the rule or generalization.

    c. Children see if they can find additional words in their reading or elsewhere in the classroom that fit the categories they have discovered.

3. Words in context:

    a. Children develop some form of written text using each of the words on their lists, underlining the focused word. This can take any form the child wishes—a story, individual sentences, a poem, an ad, a limerick, and so on. The targeted spelling words are underlined or highlighted in the text. These are later used in the buddy posttest described next.

Spelling Pretest	Pretest List	List from Which to Select
(Fold on the dotted line) →		
	recess	class
	still	small
	miss	jell
	will	dress
	yell	shall
	grass	baseball
	ball	add
	kiss	spill
	mall	grass
	drill	fell

Figure 6.5   Pretest and Word Bank Sheet.

Source: Adapted from French and Wheaton (1997:25).

      b. Children participate in various activities during the rest of the week that the teacher devises to engage them in using and having fun with the pattern or rule that serves the basis of the words under study. This can include use of reference materials.

4. Buddy posttest:

      a. Children select a buddy for this part of the exercise. Each child takes a posttest and gives one to his or her buddy. The buddy takes the text that has been developed by the child to include the targeted words and dictates it to the other child, emphasizing the targeted word and waiting while the child writes it down.

      b. The buddies may either correct one another's test and give a score or defer to the teacher to do so if she wishes. Children who score below 80 percent accuracy should receive follow-up work on the pattern or rule that has served as the basis of the week's work.

Hints for Success

- Be sure to use a strategy to determine where the children in your classroom are with respect to the established developmental stages of learning to spell and make your weekly word lists fit a child's level. That may call for providing different lists for different groups of spellers in your classroom until you see in their everyday writing that they have moved to a new level. Periodically reassess all children in your classroom, since children's maturation in these early years is highly unpredictable.

- Refer to such spelling resources as E. H. Henderson's *Teaching Spelling* (1990) and Bolton and Snowball's *Teaching Spelling: A Practical Resource* (1993) for grade-level lists of spelling words that can be adapted to the children's level, as well as for the patterns and rules that need to be emphasized.

- As children self-select additional words to add to their lists, circulate around the room to guide that selection. Also circulate to help children in the sorting process as needed.

- Be as creative as possible in structuring related activities so that children are motivated to learn the words and apply them to their writing.

- Encourage children to use their auditory sense in addition to their sense of sight and memory by saying the words out loud before categorizing them.

- Model the sorting of the words sometime during the week for the entire class by showing each word on a card, saying it out loud, thinking out loud about the proper slot to place it in, and then placing it in a slot in a pocket chart.

GRAPHIC ORGANIZERS

Jay McTighe and Frank Lyman (1988) note that effective thinking requires a fundamental ability to organize information and ideas:

> Cognitive maps and other visual organizers are effective tools for helping students improve their organizational ability. [They] provide a visual, holistic representation of facts and concepts and their relationships within an organized framework. They help students to:
>
> - Represent abstract or implicit information in more concrete form.
> - Depict the relationships among facts and concepts.
> - Generate and elaborate ideas.
> - Relate new information to prior knowledge.
> - Store and retrieve information.

Graphic organizers (Tierney, Readence, & Dishner, 1999) are a primary tool for cognitive organization and analyzing discourse structure in both narrative and expository text, making concepts concrete and explicit. The form of the organizer varies (see Figure 6.6), depending on the analysis to be made, and may include charts, tables, webs, Venn diagrams, and various kinds of flowcharts. Because they can be used as effectively in organizing writing as in trying to understand what someone else has written, they help

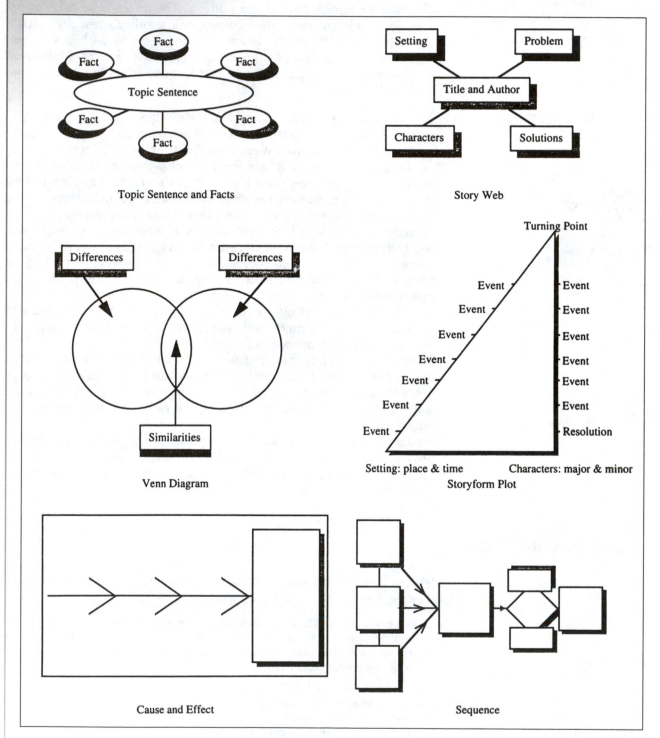

Figure 6.6 A few types of graphic organizers.

students to conceptualize the inclusive linkages between the various aspects of language arts.

Main Purpose To promote metacognition in children and the ability to conceptually organize information found in text to discover relationships, concepts, concept features, and concept examples

Materials Graphic organizer form (see Figure 6.6)
Narrative or expository text to be analyzed
Writing implements

Procedure
1. Discuss with students the value of using a strategy to organize component parts in a piece of text (finding relationships, main ideas, etc.).
2. Choose a particular graphic organizer from the forms available, and demonstrate how it can be used by taking students through the process of organizing a familiar story.
3. Read a new story and follow it by class discussion of the various parts.
4. Have children work in pairs to fill out a graphic organizer of the story.
5. Follow with a variety of other experiences using other types of graphic organizers (see Figure 6.6).

Hints for Success
- Be sure to have children discuss their graphic organizers after they have developed them so they can clarify their thinking and practice using the vocabulary involved in such organization. In this way, children begin to internalize the process so that they begin "thinking that way," even when not going through the process of putting the components on papers.
- Use a variety of organizers so that children widen their understanding of the many ways information can be structured.
- Use graphic organizers for a variety of purposes in understanding new concepts, vocabulary, relationship building, and articulation of ideas.

Creating a visual organizer.

READER'S THEATER

Even adults love to do this activity. In any community, one can find increasing numbers of small groups of people getting together for a social evening to take roles and read through a favorite play. The basic definition of a Reader's Theater is a student performance of a story that has been read together. However, it is a much richer and more complex activity than that, but one that also eliminates many of the difficulties of staging theatrical productions: Students do not have to memorize their parts; elaborate costumes and backdrops are not needed; and long, tedious hours are not spent rehearsing (Tompkins, 1997:494). Children at this age love to put on a show, and this activity is a great way to reinforce oral reading skills such as expression and delivery of text. Children also develop a better understanding of how quotation marks are used in reading and writing dialogue.

Reader's Theater promotes an awareness of communication skills, facial and voice expression, and delivery of speech. It may take on many grouping forms and may be done with or without props but is usually an informal, impromptu performance. Thus, it is not necessary to spend hours working with children to make sure they learn their roles or have everything exactly perfect. Instead, allow them a few practice runs, and then tell them to "break a leg!"—sharing with them the old show-biz expression (they may even want to delve into this to see where it originated).

Main Purpose For children to develop storytelling skills, both original and those that are heard from others or from books

Procedure

1. Choose a favorite narrative story that contains a relatively simple story line, preferably one with a variety of speaking and acting parts or characters. Retype it into a "play" so that children can easily identify the parts.
2. Read the original story and follow it up with guided discussion and other related reading strategies (graphic organizers, etc.) so that there is good understanding of the story line and characters.
3. Tell the children, "We are going to make this story come alive!" Present the idea of Reader's Theater to them and pass out duplicated copies of the story that has been transformed into a play. Have the children note the differences in the way the text is presented in the original narrative form and in the play.
4. Discuss the various roles that people play in producing a play, including those of the narrator, character roles, prop person, makeup person, musical director, set director, and wardrobe person.
5. Have the children choose a part they might like to play, including that of a prop person or other backstage worker. Show them how to highlight their parts on the individual copies. Have them practice their parts in small groups with the intention of presenting the story in large group to the rest of the class, to another class in the school, or to family members.
6. Discuss ways in which they can use their voices, gestures, and body language to make their character more believable.
7. If the children wish to do so, they may make some simple props. For example, at Sheridans School, the third graders in Mrs. Kate Currin's room presented a *Magic Schoolbus* story about what is below the earth's surface. Each child had made some digging tools and integrated these into the reading, a great addition.

8. Hold rehearsals until the presenters are comfortable, and then invite real audiences, including parents and other classes, for the performance.

Hints for Success

- Make sure every student in the class has some type of job in the production of Reader's Theater. Some options include having more than one child be the narrator, alternating with another child between paragraphs of the story line.
- Talk about the value of having everyone experience the different roles at one time or another during the year. Encourage children who always want to be in the spotlight to experience what it is like to take a different responsibility, such as creating a setting. Encourage children who never want to be in the spotlight to take on a small role "just to see how much fun it can be to be someone else for a brief period of time."
- Have prop makers create a sign that includes the title of the performance or the story title. This should be displayed on an easel as the presenter or narrator introduces the production to the audience.
- Prior to the performances, emphasize oral speaking skills, discussing the need to speak loudly enough for all to hear, to use effective expression and body language to get across points, and to make eye contact with the audience when appropriate.
- Demonstrate the possible actions that correspond with the speaking parts, so students have a model to ensure a successful performance.
- Allow children to try their hand at creating their own scripts.

DIRECTED READING/THINKING ACTIVITY (DRTA)

DRTA (Stauffer, 1975) is a strategy used in conjunction with expository text and easily adaptable to any factual topic. This is a procedure used to guide students in activating prior knowledge for the topics to be read, making predictions about what might be addressed in the text, and establishing a purpose for reading. As the child progresses through the passage being read, he or she is confirming, revising, and rejecting hypotheses. This is a useful strategy for guiding student comprehension of expository text, which tends to be difficult. Readers who have specific strategies for reading this type of text are more efficient and able to make better use of the information.

Main Purpose

For children to develop strategies for understanding expository text and images: components, facts, organization, purpose, and main idea

Materials

Paper and pencils
Chart paper and easel for recording brainstorming ideas
Highlighters (optional)
Informative articles

Procedure

1. Introduce the topic to be studied before displaying the informative article or chapter to be read. Ask and list responses about the topic: "What do you know about _____?" "What do you think about _____?" "What would you like to know about _____?" Brainstorm as a whole group or in small groups to generate and list prior knowledge and to set a purpose for reading.

2. Ask the group to "star" the facts that they are **absolutely sure of** as being true. If the children are working in small groups, have them complete this step and then list the facts they are sure of on the chart paper for the entire class to review.

3. Once children have had a chance to establish prior knowledge, provide the information article to be read. This can be done independently, with a partner, in small groups, or as an entire class, depending on the amount of guidance you think you need to provide and the amount of experience the class has had with this activity. As students read the article, ask such questions as, "See if you can find where it says that _____," or "See if you can find the answers to your questions about _____."

4. After the children have completed the article, go back to the ideas listed on the easel. Ask them to confirm, reject, or add to their prior knowledge or list of questions. See if you can motivate them to want to find out more.

Classroom Application   Ms. DeShambo's class is beginning a study of crocodiles. She writes the topic "Crocodiles" on the board and asks students what they already know about these creatures. As they brainstorm, she numbers and records their ideas:

1. Crocodiles have legs out to the side.
2. Their eyes are on the side.
3. People sometimes mix them up with alligators.
4. Their babies are born from eggs.
5. They like to go in water.
6. They are cold-blooded.
7. They are about 10 feet long.
8. They are reptiles.
9. They can breathe underwater.

"This is quite a list," says Ms. DeShambo. "Before we take a look at the informational article I have for you, tell me which of these facts that you absolutely *know* are true. I'll star those." The students ask Ms. DeShambo to star items 1, 3, 6, and 9. She then distributes the informational article on crocodiles and asks the children to read through it silently first. When they are finished, she guides them through a second reading of the article, asking such questions as, "Can someone read the part where it says that crocodiles lay eggs?" She points out aids to the reader, such as when the writer uses italics or boldface type for subheadings to help point out an important section or idea. She also encourages the children to practice the strategy of looking back or using their highlighters to identify key sentences in which their listed hypotheses are either confirmed or rejected. They are delighted when they find that some of their hypotheses are true; they are also amazed to find some of them to be otherwise.

Hints for Success   • This activity works best with topics that the students will likely know *something* about but also may hold some misconceptions about.

• As children gain confidence with this strategy through repeated practice, less guidance may be necessary. Rather, the activity may be used in guiding small groups by presenting them with a purpose as they read through an article.

• As with other developing skills, a single use of this activity will not accomplish the internalized skills we want in children. Thus, the teacher will want to plan to use it periodically to assess how well all children in the classroom have picked up on and are using the strategies.

SQ3R (Robinson, 1946) has become a traditional reading strategy. We include it here in our list of highly effective activities even though some of the more experienced teachers reading this book are probably well acquainted with it. We simply don't want you to forget about it because you're continually being introduced to newer strategies that are receiving more attention today.

SQ3R consists of a five-step plan with the purpose of helping children organize their approach to studying informational text and becoming more effective in comprehension of factual text. SQ3R is an acronym for the following strategies: Survey, Question, Read, Recite, Review. The instructional benefit of the strategy is that it uses all the elements of effective learning: (1) asking questions, (2) making predictions, (3) setting purposes, and (4) monitoring and evaluating comprehension. It may be introduced during a guided reading session, and, as students have repeated practice with the activity, it may become a technique used in small study groups or at an independent level. Obviously, the technique takes a good deal of time to learn and use. Because of its metacognitive qualities, it's a strategy that should be introduced thoroughly, with adequate time given to each of the steps.

Main Purpose For children to develop metacognitive skills: to think about what is being read; to try to make sense of the text; to make connections between personal experiences and text read

Materials Informational text
Paper and pencil
Chart paper
Highlighter (optional)

Procedure The following steps have been divided into the areas of focus: Survey, Question, Read, Recite, Review. These general strategies may be applied and adapted to fit with any informational type of text.

Survey:

1. Think about the title. Ask yourself, "What do I know?" "What do I want to know?"
2. Look over the heading and skim the first few sentences of paragraphs.
3. Look at the illustrations and graphic aids.
4. Read the first paragraph.
5. Read the last paragraph or summary.

Question:

1. Turn the title into a question.
2. Write down any questions that come to mind during the survey.
3. Turn the heading into a question.
4. Turn the subheading, illustrations, and graphic aids into questions.
5. Write down unfamiliar vocabulary and guess at the meaning of each word.

Read actively:

1. Read to search for answers to the previous questions.
2. Respond to questions and use context clues for unfamiliar words.
3. React to unclear passages, confusing terms, and questionable statements by listing additional questions for yourself.

Recite:

1. Look away from answers and the text to recall what was read.
2. Recite answers to questions aloud or in writing.
3. Reread text for unanswered questions. Repeat the following steps for each section: Question, Read, Recite.

Review:

1. Answer the main purpose question.
2. Look over answers and all parts of the chapter or text to organize information.
3. Apply your answers in one or more of the following ways: draw flowcharts, write a summary, develop a graphic organizer, participate in a group discussion, study for a test.

Classroom Application

"I want to show you something that I think is really a great way to get the most out of informational text," says Mr. Rehman to the small group of children. "Until I learned some of these little study secrets, I had a hard time remembering things I read. It's a five-step process called SQ3R, and I'm going to let you in on it. SQ3R is an acronym—remember, that means a word formed out of the first letters of other words. Watch."

He lists the five words on a white board, using a red marker to stress the initial letters. "SQ3R stands for **S**urvey, **Q**uestion, **R**ead, **R**ecite, and **R**eview."

He has the children repeat the list a couple of times. "Let's go ahead and see how it works with a two-page handout I have from Helene Lerner's book *Stress Breakers.*

Mr. Rehman distributes the information sheets to the children. "Let's look at the title. What do you know about stress?" he asks.

"School is stress!" says Vincent, laughing. "Sometimes," agrees Mr. Rehman as he leads the children through a brief discussion about stress and then into the Survey phase of the process. The children work with him to turn the title into a question, "Will Stress Break You—or Can You Be a Stress Buster?"

"That's actually pretty creative," encourages Mr. Rehman. "Let's do the same thing with the headings, graphic aids, and even that illustration of the man sinking into quicksand. Let's start with that. What do you read from the picture?"

"Well, all that stuff floating around the guy's head looks like he's gotta lot of worries," offers Enrico.

"Yeah," adds Carrie, "Look at the way his face looks—like he can't take it anymore!"

Once the children and Mr. Rehman have written down a number of questions, they look for unfamiliar vocabulary words. Three are identified—*affliction, equilibrium,* and *constructive*—and Mr. Rehman surveys the group for possible definitions. The group then reads through the handout, searching for answers to their questions and to confirm their tentative definitions for the three vocabulary words. Once the group has responded to the questions posed, Mr. Rehman removes the chart paper on which they are listed and says, "All right—let's finish up with the last two components of the process." Moving through the Recite and Review steps, Mr. Rehman closes the session by saying, "Well, either we all know more about stress, or we're just more stressed. What do you think? While I meet with the next group, I'd like to have you complete this by writing down your understanding of this process in your journal—or draw a flowchart of the process. If you choose to do that one, be sure to provide an example next to each component."

Hints for Success	• Begin by introducing the SQ3R technique to the entire class, modeling the steps to be taken when reading and comprehending informational text.

- Begin by introducing the SQ3R technique to the entire class, modeling the steps to be taken when reading and comprehending informational text.
- Allow much guided practice, followed by small study group use, before expecting independence with this strategy.
- Decide how and when the strategy will be implemented, depending on the familiarity and difficulty level of the given text. Will it be used before reading? During reading? After reading?

LITERACY CIRCLES

We couldn't bring our fluency-level activities to a close without including Harvey Daniels's (1994) superb strategy for getting children to really appreciate what reading is all about. We've seen teachers using this with second graders who absolutely love being involved, and we've been involved ourselves in similar adult groups where we felt exactly the same way. Not only are these good places to talk with someone about something just read and enjoyed; members (both younger *and* older) gain enormously from listening to one another's perspectives about a piece—and profit from the good fellowship involved in sharing deeper ideas on a regular basis. In *Literature Circles: Voice and Choice in the Student-Centered Classroom,* Daniels (1994:13) writes:

> Literature circles are small, temporary discussion groups who have chosen to read the same story, poem, article or book. While reading each group-determined portion of the text (either in or outside of class), each member prepares to take

Literacy circles: group discussion taking place.

specific responsibilities in the upcoming discussion, and everyone comes to the group with the notes needed to help perform that job. The circles have regular meetings, with discussion roles rotating each session. When they finish a book, the circle members plan a way to share highlights of their reading with the wider community; then they trade members with other finishing groups, select more reading, and move into a new cycle. Once readers can successfully conduct their own wide-ranging, self-sustaining discussions, formal discussion roles may be dropped.

In the words of Sandy Niemiera, a fourth-grade teacher who used this strategy: "This structure allowed me the freedom to turn ownership over to the students. Students gained greater insight by sharing literature instead of reading in isolation. Students who never participated before during whole-class discussion found a voice." And, of course, the proof of how well literature circles work rests in the perspectives of the children who are involved in them: "Literature circles are really fun!" says Stacy, a fifth-grade student. "Lit circles are very neat. They are very, very awesome. Lit circles are very, very complicated, though."

Main Purpose   To build metacognitive capacity in children, particularly with respect to understanding narrative text and images

Materials   Wide choice of good books and multiple copies
Role sheets (see Figure 6.7)
Writing implements

Procedure   The following is a description of the quick training procedure described by Daniels (1994:52–53, 62–63). A more in-depth description can be found in his text *Literature Circles*.

1. Provide a wide choice of good books, and invite everyone to "choose themselves" into a group of four people who want to read the same book. This will take a few minutes of informal negotiation.
2. Hand out sets of role sheets and let people in each group divide them up however they want. (It's fun to watch art-phobic older kids try to get rid of the illustrator role, which of course is primary kids' favorite.) The roles that are *required* and that ensure four different "takes" on the text are:
   a. **Discussion director:** Has official responsibility to think up some good discussion questions, convene the meeting, and solicit contributions from the other members.
   b. **Literary luminary/passage master:** Takes readers back to memorable, important sections of the text and reads them aloud.
   c. **Connector:** Takes everyone from the text world out into the real world where experiences in their own life, happenings at school or in the community, or other people and problems they are reminded of are connected with the literature.
   d. **Illustrator:** Adds a graphic, nonlinguistic response to the text— a sketch, cartoon, diagram, flowchart, or stick-figure scene.
   Optional roles include:
   a. **Summarizer:** Prepares a brief summary of that day's reading, a quick one- or two-minute statement that conveys the key points and main highlights.
   b. **Vocabulary enricher:** Is on the lookout for a few especially important words in the day's reading, words that may be puzzling or unfamiliar; marks them down when reading, looks them up in

Discussion Director

Name: _____

Group: _____

Book: _____

Assignment: Page _____ to page _____

Discussion Director: Your job is to develop a list of questions that your group might want to discuss about this part of the book. Don't worry about the small details; your task is to help people talk over the big ideas in the reading and share their reactions. Usually the best discussion questions come from your own thoughts, feelings, and concerns as you read, which you can list below, during or after your reading. Or you may use some of the general questions below to develop topics for your group.

Possible discussion questions or topics for today:

1. _____

2. _____

3. _____

4. _____

Sample questions:

What was going through your mind while you read this?

How did you feel while reading this part of the book?

What was discussed in this section of the book?

Can someone summarize briefly?

Did today's reading remind you of any real-life experiences?

What questions did you have when you finished this section?

Did anything in this section of the book surprise you?

What are the one or two most important ideas?

Predict some things you think will be talked about next.

Topic to be carried over to tomorrow:

Assignment for tomorrow: Page _____ to page _____

Figure 6.7   Literature circle role sheet.

Source: Daniels (1994).

a dictionary, and records definition; marks words that are repeated a lot as keys to meaning of text.

c. **Travel tracer:** Keeps track of when the setting changes, where the action takes place in the day's reading. Describes each setting in detail, either with words or with an action map or a diagram that can be shown to the group (includes page locations where scene is described).

   d. **Investigator/researcher:** Digs up background information on any topic related to the book. Might include information about the author, time period portrayed in book, geography, weather, culture, or history of the book's setting—not a formal research report.

3. Have someone serving in each role read aloud its description for the whole class, so that everyone hears what other roles will be part of the group. At this point, you can clarify the nature of each role and answer any questions.

4. Give a set amount of time for reading and role-sheet preparation (20 to 30 minutes is plenty; you'll need less if you're using poems, obviously). Tell the groups to assign themselves a section of the book that everyone feels can comfortably be finished in *five minutes less than the allocated time*. The remaining five minutes will be used to prepare the role sheet (this can be done either during or after reading, but there needs to be time for stopping to write).

5. When everyone has done the reading and prepared the sheets, invite groups to get together for 15 or 20 minutes. Clearly explain that the main goal is to have a natural conversation about the book.

Hints for Success

- During the conversations, visit each group unobtrusively for a few minutes, strictly as an observer. Be sure not to "steer" the discussion. Jot down specific examples and comments to make during the debriefing.

- Encourage each role player to chip in as the conversation unfolds. Everyone should look for a spontaneous opening. The discussion director is supposed to moderate, keep an eye on the clock, and invite members who haven't joined in to share their ideas.

- Follow up these during-reading activities with after-reading extensions such as having children:
  —Create a poster advertising the book
  —Create an oral or written book review
  —Write a sequel to the story and perhaps perform it
  —Prepare a Reader's Theater script from the original story and perform it
  —Create a collage of book characters or settings
  —Create a puppet show about the book
  —Create a song or dance about the book
  —Create an original piece of art work (drawing, painting, sculpture) from some aspect of the book
  —Create a diorama of a story scene
  —Create a news broadcast reporting an event from the book
  —Create a newspaper story about the events
  —Create a creative biography of one of the characters

Final Thoughts

Growing numbers of educators across the country are striving to create learning contexts much like those described earlier in this chapter. These are learning environments where teachers do not *expect* all children to be alike in the literacy skills and concepts they hold—but expect that all children will make significant progress. These teachers have the capacity to work with a range of abilities along the literacy continuum, keeping as many children as possible excited and interested in moving to the next step and always with an eye toward fluency. They use the developmental tasks of middle childhood—the child's need to do well, to do something meaningful, and to fit into the peer group—as catalysts for engaging children in building literacy capacity.

Like the children in middle childhood, we ourselves have advanced to a new stage, one that better serves our needs as educators. We share the same needs as the children we teach: strong, psychological needs for belonging, power, freedom, and fun. We want to know that we are members of that class of professionals who are on the cutting edge of best practices in literacy teaching; we feel a sense of pride and accomplishment when we put into practice strategies that make a positive difference in the children who come to us; and we most enjoy our teaching when we are equipped with the knowledge and skills that allow us to react spontaneously and creatively to whatever it is that children need to be successful. That's when we can look back at a year's worth of teaching—or a lifetime of teaching—and know all of our investment has made a distinct difference.

In the chapters that follow in Part Three of this text, you will find a variety of assessment and evaluation strategies that can help you determine whether children are achieving in your classroom. These include performance-based assessments, collection of work samples, child self-appraisal tools, and many other authentic assessment and evaluation strategies. Evidence of growth can be collected by both teachers and children, stored in portfolios, and then shared with interested others.

Challenge Yourself

1. Keep a record for one week to see exactly how much time you are spending on literacy in your classroom and how balanced your objectives are relative to teaching good skills and concepts in speaking, listening, reading, and writing. Have you included activities that specifically target each component?

2. Try out some of the activities listed in this chapter. Observe children's responses, and think about how you would adapt the activity to better meet the needs of children who are developing more slowly. What could you add as an extension for the student who needs a greater challenge?

3. Take steps to learn more about a child in your classroom who is lagging behind. Interview the child to find out what literacy tasks he or she finds particularly enjoyable and which ones are most difficult—in other words, what works and doesn't work for the child. Identify which stage of literacy the child is in. List three basic skills that need work so the child can move forward. Identify two activities from Chapters 4, 5, or 6 that would be useful in developing those particular skills. Set a time for one-on-one intervention with the child, bringing in a volunteer if necessary.

Suggested Resources for Additional Information

Books

Daniels, H. (1994). *Literature circles: Voice and choice in the student-centered classroom.* York, ME: Stenhouse.

Galda, L., Cullinan, B. E., & Strickland, D. S. (1993). *Language, literacy and the child.* Fort Worth, TX: Harcourt Brace Jovanovich College.

Kostelnik, M. J., Whiren, A. P., Soderman, A. K., Stein, L., & Gregory, K. (2002). *Guiding children's social development.* Albany, NY: Delmar.

Tompkins, G. E. (2000). *Literacy for the 21st century: A balanced approach.* Upper Saddle River, NJ: Merrill.

Children's Technology

The Cat Came Back, ages 7–11, Sanctuary Woods.
Creative Writer, ages 8–14, Microsoft Corporation.
My Own Stories, ages 8–14, MECC.
Once upon a Time, Bytes of Learning.
Worlds of Enchantment, Exploring Nature, Journey through Time, Passport to Discovery, ages 6–12, Compu-Teach.
Storybook Maker, ages 5–12, Josten's Home Learning.
Storybook Weaver and *Storybook Weaver DELUXE,* ages 6–12, MECC.
The Student Writing Center, ages 10+, The Learning Company.
Talking Textwriter, ages 3–12, Scholastic New Media.
Timeliner, all ages, Tom Snyder Productions.
Ultra Writer, ages 8+, Bytes of Learning.

Documenting Skills and Competencies

Authentic assessment, done in the familiar context of the classroom, is at the heart of teaching and learning. . . . Only through knowing children's current knowledge and understandings, their skills, interests, and dispositions, can we develop curriculum that builds on their strengths and provides experiences that support their continued development and learning. (McAfee & Leong, 2002:xv)

During this past decade, with its intensive focus on a more rigorous assessment agenda in our schools, conscientious educators have turned their attention toward developing, validating, and protecting the practices associated with *authentic assessment.* Designed to bring relief from an overreliance on workbooks, end-of-the-unit basal tests, and one-shot-only test scores that tell us precious little about planning solid literacy instruction, authentic assessment practices are based on documenting children's everyday performances in the classroom. When carefully designed and implemented, these performance assessments of children's oral language use, reading, and writing produce far better data for understanding whether the children in our classrooms are developing more complex literacy skills and concepts and, if not, where we need to strengthen our instruction. In this chapter, we intend to expand on the usefulness and importance of authentic assessment and to provide guidelines for the use of more formal tests.

As you read, keep the following questions in mind:

- What should a quality literacy assessment package look like? How close is that to the assessment and evaluation procedures in your own classroom and school? What components are missing?
- How much time do you allocate in your teaching day or week for observing children? What strategies do you use for documenting your observations? How have these observations been useful to you?
- How have you involved children in their own self-appraisal? Why is it valuable to do so?
- What strategies are you using to assess each child's developing writing skills and concepts? How often do you do this? How are the data stored and used?
- In your workplace, is any kind of standardized assessment conducted that looks at children's skill levels in speech, language, and emergent literacy? How appropriate are these tests? How do children react to them? How have you *personally* used the results for planning more effective instruction for children? How are these results shared with parents? How are they shared with children?

Our aim in this chapter is to share with you the principles of a developmentally appropriate assessment package and a number of theoretically sound and useful strategies for assessing language and literacy acquisition in your own classroom. Included will be a compendium of observation strategies, because we consider observation the most powerful assessment tool for understanding children's behavior in any developmental area. In addition, we will look at a number of other classroom-based strategies to evaluate children's literacy progress. Because children are the real stakeholders in our teaching of literacy, we will suggest ideas for getting them involved in self appraisal. Finally, we will list and summarize a number of standardized tests that are often used in the field to assess literacy growth. Our purpose is to make you acquainted with these so you can better weigh their appropriateness when they are used for diagnostic or research purposes with any child in your classroom.

We hope the information in this chapter will be helpful in your day-to-day effort to determine the best instructional approaches for scaffolding the literacy skills and concepts of each child in your classroom. If so, and if you share the outcomes with parents and others in your community, they will come to appreciate that test scores are not the only measure of what children are learning.

A Quality Assessment Package: What Does It Look Like?

Moving from assessment practices that center on grading, ranking, sorting, and grouping to those that guide, assist, and participate in children's progress is not only our challenge but also our responsibility (McAfee & Leong, 2002), and we have made a great deal of progress. Terms such as *authentic assessment, child-centered assessment,* and *performance assessment* have made their way not only into professional jargon but also into the classroom. In the past decade, portfolio assessment has caught fire, and thousands of teachers across the country have replaced or are supplementing traditional parent–teacher conferences with student-led conferencing (see Chapter 8).

Instead of relying only on the scores provided by standardized achievement testing, increasing numbers of teachers are doing their own data collection to determine whether children are making progress in their classrooms. They have come to believe that in order for assessment to be of real value for instructional purposes, it must involve teacher-selected and teacher-implemented methods. Instead of a "snapshot" of the child's skills taken only once or twice a year by someone who is unfamiliar with the child, quality assessment is based on many data points gathered over time. These assessment tasks must be part of what children do in the classroom on an ongoing basis, and should sample children's *best* work and effort. This approach to assessment allows teachers to use baseline data on individual children to carefully scaffold an effective teaching plan that is centered neither above nor below the child's learning capabilities. It also includes getting children involved in their own self-appraisal so that they can take more responsibility for their own learning. These teachers also know that parents must be brought more actively into the process.

Developmentally Appropriate Assessment and Evaluation

The National Association for the Education of Young Children (NAEYC) has developed a set of guidelines for developmentally appropriate assessment that we believe could be extended to encompass assessment from the very early primary years through the elementary years (Bredekamp & Copple, 1997:22):

a. Assessment of young children's progress and achievements is ongoing, strategic, and purposeful. The results of assessment are used to benefit children—in adapting curriculum and teaching to meet the developmental and learning needs of children, communicating with the child's family, and evaluating the program's effectiveness for the purpose of improving the program.

b. The content of assessments reflects progress toward important learning and developmental goals. The program has a systematic plan for collecting and using assessment information that is integrated with curriculum planning.

c. The methods of assessment gathering are appropriate to the age and experiences of young children. Therefore, assessment of young children relies heavily on the results of observations of children's development, descriptive data, collections of representative work by children, and demonstrated performance during authentic, not contrived, activities. Input from families as well as children's evaluation of their own work are part of the overall assessment strategy.

d. Assessments are tailored to a specific purpose and used only for the purpose for which they have been demonstrated to produce reliable, valid information.

e. Decisions that have a major impact on children, such as enrollment or placement, are never made on the basis of a single developmental assessment or screening device but are based on multiple sources of relevant information, particularly observation by teachers and parents.

f. To identify children who have special learning or developmental needs and to plan appropriate curriculum and teaching for them, developmental assessments and observations are used.

g. Assessment recognizes individual variation in learners and allows for differences in styles and rates of learning. Assessment takes into consideration such factors as the child's facility in English, stages of language acquisition, and whether the child has had the time and opportunity to develop proficiency in his or her home language as well as in English.

h. Assessment legitimately addresses not only what children can do independently but what they can do with assistance from other children or adults. Teachers study children as individuals as well as in relationship to groups by documenting group projects and other collaborative work.

Principled Data Gathering

Rob Tierney's contributions to assessment reform have been considerable and, because he bases them on a mix of child-centered views of teaching, pluralistic and developmental views of children, constructivist views of knowing, and critical theoretical views of empowerment (Tierney, 1998), his ideas about literacy assessment and evaluation could not be more closely aligned with our own. He reminds us that it's not enough to say that our assessment practices are authentic and responsive. Regardless of the label, he says, they may be compromised if they are inconsistent with the ideals that have shaped that reform. He proposes a list of principles designed to promote thoughtful rather than faddish acceptance of new reforms. Many of them are consistent with the guidelines proposed by NAEYC—that is, that they should take place in the course of normal classroom activity, involve children in self-analysis, and be culturally sensitive. Assessments also should be devised to obtain the best possible results from a child rather than being generic and group-focused—and they should be complex and flexible enough to get at the many attributes that constitute children's *literacy abilities* rather than at a single *literacy ability*. We need to be careful, he notes, not to limit our assessment to those abilities and strategies that are easily tested (e.g., spelling) while failing to get at abilities more difficult to assess, such as writing style or self-questioning in the reading process. Our approach should be formative rather than rigid and fixed, and there needs to be coordination of all aspects of assessment, including classroom assessment, report cards, conferences, and a child's ongoing records.

Assessing Language and Literacy Acquisition

Let's see how we can apply the general practices and principles just described to assessing children's language and literacy acquisition. In this section, we will look at a variety of observation strategies, specific methods for assessing reading accuracy and comprehension, and tools for evaluating spelling and writing skill acquisition.

Becoming a Kid-Watcher: Systematic Observation

We're very taken with the term *kid-watching,* which Yetta Goodman coined back in 1978 when she first proposed it as an alternative to testing children. She wrote:

> It is assumed that tests of reading measure the reading process; that tests of writing measure writing achievement; that tests of language measure language ability; that tests of intelligence measure thinking—even though such assumptions have been challenged by knowledge that is emerging from the study of language development. . . . Whether children expand their language effectiveness in the classroom or narrow their vistas to minimum competencies depends on the teacher. The school environment must support teachers to advance their own professionalism by developing the ability to observe children and understand their language strengths. (Goodman, 1978:213–218)

When teachers have a well-developed bank of knowledge related to developmental benchmarks and also sufficient knowledge about curriculum content, their minds and eyes become invaluable assessment and evaluation tools. For example, a teacher who wants to learn more about children's literacy acquisition, rather than just whether they can simply decode words, is interested in observing how children are integrating the various components of language arts as they process their learning in other areas of the curriculum. Observations will also include watching how each child responds to literature, the range and content of the child's literacy choices, and the purposes for which children create print.

Because simply looking at children does not guarantee *seeing,* systematic observation calls for identifying a particular behavior, situation, problem, or progress toward an identified goal we are interested in assessing in a child (McAfee & Leong, 2002). During the observation, the focus should be on the child's targeted behavior rather than on making interpretations. What is recorded should be objective, accurate, and thorough enough to shed some light on the targeted behavior or some ideas for subsequent observation. The observation reports just the facts.

Strategies for recording observational data include anecdotal records, checklists and inventories, dynamic assessment, and the use of rating scales and rubrics. Let's look at what each one entails.

ANECDOTAL RECORDS   Taking the time to document an informal observation of children is particularly helpful in having teachers become more reflective about what went on and the effectiveness of their responses in any given classroom interaction (Winograd, Flores-Duenas, & Arrington, 2003). If done on a regular basis, these jottings can be analyzed for patterns of child behavior, abilities, knowledge, attitudes, and growth. They should be written down as soon as possible after an event, preserving the incident, its context, and exactly what was said or done by the participants in a factual way (Puckett & Black, 2000). For example, the following events were recorded about Marvin, a child who had been highly dependent on others to spell words for him during journal writing. He was observed on November 19 asking Kim how to spell *father.* "Look on the word wall," Kim mumbled, continuing with her own writing. Walking up closer to the word wall, Marvin recorded the word and then, going back to his table, sat down and entered it into a story he was writing. His teacher took a sticky note from a pad she always had in her pocket, recorded the event, and placed it in Marvin's folder.

In a subsequent record written on November 29, the teacher noted that Marvin "looked up from his writing, apparently thinking about a word that was difficult, and then took out his class-developed dictionary of familiar words and paged through it until he found what he was looking for. He copied down the word without asking for anyone's help and continued with his writing." She placed this into his folder along with the previous written observation. Later that day, the teacher mentioned to Marvin what she had observed. He grinned broadly when she said, "You're becoming pretty independent, aren't you?"

When anecdotal record keeping is introduced, teachers may be inclined to view it as overwhelming. "How can I do this when I have 25 children to deal with every day?" is a common response. First of all, we engage in a great deal of informal observation of the children in our classrooms every day and develop a good internal sense of what's going on with each one of them. If we can devise a method to get some of this committed to paper, we can begin to use it as a valid assessment strategy. West (1998) suggests reducing the complexity of this by centering specifically on only five children each day. These may be the five that a teacher meets with during writing workshop for a brief mini-conference. The teacher also pays special attention to what each of these five children volunteers in large- and small-group sessions, their attitudes toward task completion, work habits, interaction in cooperative work assignments, and all other aspects that affect their progress—in literacy and all other domains. Very brief notes can be recorded on sticky notes or a ring of individual cards kept in the teacher's pocket. At the end of the day, the teacher spends a couple of minutes writing down what has been observed about each of the children.

The implications of doing this on a regular basis are profound. At the end of a 36-week school year, the teacher will have 36 observation-based mini-reports on each child. These carry tremendous potential for use in structuring developmentally appropriate instructional tasks for the child and selecting valid materials for those tasks.

DOCUMENTATION   In 1991, *Newsweek* identified what they believed were the 10 best school systems in the world. One of them is one we're sure you've heard of—Reggio Emilia in northern Italy. It is a model that has spurred tremendous curiosity in the United States. The popularity of the method is increasing, not only among professionals in the preprimary years but also among those teaching the early primary grades.

One of the many lessons we learned when we actually visited those schools is their regard for the *hundred languages of children*. The children in Reggio Emilia engage in project work that revolves around investigating events and phenomena of interest to them in their school and community environments. Because these preschoolers are not yet writing, they use what are called *graphic languages* to record many of their ideas, observations, memories, and feelings about these investigations (Edwards, Gandini, & Forman, 1995). Surely, this is what we are talking about when we discuss emergent literacy prior to independent reading and writing. The many *languages* used by these children to express themselves include such representations and constructions as sketches, painting, clay sculpture, collage, murals, dance, dramatic play, singing, storytelling, photos, video and audio recordings, puppetry, and building of all kinds.

Edwards et al. (1995:21) say that these various constructions wouldn't mean very much for assessment purposes without teachers' observation of children as they construct and also without teachers' written documentation of children's comments about what they observed and experienced. When observing, teachers are able to gauge children's levels of understandings and misunderstandings of what they had studied. In these schools, observation and documentation are the two chief assessment strategies used.

For example, Pat Schulze, a teacher in Michigan State University's Child Development Laboratories, uses three-sided panel boards, approximately 2 × 5 feet each, to capture project and theme work with her children. These colorful boards, which contain descriptions of the particular curricular goals and objectives highlighted during a project, line the school's hallways outside of each classroom during student-led conference days. Parents are intrigued and delighted with pictures of their children, busy working with others in the classroom. Parents learn a lot about the many concepts and skills their children are learning as they read the brief narratives written by the children and teacher that are attached to the photos and samples of the children's work. Often displayed nearby these boards are three-dimensional objects produced by the children.

Wendy Lee and Margaret Carr, New Zealand educators, enthusiastically advocate the use of video to capture what they call "narrative assessments." These reflect the reciprocal relationship between the children, adults, and the learning environment and the progress children make from initial understandings of a phenomenon toward more sophisticated concepts. These videos document lively conversations between children and adults and among children as they verbalize what they are thinking when problem solving and skill building. Very early snippets can then be combined with later film to show sequential changes in the children's thinking, correction of earlier misunderstandings, and sequential growth in performance. These very rich assessment records can become a part of a child's individual portfolio or combined into a classroom artifact to illustrate to others the manner in which children's learning evolves over time relative to a particular skill or concept. This qualitative approach to assessment also becomes a powerful resource for the teacher in scaffolding children's learning in that the process over time is included, rather than just the outcome (Lee & Carr, 2003).

CHECKLISTS AND INVENTORIES   Figure 7.1 depicts a developmental inventory of writing skills created by a group of teachers to match the curriculum on which they base their instruction and also to match the report card that is marked four times during the school year. This is an example of a skill-sequenced, criterion-referenced

Writing: Emergent to Fluent Skills

Child's Name: _____ Grade: _____ Date: _____ Test Age: _____ Teacher: _____

Emerging

0   25   50   75   100

_____ Draws simple picture
_____ Scribble-writes
_____ Begins to understand purpose of writing
_____ Makes letter-like forms
_____ Uses one letter to stand for word
_____ Writes own name
_____ Draws picture and can dictate a story about the picture
_____ Is learning letter names and letter sounds
_____ Copies words needed to make a message
_____ Uses initial consonants
_____ Uses approximations
_____ Leaves spaces
_____ Writes upper- and lowercase letters
_____ Spells some simple high-frequency words correctly
_____ "Sound-spells" unfamiliar words
_____ Writes sentence to describe a picture or topic
_____ Chooses own topic
_____ Writes title for story
_____ Able to write and read own story
_____ Use of sentence structure emerges
_____ Uses writing to communicate wants

Early

0   25   50   75   100

_____ Uses end sounds of most words correctly
_____ Knows letter names and letter sounds
_____ Uses vowels
_____ Able to put thoughts and ideas into writing
_____ Can prepare a rough draft and final copy
_____ Writes two or more connected sentences
_____ Able to spell many heavy-duty words correctly
_____ Can identify nouns, verbs, and descriptive words and use them in writing
_____ Uses more correct spellings than approximations
_____ Uses initial blends
_____ Uses capitals and periods
_____ Uses beginning editing skills
   • Circles words misspelled
   • Underlines approximations
   • Able to read and understand proofreaders' marks

Fluent

0   25   50   75   100

_____ Uses reference sources to correct approximations
_____ Can identify and use the three types of sentences
_____ Writes a complete paragraph relating to one topic
_____ Can write narrative and expository text
_____ Able to edit and proofread the writings of peers
_____ Uses final blends
_____ Uses suffixes correctly (e.g., -s, -ing, -ed, -ly)
_____ Can define syllables
_____ Uses editing skills well
_____ Correctly places quotation marks
_____ Correctly places question marks
_____ Correctly places apostrophes
_____ Correctly places commas
_____ Correctly divides story into paragraphs
_____ Indents
_____ Appropriately divides by topic
_____ Expresses and writes in complete thoughts
_____ Legible cursive and manuscript handwriting
_____ Able to write analytically
_____ Publishes correct articles of work
_____ Varies sentence beginnings
_____ Able to write expository text and expressions of others
_____ Sequences ideas logically
_____ Self-corrects run-on sentences
_____ Displays ability to use the writing process to create original stories, poems, and informational pieces
_____ Can word-process on computer

Figure 7.1 Developmental inventory of writing skills.

checklist that helps the teacher keep track not only of where individual children are but also of the specific skills on which he or she should be focusing when developing individual, small-group, and large-group classroom experiences.

Instead of trying to fill out checklists for all the children in her class prior to marking report cards, Shirley Hodgson, a second-grade teacher, tries to target four or five children during a particular exercise to observe skill levels in their reading and writing. Periodically, she sits down with individual children to elicit responses from them to provide information that she has been unable to collect simply by watching them work.

A major advantage of keeping checklists for several years is that teachers develop extraordinary expertise with respect to knowing when most children in a certain grade will acquire particular skills. In doing so, these teachers develop a better understanding of what constitutes a "red flag" in literacy acquisition. Because checklists provide little information other than that the skill or behavior has been observed in a child, they constitute only one piece of data in a more complex determination of a child's progress.

DYNAMIC ASSESSMENT   Small mini-conferences, which involve teachers interacting with children in a scaffolding situation to provide prompts and hints, allow teachers to gather information about where a child is functioning—both at an unassisted level and at a level where maximum assistance is needed. For example, Mr. Seaman is trying to determine Sanjoo's level of comprehension about a story that has just been read to him. Sanjoo is a child in his kindergarten classroom who has limited English skills. He is not yet able to communicate expressively in English, although his receptive English language appears to be growing. Using a series of cards with pictures sequencing the story line, Mr. Seaman asks Sanjoo to line them up according to the way the story happened. When Sanjoo does so quickly and confidently, Mr. Seaman is satisfied that the child's receptive language, attention to shared reading experiences, and concepts about literature are developing satisfactorily, despite Sanjoo's inability to verbalize what he is learning. Dynamic assessment has been shown to be a better predictor of literacy achievement than standardized tests (Spector, 1992) and is also highly effective in addressing the cultural differences that are sometimes problematic in assessment (Stanley, 1996).

Recording Inferences, Judgments, and Reflections: Rating Scales and Rubrics

McAfee and Leong (2002) describe two additional procedures for documenting observations: rating scales and rubrics. These can be used by teachers or parents to convert their opinions or feelings about a child's behaviors, products, or performances related to literacy acquisition,

as well as by children to evaluate their own progress in reaching toward a curricular goal.

Rating scales are constructed by including and listing brief descriptions of the targeted behavior and then a scale using words or numbers ranging from low to high frequency. Although developed scales frequently have five words or numbers, it is sometimes wise to have only four and an added category of N/A (not applicable). This produces a forced-choice situation and gets rid of the middle, fence-sitting option (e.g., "sometimes," "not sure") that allows raters to avoid making a decision (see Figure 7.2).

A disadvantage of rating scales is that they are clearly more subjective measures for documenting global impressions than are descriptions of actual behaviors. Because scoring depends on the observer's interpretation and is subject to bias, these scales should be interpreted cautiously. Children who are popular, extremely likable, cooperative, or attractive may receive higher ratings than deserved. To modify these possibilities, it helps when constructing scales to avoid terms that imply value judgments (e.g., *excellent, average, poor*). Terms such as *never, sometimes, usually,* and *always,* though still qualitative, can identify more clearly the differences in the characteristics being considered and avoid observer bias. While we're discussing rating scales, we should mention here that teachers will want to rate their own professional effectiveness in preparing the teaching environment and interacting with parents and children. A couple of classroom rating scales that have good validity and reliability are the *Early Childhood Environment Rating Scale* (Harms & Clifford, 2002) and *Assessment of Practices in Early Elementary Classrooms (APEEC)* (Hemmeter & Ault, 2001). Both are available from Teachers College Press.

Rubrics, which more clearly spell out particular characteristics of a behavior, are becoming increasingly popular tools to assess performance. Many states are creating sophisticated authentic assessment and evaluation methods that measure the *quality* of a child's product, rather than the child's ability to choose one correct answer from a number of options. For example many states have now begun to assess children's writing abilities as rigorously as their abilities to read. This calls for having children demonstrate the writing process by creating products that must then be scored qualitatively by evaluators. Readers are trained for this evaluation task by practicing on samples of papers, which they compare to a set of qualitatively different "anchor" papers. The score given to the writing on a particular anchor paper directly matches the standards outlined in the state-developed rubrics for students' writing at that grade level.

Teachers are also using rubrics for performance assessment in the classroom. This can begin as early as preschool and kindergarten, where children are asked to evaluate their own work or feeling about a task or the day by simply drawing or encircling a smiling or frowning

Name: _____   Date: _____

Independent Writing Behaviors: Rating Scale

Behavior	1 = Never observed		4 = Frequently observed	
1. Selects own topic for writing.	1	2	3	4
2. Uses webbing to develop character and plot.	1	2	3	4
3. Uses invented spellings rather than asking for help; progressing in conventional spelling.	1	2	3	4
4. Stays on task without reminders.	1	2	3	4
5. Uses reference material.	1	2	3	4
6. Uses word wall and theme charts for help.	1	2	3	4
7. Tries out ideas discussed in writers' workshop.	1	2	3	4
8. Is improving legibility.	1	2	3	4
9. Chooses to write for real purposes; visits writing center independently.	1	2	3	4
10. Chooses to share writing in author's chair.	1	2	3	4

Figure 7.2   A rating scale to document independent writing behaviors.

Copyright © 2005 by Allyn and Bacon

face. Other early childhood educators are engaging older children in the development and/or evaluation of the rubric set. In Ms. Nyswaner's room, she and her second graders talked about the factors involved in producing a well-written story. On the overhead and at the writing center, she shared a variety of second-grade work samples obtained from a colleague in another school. (It is important that teachers do not use children's work from their own classrooms.) Maintaining the anonymity of the original authors, Ms. Nyswaner and the children voted on the two papers they considered the best, two they considered the worst, another two they considered not so bad, but not the best, and two they felt were not the worst, but almost. Afterwards, taking one category of papers at a time, they talked about why they felt the two papers were characteristic of the particular category and listed some descriptors or standards for each category.

This interactive experience between teacher and children took a considerable amount of class time. However, children's products following the experience clearly indicated that children were much more aware of what constituted good-quality and poor-quality story writing. Because they had helped construct the rules—or rubrics—for qual-

ity writing, they were more inclined to observe them, particularly out of a desire to avoid what the children came to call the "crummy categories."

Children's Art as an Observational Literacy Assessment Tool

In the preprimary and early primary grades, children's drawing abilities often parallel their emerging literacy concepts and skills. During this period, their drawings can be used as a fairly accurate window to gauge their ability to deal with writing tools and symbols to express themselves.

Children's capabilities to hold and employ a variety of writing and drawing tools increases markedly as the strength and cartilage in their hands develop during this period. Their cognitive perspectives of lines, circles, shapes, dots, directionality, visual motor integration, memory, and resulting ability to depict abstract ideas all seem to be linked in the early years to their emerging writing ability. For example, look back in Chapter 1 at Figures 1.2 and 1.3. The drawings of Matthew, who was 7 years and 10 months, when compared to Joel's, a peer who was an entire year younger, demonstrate the older child's far greater ability to

Children's art is a legitimate early expression of ideas.

Assessing Reading Accuracy and Comprehension

RUNNING RECORDS OR MISCUE ANALYSIS A highly efficient and effective method for assessing reading accuracy and comprehension at any grade level is to take a running record or miscue analysis (Clay, 1993a). This can be used to determine what kinds of errors a child is making and the strategies he or she is using to decode in oral reading. The teacher selects a text from a recognized listing of children's literature such as Regie Routman's (2000) lists of recommended literature by grade level. While the child reads from the actual text, the teacher follows along on a copy (see Figure 7.3) and notes any repetitions, substitutions, insertions, omissions, reversals, self-corrections, and words that must be supplied to the child. A simpler method is to just underline or circle all errors and to place a *C* over all words self-corrected by the child. Notes about the strengths and limitations of the child's approach can be made in the margins.

Along with what the teacher observes about the child's capabilities, the following three scores are produced from a miscue analysis:

1. *Reading accuracy score:* This is obtained by subtracting all errors not self-corrected by the child from the total number of words read and then dividing by the total number of words read (see Figure 7.3).
2. *Self-correction score:* This is obtained by dividing the number of self-corrected errors by the total number of all errors.
3. *Comprehension score:* This is obtained only if the child reads the entire selection by asking a set of three or four standard questions developed for that particular text and then, depending on the child's responses, assigning one of the following scores:

> 1 = fragmentary understanding
> 2 = partial understanding
> 3 = fairly complete understanding
> 4 = full and complete understanding

For example, for the story "The Biggest House in the World," the teacher devised the following questions to determine comprehension: (1) Who was telling the story? (2) If you were going to retell this story to the class, what would you tell them? (3) What problem did the little snail have, and how was it solved?

Although some teachers argue that grade-level reading lists such as Routman's are arbitrary, reliability can be obtained by choosing a text or two at each grade level and then keeping them aside for assessment purposes to be used with all children at the same grade level. In this way, a child's performance can be gauged against his or

remember and depict detail related to what he had just seen in an assembly with Ronald McDonald. The same differences can be seen in the two children's abilities to remember how letters, words, and sentences are constructed. Also obvious were distinct variations in their steadiness relative to controlling the drawing or writing tool, their recognition of spaces between words, degree of sophistication in creating features of letters and also human features, and relative facility in depicting the abstract qualities of the assembly experience in their drawings and in telling the story with letters.

The Reggio Emilia perspective of "The Hundred Languages of Children" (Edwards, Gandini, & Forman, 1998) honors the important role of children's art as a legitimate early expression of ideas preceding and accompanying earliest efforts at writing. These artifacts that children produce can be maintained as dated work samples in their ongoing portfolios (described in Chapter 8), serving over time as illustrations of both cognitive growth and evolving abilities to remember and produce symbols.

Assessing reading accuracy.

her previous attempt and also against that of other children at the same level. This type of information can be used by the classroom teacher to gauge how well literacy instruction techniques are working in moving all children in the classroom toward a higher percentage of reading accuracy. Data also can be used as a formative and summative measure to weigh skill development of children at baseline levels and at subsequent points in time when new programs or approaches are being implemented or for research purposes.

Texts in which a child is reading at 95 to 100 percent accuracy can be used for independent reading or partner reading activities. For instructional purposes and scaffolded learning activities, however, we will want to move the child to the next level of difficulty and provide needed assistance. Each time children move to a higher level of difficulty, you can expect a drop in accuracy and also in the self-correction rate. Therefore, the level of difficulty should always be noted in the child's ongoing literacy record. Every assessment should be dated.

This brief analysis takes only about four minutes per child if you only intend to check accuracy. It is useful not only for instructional purposes but also for research purposes to look at intervention methods with entire classes or schools of readers. Group scores can be transferred to means and standard deviations for more in-depth analysis.

Using the running record miscue analysis for assessing developing reading skill and comprehension allows teachers to use literature that is not "basal bound"—that is, not narrowed in vocabulary and not overly familiar to the child. It also allows children to use picture clues and

syntax, which are important strategies for the child to use in emerging and early acquisition of literacy but are unavailable in most standardized reading tests. Most of all, it's based on what the child does normally in the classroom. It is not a "test," with all of the anxiety and stress that can accompany an unfamiliar experience. Once children begin reading, an analysis should be done three or four times per year for instructional purposes. For the child who is struggling to keep up with others or moving far ahead of others, analysis should occur more frequently, with texts nearer the child's ability level. This motivates these children to keep trying because they are within their own unique zone of proximal development, are achieving success, and are receiving reinforcement. Oral reading samples can be taped so that children and others can listen to determine if there are increased fluency, phrasing, and overall reading gains.

At least informally, we need to obtain a sense of whether children are developing a sight list of 25 common words, sometimes referred to as *anchor words* (Clay, 1993a). Eleven of these words constitute 25 percent of all words used in spoken language, as depicted in Figure 7.4 (Lederer, 1991). A complete listing of the 1,000 most common words identified by Dolch (1948) can be found in the Appendix.

These are not necessarily easy words for children to learn, *especially when they are out of context.* In the emerging phase, they should be pointed out frequently in the big books that we are using in large- and small-group activities, and children should be given frequent opportunities to play "detective" and identify them when asked. Teachers will want to make sure that the words are handy

Name: _____ Date: _____

Evaluator: _____ Level of Difficulty: _____

The Biggest House in the World
By Leo Leonni (New York: Alfred A. Knopf)

	Number of words
Some (snails) lived on a (juicy) (cabbage.) [C]	7
They moved (gently) around, (carrying) their	13
(houses) from leaf to leaf, in (search) of [C]	21
a (tender) spot to (nibble) on. [C]	27
One day a little (snail) said to his father,	36
"When I grow up I want to have the ^great biggest	46
(house) in the world."	50
"That's silly," said his father, who	57
(happened) to be the (wisest) snail on	64
the (cabbage.) "Some (things) are better [C]	70
small." And he told this story.	76

SCORING

Total number of words read:	76
Total number of uncorrected errors:	12
Reading accuracy score: (76 − 12 = 64 ÷ 76 = .84)	84%
Self-correction rate: (4 ÷ 16 = .25)	25%

Comprehension score: N.A. Did not finish selection.

Comments: Is using pictures and context for help. Self-correction rate is increasing (sounding out words). Move to lower difficulty level for independent reading.

Figure 7.3 Running record of second grader's reading of Leo Leonni's *The Biggest House in the World.*

*I	look	here
*is	this	up
am	*a	go
come	*in	*it
see	*to	*you
*the	like	*of
we	me	*that
at	my	
on	*and	

Figure 7.4   Twenty-five anchor words, of which eleven (*) constitute 25 percent of all spoken language.

Sources: Clay (1993) and Lederer (1991).

for children by posting them at a writing center or supplying individual dictionaries for children to use at their tables. Assessment of whether children are learning these frequently used words can be documented by their ability to sound out the words easily when they come to them in their reading or when they appear in their written work samples. Again, although it would be inappropriate for children to learn these words out of context, some assessment should be done to see whether children are beginning to recognize them on sight and also to make progress in spelling them correctly in their written work.

CLOZE PROCEDURE   If someone were to give you the following sentence: "Tonight, when I get home from work, I will cook _____," what is the first word that you would think of to complete the sentence? If you said something like "dinner," this would tell the speaker that you are able to use syntax and semantics correctly. In other words, you are able to *audiate* mentally the kinds of words that should come next in the sentence based on the way sentences are commonly structured or ordered in English—in this case, subject, verb, and direct object—even if you couldn't specifically name the parts of speech. You also would be supplying a meaningful word that fit with the first part of the utterance. Syntax and semantics are important cueing systems that children internalize first in their spoken communication with others and then later expand into their reading. If children have not developed good understandings of this, they are less able to comprehend reading materials that contain some unfamiliar words.

Teachers of preprimary and kindergarten children can assess this kind of knowledge by first using a familiar rhyme or poem and holding an index card over certain words to see if the children can remember them and fill

them in. This gets the children used to the procedure. Later on, to assess whether children are developing an understanding of syntax and semantics in print and not just using memorization, a small section could be taken from a big book that has been read to them. The teacher can develop sentence strips, place them in a pocket chart, and place index cards over strategic words to see if children can fill in some that would make sense when the sentences are read aloud.

For individually testing children who are reading and writing, teachers can again construct their own tests, as follows (Tompkins, 2001:478):

1. Select a passage from a textbook or trade book. The selection may be either a story or an informational piece.
2. Retype the passage. The first sentence is typed exactly as it appears in the original text. Beginning with the second sentence, one of the first five words is deleted and replaced with a blank. Then every fifth word in the remainder of the passage is deleted and replaced with a blank.
3. Have students read the passage all the way through once silently and then reread the passage and predict or guess the word that goes in each blank. Students write the deleted words in the blanks.
4. Score the student's work, awarding one point each time the missing word is identified correctly. The percentage of correct answers is determined by dividing the number of points by the number of blanks.
5. Compare the percentage of correct word replacements with this scale:

> *61 percent or more correct:—independent level:* Children are able to read the text comfortably and without assistance.
>
> *41–60 percent correct:—instructional level:* At this level, children need scaffolding assistance from the teacher.
>
> *Less than 40 percent correct:—frustration level:* At this level, the reading materials are too difficult, seriously undermining the child's ability to understand what is being read.

INDIVIDUAL READING INVENTORIES (IRIs)   IRIs are individually administered tests to determine a child's reading level or grade-level score. Such a score may be needed for research purposes or for diagnostic purposes when children are not making progress. We want to underscore that the tests themselves do nothing to improve the child's skills; they only give us more information to think about where and how we can provide more helpful instruction. Teachers may construct their own inventories as described in our miscue example. They also may elect to use those that accompany basal texts or to take advantage of any number of commercial tests available to determine a child's reading level or grade-level score. They yield the following information about a child:

- Reading strengths and weaknesses
- Ability to use strategies in context
- Ability to identify unknown words
- Comprehension of main ideas, inferences, vocabulary
- Independent, instructional, and frustration reading levels
- Children's listening capacities as they respond to the teacher's questions about what they have just read

Children typically are asked to read from a list of words until they begin to have difficulty decoding. An additional task is to read orally or silently from a series of narrative and expository passages that become increasingly more difficult and then to answer a series of comprehension questions.

One of the most comprehensive IRIs we have seen is the Bader Reading and Language Inventory (Bader, 1998). Now in its third edition, it contains a graded series of reading passages from a preprimer to twelfth-grade difficulty level, graded word recognition lists, and an English as a second language screening test. Also included are spelling tests to obtain information about children's abilities in auditory and visual discrimination and memory, cognitive language development, sound–symbol association, and knowledge of spelling conventions. There is a section to test emergent literacy skills (literacy awareness, blending, segmentation, letter knowledge, hearing letter names in words, and syntax matching) and another to analyze phonics and structural analysis knowledge (with age-appropriate cautions about utilization). Four cloze tests are included to look at semantic, syntactic, and grammatical processing. Checklists for evaluating language abilities and ideas for constructing open-book reading assessments are also available.

Assessing Spelling and Writing Acquisition Skills

In our estimation, two errors are commonly committed in teaching young children how to write. First, some teachers teach spelling words by having children memorize a list of words each week and then take a test on them at the end of the week. Research indicates that this method is ineffective and that children may remember for the test but not be able to remember how to spell the word when they need it in their writing. The second error is in having children spending writing time copying letters, words, and sentences—or practicing handwriting—and calling that "writing time." As pointed out in earlier chapters, invented spelling is necessary during emerging and early stages of literacy acquisition if children are going to develop a sense of how words are put together and how they are used to construct meaning. To assess writing progress, a child's work samples are

the most useful assessment products. In comparing writing production from one time to another, the children themselves and their parents and teachers can note growth in fluidity (increase in vocabulary), movement toward conventional spelling, and skill in sentence generation.

Although there are many methods for assessing these skills, there are two that we might suggest here—"repetitions" and "attribute-naming" activities. The first is simply using the same stimulus each time, for example a familiar rhyme such as "Humpty Dumpty" or a well-known song, and asking the child first to draw a picture of the character and then to write the rhyme or song from memory (see Figure 7.5). For comparison purposes, the same poem or song should be used to assess growth at least three or four times during the school year, although the exercise might be varied with other poems or songs in between the assessments. The method should always be demonstrated in large group to the children before asking them to produce individual samples, and any large-group sample should be removed from viewing before asking the children to produce their own sample so that copying does not occur.

A similar strategy is to use a picture stimulus of a familiar object (e.g., a house) or living thing (e.g., a dog) and ask the children in large group to see how many words they can generate about the picture. The teacher writes each of the words they suggest, prompting them to help her spell them correctly. The group product is then removed, and the children are provided with their own page with a smaller version of the same stimulus on it. Ten minutes are allocated to producing as many words as they can think of. Children are asked to spell the words as well as they can, using invented spelling when necessary, and not to refer to reference materials for this exercise or to ask for help from another child. Another 10 minutes are then allocated for children to write a story about the stimulus. Figure 7.6 shows Britanny's early attempts at word generation in November of the first grade. This sample, along with the story she generated about "Clifford," was saved in her portfolio, and subsequent efforts through second grade were collected for comparison. Britanny's appreciation of her own progress was evident in her comments at the end of second grade, when she compared later and earlier samples over the two-year period: "I was such a baby then!"

Although the validity of this technique is apparent, it is possible to construct a scoring system to rate growth for the purposes of research or group comparisons. For example, in measuring fluidity—the numbers of words generated from time to time on the same stimulus—numbers can be totaled each time and compared for the same child over time or compared across groups of children. In assessing growth toward conventional spelling on a three-point scale, one point can be given for a consonant stage (few or no vowels being used) in generating a word, two points for the alphabetic stage, where vowels are present,

Kayla, age 4.10:

"Humpty Dumpty sat on a wall.
Humpty Dumpty had a great fall.
And all the King's men . . ."

Figure 7.5   Writing assessment—using one nursery rhyme for comparison at each assessment period.

and three points for a word that is spelled correctly. The total is divided by the number of words assessed, for a score range of zero to three. In sentence generation, one point can be given for a noun and verb; two points for a noun, verb, and modifiers; three points for the correct addition of a capital letter or ending punctuation; four points for a capital letter and ending punctuation; five points for two connected, well-constructed sentences; and six points for three or more connected, well-constructed sentences, for a scoring range of zero to six. An alternative point value system could also be constructed; however, what is important is that the implemented system is used consistently by all who teach in the same building (better yet, all who teach in a particular school system) so that the interpretation of what scores mean is common across educators who might be involved with the child on an ongoing basis and can also be shared with parents and other professionals.

Hayward (1998) has devised a system that can be used by the classroom teacher to monitor each child's spelling development and to plan instruction leading toward conventional spelling. The technique involves de-veloping listings of the high-frequency words targeted at each grade level (or at progressive levels). He then creates a computer-generated spreadsheet, labeling each of the rows with the names of the children in his class, and lists the 25 high-frequency spelling words under each child's name (see Figure 7.7 for Hayward's first-grade listing). At the beginning of each month, he individually assesses each child's ability to recognize the words and highlights these in yellow. Children delight in building up the number of yellow marks, and he can see at a glance which words he needs to stress more frequently in the context of children's classroom literacy experiences. He discusses the purpose of the exercise with the children—that it is not meant to be a "test" but is a strategy to get information to help him be a better teacher. While the children are expected to learn the words, Hayward points out that children should be provided *authentic literacy experiences* to learn the words through daily writing, guided reading, and independent reading. These words can constitute the words that are chosen for the word wall and, once they are discussed in context and put up on the wall, children are

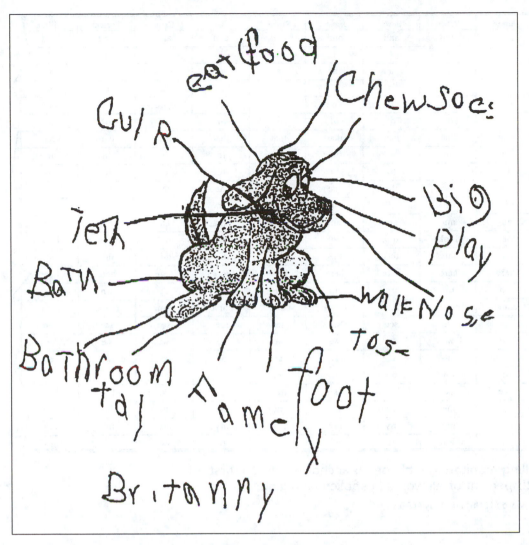

Figure 7.6   Attribute-naming writing sample.

expected to spell them correctly in their writing (see Chapter 5).

Self-Appraisal by the Child

When we talk about authenticity in assessment and evaluation, a key component is making sure that children are drawn into the process so that they have ownership and investment in their own learning and progress. This leads to developing *metacognition*—children's understanding of their own capabilities and the positive outcomes that can result from practice and *independent, strategic* application of what they are learning. For example, Ms. Grey talked with her second graders about seeing whether they could spot some smaller words in larger, unfamiliar words they were having trouble decoding. She demonstrated it in large group by taking some of the compound words out of a poem they had been reading. She listed several of these on the easel and then took an index card and covered first the front half and then the second half to show the children that the longer word was actually made up of two smaller words they already knew. She then took time to have children find some additional compound words in a reading passage, list them, and practice the technique. Afterward, she observed several of the children during silent reading holding a finger over parts of words in order to figure them out and then going on with their reading. These metacognitive strategies evolve from clear demonstrations by teachers or more knowledgeable peers, followed by independent practice by the child. It is as important to assess whether children are employing these strategies independently, as when they are asked to do so in a specific task. One way to do this is not always to provide the suggested strategy but, instead, to ask a child which strategies he or she might use when needed for decoding or comprehension (Cunningham et al., 2000).

The process of having children involved in keeping portfolios and student-led conferencing is outlined carefully

Rhashan	Kaitlyn	Aimee	Robert	Boyce	Jeanne	Rossie	Gary	Carrie	Tomeka	Milton
and	and	and	and	and	and	and	and	and	and	and
I	I	I	I	I	I	I	I	I	I	I
a	a	a	a	a	a	a	a	a	a	a
is	is	is	is	is	is	is	is	is	is	is
you	you	you	you	you	you	you	you	you	you	you
of	of	of	of	of	of	of	of	of	of	of
that	that	that	that	that	that	that	that	that	that	that
in	in	in	in	in	in	in	in	in	in	in
to	to	to	to	to	to	to	to	to	to	to
the	the	the	the	the	the	the	the	the	the	the
it	it	it	it	it	it	it	it	it	it	it
am	am	am	am	am	am	am	am	am	am	am
look	look	look	look	look	look	look	look	look	look	look
this	this	this	this	this	this	this	this	this	this	this
here	here	here	here	here	here	here	here	here	here	here
up	up	up	up	up	up	up	up	up	up	up
come	come	come	come	come	come	come	come	come	come	come
see	see	see	see	see	see	see	see	see	see	see
we	we	we	we	we	we	we	we	we	we	we
at	at	at	at	at	at	at	at	at	at	at
on	on	on	on	on	on	on	on	on	on	on
like	like	like	like	like	like	like	like	like	like	like
me	me	me	me	me	me	me	me	me	me	me
my	my	my	my	my	my	my	my	my	my	my
go	go	go	go	go	go	go	go	go	go	go

Figure 7.7 A spelling monitoring table of 25 anchor words, the first 11 of which make up 25 percent of all words in spoken language.

Sources: Adapted from Hayward (1998) and Clay (1993).

in Chapter 8. A couple of self-appraisal examples related to literacy acquisition that might be included in the portfolio can be seen in Figure 7.8 ("Look! I'm Making Progress in My Writing. I Can . . . "), Figure 7.9 ("My Conference Report"), and Figure 7.10 ("Look at Me!"), contributed by Dolores McFadden, kindergarten teacher at Gundry Elementary School in Flint, Michigan.

In constructing a self-evaluation checklist of literacy skills, we should always include some skills that we know the child can do or is on the brink of accomplishing with some scaffolding help from an adult or more developed peer. The skills listed should always be *observable*—that is, skills for which direct observation or work samples can be obtained to document performance or ability. The checklist can be developed for an entire class of children or for individual children and can be used to assess children weekly, monthly, or trimonthly, depending on the assessment goal. To mark the checklist, the child meets individually with the teacher for several minutes to go over each of the variables. The checklist is dated each time, and the child simply colors in or checks off the skills

that have been achieved. If the child wishes to mark a skill that has not been demonstrated by way of a work sample, the teacher can ask for an on-the-spot demonstration. The mini-conference format of this assessment procedure allows the teacher and child to collaborate together in the assessment process and gives the teacher an opportunity to reinforce the child's progress. An important aspect of the procedure is that the child is asked which skill he or she will be working on for the next time so that both teacher and student are aware of the goal.

Using the same idea, children can be asked to fill out a preconference report one or two days before a parent–teacher conference or student-led conference. It might be a listing of general skills over all domains or might assess only the literacy skills being acquired. Again, the child and teacher talk about the particular item that should be an observable skill, focusing the child's attention on what he or she has already accomplished and on some areas of progress to target for the next assessment period.

The literacy, math, and science logs and journals that were described in Chapter 6 are another way that children

Name: _____ Grade: _____

Look! I'm Making Progress in My Writing. I Can . . .

Skill	Date	Date	Date	Date	Date	Date	Date
Write my first name							
Write my first and last name							
Write five words							
Write a sentence							
Put uppercase letters at the beginning of sentences							
Put periods at the end of sentences							
Put spaces between words							
Put question marks at the end of questions							
Write the word *I* with an uppercase letter							
Put a vowel in every word							
Use describing words							
Write legibly							

Don't forget to target at least one skill to work on for next time!

Figure 7.8   Child's self-appraisal writing inventory.

Name: _____ Grade: _____

Date: _____

My Conference Report		
I can recognize my name. _____ Yes _____ Not Yet	I can write my first name. _____ Yes _____ Not Yet	I can write my first and last name. _____ Yes _____ Not Yet
I can recognize the names of two friends. _____ Yes _____ Not Yet	I leave spaces between words that I write. _____ Yes _____ Not Yet	I always capitalize someone's name. _____ Yes _____ Not Yet
I can write a sentence. _____ Yes _____ Not Yet	I can recall and tell a familiar nursery rhyme. _____ Yes _____ Not Yet	I can read a familiar nursery rhyme. _____ Yes _____ Not Yet
I put a vowel in every word. _____ Yes _____ Not Yet	I can write some whole words. _____ Yes _____ Not Yet	I can write the first and last letters in a word. _____ Yes _____ Not Yet
I put periods in the right places. _____ Yes _____ Not Yet	I put capital letters at the beginnings of my sentences. _____ Yes _____ Not Yet	I can think of a story to write. _____ Yes _____ Not Yet

Figure 7.9 My conference report.

can be involved in self-assessment of what they are learning. These provide a written work sample that can be used to assess the conceptual learning of the child as well as his or her literacy capabilities over time. This is an excellent way of integrating literacy across the curriculum and carrying out useful assessment at the same time. Information gleaned from close analysis of products such as these helps not only to assess literacy, but also to reveal the child's conceptual understanding in other domains. It also assesses the child's written ability to synthesize and interpret meaning from silent reading or oral discussion, skills very different than those demonstrated in oral reading (Routman, 1996).

In addition to these activities, children may be given such tools as editing checklists (see Figure 7.11, "My Good Writing Checklist") to help them organize and evaluate the quality of their work before turning it in to the teacher or sharing it with others. Teachers should work with children to make sure they know how to use each of these self-evaluation tools for skill improvement and also as mechanisms for appreciating their own progress.

All of these activities are only suggestions that may be altered to make them more appropriate, depending on the variables of interest and the children's levels of development in your classroom. In addition, all of the authentic assessment strategies are also useful for assessment across other domains.

The Status of Standardized Testing

Recently, a professor in early childhood education was observing her student teachers from an observation booth. Standing next to her was the mother of one of the children in the classroom, a child with Down syndrome. As the mother watched the teacher reminding her daughter Sammy to be gentle with another child, she sighed and said, "It's tough dealing with a child who has a 5-year-old body and a 2-year-old mentality."

"I'm curious," said the professor, knowing that children with Down syndrome differ as much with re-

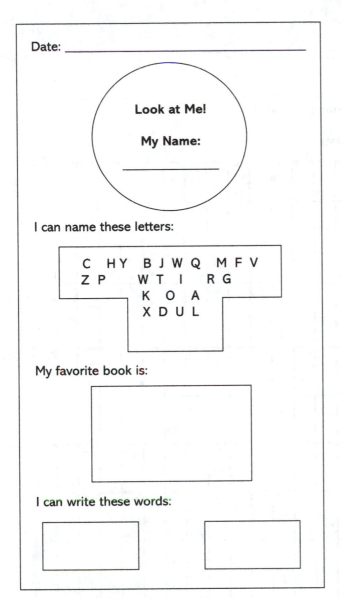

Figure 7.10   Child's self-appraisal.

Copyright © 2005 by Allyn and Bacon

spect to intelligence as all children, "How was the '2-year-old mentality' diagnosed? I've seen Sammy at work in the classroom, and she's obviously much more capable than that."

"Well," said the mother, "she was tested . . . and even though I agree that she can do so much more than what was on the test . . . that's the conclusion they came to." A discussion between the two followed in which the mother related her fear that the test score would follow her daughter and make a difference in the way her potential would be viewed, particularly until others became better acquainted with what she could really do.

Today, federal legislation and the millions of dollars being poured into early childhood education to support literacy

frequently come with a mandate of standardized testing. A major provision of the No Child Left Behind Act of 2001 is that all children in grades 3–8 must be tested every year with a standardized tool. Those schools receiving Reading First grants from the U.S. Department of Education are required to select a standardized test to assess children prior to grade 3 in an effort to ensure that every child will be reading at the end of grade 3 (Ysseldyke, 2004).

These requirements are based on a belief that standardized tools with established psychometric properties are a more reliable and efficient way of measuring children's progress. Wise school systems have chosen to use these measures judiciously, along with maintaining teacher-constructed and informal strategies that are often more understandable to parents and children and more useful for instructional planning.

Still, in other school districts, norm-referenced and criterion-related tests remain the most important "pillars of assessment" used to gain information and make decisions about young children. In fact, it's been estimated that U.S. students now take more than 300 million standardized tests each year (Ysseldyke, 2004). When this happens, the possibility exists that decision making about curriculum, instruction, and assessment can be taken out of the hands of those working daily with children and placed in the hands of district office administrators, textbook publishers, and outside policy makers. Feeling powerless to disagree, teachers often fall in line despite their gut feelings that the high stakes testing process may be consequential to children and not very useful in making instructional decisions (Barrentine, 1999).

Professionals working with young children need to be familiar with the properties of these instruments and also their limitations, whether they are administering the tests themselves, participating in research projects, or consulting with other professionals who are testing children referred from their classrooms. Particularly, professionals need to be concerned about a chosen instrument's *reliability*—that it consistently measures what it is supposed to—and also its *validity*—that it provides accurate, reasonable, and fair information about what is being assessed. When these instruments have been normed carefully, and reliability and validity have been adequately attended to, they can be useful for *diagnostic* and *research* purposes to look at how individual children and groups of children vary with respect to their developmental functioning or in terms of educational achievement.

Standardized tests, which are usually normed on such characteristics as age, grade, urban/rural, status, racial and ethnic group, and gender, were originally constructed to look at *abnormalities* in development, particularly in intelligence. After their debut in the United States at the 1893 Chicago World's Fair, where visitors could take tests in "mental anthropometry and compare their performance with that of others," intelligence tests and achievement tests flourished (Sattler, 2002). Beginning in the 1960s,

| My Good Writing Checklist | | | | | | | | | | | | | | | | | | | | | | |
Date																						
I have checked these things:																						
All my sentences end with a period (.), exclamation point (!), or question mark (?).																						
Each sentence or name begins with a capital letter.																						
Each word has a vowel in it.																						
My handwriting is readable.																						
I used some describing words.																						
I read the story to a friend.																						
I read my story to myself, and it made sense.																						

Name: _____

Figure 7.11   My good writing checklist.

Copyright © 2005 by Allyn and Bacon

they gained enormous popularity and power with the public, parents, researchers, and policymakers. However, because of growing criticisms in the 1980s about technical and educational inadequacy, overuse and misuse, unsuitability for the population being tested, cultural bias, and undue influence on education, educators began looking for alternatives that might have better payoff in terms of instructional planning for individuals or groups of children (McAfee & Leong, 2002).

Tierney (1998:383–387) argues against the rigidity of current assessment practices and the overdrive for uniformity, suggesting that children's skill acquisition is rarely so

"neatly packaged." Some broad based benchmarks may be possibilities for all students; however, there may be some which can be achieved by very few students, realistically. The latter happens when standards and assessment practices are "preset, prescribed, and mandated" in a restrictive manner without enough consideration for where students are or whether learning routes and possibilities have been aligned.

Research-based best practices in literacy assessment should be grounded in knowledge of child development, centered in the classroom rather than imposed from outside, start with what children currently know and can do, provide information that is supportive rather than penalizing to children, be integral to instruction, and continually undergo review, revision, and improvement (Winograd, Flores-Duenas, Arrington, 2003: 209). If any of these principles is violated, those who advocate for education in the best interest of children must challenge the ingegrity of the process and ask for reform.

If you are working in a school or district that still requires achievement tests to be given in the classroom below third grade, do whatever you can to help administrators and board members be aware of the problems in paper–pencil testing of young children. If you can't steer them toward more authentic strategies, then at least prepare children in advance for the testing experience. You can do this by providing experiences similar to the ones they will have in the actual testing situation (marking bubbles, following directions, working under a time constraint, using a separate answer sheet or machine-scorable sheet). You can also talk about "appropriate" testing behaviors, such as working quietly, doing their own work, and guessing. One caution: It will be important to exercise integrity with respect to the amount of time you allocate and spend on test preparation in your classroom, because it is time that will be taken away from children for other, more meaningful learning opportunities.

An alphabetical listing of some of the standardized screening and assessment instruments most often selected for isolating specific aspects of language development or special problems is provided here so that you can be familiar with typical instruments used, consider the appropriateness of their use, and advocate for alternatives or additional information when they do not seem appropriate.

Formal Literacy Assessment Tools

Measure	Description
Auditory Discrimination Test	Individually administered listing of 40 pairs of words from which children distinguish whether they are the same or different. Ages 5–8.
Dynamic Indicators of Basic Early Literacy Skills (DIBELS)	One-minute timed tests of alphabetic understanding, phonemic awareness, letter naming, and fluency. Scored on specific number of responses in one minute.
Early Language and Literacy Classroom Observation Toolkit (ELLCO)	Addresses the role of environmental factors in early literacy and language development. Contains three assessment tools: literacy environment checklist; protocol to conduct classroom observations and administer teacher interviews; and a literacy activities rating scale. Preschool–grade 3.
Expressive One-Word Picture Vocabulary Test (EOWPVT-R)	Assesses expressive vocabulary (children name pictures). Scores: Raw, standard, stanines. Normed on 439 California children. Concurrent validity. Spanish and English. Ages 2½–grade 3+.
Gates MacGinitie Reading Tests, Third Ed.	Assesses children's strengths and weaknesses in reading comprehension. Parallel forms. Results reported in gain scores; links weaknesses to specific instructional strategies. Grades K–12.
Gray Oral Reading Test, Third Ed.	Screens for ability to retrieve sight words from memory and use phonetic strategies to read new words in passages, each followed by five comprehension questions. Grades 1–12.
Kaufman Assessment Battery for Children	Wide-range screening test. Includes subtests to measure vocabulary, reading/decoding, word naming, and comprehension. Scores: Raw, scaled, standard. National and sociocultural percentiles. Normed on nationwide sample of 2,000 children. Spanish and English. Ages 2½–grade 3.
Lindamood Auditory Conceptualizaton Test	Assesses phonological awareness and processing deficits. Yields age equivalents. K–adult.
Observation Survey of Early Literacy Achievement (Concept of Print)	Running records, letter identification, concepts about print, word tests, writing, hearing sounds in words; detailed diagnostic information. Beginning grade 1.
Peabody Picture Vocabulary Test-R (PPVT-R)	Tests receptive vocabulary. Equivalent forms. Raw scores, standard scores, percentiles, stanines. Standardization based on 4,200 children. Good reliability and validity. Age 2½–40+.

Measure	Description
Preschool Language Scale-3 (PLS-3)	Language acquisition and prelanguage skills. Subscales for auditory comprehension and expressive communication. Standard scores and percentiles by age. Normed on 1,200 children. High test-retest reliability; moderate validity. Spanish and English. Birth to age 6.
Stanford Diagnostic Reading Test-4 (SDRT-4).	Phonetic analyses, vocabulary, comprehension, and scanning. Alternative forms. Norm referenced. Raw and standard scores. Grades 1–12.
Test of Auditory Analysis Skills (TAAS)	Evaluates children's auditory perceptual skills, abilities to break spoken language into separate parts and to recognize sequence of each of parts. Raw scores, grade-level equivalencies. No normative data, validity, or reliability information. Grades K–12.
Test of Early Language Development (TELD-2)	Receptive and expressive language, syntax, semantics. Alternate forms. Raw scores, language quotient, percentiles, normal curve equivalents, age equivalents. Normed on 1,329 children. Ages 2–7.
Test of Oral Reading Fluency	Screens with one-minute timed passages. Alternate forms. Score based on words read correctly in one minute. Age equivalents. Grades 1–6.
Test of Phonological Awareness	Measures phonemic awareness, ability to match pictures according to beginning and final sounds. Raw scores, standard scores, percentiles. Grades K–2.
Test of Reading Comprehension-3 (TORC-3)	Eight subtests to assess general reading comprehension, vocabulary, ability to read directions. Scores: standard, percentiles, stanines, normal-curve equivalents, age equivalents. Grades 1–12.
Test of Written Spelling-3 (TWS-3)	Predictable and unpredictable words. Raw scores, percentiles, standard scores, age and equivalents. Grades 1–12.
Woodcock Johnson Reading Mastery Tests-R	Screens for visual and auditory learning, letter identification, word identification, word attack, word and passage comprehension. Grade and age equivalents. Relative performance index; instructional ranges, percentile ranks, standard scores. Grades K–12.
Woodcock Johnson Psychoeducational Battery-R (WJ-R)	Cognitive ability (memory for names and sentences, visual matching, incomplete words, visual closure, picture vocabulary, analysis-synthesis). Supplementary battery measures visual-auditory learning, memory for words, visual processing speed, sound blending, picture recognition, oral vocabulary, concept formation, delayed recall-memory for names, delayed recall-visual/auditory learning, short-term memory and attention, sound patterns, spatial relations, listening comprehension, verbal analogies. Second section comes in two parallel forms, nine subtests. Supplemental battery consists of word attack, reading vocabulary, quantitative concepts, proofing, writing fluency, punctuation, capitalization, spelling, and handwriting. Standard scores, percentile ranks, age and grade equivalent scores. Ages 2–adult.

Following are issues to consider whenever you are deciding about the use of standardized tests with young children:

1. Who should determine what literacy skills and concepts are to be assessed? How often should assessment take place? Who should complete the assessments? How do assessments link together from year to year? The answers to these questions reveal a great deal about what the stakeholders in a school district and community be-

lieve is most important relative to children's short- and long-term literacy development. A philosophy of assessment and evaluation is always reflective of viewpoints about learning, perspectives about what should occur in the classroom, the role of teachers and children in the assessment process, and allocation of resources.

2. Before selecting a test, or allowing a test to be given to children in your classroom, you should become familiar with the appropriateness of the test for those children. How psychometrically sound is it? How valid? How reliable? Is training required or recommended for administration of it?

3. How will the test be administered? In grades 2 and below, group-administered tests are not appropriate. There are too many confounding factors that can get in the way of a true score. Children may lose their place or not understand directions adequately. Diagnostic tests should be given on a one-to-one basis. Tests that are inordinately long and stressful to children are also not appropriate, no matter how well known or popular the tests are or how technically "sound." In short, assessment should not be harmful to children.

4. How useful will the results be, and how will the results be used? Will they yield information to improve instruction of the children? To generate additional knowledge about skill emergence in young children (research)? To evaluate the usefulness of a particular pedagogical approach to literacy? Will children (or classes or schools of children) be unfairly compared with children who come from more af-

fluent learning communities? Will the publicized results embarrass such groups? If the assessment is for research purposes, it may be that not all children need to be tested every year to obtain good and useful information. If no good use of the results can be determined, the testing is probably a waste of children's valuable time and should be reconsidered.

5. One, or even two, standardized scores per year per child is not enough assessment to be helpful to adequately measure literacy growth in a dynamically changing child. What kinds of informal assessment strategies are in place to evaluate progress in between and to support instruction? What other factors within or surrounding a child could negatively influence the child's performance on the day a test is given? How comprehensive, ongoing, reasonable, useful, and developmentally appropriate is the overall assessment and evaluation approach for protecting every child's acquisition of strong literacy concepts and skills?

Final Thoughts

Good assessment of young children is always *context-responsive*. According to Jessie Roderick (1991), this means that it is collaborative and social. It also values planned and unplanned curricular experiences that give the teacher opportunities for continuous data collection and instructional decisions while interacting with children. Finally, it helps us view children as important key participants in shaping and evaluating their own learning. The authentic assessment strategies that we have described fit well within this definition and also within the definition of developmentally appropriate practices.

In designing your own strategies and tools for assessment, you will still want to consider validity and reliability. Determine exactly what literacy skills you want

children to develop, and then find the best possible ways to measure whether this is happening. Be sure that the strategies and procedures you use are fair, and be cautious in interpreting and sharing outcomes. Data should be collected consistently by both teachers and children, always dated, and reviewed periodically with an eye to modifying instructional practice in a way that will benefit the child.

The children being evaluated and their families deserve to be involved in these processes and fully privy to what is learned. In the next chapter, we will provide in-depth descriptions of the portfolio process and student-led celebrations—absolutely the most effective ways to organize and share what we are learning about each child's emergent literacy.

Challenge Yourself

1. Look at the cumulative school folders of three children in your classroom who differ widely in their reading and writing abilities. What information do you see that tells you about their current levels of skills and concepts relative to literacy? What weaknesses are apparent? What strengths are apparent? How would you change your instructional planning for these children on the basis of the information presented? What could be added to the cumulative folders to provide helpful information about acquired literacy?

2. Analyze the amount of involvement by children in the assessment process. Construct a self-appraisal checklist that might be used by all children in the classroom at the beginning of the year and another

for the end of the year based on your knowledge of how children generally acquire skills during the school year. How does the listing of skills vary from time to time? Which skills overlap? Have children in your classroom use the appropriate checklist for self-appraisal.

3. Select an appropriate, grade-related text from a listing of children's texts. Following the procedure outlined in this chapter, complete a brief running record of each child in your classroom. Then construct a graph of your results, indexing children by chronological age and reading accuracy percentages. Is chronological age the best predictor of results? What other factors appear to be important?

Suggested Sources
for Additional Information

Goodman, Y. M. (1996). *Notes from a kidwatcher: Selected writings of Yetta M. Goodman* (S. Wilde, Ed.). Portsmouth, NH: Heinemann.

McAfee, O., & Leong, D. (2002). *Assessing and guiding young children's development and learning.* Boston: Allyn and Bacon.

Puckett, M. B., & Black, J. K. (2000). *Authentic assessment of the young child* (2nd ed.). New York: Merrill.

Sattler, J. M. (2001). *Assessment of children—cognitive applications* (4th ed.). San Diego, CA: Jerome M. Sattler.

Portfolios and Student-Led Conferencing
Celebrating the Stages of Development

Portfolios: Empowering the Learner

The letter shown in Figure 8.1 was written by a first-grade student in the middle of the school year in which portfolios played an integral part in the classroom. It expresses the high degree of possessiveness and the feelings of pride and ownership that keeping a portfolio can instill in a child who has participated actively in learning. Portfolios offer unique opportunities for students to discover how to think for themselves and how to assess their own progress—crucial steps on their way to becoming lifelong learners. When these opportunities for initiative occur, students are likely to work to their full potential and in a creative fashion to accomplish the tasks at hand. Moreover, portfolios provide a venue for students to take responsibility for their learning. The portfolio experience helps learners take pride in their work and gives that work new meaning and purpose for every student.

As you investigate the concept of portfolios, ask yourself these questions:

- What is the definition and purpose of a portfolio?
- What are the unique benefits for children, teachers, and parents as a result of portfolio implementation?
- How does one implement and manage a portfolio program?
- How are students involved in the selection and evaluation process of the portfolio components?
- What are the unique formats that will allow students to share their portfolio collection effectively?

In this chapter, we will define the concept of a student portfolio and explore the benefits of its use. We will share with you a variety of methods of implementation, dependent on your knowledge and comfort level with the topic. The chapter will explore several types of portfolios

Figure 8.1 To the reader of this portfolio.

including working, showcase, and electronic. In our discussion of portfolios, we will show you ways to introduce the portfolio idea to your students, how to manage a portfolio program, how to facilitate the selection and evaluation process, and, finally, how to share the portfolio collection with others.

What Is a Portfolio?

Portfolios are tools for children to learn how to tell their unique story of learning. Students gain insight into their own abilities and interests by collecting and reflecting on samples of their own work (Herbert, 2001). The portfolio concept views learning as a process that is always evolving, growing, and changing. Learning is never complete, but is a lifelong endeavor. Therefore, assessment also must be an ongoing process. It is the goal of the portfolio to assess this continuous learning process by capturing a rich sampling of student performance in all areas during the school year.

The portfolio provides a vehicle for ongoing, collaborative reflection between the student, teacher, and parent(s), enabling each to become a partner in the learning process. Most important, a portfolio should be a celebration of the child's unique abilities, achievements, and progress, displayed through authentic samples. Portfolios are unique to each child and demonstrate very specifically what each child has learned.

Who Can Use a Portfolio?

Anyone can use a portfolio. They have been successfully used in homes, child care centers, and preschools, as well as in elementary, middle, and high schools. Today, even colleges and certain professions require the use of portfolios to document growth and potential. Once you consider all of the benefits portfolios can offer learners, you will probably ask yourself, "Who *wouldn't* use a portfolio?"

What Are the Benefits of Portfolios?

Portfolios provide numerous and varied benefits to the teacher, child, and parent. An effective portfolio program builds a strong bond among these partners.

Portfolio implementation allows the teacher to become an "objective" observer of a child's abilities and successes. As noted by Shaklee et al. (1997:23), "The teacher clears the lenses through which he or she views children."

Such perceptual change is truly the driving force behind the power of portfolio assessment. Teachers who use portfolios gain new knowledge about students' strengths and needs. In addition, they typically establish a more equal learning relationship with their students and find this has a positive effect on their abilities as teachers. Analyzing a portfolio's contents for evidence of student growth and strengths fosters awareness of the patterns and trends that occur throughout the year.

As Evangeline Stefanakis (2002:10) states:

Imagine a class in which teachers regularly look at students' work and look at how students do that work to better understand the multiple intelligences of these individuals. This ongoing practice of examining daily classroom work allows teachers and students to be **co-learners,** to discover, to use, and to build on an individual child's abilities. Teachers and students in these classrooms use portfolios, or collections of student work, to guide their interactions related to teaching, learning, and assessment. Portfolios are a powerful tool that can help teachers in their efforts to reach and teach every child, including those who are bilingual or may have special needs.

Besides providing new insights for teachers, portfolios empower and motivate learners. First, portfolios encourage students to be thoughtful evaluators of their own work. Second, through the sense of ownership that portfolios instill, students give greater value to their work and to the processes involved in learning. Third, portfolios respect each child's individuality, fostering creativity, independent work habits, and improved self-esteem. Finally, portfolios complement the ways in which early childhood educators believe that children learn best. Children learn best when:

- They receive tasks that are developmentally appropriate for their level of learning.
- They have numerous and varied learning opportunities.
- They feel confident as a result of previous successes.
- They are active and involved in learning—discovering, solving problems, and explaining what they are doing and why.

Besides helping in the classroom, portfolios strengthen the connection between home and school. Not only do portfolios give the teacher a more complete picture of the child, including the developing growth and areas of strength and improvement, but the portfolio also does the same for the parent.

Used as a communicative tool, the portfolio presents parents with vivid, tangible evidence of their children's experiences in school. The question "What did you learn in school today?" is most often met with the reply, "Nothing!" Discussing the contents of a portfolio together, while noting what the child has learned and achieved, allows a parent to reinforce the importance of the child's work.

One parent of a child who was involved in a portfolio program had this to say about the value of the portfolio (1996):

As our children bring home their work, it is usually looked over and then thrown away. Even though we realize they have progressed, it's difficult to actually realize how much. Through this method, I gained a greater appreciation of what my son had learned. Also, by evaluating himself on his needs, I think it has a greater impact than if I tell him. At that point, it becomes criticism and makes him feel bad.

Now that we have presented the many reasons for using portfolios in the classroom, you may be wondering how this approach can work for you. The next section discusses the purpose of portfolios and the direction that a portfolio program may take, depending on your comfort level and experience with portfolios, as well as on the needs and interests of your students.

The Portfolio Approach: Stepping in the Right Direction

There has been much debate in recent years over the various means used to assess student achievement. Some educators support standardized tests; others champion portfolios. There are both criticisms and words of support for each side. Gilman and Hassett (1995) list the following criticisms of standardized tests:

1. They often measure unimportant curriculum content.
2. They may measure what was *not* taught.
3. They usually rank student aptitudes at one moment but ignore how much an individual has progressed over time.
4. They may have a racial, gender, or other bias.
5. They produce results that are often filed away and forgotten.

Despite the ongoing debate, only a few school districts have eliminated standardized testing and many are adding it. This has led teachers to seek an alternative method of assessing what students in their classrooms truly know and understand. A common choice for alternative assessment is the portfolio. Gilman and Hassett (1995:311) find that portfolios are an appropriate way to meet the new standards for reading and writing assessment:

> The eleven standards for assessment created by the International Reading Association (IRA) and the National Council of Teachers of English (NCTE) committee reflect the belief that teachers should be focused on student learning more than content coverage; that reading and writing activities should be integrated with other activities in the student's home, school, and community; and that reflection and critical inquiry are a vital part of every student's academic growth and progress.

Unlike many norm-referenced and criterion-referenced tests, **assessment portfolios** do not exclude certain student populations, such as English language learners. Such portfolios can be designed to measure any observable skill or content-area knowledge needed for systemwide assessment purposes, as long as predetermined scoring criteria are in place. To implement, a designated group of professionals decides on common goals for student achievement and performance, develops rubrics and checklists for scoring purposes, and agrees to the standards of performance to be reached. Including English language learners through the use of assessment portfolios not only provides improved information about student achievement but it also impacts teaching and student learning in a positive way (Gomez, 2000).

Birrell and Ross (1996:285) justifiably argue against viewing standardized testing and portfolio assessment as "oppositional methods for determining student growth and teacher effectiveness, as some seem to be implying."

Instead, they contend, we should see them as "different, yet complementary means of gathering and interpreting information that can lead to more holistic evaluations of student achievement in school."

We propose, then, that regardless of any personal or institutional commitment you may have to standardized testing, you should strongly consider using portfolios in your classroom to add a new dimension of reading and writing assessment. The beauty of this assessment tool is that it is a learning tool as well, empowering you, the teacher, with unique assessment criteria while encouraging your students to be lifelong learners—responding to and reflecting on each step of the educational process.

How Do Portfolios Work?

> The power of any tool lies not in its creation, but in its use. A sculpting tool is useless unless it is used by a sculptor. At first, the tool is awkward, even unwieldy, until the sculptor learns the most effective ways to use it. Interaction with the tool must accompany its use because feedback makes the tool dynamic and powerful. The tool eventually seems to be part of the sculptor's hand and he wonders, "How could I ever do my work as well without this wonderful tool?" (Stone, 1995:232)

Stone presents this analogy as words of encouragement for using the portfolio as a tool in your own classroom. She reminds us that, in the beginning, you may think that a portfolio program seems "awkward and unwieldy." With experience, however, you'll find that portfolios soon become one of the most powerful and rewarding tools you can use.

Before you start, it is important to determine the goals for a portfolio program in your classroom. Certainly, it is neither feasible nor desirable to save vast amounts of a student's work. Instead, the teacher should examine the goals of a portfolio program, then decide what kinds of work should be saved to achieve those goals. Teachers should discuss portfolio goal setting with students, either as a group or individually. Ideally, teachers and students should work together to set portfolio goals.

In determining goals for a portfolio, Shaklee et al. (1997) suggest that teachers ask themselves these questions:

- Will the portfolio be comprehensive, serving to evaluate overall student performance, or will it merely record one aspect of learning?
- Will the portfolio be used as feedback, to guide instruction?
- Will the portfolio be used as a periodic progress report to identify special needs or to check program effectiveness?
- Will the portfolio include a student's best work, typical work, or all kinds of work?

As you contemplate your goals for portfolio development, keep in mind that there is no one right way to select student work. The actual process depends on your teaching philosophy, your experience with portfolios, and your views of the best methods for assessing student growth and achievement in your classroom.

Now, let's take a look at the types of work you may wish to include as you guide your students in the development of their portfolios.

What Goes into a Portfolio?

Portfolios may be developed in a variety of ways. One possibility is to represent the whole child by including work representative of all the subject areas. Or you may wish to start small, choosing one subject area such as language arts on which to focus throughout the selection process. In either case, be sure you involve your students in the selection process. One effective way to do that is to brainstorm with them, discussing the items that they feel would be important to include in their portfolios. For example, brainstorm with the class the things they have learned in math that week, whether they were particular concepts or problem-solving techniques. Then guide them in selecting those math pieces that reflect that learning.

As mentioned, Lipton and Hubble (1997) favor collecting examples of both the learning process and the finished product. Examples of the learning process might include taped readings, self-assessment forms, photographs or videos of students at work throughout the school year, revised drafts of student writing, and inventories or checklists. Examples of the finished product might include published pieces of writing, book logs, learning logs, story maps, drawings and artwork, self-reflections, and photos of favorite projects.

Attached to each selected piece should be some type of response form, either filled out by the child or dictated to an adult, indicating the child's reason for including that particular selection in the portfolio. As one selection process, you might ask the children to choose pieces from the week each Friday. One or more pieces may be picked each week, attaching a short response form to each individual piece. More on guiding the self-evaluation and reflection process will be included later in the chapter. The next section provides a brief description of some of the items typically found in a student portfolio. This list is certainly not all-inclusive. Rather, it just contains some ideas to get you started.

READING SAMPLES   Evidence of a child's growth in reading may take several forms in a portfolio. The child might include completed literature logs, reading logs indicating books that have been read, and book reports. In addition, recorded oral readings offer an effective measurement of growth in word attack skills and in developing fluency. We suggest that taped sessions be conducted three to four times a year, using an electronic portfolio format on a program such as Microsoft PowerPoint. An

electronic portfolio is a nice complement to the paper portfolio format discussed here, and will be addressed in further detail later in the chapter.

A template may be created in slide format on Power Point, including information such as the title of selected literature, date, and pages read for the recording sessions. Utilize your parent volunteers to assist children in recording their reading throughout the year, including the necessary information to demonstrate growth over time.

WRITING SAMPLES   Writing samples included in a portfolio should demonstrate evidence of the stages of the writing process as well as examples of a completed written assignment. For example, include all the writing steps that a child takes along the way, such as the created list of brainstormed ideas, the "sloppy copy" of that piece, the evidence of the conferencing stage, the revised piece, and finally the finished product.

At the emerging level, the writing may be samples of children's name writing, simple sentence formations collected at different points throughout the year, or even their stories, which may be recorded using any stage of the writing progression discussed in Chapter 2. It is ideal if both the pictures and stories are collected along with transcripts of the language that surrounded the separate writing pieces. Writing samples collected by children at the emerging-to-early levels of development will often demonstrate great degrees of growth. You will notice vast improvements in the use of capital letters, punctuation marks, and spelling, and in the spacing between letters and words (see Figure 8.2).

The writing samples collected from students at the early-to-fluent level of learning may display evidence of growth in the development of written ideas, the mechanics of writing, and the sequencing of story ideas. To indicate growth over time, it is crucial that all items placed in the portfolio are dated. Simply placing a dating stamp next to the storage container of portfolios helps to remind students to date their work before adding it to their collection, while reinforcing the idea that this is a responsibility of the *student*.

Other kinds of writing you could include in a portfolio might be journals, self-reflections, and response forms from field trips, scientific experiments, and literature (see Figure 8.3).

ORAL LANGUAGE SAMPLES   For children of all ages, it is important to not overlook the role that samples of oral language can play in a portfolio. Such samples can document children's growth in the important areas of oral language discussed in Chapters 2 and 4. Some examples you may wish to use include children: telling and retelling stories, playing in various situations, conversing during snack or lunch time, conversing during group time, singing songs, explaining how something was created, defining words, describing events at a field trip or special day.

Figure 8.2   Writing sample demonstrating progress over time: "The big green frogs are jumping in the lake."

SELF-ASSESSMENTS AND OTHER INVENTORY ITEMS   Self-assessments are crucial for children to learn the fine art of self-evaluation. When children are engaged in self-assessments, they must think about their thinking. This **metacognitive process** is linked directly to children's literacy learning. Therefore, when we engage children in self-assessments in any curricular area, we are furthering their literacy growth. Self-assessments can include both behavioral and academic checklists. These checklists ask students to evaluate themselves as to their conduct and levels of various skills. These self-assessments should be conducted three to four times each year, so that each student is able to identify areas of growth and success as well as some areas needing improvement. Teachers often find that these self-assessment checklists are an invaluable tool for understanding student behavior problems and for motivating improvements.

Other inventory items you can include in a portfolio are: student surveys, reflective journal entries, conference reports, and progress charts. The students should be encouraged to be thoughtful evaluators of their progress. Students are typically quite honest when assessing themselves in this way (see Figure 8.4).

OTHER EVIDENCE OF GROWTH AND ACHIEVEMENTS   Should you choose to represent the *whole* child using the portfolio as a tool, collections of student work from all curricular areas should be included. This might mean selecting samples of math concepts or problem-solving techniques, results of scientific experiments, learning logs, or research reports.

PHOTOGRAPHS   Including photographs of student constructions, artwork, or group projects in a portfolio is a wonderful way to remember important achievements that are just too bulky to fit into a portfolio. At the same time, photographs capture moments of learning that parents and children are sure to treasure for years. Taking photos of creations, which are often three dimensional, and other large projects will preserve those masterpieces for the student's portfolio while allowing a child to take the items home. That frees up space in your classroom and allows you to share tangible examples of the children's work with parents.

VERY IMPORTANT PERSONALS (VIPS)   The pieces in this section of the portfolio have unique personal importance for the owner. This section often serves as a link between the school and home because the pieces included here typically reflect achievements and interests from outside the classroom. Examples might include photos of performances in sports activities or plays, musical achievements, contests, awards, artifacts from trips, or anything else that gives the viewer of the portfolio a fuller sense of its owner.

What Are the Various Types of Portfolios?

Portfolios may take many forms. The following forms will be discussed here: working, showcase, and electronic portfolios. Although each portfolio format may have a different appearance, and the implementation may vary, the overall purpose for each is the same: Every successful portfolio serves to document achievement and areas of growth over time.

Working Portfolios

The working portfolio includes any and all work in progress—projects and papers, drafts attached to final products, homework, notes, logs, reflections, and most selected work. It is suggested that students build these first, adding a couple of pieces to the folder each week. Then, as the student-led conferences draw near, students may be guided in the selection process of choosing items from their working portfolio to add to the showcase portfolio. The steps taken to prepare for the student-led conference are discussed later in the chapter. The portfolios should be placed in an area of the room that is readily accessible to students, allowing them the freedom to add work as they wish throughout the week. The typical form of a working portfolio is that of a manila folder, labeled and decorated by the student. The folders may be kept as hanging files, placed alphabetically for organizational purposes.

Reading Survey

Name:_____ Date:_____

1. If you had to guess . . .
    How many books do you own? _____
    How many books are in your house? _____
    How many books have you read in the last month? _____

2. How did you learn to read?

3. Why do people read?

4. What does someone have to do in order to be a good reader?

5. What kinds of books do you like to read?

6. Do you think reading is important? Tell me why.

7. Do you like your parents and teacher to read to you? Tell me why.

8. Is reading important for adults?

9. How does a teacher decide which students are good readers?

10. How do you feel about yourself as a reader? Tell me why.

Figure 8.3 Self-evaluation form, reading.

School Feelings

Name: _____ Date: _____

I feel the best about myself in this class when _____

_____

I have the most fun in this class when _____

_____

I feel proud of myself in this class when _____

_____

I am the most relaxed in this class when _____

_____

The best thing I contribute to this class is _____

_____

A picture of me at school:

Figure 8.4   Student survey.

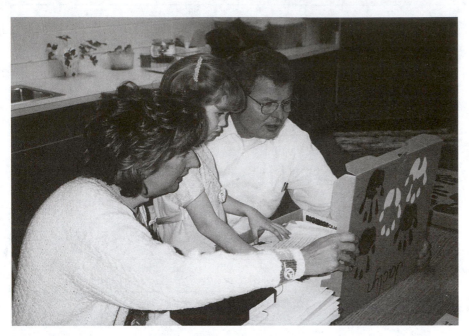

Child sharing showcase portfolio.

Showcase Portfolios

The showcase portfolio is a collection of the student's best work. Components may include final drafts, improved performances, self-assessments, peer assessments, reflections, and goals. The showcase portfolio will serve as the vehicle for communicating to parents the student's efforts, achievements, and areas of growth throughout the year. It is suggested that students choose about two pieces per subject or topic to pull from their working portfolio and add to the showcase portfolio. A more detailed discussion of preparing for student-led conferencing appears later in the chapter. The folder used for the showcase portfolio is entirely up to the teacher and students, so **be creative!** A commonly used form is the three-ring binder, with inserted tabs separating labeled sections.

Electronic Portfolios

Discussion of the storage of portfolio contents leads us to yet another type: the electronic portfolio. Electronic portfolios contain similar information as the portfolios discussed earlier, with the difference being that the information is collected, stored, and managed electronically.

In this age of technology, the concept of the electronic portfolio has arisen in response to the notion that there had to be a more space-efficient way to store all that a complete portfolio may contain. Software has since been developed with the multimedia input capability to enter student work in digital form through word processing, scanning, or digitizing audio or video. For example, Microsoft PowerPoint allows students to create several slides to highlight particular areas of learning, such as writing samples, solutions to mathematical problems, samples of art work, science projects, and multimedia presentations all in one document. Completed class work or projects may be scanned into the program; digital photos taken throughout the year may be inserted from a disk; and goals, reflections, or other information pertinent to the student's growth may be entered manually into a slide format.

Younger students benefit from a given template onto which they enter their information throughout the year. This provides the structure and guidance they need to efficiently address their areas of learning, while gaining exposure to a new technological tool. Adding such finishing touches as recorded voice, sound bytes, and slide transitions or animations gives the electronic portfolio an exciting, polished look. Not to mention, years of documented student growth and achievement can all be saved on one tiny disk or CD-ROM to transport from teacher to teacher or school to school.

Now that you are aware of the varied forms that a portfolio may take, let's discuss the classroom strategies to use for introducing a portfolio program.

How Do You Get Started?

When taking the plunge into portfolios, it's not enough simply for teachers to be aware of the many benefits of such a program. It is equally important for *students* to recognize the benefits they will enjoy. When they do, students will develop the interest and enthusiasm that lead to a successful portfolio program in your classroom.

How Can You Introduce the Portfolio Concept?

Possible methods of introducing the portfolio idea to children include showing them actual portfolios, perhaps constructed by an artist, a member of the community, or even their teacher. This is a necessary step in developing an appreciation for the benefits that a portfolio will bring to its owner. Lead the students in a discussion of why particular pieces may have been included or why they might be of importance to the owner, as they are presented in the portfolio.

How Can You Manage Storage and Time Issues?

I store my student portfolios in cardboard pizza boxes! I teach first grade, and at the early elementary levels, their artwork and writing isn't always small. I found that I needed a bigger container to store their work in. Pizza boxes work wonders! (Shelly Novotony, first grade)

Before beginning a portfolio program, you'll need to choose an organized method for collecting and storing student work. This method may be as simple as having a manila file folder for each student, placed alphabetically in a crate of hanging files. Other methods include boxes, such as those for boots, shirts, or pizza; expandable files; mailboxes; or three-ring binders. Involving the parents with supplying such storage materials is an effective way to inform them of the process itself (see Figure 8.5).

Regardless of which storage method you choose, it is important to note the difference between a collection of student work and a *portfolio* collection. That difference is that every piece of work in a portfolio is there for a reason; namely, it helps achieve the goals set for the portfolio. The portfolio is not simply a summary of everything the student has completed over the year. Instead, it is "a representative sample selected to demonstrate growth and achievement in a particular dimension of learning (e.g., mathematics, literacy, science, etc.)" (Shaklee et al., 1997:78).

Time is another management issue to address when beginning a portfolio program. You may be under the impression that maintaining a portfolio program will require a great deal of planning, preparation, and time on the part of the teacher. Not so. That is, not if the portfolio program puts the responsibility for learning where it should be—in the hands of the student. Remember, a main goal of any portfolio program is to empower learners. As children collect

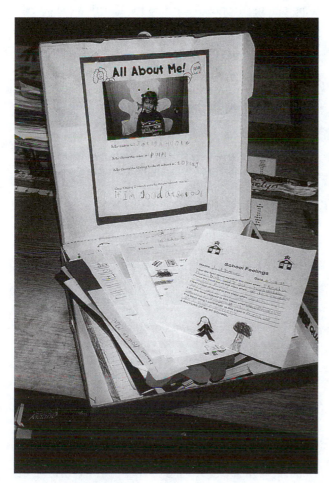

Portfolio storage.

PORTFOLIO STORAGE

The portfolio is a purposeful collection of student work that exhibits student effort, progress, and achievements in one or more curricular areas. The purpose of a portfolio is to demonstrate each student's progress in the selected areas, while also allowing students to assume ownership of their learning by requiring them to collect work regularly and to reflect on that work.

Portfolio contents for assessment and evaluation are consistently gathered over time. The process emphasizes what kids know. The portfolio itself is unique to each child. This sampling of work becomes quite precious and important to the owner. An appropriate method of storage for such treasured pieces is essential to the portfolio process.

Portfolios may come in many different shapes and sizes. The preferred method of storage f   this year will be in the form of a binder. The binder will be divided into designated sections, encouraging students to organize their pieces in a systematic manner.

The following is a list of items that your child will need to efficiently store his or her portfolio pieces:

✔ 2" clear view binder (with room for a picture as a cover insertion)
✔ 5 dividers with the following labels: Literacy, Math, Reflections, Life Skills, V.I.P. (very important personals)
✔ Blank cassette tape (labeled with the child's name)
   We will use the tape to record the child's oral reading skills at various points throughout the year.

Thanks so much for your prompt response to these requests!

Figure 8.5   Parent letter detailing portfolio storage.

evidence of their learning, they begin to see particular samples of their work as evidence of progress toward their individualized goals (Herbert, 2001). Most importantly, students show that they are genuinely excited about taking responsibility for collecting their own work.

As with any new experience, the initial steps toward success with portfolios may seem awkward and time consuming. But documented experience with countless hours of teaching shows that, with the management skills suggested in this chapter, the students in your classroom can ultimately take over much of the portfolio process themselves. They will become active participants, appropriately selecting portfolio pieces, organizing their work, and reflecting on that work. Once you have established the necessary routines for portfolio implementation, the responsibility and accountability shift from a teacher-centered approach to a student-centered one.

Shaklee et al. (1997) support this theory via interviews with teachers who had recently been given the time to make the shift from traditional forms of assessment to portfolio assessment. The teachers reported that portfolio assessment had not added to their burden, but, in fact, found that the time it took to provide more student-centered curriculum decreased because more individuals were involved in the contribution of data to the assessment process.

Take comfort in knowing that you are not alone if you feel uncertainty and trepidation as you set forth on the path to portfolios and student empowerment. However, we strongly believe that soon after you introduce portfolios you will begin seeing their value in the classroom. The next section will get you started on the right foot.

Here We Go . . . Implementing Portfolios

We previously discussed the importance of showing students a model portfolio. Once they see what a portfolio might look like, and once they learn about the benefits they'll enjoy, students are ready to begin assembling their own. Following the session during which sample portfolios are shared with students, present them with their own portfolio folders, ready and waiting to be filled with their own work. This is the first step in initiating ownership.

Students enjoy creating a cover for their portfolios. You might encourage them to give their portfolio a title, such as "My Best Work" or "Portfolio Portraits." Then lead the students in a brainstorming session of ways to decorate the cover that will illustrate for the viewer their style and personality.

Another nice introduction to the viewing of the portfolio is to ask the students to draw a self-portrait (see Figure 8.6). Place this at the front of the portfolio, and be sure to date it. An effective follow-up as a measurement of growth is to ask the students to draw a second self-portrait at the end of the school year. They will be sure to note the artistic differences evident in the two pieces, usually with much surprise and amusement!

Figure 8.6   Student self-portrait included in the portfolio.

To effectively carry out the selection process involved with the other pieces that are added to the portfolio, it is important to structure a set time for selection each week. During this time, students are asked to look over their work from the week and to choose one or two items to add. Students should be encouraged to look over all subject areas, remembering to check for favorite journal entries, a drawing they are especially proud of, or even work that has yet to be completed. If your goal setting includes the need for a comprehensive view of each child's progress—the "whole child" approach—you may want to direct this selection session at times, asking students to focus on one subject area, such as writing, in their selection process.

One hint for those of you just beginning with a portfolio program—start small. Developing your portfolio assessment around one designated curricular area, such as literacy or math, before moving onto other areas, will allow you to get your feet wet without causing overwhelming anxiety (Stone, 1995).

The actual selection process may be carried out in a variety of ways, three of which will be mentioned here:

1. The pieces for the portfolio may be student-selected (otherwise known in the classroom as a "free pick") after a brainstorming session listing all of the things they had learned that week. Together, through discussion, the students begin to narrow their choices down to a final selection or two that they feel are valuable pieces to add to their portfolios.

2. The selected pieces might be referred to as a "negotiated pick." The teacher may make the suggestion, "This would be a great piece to add to your portfolio." However, the student continues to have the final say in this decision.

3. There may be pieces added to the student portfolio known as "teacher picks." The teacher, for any number of reasons, may feel that a particular selection effectively demonstrates growth, or signifies either an area of strength or of concern.

Regardless of the selection process employed, it is important, even critical, to the overall success of the portfolio program that students take time to reflect on the selected works.

Portfolio Evaluation: Reflecting and Responding

The reflection component of the portfolio program is instrumental in teaching children to examine their work closely and to focus on the decision-making process involved in selecting that work. The reflection process may be taught either through oral discussions in small groups or one-on-one, using student response journals or written response forms, which are directly attached to the selected piece for the portfolio. We have offered samples of response forms that may be adapted to fit the needs of all learners (see Figure 8.7). With emerging-to-early learners, students could be asked to *dictate* responses that reflect their work to the teacher or another adult. The adult would

record these responses, then attach the form to the selected piece. This simple modification of the reflection process is also useful for those students who are English language learners or those for whom written expression is a challenge (Stefanakis, 2002).

The reflective conversation takes on greater significance when connected to the purpose of creating a portfolio (Herbert, 2001). Portfolios provide the opportunity for students to express their individuality and to give evidence of their metacognitive understanding about learning through interactive conversation, which is needed at both the selection and reflection stages of the portfolio process.

A helpful hint to keep in mind while attempting to develop your students into thoughtful self-evaluators and lifelong learners is this: Reflection is a skill that needs to be *taught,* with much initial guidance, providing examples along the way.

Teaching Self-Reflection

One way to teach self-reflection is to arrange for either a parent volunteer or an older student to work with small groups of students as they write the response forms that are to be attached to their selected pieces. As the students share their reflections with the group, the adult or older student is there to offer suggestions as to how they might

---

My Showcase Portfolio Selection

Title of piece selected: _____

Date: _____

I chose this piece because _____

_____

_____

From this piece I learned _____

_____

Next time I do this, I would like to try and/or learn _____

_____

_____

_____

_____

Name: _____

Date: _____

I chose this piece because _____

_____

_____

I learned _____

_____

_____

One way I could improve in this area is

_____

_____

_____

_____

Figure 8.7   Response forms for use with reflecting on pieces.

be more specific and detailed in their responses. This helps to avoid such responses as, "I picked it because it was good!" At this point, the volunteer might step in and ask: "*Why* was it good? What do you feel you did well here?" One classroom teacher planned weekly meetings such as these during a period of the day when the students were participating in center-based activities or choices, which proved to be less disruptive to the schedule. If the volunteer meets with a group of four or five students at a time, such weekly sessions typically take no more than 30 minutes, especially as the students become more adept at assessing their own work.

One first-grade teacher taught students to reflect on their writing development through the use of mini-lessons. She decided to have her students evaluate their writing based on the following criteria: ideas, organization, voice, word choice, sentence fluency, and conventions. As the students periodically reviewed their work and wrote reflections, this teacher supported the process by teaching mini-lessons on each of the criteria. She modeled self-assessment by talking about her own writing, and she asked her students to point out elements of good writing during their conferences.

Another suggestion for teaching students to assess their own work is to give them prompts or "sentence starters" to encourage more thoughtful responses to their learning. Encourage students to use a different prompt each week when reflecting on their pieces. It's a good idea to have these prompts posted somewhere in the room or to include them at the beginning of their portfolios, to be used as a reference when needed. The following are a few ideas for such prompts:

- Next time I do this, I will try to . . .
- Something I want you to notice about this piece is . . .
- I am the most proud of _____ because . . .
- This was hard for me because . . .
- Something I need to work on here is . . .

Holding regular portfolio conferences with students is an effective way to measure their abilities to assess their own work, as well as to check their understanding of subject-related concepts. Figures 8.8 and 8.9 offer sample conference guides for student use during this process.

Lipton and Hubble (1997) offer a fun method of allowing students to review their entire portfolios and draw conclusions about their learning and progress. Using this method, students write an "autobiography" of the work inside, describing how it has changed over time. One suggested way to begin the "Autobiographies of Work" process is to have students choose an area where they can spread out the contents of their portfolio and organize them into categories. As they review the contents, students should consider the following:

- Why is this piece better than that one?
- What did I do differently in this piece?
- What can I say about my improvement from my least successful piece to my most successful?
- How have I grown?

Lipton and Hubble (1997) acknowledge that the depth of their conclusions depends on the maturity level of the students. However, all students are capable of some form of self-evaluation. Again, with the emerging learner, this activity may take the form of a discussion rather than a written assignment. Once students have analyzed and reflected on their pieces, ask them to write an autobiography of the work inside, incorporating their reflective responses. Take this piece through the writing process, to be kept as an assessment of growth for the portfolio.

Still another method of teaching self-evaluation is through the use of time planners. Time planners help students to organize themselves and evaluate how they have spent their day. Time planners are also effective in fostering good homework habits with older children (see Figure 8.10 on p. 224 for an example of a time planner to be used with early-to-fluent learners).

From this discussion, it appears that educators can encourage self-reflection among their students in a variety of ways. These methods are noted in the following applications section.

APPLICATIONS FOR SELF-REFLECTION DEVELOPMENT

1. Arrange for a parent volunteer or an older student to work with students in generating more specific and detailed responses to their work. It is suggested that sessions such as these be held weekly, for approximately one half an hour at a time.
2. Develop the reflective process by holding mini-lessons in which the teacher models self-assessment by talking about her or his own writing. During conferences, ask students to point out elements of good writing. Students evaluate their writing based on the following criteria: ideas, organization, voice, word choice, sentence fluency, and conventions.

3. Give students prompts or "sentence starters" to encourage a more thoughtful response to their learning.
4. Hold regular portfolio conferences with students to measure their abilities to assess their own work. In this way, the teacher is able to make regular observations and set goals with students.
5. Allow students to create an "autobiography" of their portfolio collection, taking into consideration the growth and learning that has taken place.
6. Make use of time planners to help children to organize themselves and evaluate how they have spent their day.

As indicated, self-reflection is a skill that must be taught, as is the concept of goal setting. Both skills are important steps in the portfolio process.

Teaching Goal Setting

In addition to teaching self-reflection, teaching children to set goals for themselves is another effective way for them to develop into independent learners, periodically assessing their progress (see Figures 8.11 and 8.12 on p. 225). Goal setting may be discussed initially as a whole group, with individual goals planned and assessed at later points in the year. Incorporating goal setting into a conferencing format in which goals are shared, discussed, and evaluated, allows parents to view their child's learning from the child's perspective. Together, the teacher, parent, and student can develop strategies to ensure success in reaching the designated goals. We suggest that the goal setting process be posted to assist students as they select and set their individual goals. Children are often very adept in identifying the areas that they could improve on. It is important to follow up on those goals set by the students by asking: "Who has achieved his or her goal? How did you achieve it? What is your new goal in literacy?" As mentioned earlier, the identified goals may be discussed within a conferencing framework at different points throughout the year.

The preceding suggestions are all effective means of preparing students to eventually share the contents of their portfolio with others. These opportunities instill in children the confidence needed to proudly convey their areas of strength and improvement noted in the portfolio. "When we teach, we need celebrations. Writing and reading achievements can be lauded by framing, fridge decoration, publishing, sharing, and performing—to amaze children with their own capabilities. Celebrations create a willingness to continue learning. Special days lift the spirits, renew ambition and set new goals" (Fox, 1997:128).

Sharing the Portfolio: A Celebration of Learning

There are a number of ways in which you can highlight and share children's portfolios with their families. Gaining great popularity in this genre is the student-led conference. While this format works well, the beauty is that you can design any type of celebration to share children's work. Other options include the three-way conference (involving parent, student, and teacher), the take-home conference, and end of the year learning celebrations using storyboards or portfolios. Though each may be implemented differently or adapted to fit your specific classroom needs, all have a common purpose: to instill in the students a sense of responsibility and ownership for their learning, and to rejoice in children's learning!

Student-Led Conferencing

In the past, my conferences have averaged a 75 percent level of parent participation. This year, with the student-led conferences, I had 100 percent parent participation! (Rene Fox, first grade teacher)

The developed showcase portfolio, representing a student's best work, is the communicative tool in the conferencing process. As teachers begin to work with their students in assembling their showcase portfolios, they need to first determine the subject areas that they would like represented. Remember our earlier tip? *Start small.* When first experimenting with student-led conferencing, you may want to focus in on one subject area, such as literacy, or perhaps turn to a favorite theme taught over the past year. As you become more comfortable with the conferencing procedure, you may wish to then represent the *whole* child, guiding students in selecting pieces from all subject areas.

Once the topics of focus have been determined, brainstorm as a group what has been learned relative to that topic and post the suggested ideas around the room, perhaps in a web format.

Portfolio Conference Guide

Name: _____   Date: _____

Reading and Writing 
My Stars: Your Stars:

Math
My Stars: Your Stars:

Science and Social Studies
My Stars: Your Stars:

Friends
My Stars: Your Stars:

Goals

My Goals: Your Goals:

1. _____   1. _____

2. _____   2. _____

Figure 8.8 Conference guide (to be filled out by student and teacher or student and parent, depending on the type of conference), emerging to early.

Source: Adapted from work by Colleen Monroe, Delta Kelly Elementary, Rochester Hills, Michigan.

_____'s Conference Reflections

My Stars
(Things I Do Really Well)

Two things I have done really well these 10 weeks are:

1. _____

2. _____

The most important thing in our classroom that I am trying to do well is _____

_____

This is important to me because _____

_____

Something that I am proud about these 10 weeks is _____

_____

Two wishes for myself or things I'd like to improve on:

1. _____

_____

2. _____

_____

My goals for each area are:

Reading _____

Writing _____

Math _____

Life Skills _____

Figure 8.9   Conference guide (to be filled out by the student), early to fluent.

Suggested Use: Hand out each Monday for students to keep in their homework folders. Students keep track of their assignments during the week, and parents are asked to participate by signing the planner each night. On Friday, part of their homework is to fill out their reflections at the bottom of the planner. Follow up by discussing these reflections as a class, asking: "Who had a good reflection?" "Share it with us." "What did you like about it?" "What do others like about it?"

Time planner for the week of: _____ Name: _____

Homework	**Parent Signature/Comments**
Monday	
Tuesday	
Wednesday	
Thursday	
Friday	

The most important thing I learned this week was _____

The things I need to work on are _____

I will improve by _____

The thing I am most proud of is _____

Figure 8.10   Time planner for early-to-fluent learners.

Reaching My Goals

To reach my first goal, _____

_____,

I will _____

_____.

To reach my second goal, _____

_____,

I will _____

_____.

Signed by

_____ (Teacher)

_____ (Student)

_____ (Parent)

Figure 8.11   Goal-setting form, lower elementary.

Copyright © 2005 by Allyn and Bacon

It is suggested that students choose about two pieces per subject or topic to pull from their working portfolio and add to their showcase portfolio.

Preparing for the "Big Day"

Remember: Preparation is 90 percent of the process!

There is nothing more exciting than watching students take charge the day of conferences, explaining their work and the learning process to their parents or guardians with a great sense of pride. Grades are no longer a secret or a surprise to them. They now feel a sense of ownership over their learning.

Although student-led conferences began with older children, many teachers of preschoolers are now using them effectively. For the youngest students, prior to the conference or "celebration of learning," you will want to go

Reaching My Goal

Goal: _____

_____

The way that I will measure the achievement of this goal will be (how often, how long, grade, etc.):

_____

_____

The evidence that I will use to indicate my achievement of this goal will be (chart, checklist, actual written work, parent signature, etc.):

_____

_____

Steps to help me reach my goal:

_____

_____

_____

_____

_____

_____

_____

_____

_____

Student Signature: _____

Date: _____

Teacher Signature: _____

Date: _____

Figure 8.12   Goal-setting form, upper elementary.

Copyright © 2005 by Allyn and Bacon

through the portfolio with the child, enjoying the changes that have occurred. You will of course help the young child focus his or her plans for sharing the tremendous changes in learning with his or her family. You will want to plan open-ended questions you can ask the child about the portfolio. You will use these same questions two times. Once during your meeting time and again when you and the child are with the parents. If the celebration is more informal and the children will be visiting the classroom areas and exploring the portfolio only with their families, consider attaching the same open ended questions to the front of each portfolio to assist families in their exploration of the work.

For older children, a teacher will need to spend approximately 30 minutes to an hour each day, two weeks before the conference—organizing, planning, and rehearsing with students through role playing. On the actual conference day, however, teachers have the pleasure of being able to step back, allowing their students to display their achievements.

After mapping out what has been learned in each of the subjects of focus for the showcase portfolio, it is time to begin guiding students in filling out a type of conference organizer that will be used as a script for the student to follow during the student-led conference.

A suggested time format for this type of preparation is to focus on a different domain every couple of days a few weeks before the conference, spending about 30 minutes each day, completing the organizer and pulling appropriate

pieces from the working portfolio that will reflect what has been learned in that subject area. In guiding students through this organizational process, one may want to model for his or her students as a whole group first, and then assign the organizers to be completed individually. An example of a conference organizer has been included here. The top half of the organizer may be seen as a process that allows the student to think things through. The bottom half is the actual script that the student may follow during the conference (see Figure 8.13). After going through the script, the student would conclude by saying, "Here are some examples of my work in reading. . . ."

Student Preparation

Role playing with the students is an essential part of preparing them for the conference. Sample scripts that may be used in role-playing situations have been included. Adjust these lessons to fit your own time frame and needs. Expect to feel overwhelmed at first. But you *can* do this! You will be amazed at how it all falls into place at conference time. Remember, *good preparation* is the key.

Role Playing with Older Students

LESSON 1: MAKING INTRODUCTIONS When the teacher stops by the conference to check on the progress, the students introduce their parents to the teacher. A lesson

Child created web of writing goals for the current semester: punctuation, capital and lowercase letters, picture to match words, and spaces between words.

Student-Led Conference Organizer

Three Things I've Learned
(Star the most important one)

_____

_____

_____

Two to Three Things I Want You to Notice
(Star the most important one)

_____

_____

_____

Three Things I've Enjoyed
(Star the most important one)

_____

_____

_____

Two to Three Ways to Improve
(Star the most important one)

_____

_____

_____

Topic: _____

The most important thing I learned on this topic was _____

_____

I especially enjoyed _____

_____

The most important thing I want you to notice about my work is _____

_____

The thing I need to work on most is _____

_____

The way I will improve in this area is _____

_____

Would you please comment here on my work? _____

Student signature: _____   Parent signature: _____

Figure 8.13   Portfolio conference organizer.

on how to conduct proper introductions is important as it ensures quick success and a good starting point for students. The key points to stress include good eye contact and a clear voice.

Sample: "Mrs. Johnson, I'd like to introduce you to my parents. Mom and Dad, this is my teacher, Mrs. Johnson."

LESSON 2: BRAINSTORMING IDEAS FOR THE CONFERENCE ORGANIZER   Allow time for your students to suggest ideas of things to share with their parents about their work. Focus on the learning objectives you have set for your class. Post these ideas around the room so that students may refer to them as they assemble their showcase portfolios.

Sample: "We want to show your parents how your writing skills have improved from the beginning of the year until now. What evidence can we show of that?"

LESSON 3: FILLING OUT THE CONFERENCE ORGANIZER   Model for the students the way to organize their thoughts and their pieces to add to their portfolio.

Students then independently complete the organizer, with your guidance as needed.

LESSON 4: ROLE-PLAYING THE CONFERENCE Have students practice making the introductions in small groups of three or four. Remind students of the items needed to complete their portfolio. Review their final portfolio and organizer with them.

Role-Play: It is beneficial to have two adults assisting in the role playing of the conference. Tell students that you will demonstrate what the conference will look like by modeling it for them, and then they will have a chance to practice it.

Modeling how to talk about students' work is very important. Spend time demonstrating for your students how to do this, and give them time to practice. Call on students to role-play with you in front of the class. You act as the parent. Ask the other students to comment on strengths and areas needing improvement in the role playing. Then, allow students to work in groups of three or four to role-play their conference, rotating the following roles as they practice: student, parent, parent, teacher/observer.

APPLICATIONS FOR STEPS IN A STUDENT-LED CONFERENCE

1. The student enters the classroom and gets his or her portfolio from a designated area of the room.
2. The student goes to a conference table and sits next to his or her parents.
3. The conference organizer should be on top of the portfolio. Students use the organizers to guide them through their discussions of their work.
4. Sometime during the conference, the teacher will stop by the conference to see how things are going. At this point, the student stops to make an introduction and lets the teacher know how the conference is progressing.
5. The teacher then moves on, continuing to facilitate at other conferences in the room.
6. Once the student has gone through the contents of his or her portfolio, the student returns the portfolio to its designated area.
7. At the conclusion of the conference, parents may be asked to fill out an evaluation form regarding the conference procedures. They also are offered the opportunity to sign up for another appointment with the teacher if needed (most of the time it's not).

Student-Led Conferencing Procedures and Goals

Virtually any student, from preschool on up, can carry out a student-led conference if properly prepared. We have just shown you how to prepare students at the early-to-fluent level for conferencing. Figure 8.14 offers an example of how the conferencing procedure might look for those children operating at the emerging-to-early level. The procedures addressed in the "applications to follow during a conference" are important to teach all children prior to a student-led format.

APPLICATIONS FOR CHILDREN TO FOLLOW DURING A CONFERENCE

1. Find your portfolio.
2. Go to a designated spot.
3. Sit next to your parents or guardians.
4. Review your organizer/portfolio pieces.
5. When the teacher arrives at your spot, introduce your teacher to your guests.
6. Thank your guests for coming to the conference; then return the portfolio to the file.
7. Encourage your guests to fill out the evaluation on the student-led conference procedure.

Portfolio Conferencing with Preschool–Grade 1 Children

Activities:
- Centers available for children to take parents to and to do activities.
- Big books and little books available to share reading techniques with parents.
- Journals set out for children to read, reflect, and share with parents.
- A group project—child explains process and his or her part in the project.
- A table of portfolios that children bring their parents to as part of their "portfolio conferencing program"—the teacher is here to discuss the portfolio with the child and the parent. (The teacher and child have recently held a conference on this.)

Children participate by:
- Inviting the parents with an invitation.
- Introducing the parents to the learning stations in the classroom.
- Demonstrating their understanding with explanations and examples such as reading a favorite story or retelling a familiar tale with puppets.
- Sharing portfolio reflections with parents using the teacher as a guide.

Teachers prepare by:
- Setting up the classroom in advance. Include at each station an explanation of the developmental and curriculum learning that is taking place for the adults to read.
- Conferencing with the children ahead of time.
- Preparing a conference overview to use as a guide during the session.
- Confirming the conference times with the parents.

Figure 8.14 Planning the portfolio conference with young learners.

When children and their parents participate in a successful student-led conference, the following goals are met:

Conference goals for students
- To accept ownership and responsibility for their learning
- To learn to communicate effectively with others about their progress

Conference goals for parents
- To see a holistic view of their child's achievements and strengths in school
- To be positive and accepting of their child's efforts

Scheduling Conferences

It is suggested that teachers conduct the typical parent–teacher conference in the fall, notifying parents at that time about the student-led procedure to take place in the spring. The format used in scheduling the student-led conference really depends on a teacher's comfort zone as well as the building's schedule. Some may wish to have one family in the room at a time, conferencing every 15 minutes or so. Or, one may wish to have three to four families in the room at the same time for a scheduled block of 45 minutes. At this time, the teacher's role changes to that of a facilitator, periodically checking on the progress of each conference.

Conference Attendance

Better attendance has been recorded with student-led conferences. "It would be as if the parents were to miss their child's school play!!" (Shelly Potter, Potter Press, Inc.). If for some reason the parents are unable to attend the conference, arrange for another teacher, a principal, a custodian, or a special friend to sit in on the conference. The important thing is that there is someone there who will listen and share in the child's efforts and achievements.

Three-Way Conferences

A three-way conference is quite similar to a student-led conference. The biggest difference between student-led and three-way conferences is the role of the parent (see Figures 8.15 and 8.16). By using a planning sheet such as those found in Figures 8.8 and 8.9, parents and children take responsibility together for the event. Parents, children, and teachers all set goals for future learning while celebrating all that has already happened.

Take-Home Portfolio Conferences

Because it is so important that children get a time to share their work, it may be a better option for your students to en-gage in what is known as a Take-Home Portfolio Conference (Paris & Ayres, 1994). These are exactly what they sound like. Portfolios are sent home with students for families to share together (see Figure 8.17). When a guide such as Figure 8.18 is provided, families are more strategic in their perusal of the portfolio. Many families truly appreciate the less formal format of this type of conference and it still allows for a true celebration of children's growth.

Storyboards (Presentation Boards)

An alternative to presenting portfolios at an end of the year learning celebration is to use storyboards (also known as documentation or presentation boards). Storyboards are comprised of selections from a child's portfolio that he or she and the teacher feel are important representations of the student's literacy learning. These items may consist of pictures of constructions or big projects, samples of writing or artwork with narrative, samples of dialogue from snack time, a favorite story which was created, and so on. Anything that can be included in a portfolio is also possible for a storyboard. Each item selected for the board is accompanied by the story behind it. This explanation can be composed by the student or in cooperation with the teacher. The creation of storyboards is a powerful way to document literacy "in action" because they incorporate all

---

Three-Way Conference

Dear Parent/Guardian,

Conferences are coming up! Our class will be participating in a three-way conference this year, involving the student, parent, and teacher. This is what you can expect when you attend your child's conference:

- Please plan to arrive with your child at least 10 or 15 minutes prior to your scheduled conference time to look over his or her collection of work in the portfolio. Your child will demonstrate what he or she knows as he or she shares his or her accomplishments.
- You and your child will then meet with me to discuss your child's strengths, any concerns, and to set new learning goals for the next several weeks.
- Your child is prepared to take an active part. There will be opportunities for you to ask questions, make comments, or express concerns and ideas.
- I will support the learners AND the parents by clarifying, elaborating, and responding to specific questions and concerns.
- Should you have any issues you wish to discuss privately with me following the three-way conference, a sign-up sheet will be available by the door.

I believe that a three-way conference is one important way to support student learning. I look forward to meeting with you.

Sincerely,

Figure 8.15   Three-way conference format, upper elementary.

Three-Way Conference

You have been invited to participate in a highly interactive form of conferencing involving the student, parent, and teacher. Within this format, students will demonstrate responsibility for their learning in sharing their achievements thus far and in setting goals for themselves. Following the conference, your child will keep track of the progress he or she makes toward reaching his or her goals.

On the night of your child's conference, please plan to arrive 10 minutes prior to your scheduled conference time, so that your child may walk you through his or her portfolio located outside the classroom. At your conference time, I will meet with you and your child to discuss progress in studies. Your child and I have indicated the "stars," or things he or she is very good at, in each of the curricular areas. Your child will share the stars he/she gave himself/herself, and I will share the stars that I gave your child. Please be thinking about the stars that *you* would like to give your child (whether they are things your child is good at in the home or school setting). You will be asked to share these stars with us during the conference. Once all the stars have been shared, your child will share the goals that he or she has identified for him- or herself for the remainder of the year. I will then discuss ways in which we can help your child to reach his or her goals.

I hope you enjoy this form of conferencing. Should you have a concern that you feel would best be discussed without your child present, you will be given the opportunity to sign-up for a follow-up phone conference. I look forward to sharing this time with you and your child!

Sincerely,

Figure 8.16   Three-way conference format, lower elementary.

Copyright © 2005 by Allyn and Bacon

Take-Home Portfolio Conference

Dear Parents,

As you are aware, the children have been collecting samples of their work, representative of all areas of the curriculum, throughout the school year. This selection process has involved careful reflection and evaluation on the part of the student. These pieces have been compiled into a showcase portfolio, with the purpose of presenting a clear picture of the growth and development that has taken place over the last several months.

To provide practice for the upcoming Portfolio Celebration held in the spring, in which the students will be leading a conference type of format using the portfolio as a tool, the students are now being asked to share their developing portfolios with you at home. The Take-Home Portfolio Conference is an excellent means of practice and instills in the children the confidence to assess their own work and discuss it with one or more adults.

Please set aside 30 minutes or more of quiet time during which your child has your full attention. Your child will take you on a "tour" of his or her portfolio, sharing his or her treasured selections. At this time, your interest and probing questions about the individual pieces that are shared will encourage your child to elaborate and extend his or her thoughts about his or her learning.

A guide has been provided for you and your child to fill out as you look over the contents of the portfolio. Please be sure to return the portfolio and completed form to school the following week.

Enjoy this special time with your child!!

Figure 8.17   Take-home portfolio conference format.

Copyright © 2005 by Allyn and Bacon

Student and Parent Reflections
(Take-Home Conference Guide)

Take a guided tour through the contents of your portfolio. Together, select three pieces of work from different subject areas that you treasure the most. Share your choices with each other and explain why you picked them.

Student Favorites	Parent Favorites
1. _____	1. _____
2. _____	2. _____
3. _____	3. _____

Now, choose an area of your portfolio that you feel you have really improved on over the last few months. Select a piece from that area that demonstrates your improvement. Be ready to discuss the ways that you have improved in this area. Ask your parents to choose a piece that they feel shows improvement.

Student Choice	Parent Choice

Think about the goals that you have for yourself for the remainder of the school year. Discuss with your parents a goal that you hope to achieve, and the steps you could take to reach that goal.

Student Goal	Ways that Parent(s) Can Help You Achieve This Goal

Figure 8.18   Take-home conference guide.

Source: Adapted from Paris and Ayres (1994).

Sharing the snowman story in the take home portfolio.

five areas of literacy. Once the storyboards are ready, families are invited to attend a fair or celebratory party in which these are displayed and enjoyed by all.

End of the Year Literacy Learning Celebrations

Beyond storyboards, there are numerous ways to celebrate children's learning progress using portfolios. The set up that you choose for the celebration will be based, of course, on the situations specific to your students and their families. Some teachers host the parties. Others share the responsibility for the party with their students and families (see Figure 8.19). Of utmost importance is that the students are an integral part of the festivities and that their sense of pride over their work are able to shine.

Parents and Portfolios

It is important that parents be aware of the many benefits of portfolios and the processes involved. Through active parental involvement and understanding, portfolios have the ability to provide a clearer, more holistic picture of what children can do than typical report cards or traditional assessments usually achieve. Grades are no longer the focus with portfolios.

According to the Association for Childhood Education International (ACEI), parents can be involved in this type of authentic assessment by:

- Attending portfolio conferences and providing information on the child's strengths and needs
- Reflecting on the child's portfolio contents and making supportive comments and suggestions
- Remaining active in the child's school to observe progress and work habits

Parents need to be informed not only about the portfolio program itself (i.e., reminding them that some student work will be kept at school for the portfolio rather than being sent home) but also about the format to be used for the student-led conferences, in hopes of alleviating any confusion. Preparing both students and parents will ensure a successful experience for all.

Evaluation is a necessary component to any new program. Parents can be a valuable source for future suggestions or comments on the portfolio program and student-led conference.

Celebrating Our Successes in Learning and in Life!

Mark your calendars now for the Poetry and Portfolio Pizzazz! Please plan to join us for this special event highlighting areas of strength and improvement, surprises and curiosities along the way, and demonstrating overall growth as individuals.

The big day is scheduled for Thursday, May 22, in the Media Center, from about 1:30–3:00. We will begin our afternoon with class poetry readings. Following the poetry readings, families will break into two groups, so that portfolio conferencing may take place in the classroom, while in the computer lab, students will demonstrate their completed Electronic Portfolios completed on the Microsoft PowerPoint program.

This is an important and special day in wrapping up our year together. If neither parent is able to attend, a "substitute" special someone is suggested, such as an older sibling, relative, or a neighbor. Children look forward to sharing their efforts and achievements.

I am encouraging the children to dress like little professionals for their time in the spotlight. Your continued encouragement of this at home would be appreciated.

Invitations created by the children will be sent home shortly before May 22 as a friendly reminder to all. We are in need of a few dessert and drink donations for that day. Please let me know if you are willing to send in a simply prepared dessert or drink on the morning of that school day. Thanks so much!

I'm looking forward to sharing this time with you and your child. It's exciting to watch as the students take ownership and pride in their learning. It definitely makes it all worth it!

See you May 22 at 1:30 in the Media Center!

Figure 8.19   Sample year-end portfolio celebration invitation.

Copyright © 2005 by Allyn and Bacon

Final Thoughts

Wishing You Success

We hope that this chapter has provided you with both the knowledge and the incentive to go forth with a portfolio program of your own! Here, we have discussed portfolio implementation, management, and types, along with the necessary reflection and evaluation components. We have detailed a variety of methods that allow students to share their growth and achievement, using the portfolio as a tool in this process. Know that when you introduce portfolios to your students, you are providing them with an effective tool for becoming enthusiastic, independent, and self-regulated learners.

Challenge Yourself

1. Design your own electronic teaching portfolio using a program such as Microsoft FrontPage or Netscape Navigator. This portfolio will display your teaching talents and proficiencies and demonstrate your knowledge and skills. The question that you should ask is "What am I trying to tell the viewer about myself?" How you answer this question depends on your targeted audience. Keep in mind that your portfolio is a personal reflection. The following are suggestions as to what you might include: a brief biographical sketch; your resume, copies of licenses, and documents; your teaching philosophy and style; copies of lesson or unit plans you have implemented, along with photo documentation; samples of student work; letters of recommendation, evaluations, recognition or honors you've received.

2. Choose one subject area. Decide on the *types* of pieces a student and teacher might collect to represent that subject.

3. Outline a plan detailing how you would get started on a portfolio program in your classroom. Specify the subject areas you will focus on, the management system you will use, and the conferencing formats.

Suggested Sources for Additional Information

Grant, et al. (1995). *Student-led conferences: Using portfolios to share learning with parents.* Markham, Ont.: Pembroke Publishers, Ltd.

Shaklee, B., et al. (1997). *Designing and using portfolios.* Boston: Allyn and Bacon.

Shannon, K. (1997). Student-led conferences: A twist on tradition. *Schools in the Middle, 6*(3):47–49.

Sloan, M. (1996). I love this piece because . . . Strategies to help kids evaluate their own work. *Instructor, 105*(7):30–31.

Stone, S. (1995). Teaching strategies. Portfolios: Interactive and dynamic instructional tool. *Childhood Education, 71*(4):232–234.

Sullivan, M. (1995). *Making portfolio assessment easy.* Canada: Scholastic, Ltd.

Organizations

International Reading Association. *Phone:* 1-800-336-7323

National Association for the Education of Young Children. *Phone:* 1-800-424-2460

Association for Childhood Education International. *Phone:* 1-800-423-3563

Alphabetical Listing of the First Thousand Words for Children's Reading

A

a
about
above
accident
ache
across
act
address
afraid
after
afternoon
again
against
ago
air
airplane
all
almost
alone
along
already
also
always
am
an
and
angry
animal
another
answer
ant
any
anything
apple
are
arm
around
as
ask
at
ate

aunt
automobile
awake
away

B

baby
back
bad
bag
bake
ball
balloon
banana
band
bandage
bank
bark
barn
basket
bath
bathe
be
beans
bear
beat
beautiful
because
bed
bee
been
before
began
begin
begun
behind
believe
bell
belong
bend
beside
best

better
between
bicycle
big
bill
bird
birthday
bit
bite
black
blackboard
bleed
bless
blind
blood
blow
blue
board
boat
body
bone
book
born
both
bottle
bottom
bow
bowl
box
boy
branch
brave
bread
break
breakfast
brick
bridge
bright
bring
broke
broken
broom

brother
brought
brown
bug
build
building
built
bump
burn
burnt
bus
busy
but
butcher
butter
butterfly
button
buy
by

C

cake
calf
call
came
camp
can
candy
cap
captain
car
card
care
careful
careless
carry
case
cat
catch
cause
cent
center

chain
chair
chalk
chance
change
cheek
chicken
chief
child
children
chimney
chin
chocolate
choose
Christmas
church
circle
circus
city
class
clean
clear
climb
clock
close
cloth
clothes
cloud
clown
coal
coat
cocoa
cold
color
come
company
cook
cookie
cool
copy
corn
corner

cost
cough
could
count
country
course
cousin
cover
cow
crackers
crayons
cream
creek
cross
crowd
crown
cry
cup
cupboard
curtain
cut

D

dance
danger
dark
date
day
dead
dear
deep
deer
dentist
desk
did
die
different
dig
dime
dining
dinner
dirt

dirty
dish
do
doctor
does
dog
doll
dollar
done
don't
door
double
down
draw
drawer
dream
dress
drink
drive
drop
drug
dry
duck
dust

E

each
ear
early
earth
east
Easter
easy
eat
edge
egg
eight
either
elephant
eleven
else
empty

Source: Adapted from Dolch (1948).

end
engine
enough
eraser
even
evening
ever
every
everything
except
expect
eye

F

face
fair
fall
family
far
farm
farmer
fast
fat
father
feather
feed
feel
feet
fell
fellow
felt
fence
few
field
fight
fill
find
fine
finger
finish
fire
first
fish
fit
five
fix
flag
floor
flower
fly
follow
food
foot
for
forget

forgot
fork
forth
found
four
fresh
friend
frog
from
front
fruit
full
funny
fur
furniture

G

game
garage
garden
gate
gave
get
gift
girl
give
glad
glass
go
goes
going
gold
golden
gone
good
goodbye
got
grade
grain
grandfather
grandmother
grass
gray
great
green
grew
grocery
ground
grow
guess

H

had
hair
half

hall
hammer
hand
handkerchief
hang
happy
hard
has
hat
have
he
head
hear
heard
heart
heavy
hello
help
hen
her
here
herself
hid
hide
high
hill
him
himself
his
hit
hold
hole
home
hope
horse
hot
hour
house
how
hundred
hung
hungry
hunt
hurry
hurt

I

I
ice
if
in
indoors
inside
instead
into

iron
is
it
its

J

juice
jump
just

K

keep
kept
kick
kill
kind
king
kiss
kitchen
kitten
knee
knew
knife
knock
know

L

lady
laid
lake
lamb
lamp
land
lap
large
last
late
laugh
lay
lead
leaf
learn
leather
leave
leaves
led
left
leg
lemonade
lesson
let
letter
lettuce
lie
lift

light
like
line
lion
lip
listen
little
live
load
long
look
lost
lot
loud
love
low
lunch

M

made
mailman
make
man
many
march
mark
market
matter
may
me
mean
meat
medicine
meet
men
mend
met
middle
might
mile
milk
mill
mind
mine
minute
mirror
miss
Miss
money
monkey
month
moon
more
morning

most
mother
mountain
mouse
mouth
move
Mr.
Mrs.
much
music
must
my
myself

N

nails
name
nap
napkin
near
neck
need
neighbor
neither
nest
never
new
next
nice
nickel
night
nine
no
noise
none
noon
nor
north
nose
not
note
nothing
now
number
nurse
nut

O

oak
ocean
of
off
office
often
oh

old
on
once
one
only
open
or
orange
other
ought
our
out
outdoors
outside
over
overalls
own

P

page
pail
pain
paint
pair
pan
pants
paper
parade
part
party
pass
past
paste
path
pay
peach
peas
pen
pencil
penny
people
pet
pick
picnic
picture
pie
piece
pig
pillow
place
plain
plant
plate
play
please

pocket
point
policeman
pond
pony
poor
porch
post
pot
potatoes
pound
present
press
pretty
pull
puppy
put
puzzle

Q

quarter
queen
question
quick
quiet
quite

R

rabbit
race
radio
rag
rain
ran
rather
reach
read
ready
real
reason
red
remember
rest
ribbon
rich
ride
right
ring
river
road
robin
rock
roll

roof
room
rooster
root
rose
round
row
rub
rubber
rug
ruler
run

S

said
sail
salt
same
sand
sandwich
sat
save
saw
say
school
scissors
scooter
sea
season
seat
second
see
seed
seem
seen
self
sell
send
sent
serve
set
seven
several
shadow
shake
shall
shape
she
sheep
shine
ship
shirt
shoe

shook
shop
short
should
shoulder
show
shut
sick
side
sign
silk
silver
sing
sir
sister
sit
six
size
skates
skin
skirt
sky
sleep
slip
slow
small
smell
smile
smoke
snow
so
soap
socks
soft
sold
soldier
some
something
sometime
song
soon
sore
sorry
sound
soup
south
space
speak
spoke
spoon
spot
spread
spring

square
squirrel
stairs
stand
star
start
station
stay
step
stick
still
sting
stocking
stomach
stone
stood
stop
store
storm
story
stove
straight
street
strike
string
strong
such
sugar
suit
summer
sun
supper
suppose
sure
surprise
sweater
sweep
sweet

T

table
tail
take
talk
tall
taste
teach
teacher
tear
teeth
tell
ten
tent

than
thank
Thanksgiving
that
the
their
them
then
there
these
they
thick
thin
thing
think
third
thirsty
this
those
though
thought
thousand
three
throat
through
throw
thumb
ticket
tie
till
time
tire
tired
to
today
toe
together
told
tomatoes
tomorrow
tongue
too
took
tooth
top
touch
towel
town
toys
trade
train
tree
tried

trip
truck
true
try
tub
turn
turtle
twelve
twenty
two

U

ugly
umbrella
uncle
under
until
up
upon
us
use

V

valley
very
visit

W

wagon
wait
wake
walk
wall
want
war
warm
was
wash
waste
watch
water
wave
way
we
wear
weather
week
well
went
were
west
wet
what

wheat
wheel
when
where
whether
which
while
whisper
white
who
whole
whom
whose
why
wide
wild
will
win
wind
window
wing
winter
wish
with
without
woman
women
wonder
wood
wool
word
wore
work
world
would
wrap
write
wrong

Y

yard
year
yellow
yes
yesterday
yet
you
young
your

Z

zipper

References

Adams, M. J. (1990). *Beginning to read: Thinking and learning about print.* Cambridge, MA: MIT Press.

Adams, M. J. (2001). Alphabetic anxiety and explicit, systematic phonics instruction: A cognitive science perspective. In S. B. Neuman & D. K. Dickinson (Eds.), *Handbook of early literacy research.* New York: Guilford Press.

Airasian, P. W., & Walsh, M. E. (1997, February). Constructivist cautions. *Phi Delta Kappan,* pp. 444–449.

Au, K. H. (2000). Literacy instruction for children with diverse backgrounds. In D. S. Strickland & L. M. Morrow (Eds.), *Beginning reading and writing* (pp. 35–44). New York: Teachers College Press.

Ayres, L. (1994). The efficacy of three training conditions on phonological awareness of kindergarten children and the longitudinal effect of each on later reading acquisition. *Dissertation Abstracts International.* Ann Arbor, MI: University Microfilm Inc.

Bader, L. A. (1998). *Reading and language inventory* (3rd ed.). Upper Saddle River, NJ: Merrill.

Ball, E. W., & Blachman, B. A. (1988). Phoneme segmentation training: Effect on reading readiness. *Annals of Dyslexia, 38,* 208–225.

Baron, J., & Treiman, R. (1980). Use of orthography in reading and learning to read. In J. F. Kavanagh & R. L. Venezky (Eds.), *Orthography, reading, and dyslexia* (pp. 171–189). Baltimore: Park Press.

Barrentine, S. J. (Ed.). (1999). *Reading assessment.* Newark, NJ: International Reading Association.

Beach, S. A., & Young, J. (1997). Children's development of literacy resources in kindergarten: A model. *Reading Research and Instruction, 36*(3), 241–265.

Berk, L. E., & Winsler, A. (1995). *Scaffolding children's learning: Vygotsky and early childhood education.* Washington, DC: National Association for the Education of Young Children.

Billman, J., and Sherman, J. (2003). *Observation and participation in early childhood settings.* Boston: Allyn and Bacon.

Birrell, J., & Ross, S. (1996). Standardized testing and portfolio assessment: Rethinking the debate. *Reading Research and Instruction, 35*(4), 285–298.

Block, C. C., & Pressley, M. (2003). Best practices in comprehension instruction. In L. M. Morrow, L. B. Gambrell, & M. Pressley (Eds.), *Best practices in literacy instruction* (2nd ed., pp. 111–126). New York: Guilford Press.

Bolton, F., & Snowball, D. (1993). *Teaching spelling: A practical resource.* Portsmouth, NH: Heinemann.

Bradley, L. (1988). Rhyme recognition and reading and spelling in young children. In R. L. Masland & M. R. Masland (Eds.), *Preschool prevention of reading failure* (pp. 143–162). Parkton, MD: New York Press.

Bradley, L., & Bryant, P. E. (1983). Categorizing sounds and learning to read—A causal connection. *Nature, 303,* 419–421.

Bradley, L., & Bryant, P. (1985). *Rhyme and reason in reading and spelling.* Ann Arbor: University of Michigan Press.

Bradley, L., & Bryant, P. (1991). Phonological skills before and after learning to read. In S. A. Brady & D. P. Shankweiler (Eds.), *Phonological processes in literacy* (pp. 37–45). Hillsdale, NJ: Lawrence Erlbaum Associates.

Bredekamp, S., & Copple, C. (Eds.). (1997). *Developmentally appropriate practice in early childhood programs* (rev. ed.). Washington, DC: National Association for the Education of Young Children.

Brewer, J. (2001). *Introduction to early childhood education* (4th ed.). Boston: Allyn and Bacon.

Bus, A. G., & van Ijzendoorn, M. H. (1999). Phonological awareness and early reading: A meta-analysis of experimental training studies. *Journal of Educational Psychology, 91,* 403–414.

Busink, R. (1997). Reading and phonological awareness: What we have learned and how we can use it. *Reading Research and Instruction, 36*(3), 199–215.

Calkins, L. (1997, January–February). Motivating readers. *Instruction, 106*(5), 32–33.

Cazden, C. B. (1988). *Classroom discourse: The language of teaching and learning.* Portsmouth, NH: Heinemann.

Chall, J. S. (1967). *Learning to read: The great debate.* New York: McGraw-Hill.

Christie, J. F., & Enz, B. (1992). The effects of literacy: Play interventions on preschoolers' play patterns and literacy development. *Early Education and Development, 3*(3), 205–220.

Clay, M. M. (1966). *Emergent reading behavior.* Unpublished doctoral dissertation, University of Auckland Library.

Clay, M. M. (1975). *What did I write?* Aukland: Heinemann.

Clay, M. M. (1991). *Becoming literate: The construction of inner control.* Portsmouth, NJ: Heinemann.

Clay, M. M. (1993a). *An observation survey of early literacy achievement.* Portsmouth, NH: Heinemann.

Clay, M. M. (1993b). *Reading Recovery: A guidebook for teachers in training.* Portsmouth, NH: Heinemann.

Clay, M. (2000). *Concepts about print.* Aukland, New Zealand: Heinemann.

Clayton, M. (2001). *Classroom spaces that work.* Greenfield, MA: NEFC Publishing Co.

Combs, M. (1997). *Developing competent readers and writers in the primary grades.* Englewood Cliffs, NJ: Merrill.

Coppola, J. M. (2003). Meeting the needs of English learners in all-English classrooms: Sharing the responsibility. In G. Garcia (Ed.), *English learners.* Newark, DE: International Reading Association.

Crawford, A. N. (2003). Communicative approaches to second-language acquisition: The bridge to second-language literacy. In G. G. Garcia (Ed.), *English learners* (pp. 152–171). Newark, DE: International Reading Association.

Crawford, P. A. (1995). Early literacy: Emerging perspectives. *Journal of Research in Childhood Education, 10*(1), 71–85.

Cummins, J. (2003). Reading and the bilingual student: Fact and fiction. In G. G. Garcia (Ed.), *English learners* (pp. 2–33). Newark, DE: International Reading Association.

Cunningham, P. (August, 1997). Reading clinic. *Instructor, 107*(1): 30–32.

Cunningham, P. M. (2000). *Phonics they use.* New York: Longman.

Cunningham, P. M., Moore, S. A., Cunningham, J. W., & Moore, D. W. (2000). *Reading and writing in elementary classrooms: Strategies and observations.* (4th ed.). New York: Longman.

Daniels, H. (1994). *Literature circles: Voice and choice in the student-centered classroom.* York, ME: Stenhouse.

Dickinson, D. K., Beals, D. E. (1994). Not by print alone: Oral language supports for early literacy development. In D. Lancy (Ed.), *Children's emergent literacy: From research to practice.* Westport, CT: Praeger.

Dickinson, D. K., & Tabors, P. O. (2001). *Beginning literacy with language.* Baltimore: Brookes Publishing.

Dolch, E. W. (1948). *Problems in reading.* Champaign, IL: Garrard.

Dunn, L., Beach, S. A., & Kontos, S. (1994). Quality of the literacy environment in day care and children's development. *Journal of Research in Childhood Education, 9,* 24–34.

Dutro, S., & Moran, C. (2003). Rethinking English language instruction: An architectural approach. In G. G. Garcia (Ed.), *English learners* (pp. 227–258). Newark, DE: International Reading Association.

Dyson, A. H. (1990, January). Symbol makers, symbol weavers: How children link play, pictures and print. *Young Children,* pp. 50–57.

Dyson, A. H. (2001). Writing and children's symbolic repertoires: Development unhinged. In S. B. Neuman & D. K. Dickinson (Eds.), *Handbook of early literacy research* (pp. 126–140). New York: Guilford Press.

Edwards, C., Gandini, L., & Forman, G. (Eds.) (1995). *The hundred languages of children: The Reggio Emilia approach to early childhood education.* Norwood, NJ: Ablex.

Edwards, C., Gandini, L., & Forman, G. (1988). *Hundred languages of children* (2nd ed.). Greenwich, CT: Ablex/JAI.

Ehri, L. C., & Sweet, J. (1991). Fingerpoint reading of memorized text: What enables beginners to process the print? *Reading Research Quarterly, 14*(26), 442–462.

Ellis, N., & Large, B. (1987). The development of reading: As you seek so shall you find. *British Journal of Psychology, 78,* 1–28.

Epstein, H. (1978). Growth spurts during brain development: Implications for educational policy and practice. In J. Child & A. Mersey (Eds.), *Education and the brain.* Chicago: University of Chicago Press.

Estrin, E., & Chaney, C. (1988, Winter). Developing a concept of word. *Childhood Education,* pp. 78–82.

Ferreiro, E., & Teberosky, A. (1982). *Literacy before schooling.* Exeter, NH: Heinemann.

Fields, M. V., & Spangler, K. L. (1995). *Let's begin reading right: Developmentally appropriate beginning literacy* (3rd ed.). Englewood Cliffs, NJ: Prentice-Hall.

Fowler, A. E. (1991). How early phonological development might set the stage for phoneme awareness. In S. A. Brady & D. P. Shankweiler (Eds.), *Phonological processes in literacy* (pp. 97–117). Hillsdale, NJ: Lawrence Erlbaum Associates.

Fox, M. (1997). Personal theory of whole language: A teacher-researcher-writer reflects. *The Australian Journal of Language and Literacy, 20*(2), 122–129.

Freeman, D., & Freeman, Y. (2003). Teaching English learners to read: Learning or acquisition? In G. G. Garcia (Ed.), *English learners* (pp. 34–51). Newark, DE: International Reading Association.

Fresch, M. J., & Wheaton, A. (1997, September). Sort, search, and discover: Spelling in the child-centered classroom. *The Reading Teacher, 51*(1), 20–31.

Frith, U. (1985). Beneath the surface of developmental dyslexia. In K. Patterson, J. Marshall, & M. Colheart (Eds.), *Surface dyslexia* (pp. 301–330). London: Lawrence Erlbaum Associates.

Galda, L., & Cullinan, B. E. (1990). Literature for literacy: What research says about the benefits of using trade books in the classroom. In J. Flood, J. Jensen, D. Lapp, & J. Squire (Eds.), *Handbook of research on the teaching of English language arts* (pp. 528–535). New York: MacMillan.

Galda, L., Cullinan, B. E., & Strickland, D. S. (1993). *Language, literacy and the child.* Fort Worth, TX: Harcourt Brace Jovanovich College Publishers.

Galda, L., Pelligrini, A. D., & Cox, S. (1989). A short term longitudinal study of preschoolers' emergent literacy. *Research in the Teaching of English, 23,* 292–310.

Gardner, H., Kornhaber, M. L., & Wade, W. K. (1997). *Intelligence: Multiple perspectives.* Fort Worth, TX: Harcourt Brace College Publishers.

Gates, B. (1996). *The road ahead.* New York: Penguin Books.

Gilman, D., & Hassett, M. (1995). More than work folders: Using portfolios for educational assessment. *Clearing House, 68*(5), 310–312.

Glasser, W. (1992). *The quality school: Managing students without coercion.* New York: HarperCollins.

Gleason, J. B. (2001). *The development of language* (5th ed.). Boston: Allyn & Bacon.

Goldhaber, J., et al. (1996–1997). Books in the sandbox? Markers in the blocks? Expanding the child's world of literacy. *Childhood Education 73*(2), 88–91.

Gomez, E. (2000). *Assessment portfolios: Including English language learners in large scale assessments.* Washington, DC: ERIC Clearinghouse on Languages and Linguistics.

Goodman, Y. M. (1978). Kid watching: An alternative to testing. *National Elementary Principal's Journal, 57,* 41–45.

Goodman, K. S. (1992). Why whole language is today's agenda in education. *Language Arts, 69*(5), 354–363.

Gordon, A. M., & Williams-Browne, K. W. (1995). *Beginnings and beyond: Foundations in early childhood education.* Albany, NY: Delmar.

Goswami, U. (2001). Early phonological development and the acquisition of literacy. In S. B. Neuman & D. K. Dickinson (Eds.), *Handbook of early literacy research* (pp. 111–123). New York: Guilford Press.

Graves, D. (1994). *A fresh look at writing.* Portsmouth, NH: Heinemann.

Graves, M., & Fitzgerald, J. (2003a). *Scaffolding reading experiences.* New York: Christopher-Gordon, Inc.

Graves, M. F., & Fitzgerald, J. (2003b). Scaffolding reading experiences for multilingual classrooms. In G. G. Garcia (Ed.), *English learners.* Newark, DE: International Reading Association.

Gregory, K. M. (2002). *Playful Literacy and You! (PLaY!): A curriculum for trainers.* Mason, MI: Ingham Regional Literacy Training Center.

Griffith, P. L., & Olson, M. W. (1992). Phonemic awareness helps beginning readers break the code. *The Reading Teacher, 45*(7), 516–523.

Guthrie, J. T., et al. (1996). Growth of literacy engagement: Changes in motivations and strategies during concept-oriented reading instruction. *Reading Research Quarterly, 31*(3), 306–332.

Hadaway, N. L., Vardell, S. M., & Young, T. A. (2001). Scaffolding oral language development through poetry for students learning English. *The Reading Teacher, 54*(8), 796–806.

Hall, N., Crawford, L., & Robinson, A. (1997). Writing back: The teacher as respondent in interactive writing. *Language Arts, 74*(1).

Halliday, M. A. K. (1975). *Learning how to mean: Explorations in the development of language.* London: Edward Arnold.

Halliday, M. A. K. (2002). Relevant models of language. In B. M. Power & R. S. Hubbard (Eds.), *Language development: A reader for teachers* (2nd ed., pp. 49–53). Upper Saddle River, NJ: Merrill.

Harms, T., & Clifford, R. M. (2002). *Early childhood rating scale.* New York: Teachers College Press.

Harrison, C. (1996). *Methods of teaching reading: Key issues in research and implications for practice.* Interchange No. 39. Scottish Office Education & Industry Dept. Edinburgh Research & Intelligence Unit. ED 395 293.

Harste, J. (1990). Jerry Harste speaks on reading and writing. *The Reading Teacher, 43*(4), 316–318.

Hart, B., Risley, T. R. (2000). *Meaningful differences in the everyday experience of young American children.* Baltimore: Brookes Publishing.

Haugland, S. W., & Wright, J. L. (1997). *Young children and technology.* Boston: Allyn and Bacon.

Hayward, C. C. (1998, February). Monitoring spelling development. *The Reading Teacher, 51*(5), 444–445.

Hemmeter, M. L., & Ault, M. J. (2001). *Assessment of practices in early elementary classrooms (APEEC).* New York: Teachers College Press.

Henderson, E. H. (1990). *Teaching spelling* (2nd ed.). Boston: Houghton Mifflin.

Herbert, E. (2001). *The power of portfolios: What children can teach us about learning and assessment.* San Fransisco: Jossey-Bass Publishers.

Heuwinkel, M. (1996). New ways of learning = new ways of teaching. *Childhood Education, 73,* 27.

Hildreth, G. (1936). Developmental sequences in name writing. *Child Development, 7,* 291–303.

Hohmann, M., & Weikart, D. P. (1997). *Educating young children.* Ypsilanti, MI: High/Scope Foundation.

Holdaway, D. (1979). *The foundations of literacy.* New York: Scholastic.

International Reading Association and the National Council of Teachers of English. (1996). *Standards for the English language arts.* Newark, DE: International Reading Association/Urbana, IL: National Council of Teachers of English.

Isbell, R. & Exelby, B. (2001). *Early learning environments that work.* Beltsville, MD: Gryphon House.

Jalongo, M. R. (1988). *Young children and picture books.* Washington, DC: National Association for the Education of Young Children.

Jett-Simpson, M., & Leslie, L. (1984). *Ecological assessment: Under construction.* Schofield, WI: Wisconsin State Reading Association.

Juel, C. (1988). Learning to read and write: A longitudinal study of fifty-four children from first through fourth grade. *Journal of Educational Psychology, 80,* 437–447.

Juel, C. (1991). Beginning reading. In R. Barr, M. Kamil, P. Mosenthal, & P. Pearson (Eds.), *Handbook of reading research* (2nd ed.) (pp. 759–788). New York: Longman.

Juel, C., Griffith, P. L., & Gough, P. B. (1986). Acquisition of literacy: A longitudinal study of children in first and second grade. *Journal of Educational Psychology, 78,* 243–255.

Kamberelis, G., & Perry, M. (1994). A microgenetic study of cognitive reorganization during the transition to conventional literacy. In D. F. Lancy (Ed.), *Children's emergent literacy: From research to practice* (pp. 93–123). Westport, CT: Praeger.

Karlsen, B., & Gardner, E. F. (1996). Directions for administering the Standford Diagnostic Reading Test, forms J/K. San Antonio, TX: Harcourt Educational Measurement.

Kirby, P. (1992). Story reading at home and at school: Its influence upon children's early literacy growth. *Reading, 26*(2), 7–12.

Koeller, S., & Mitchell, P. (January, 1997). From Ben's story to your story: Encouraging young writers, authentic voices, and learning engagement. *The Reading Teacher, 50*(4), 328–336.

Kolata, G. (1998, March 3). Scientists track the process of reading through the brain. *New York Times,* p. B13.

Kostelnik, M. J., Soderman, A. K., & Whiren, A. P. (2004). *Developmentally appropriate curriculum: Best practices in early childhood education* (3rd ed.). Upper Saddle River, NJ: Prentice Hall.

Krashen, S. (2003). Three roles for reading for minority-language children. In G. G. Garcia (Ed.), *English learners* (pp. 55–70). Newark, DE: International Reading Association.

Laturnau, J. (2003). Standards-based instruction for English language learners. In G. G. Garcia (Ed.), *English learners* (pp. 286–307). Newark, DE: International Reading Association.

Lederer, R. (1991). *The miracle of language.* New York: Pocket Books.

Lee, W., & Carr, M. (2003). Reciprocal and responsive relationships in early childhood settings: Ways in which assessment can support them. Paper delivered at the 13th Annual EECERA Conference, Glasgow, Scotland.

Lehman, J. R. (1994). Integrating science and mathematics: Perceptions of preservice and practicing elementary teachers. *School Science and Mathematics, 94,* 58–64.

Levin, D. E., & Carlsson-Paige, N. (1994, July). Developmentally appropriate television: Putting children first. *Young Children,* pp. 38–41.

Lipton, L., & Hubble, D. (1997). *More than 50 ways to learner-centered literacy.* ED 404 619. Arlington Heights, IL: IRI/Skylight Training and Publishing.

Lundberg, I., Frost, J., & Peterson, O. (1988). Effects of an extensive program for stimulating phonological awareness in preschool children. *Reading Research Quarterly, 23,* 263–284.

Lyon, G. R. (1998). What works in reading. *Learning, 24*(6), 31–35.

Maclean, M., Bryant, P., & Bradley, L. (1987). Rhymes, nursery rhymes, and reading in early childhood. *Merrill-Palmer Quarterly, 33,* 255–281.

Many, J. E., et al. (1996). Traversing the topical landscape: Exploring students' self-directed reading–writing–research processes. *Reading Research Quarterly, 31*(1), 12–35.

Marcon, R. A. (1992). Differential effects of three preschool models on inner-city 4-year-olds. *Early Childhood Research Quarterly, 7,* 517–530.

McAfee, O., & Leong, D. (2002). *Assessing and guiding young children's development and learning* (3rd ed.). Boston: Allyn and Bacon.

McCormick, S. (1995). *Instructing students who have literacy problems.* Englewood Cliffs, NJ: Merrill.

McCormick, S. (2003). *Instructing students who have literacy problems.* Englewood Cliffs, NJ: Prentice Hall.

McGee, L. (2003). Book acting. In D. M. Barone & L. M. Morrow (Eds.), *Literacy and young children* (pp. 157–171). New York: Guilford Press.

McGee, L. M., & Richgels, D. J. (200). *Literacy's beginnings: Supporting young readers and writers* (3rd ed.). Boston: Allyn and Bacon.

McGee, L. M., & Richgels, D. J. (2003). *Designing early literacy programs.* New York: Guilford Press.

McGuinness, D., McGuinness, C., & Donohue, J. (1995). Phonological training and the alphabet principle: Evidence for reciprocal causality. *Reading Research Quarterly, 30*(4), 830–852.

McGuinness, D., Olson, A., & Chaplin, J. (1990). Sex differences in incidental recall for words and pictures. *Journal of Learning and Individual Differences, 2,* 263–286.

McKinnon, S. (1998, March). 3 R's go high tech. *Lansing State Journal,* pp. 1G, 3G.

McMillon, G., & Edwards, P. (2000). Why does Joshua "hate" school . . . but love Sunday School? *Language Arts, 78,* 111–120.

McTighe, J., & Lyman, F. T. (1988, April). Cueing thinking in the classroom: The promise of theory embedded tools. *Educational Leadership, 44*(7), 18–24.

Miller, D. (2002). *Reading with meaning: Teaching comprehension in the primary grades.* Portland, ME: Stenhouse Publishers.

Mondock, S. (1997). Portfolios: The story behind the story. *English Journal, 86*(1), 59–64.

Morrow, L. M. (1989). Designing the classroom to promote literacy development. In D. S. Strickland & L. M. Morrow (Eds.), *Emerging literacy: Young children learn to read and write* (pp. 1–15). Newark, DE: International Reading Association.

Morrow, L. M., Gambrell, L. B., & Pressley, M. (2003). *Best practices in literacy instruction* (2nd ed.). New York: Guilford Press.

Morrow, L. M., et al. (1997). The effect of a literature-based program integrated into literacy and science instruction with children from diverse backgrounds. *Reading Research Quarterly, 32*(1), 54–76.

Mueter, V., Hulme, C., Snowling, M., & Taylor, S. (1997). Segmentation, not rhyming, predicts early progress in learning to read. *Journal of Experimental Child Psychology, 65,* 370–396.

Musthafa, B. (1995). *Play–literacy connections: A research synthesis and suggested directions.* ED 395 705.

Nash, J. M. (1997, February 3). Fertile minds. *Time, 149*(5), 48–56.

National Center for Education Statistics (1999). *Teacher quality: A report on the preparation and qualifications of public school teachers.* Washington, DC: U. S. Department of Education.

National Research Council. (1998). *Preventing reading difficulties* (C. E. Snow, M. S. Burns, & P. Griffin, Eds.). Washington, D.C.: National Academy Press.

Neuman, S. (1999). Books make a difference: A study of access to literacy. *Reading Research Quarterly, 34,* 286–312.

Neuman, S. B., Copple, C., & Bredekamp, S. (1998). *Learning to read and write: Developmentally appropriate practices for young children.* Washington, DC: NAEYC.

Neuman, S. B., & Roskos, K. (1991). Play, print and purpose: Enriching play environments for literacy development. *The Reading Teacher, 44*(3), 214–221.

Neuman, S. B., & Roskos, K. (Eds.). (1998). *Children achieving: Best practices in early literacy.* Newark, DE: International Reading Association.

O'Brien-Palmer, M. (1992). *Book-write.* Kirkland, WA: Micnik Publications.

O'Donnell, M. D., & Wood, M. (1992). *Becoming a reader: A developmental approach to reading instruction.* Boston: Allyn and Bacon.

O'Donnell, M. D., & Wood, M. (1998). *Becoming a reader: A developmental approach to reading instruction* (2nd ed.). Boston: Allyn and Bacon.

Ogle, D. (1986). K-W-L: A teaching model that develops active reading of expository text. *The Reading Teacher, 39,* 564–570.

Oppenheimer, T. (1997, July). The computer delusion. *The Atlantic Monthly,* pp. 45–62.

Paris, S., & Ayres, L. (1994). *Becoming reflective students and teachers with portfolios and authentic assessment.* Washington, DC: American Psychological Association.

Pelligrini, A. D., & Galda, L. (1982). The effects of thematic fantasy play on the development of children's story comprehension. *American Educational Research Journal, 19,* 443–452.

Pellegrini, A. D., & Galda, L. (1994). Early literacy from a developmental perspective. In D. Lancy (Ed.), *Children's emerging literacy: From research to practice* (pp. 21–27). Westport, CT: Praeger.

Pelligrini, A. D., & Galda, L. (1996). *Oral language and literacy learning in context: The role of social relationships.* National Reading Research Center, Reading Research Report No. 57.

Pellegrini, A. D., Galda, L., Dresden, J., & Cox, S. (1991). A longitudinal study of the predictive relations among symbolic play, linguistic verbs, and early literacy. In D. Lancy (Ed.), *Children's emerging literacy: From research to practice.* Westport, CT: Praeger.

Pelligrini, A. D., Galda, L., Stahl, S., & Shockley, B. (1995). The nexus of social and literacy experiences at home and school: Implications for primary school oral language and literacy. *British Journal of Educational Psychology, 65,* 273–285.

Polakow, V. (1986). On meaningmaking and stories. *Phenomenology and Pedagogy, 4,* 37–47.

Prelutsky, J. (1993). *A nonny mouse.* New York: Random House.

Puckett, M. B., & Black, J. K. (2000). *Authentic assessment of the young child* (2nd ed.). New York: Merrill Publishing Group.

Reutzel, D., & Wolfersberger, M. (1996). An environmental impact statement: Designing supportive literacy classrooms for young children. *Reading Horizons, 36*(3), 266–282.

Roberts, B. (1992). The evolution of the young child's concept of word as a unit of spoken and written language. *Reading Research Quarterly, 27*(2), 125–138.

Robinson, F. P. (1946). *Effective study,* rev. ed. New York: Harper and Bros.

Roderick, J. (Ed.). (1991). *Context-responsive approaches to assessing children's language.* Urbana, IL: National Conference on Research in English.

Roskos, K. (1988, February). Literacy at work in play. *The Reading Teacher,* pp. 562–566.

Roskos, K., & Neuman, S. B. (2001). The environment and its influences for early literacy teaching and learning. In S. B. Neuman & D. K. Dickinson (Eds.), *The handbook of early literacy research* (pp. 281–294). New York: Guilford Press.

Routman, R. (1988). *Transitions.* Portsmouth, NH: Heinemann.

Routman, R. (1996). *Literacy at the crossroads.* Portsmouth, NH: Heinemann.

Routman, R. (2000). *Conversations.* Portsmouth, NH: Heinemann.

Routman, R. (2003). *Reading essentials.* Portsmouth, NH: Heinemann.

Rowe, D. W. (1998). Examining teacher talk: Revealing hidden boundaries for curricular change. *Language Arts, 75*(2), 103–107.

Sattler, J. M. (2002). *Assessment of children* (4th ed.). San Diego, CA: Jerome M. Sattler.

Schickedanz, J. A. (1986). *More than the ABCs.* Washington, DC: NAEYC.

Schickendanz, J. A. (1999). *Much More than the ABCs: The early stages of reading and writing.* Washington, DC: National Association for the Education of Young Children.

Shaklee, B., et al. (1997). *Designing and using portfolios.* Boston: Allyn and Bacon.

Shanahan, T. (1997). Reading–writing relationships, thematic units, inquiry learning: In pursuit of effective integrated literacy instruction. *The Reading Teacher, 51*(1), 12–19.

Shaywitz, S. (2003). *Overcoming dyslexia: A new and complete scientifically-based program for overcoming reading problems at any level.* New York: Alfred A. Knopf.

Slavin, R. E., Madden, N. A., Karweit, N. L., Dolan, L., & Wesik, B. A. (1996). *Every child, every school: Success for all.* Newberry Park, CA: Corwin.

Smith, F. (1997). *Reading without nonsense* (3rd ed.). New York: Teachers College Press.

Smyth, G. (2003). *Helping bilingual pupils to access the curriculum.* London: David Fulton Publishers.

Snow, C. E., Burns, M. S., & Griffin, P. (1998). *Preventing reading difficulties in young children.* Washington, DC: National Academy Press.

Snow, C. E., Cancino, H., Gonzalez, P., & Shriberg, E. (1989). Giving formal definitions: An oral language correlate of school literacy. In D. Bloome (Ed.), *Classrooms and literacy* (pp. 233–249). Norwood, NJ: Ablex.

Soderman, A. K. (1995). *Brownell Community School and Gundry Elementary Reading Accuracy Assessment: A baseline study, grades 1–3.* East Lansing: MSU Flint PDS Reports.

Soderman, A. K., Beatty, L., Cooper, P., Cummings, K. E., Fleury, J., Darrow, L., Thompson, C., & Weber, M. (1995, April). *Emerging literacy in Michigan first graders.* Research Report #1: *Emerging literacy: U.S., India, and Taiwan.* East Lansing: Michigan State University.

Spector, J. E. (1992). Predicting progress in beginning reading: Dynamic assessment of phonemic awareness. *Journal of Educational Psychology, 84*(3), 353–363.

Stahl, S. (1992). Saying the P word. *The Reading Teacher, 45*(8), 618–624.

Stahl, S. A., & Murray, B. A. (1994). Defining phonological awareness and its relationship to early reading. *Journal of Educational Psychology, 86*(2), 221–234.

Stanley, N. V. (1996). Vygotsky and multicultural assessment and instruction. In L. Dixon-Krauss (Ed.), *Vygotsky in the classroom: Mediated literacy instruction and assessment.* White Plains, NY: Longman.

Stanovich, K. (1986). Matthew effects in reading: Some consequences of individual differences in the acquisition of literacy. *Reading Research Quarterly, 21,* 360–407.

Stanovich, K. (1991). Word recognition: Changing perspectives. In P. D. Pearson, R. Barr, M. L. Kamil, & P. Mosenthal (Eds.), *Handbook of reading research* (vol. 2, pp. 418–452).

Stanovich, K., West, R. F., & Cunningham, A. E. (1991). Beyond phonological processes: Print exposure and orthographic processing. In S. A. Brady & D. P. Shankweiler (Eds.), *Phonological processes in literacy.* Hillsdale, NJ: Lawrence Erlbaum Associates.

Stauffer, R. G. (1975). *Directing the reading–thinking process.* New York: Harper & Row.

Stefanakis, E. (2002). *Multiple intelligences and portfolios: A window into the learner's mind.* Portsmouth, NH: Heinemann Publishers.

Stewig, J. W., & Jett-Simpson, M. (1995). *Language arts in the early childhood classroom.* Belmont, CA: Wadsworth.

Stone, S. (1995). Teaching strategies. Portfolios: Interactive and dynamic instructional tool. *Childhood Education, 71*(4), 232–234.

Strickland, D. S., & Morrow, L. M. (Eds.). (1989a). *Emerging literacy: Young children learn to read and write.* Newark, DE: International Reading Association.

Strickland, D. S., & Morrow, L. M. (2000). *Beginning reading and writing.* New York: Teachers College Press.

Strickland, D. S., & Taylor, D. (1989). Family storybook reading: Implications for children, families, and curriculum. In D. S. Strickland & L. M. Morrow (Eds.), *Emerging literacy: Young children learn to read and write* (pp. 27–34). Newark, DE: International Reading Association.

Sulzby, E. (1985). Children's emergent reading of favorite storybooks: A developmental study. *Reading Research Quarterly, 20*(4), 458–481.

Sulzby, E., Teale, W. H., & Kamberelis, G. (1989). Emergent writing in the classroom: Home and school connections. In D. S. Strickland & L. M. Morrow (Eds.), *Emerging literacy: Young children learn to read and write* (pp. 63–79). Newark, DE: International Reading Association.

Tabors, P. O., & Snow, C. E. (2001). Young bilingual children and literacy development. In S. B. Neuman & D. K. Dickinson (Eds.), *Handbook of early literacy research.* New York: Guildford Press.

Teale, W. T., & Sulzby, E. (1989). Emergent literacy: New perspectives. In D. S. Strickland & L. M. Morrow (Eds.), *Emerging literacy: Young children learn to read and write* (pp. 1–15). Newark, DE: International Reading Association.

Thatcher, R. W., Walker, R. A., & Guidice, S. (1987, May). Human cerebral hemispheres develop at different rates and ages. *Science, 236,* 110–113.

Thomas, K. F., & Rinehart, S. D. (1990). Young children's oral language, reading, and writing. *Journal of Research in Childhood Education, 5*(1), 5–26.

Tierney, R. J. (1998, February). Literacy assessment reform: Shifting beliefs, principled responsibilities, and emerging practices. *The Reading Teacher, 51*(5), 374–390.

Tierney, R. J., Readence, J. E., & Dishner, E. K. (1999). *Reading strategies and practices: A compendium* (5th ed.). Boston: Allyn and Bacon.

Tishman, S., & Perkins, D. (1997, January). The language of thinking. *Phi Delta Kappan, 78*(5), 368–374.

Tompkins, G. E. (2001). *Literacy for the 21st century: A balanced approach* (2nd ed.). Upper Saddle River, NJ: Merrill.

Torrance, N., & Olson, D. R. (1985). Oral and literate competencies in the early school years. In D. R. Olson, N. Torrance, & A. Hilyard (Eds.), *Language and literacy learning* (pp. 256–284). New York: Cambridge University Press.

Treiman, R., & Zukowski, A. (1991). Levels of phonological awareness. In S. A. Brady & D. P. Shankweiler (Eds.), *Phonological processes in literacy* (pp. 67–81). Hillsdale, NJ: Lawrence Erlbaum Associates.

Treiman, R., & Zukowski, A. (1996). Children's sensitivity to syllables, onsets, rimes, and phonemes. *Journal of Experimental Child Psychology, 61*(3), 193–215.

Tunmer, W. E. (1989). The role of language related to factors in reading disability. In D. Shankweiler & I. Y. Liberman (Eds.), *Phonology and reading disability: Solving the reading puzzle* (pp. 91–132). IARDLM (Monograph No. 6). Ann Arbor: University of Michigan Press.

Vandervelden, M. C., & Siegel, L. S. (1995). Phonological recoding and phoneme awareness in early literacy: A developmental approach. *Reading Research Quarterly, 30*(4), 854–875.

Vukelich, C. (1994). Effects of play interventions on young children's reading of environmental print. *Early Childhood Research Quarterly, 9*(2), 153–170.

Vygotsky, L. S. (1978). *Mind in society: The development of higher mental processes* (Eds. & Trans. M. Cole, V. John-Steiner, S. Scribner, & E. Souberman). Cambridge, MA: Harvard University Press.

Vygotsky, L. S. (1986). *Thought and language* (Trans. A. Kozulin). Cambridge, MA: MIT Press.

Wagstaff, J. (1995). *Phonics that work! New strategies for the reading/writing classroom.* New York: Scholastic.

Waring, C. C. (1995). *Developing independent readers.* West Nyack, NY: Center for Applied Research in Education.

Weaver, C. (1990). *Understanding whole language: From principles to practice.* Toronto: Irwin.

Weinberger, J. (1996). *A longitudinal study of children's early literacy experiences at home and later literacy development at home and school.* United Kingdom Reading Association. United Kingdom: Blackwell Publishers.

West, K. R. (1998, April). Noticing and responding to learners: Literacy evaluation and instruction in the primary grades. *The Reading Teacher, 51*(7), 550–559.

West, T. B. (1997). *In the mind's eye* (updated ed.). Buffalo, NY: Prometheus Press.

Whitehurst, G. J., & Lonigan, C. J. (2001). Emergent literacy: Development from prereaders to readers. In S. B. Neuman & D. K. Dickinson (Eds.), *Handbook of early literacy research* (pp. 11–28). New York: Guilford Press.

Wigfield, A., & Asher, S. R. (1984). Social and motivational influences in reading. In P. D. Pearson, R. Barr, M. L. Kamil, & P. Mosenthals (Eds.), *Handbook of research on reading* (pp. 423–452). New York: Longman.

Wingert, P., & Kantrowitz, B. (1997, October 27). Why Andy couldn't read. *Newsweek, 103*(17), 56–64.

Winograd, P., Flores-Duenas, L., & Allington, H. (2003). Best practices in litracy assessment. In L. M. Morrow, L. B. Gambrell, & M. Pressley, *Best practices in literacy instruction* (2nd ed.). New York: Guilford Press.

Wood, D. J., & Middleton, D. (1975). A study of assisted problem solving. *Journal of Child Psychology and Psychiatry, 17,* 89–100.

Wortham, S. (1998). *Developmental bases for learning and teaching.* Columbus, OH: Merrill.

Wortham, S. (2001). *Early childhood curriculum: Developmental bases for learning and teaching* (3rd ed.). Columbus, OH: Merrill.

Xu, S. H. (2003). The learner, the teacher, the text, and the context. Sociocultural approaches to early literacy instruction for English language learners. In D. M. Barone & L. M. Morrow (Eds.), *Literacy and young children* (pp. 61–82). New York: Guilford Press.

Ysseldyke, S. (2004). *Assessment in special and inclusive education* (9th ed.). Boston: Houghton Mifflin.

Active listening, 114

Activities, 20

Adams, M. M., 33, 38, 40, 42, 46, 79

ADD (*see* Attention deficit disorder)

ADHD (*see* Attention deficit hyperactivity disorder)

Airasian, P. W., 13

Alliteration, 36

Alphabetic principle, 38, 79, 119

Anchor words, 194, 197

Andersen, Hans Christian, 4

Angular gyrus, 5

Antecedents

    classroom climate and, 9

    in developing literacy, 2

    responding to variations, 9

Asher, S. R., 47

Assessment and evaluation, 186–235, 194, 196, 206, 207, 210

    adapting curriculum and teaching and, 187

    anecdotal records and, 189

    authentic, 186, 187, 191

    baseline data and, 187, 205, 207

    best practices and, 204

    checklists and inventories and, 188, 189, 196, 200, 202, 204, 212, 213

    child-centered, 187

    child development knowledge and, 204

    child self-appraisal, 23, 186, 187, 199, 201

    children's art as a tool, 192

    cloze procedure and, 196

    comprehension, 193, 197

    conference report, 202

    content of, 187

    context responsive, 207

    continuous data collection and, 207

    criterion-referenced, 189

    developmental benchmarks, 188

    developmentally appropriate, 187

    developmental writing inventories, 190

    diagnostic and research purposes, 203

    documentation, 189

    dynamic, 188, 191

    formal literacy assessment tools, 205–206

    formative, 188

    individual variations in learners and, 187

    kid-watching and, 188

    means and standard deviations, 194

    methods of, 187

    NAEYC guidelines and, 187

    narrative assessments, 189

    nursery rhyme repetition and, 197, 198

    observation and, 24, 156, 186, 188, 189, 200, 202

observation-based mini-reports and, 189

observer bias and, 191

performance assessment, 13, 187, 191, 200

practices that center on grading, ranking, sorting, and grouping and, 187

portfolios and, 187, 189, 193, 199, 209–235

principled data gathering and, 187

quality assessment package, 187

rating scales and, 188, 191, 192

reading accuracy and comprehension, 188, 193

rebus, 20

reliability, 191, 193, 203

rubrics and, 188, 191

running records and miscue analysis, 193

screening and assessment instruments, 205

self-appraisal (child) and, 199–202, 203, 207

skill acquisition and, 204

skill-sequenced, 189

special learning/developmental needs and, 187

spelling, 188, 197

standardized testing and, 186, 187, 191, 202, 203

teacher-involved methods of, 187

validity, 191, 203

Assessment tests

    Auditory Discrimination Test, 205

    Dynamic Indicators of Basic Early Literacy Skills (DIBELS), 205

    Early Language and Literacy Classroom Observation Toolkit (ELLCO), 205

    Expressive One Word Picture Vocabulary Test (EOWPVT-R), 205

    Gates MacGinitie Reading Tests, 3rd ed., 205

    Gray Oral Reading Test, 3rd ed., 205

    Kaufman Assessment Battery for Children, 205

    Lindamood Auditory Conceptualization Test, 205

    Observation Survey of Early Literacy Achievement, 205

    Peabody Picture Vocabulary Test—Revised (PPVT-R), 205

    Preschool Language Scale-3 (PLS-3), 206

    Stanford Diagnostic Reading Test (SDRT-4), 206

    Test of Auditory Analysis Skills (TAAS), 206

    Test of Early Language Development (TELD-2), 206

    Test of Oral Reading Fluency, 206

    Test of Phonological Awareness, 206

    Test of Written Spelling-3 (TWS-3), 206

    Woodcock Johnson Reading Mastery Tests-R, 206

    Woodcock Johnson Psychoeducational Battery-R (WJ-R), 206

Assessment of Practice in Early Elementary Classroom (APEEC), 191

Attention deficit disorder, 4

Attention deficit hyperactivity disorder, 13

Audiovisual presentations, 158

Author! Author!, 98

Author's Chair/Author's Night, 145

Automaticity, 150, 156

Ayres, L., 34, 36, 37, 78, 102

Bader, L. A., 197

Bader Reading and Language Inventory, 197

Balanced literacy, 16

Ball, E. W., 36

Baron, J., 42

Barrentine, S. J., 203

Basal tests, 186, 196

Basal texts, 18, 19

Beach, S. A., 80

Behaviorists, 11

Berk, L. E., 11

Best practice, 16

Blachman, B. A., 36

Blends, 124,

Block, C. C., 151

Bodrova, E., 88

Bolton, R., 173

Book acting, 33

Book making, 57, 127

Books in the classroom, 20

    big books, 57

    exploration of, 46

    fiction and non-fiction, 57, 60

    joke and riddle books, 57

    labeling of, 46

    songbooks, 57, 59

Bradley, R., 33, 34, 36, 78

Brain

    and attention deficit disorder, 4

    intelligence and, 4

    and learners with special needs, 4

    motivation and, 4

    and myelinization, 113

    and neural development, 113

    organization, 4, 9, 153

    as a pattern-seeking organ, 111

    and reading disability, 4

    and sight vocabulary, 4

    visual acuity and, 4

Brain-imaging technology, 153
Bredekamp, S., 73, 187
Brewer, J., 20
Bruner, J. , 28
Bryant, P. E., 33, 34, 36, 78
Buddy Biographies, 158
Buddy reading, 116
Burke, C., 64
Busink, R., 34

Calkins, L., 117
Capitalization, 141, 160
Carlsson-Paige, N., 78
Carpenter, J., 123–124
Cazden, C. B., 32
CD-ROMS, 156
Challenge words, 134
Chaney, C., 40
Chants, 59
Chaplin, J., 38
Chapter books, 117
Children's art as an assessment tool, 192
Christie, J. F., 82
Chronological age differences, 3
Chunking, 11
Churchill, W., 4
Cipher reading, 39
Class books, 128, 129
    labeling, 105
Classroom
    adaptable time component, 53, 69, 71
    age-related literacy experiences, 4
    book corner, 57
    block area, 57, 59, 62
    catalogs in, 57
    computer center, 62
    decision making and rule setting, 54
    design and layout of, 53–57
    developmentally appropriate practice and, 16, 17, 19
    diverse learning styles, 53, 57
    dramatic play and story reenactment area, 57, 59
    flannel board, 60
    flexible layout, 53, 64–65, 71
    fostering a positive environment, 52
    integrating subject matter, 66
    labeling, 63
    learning centers, 57
    learning materials, 52, 53, 71
    library, 57
    listening centers, 57, 58
    literate environment, 52, 62
    magazines in, 57
    meeting area, 57, 60
    music center, 57, 59
    must-have materials, 65
    newspapers in, 57
    one-size-fits-all approach and, 16, 17
    organization, 52–71
    physical structure, 52, 53
    positive social environment, 53
    primary grades, 113
    print-rich 60, 62, 63, 64
    project work and, 20
    puppet theater, 60
    puzzles and manipulatives, 57, 60, 62

Reader's Theater in, 57, 59, 154, 156
reading center, 58
reference materials in, 57
routines, 66
sand and water table, 57
science area in, 57, 60
spatial areas, 57, 58, 61, 64
structural components, 53
structure for implementing themes, 20
storytelling area, 57, 60, 62
teacher's attitude, 52, 53, 71
woodworking center, 59–60
writing center, 54, 57, 58–59, 62
Clay, M. M., 32, 38, 72, 74, 119, 194, 197
Cloze procedure, 196
Cognition
    ability to think abstractedly and, 153
    cognitive maps and organizers, 173
    cognitive reorganization and, 153
    comprehension strategies and, 150
    focusing abilities, 153
    long-term memory and, 153
    inference and, 151
    logical thinking and, 153
    organizing skills, 153
Collaborative learning, 118
Combs, M., 125
Comic books, 57, 117
Complex sentences, 113
Compound words, 199
Comprehension, 20, 22, 49, 152, 191, 193, 199
Computers in the classroom, 20, 22, 152
    CD-ROMS, 22
    and developmental experiences, 21
    Internet, 22, 24, 156
    and participatory learning, 21
    talking word processers, 22
Concepts about print, 38, 74, 79, 119, 123
Concepts about words, 38–40
Consonants, 124
Constructivist theory, 13
Contractions, 124
Cooperative learning, 13, 189
Copple, C., 73
Coppola, J. M., 6
Cox, S., 33, 41
Crawford, P. A., 26, 120
Creative writing (see also Writing), 127
Cullinan, B. E., 47
Cummins, J., 119, 120
Cunningham, P. M., 122, 132

Daily message–daily news, 100
Daniels, H., 181–182
da Vinci, L., 4
Decodable text, 119
Decoding tasks and abilities, 1, 11, 110, 111, 150, 197, 199
    academic underachievement and, 16
    inside-out information systems and, 16
    outside-in information systems and, 16
    phonics programs and, 16
    whole-language programs and, 16
Developmental constructivist theory, 11
Developmentally appropriate practices (DAP), 15, 120, 207
    classroom applications for, 19

definition of, 16
    didactic settings and, 17
    integrated learning across the curriculum and, 20
    NAEYC guidelines for, 15, 19
Developmentally appropriate programs, 17, 18
    current approaches, 17
    receptive language and, 17
    verbal and listening skills and, 17
Dewey, J., 20
Dickinson, D. K., 32, 33, 73, 75, 78
Dictionaries, 196
Digraphs, 124
Directed Reading/Thinking Activity (DRTA), 177
Discovery Learning, 31
Dolch word list, 119, 194, 236–238
Donahue, J., 37
Down syndrome, 202
Dramatic play, 20
Dresden, J., 41
Dunn, L., 17
Dyslexia, 5, 6
Dyson, A. H., 41, 42, 45

Early Childhood Environment Rating Scale (ECERS), 191
Ecomap, 9, 10
Edwards, C., 80, 189
Ehri, L. C., 39, 47, 74
Einstein, A., 4
Ellis, N., 36
Emergent literacy, 27, 72, 186
    age and, 2
    alphabetic stage, 39
    awareness and exploration stage of, 73
    brain organization and, 2
    culture and, 2
    early phase of, 110–148
    emerging phase of, 72–109
    experience and, 2
    experimenting stage of, 73
    fluent phase of, 149–185
    gender and, 2
    logographic stage, 38
    orthographic stage, 39
    primary language and, 2
    skills, 197
English language
    basic components of, 113
    morphology, 114
English language learners, 5, 6, 7, 8, 58, 62, 119, 156, 211
    bilingual programs and, 6
    instructional scaffolding and, 7
    language acquisition and, 7
    monolingual classroom and, 6, 7
    oral communication, 7
    primary language, 6, 7
    sociopsycholinguistic approach, 119
    systematic word recognition, 7
English-proficient children, 7
Environmental print, 63
Enz, B., 82
Erickson, E., 3, 113
Essays, 158
Estrin, E., 40

Faraday, M., 4
Ferreiro, E., 40
Fields, M., 59, 67, 70
Fluency, 111, 120, 126, 149, 156, 194, 197, 212
    later primary child and, 153
    role of teacher, 153
    skill and concept building, 153
Fowler, A. E., 35
Freeman, D., 119
Freeman, Y., 119
Frequently used words, 124
Fresch, M., 171
Frith, U., 38

Galda, L., 33, 41, 47, 75
Gardner, H., 111
Gender differences, 4, 117
    antecedent variations in children, 9
    brain-growth periodization studies and, 3
Genres, 57, 58
Gifted and talented, 3
Gilman, D., 211
Glasser, W., 155
Goldhaber, J., 59, 61, 70
Gomez, E., 211
Goodman, Y. M., 27, 188
Gordon, A. M., 113
Goswami, U., 34, 35, 40, 78
Gough, P. B., 34
Graphic/visual organizers, 156, 173, 174, 175
Graves, D., 145, 147, 156
Graves, M., 120
Griffith, P. L., 34
Grouping
    flexible, 66, 67, 68, 69
    heterogeneous, 17, 115
    homogeneous, 115, 116
    role of teacher, 67
Guided reading, 124, 125, 198
Guthrie, J. T., 66

Hadaway, N. L., 58
Hall, D., 96, 140,
Halliday, M., 29, 32
Harms, T., 191
Harrison, C., 48
Harste, J., 28, 41
Hart, C. H., 27, 73, 75, 77, 78
Haughland, S. W., 21
Hayward, C. C., 198
Hemmeter, M. L., 191
Herbert, E., 210, 218, 219
High-stakes testing, 203
Hildreth, G., 42
Hodgins, S., 117
Hohmann, M., 110
Holdaway, D., 4
Homophones, 124
Hulme, C., 36

Idioms, 156
Imaging, 156
Individual Reading Inventories (IRIs), 118, 196
    commercial, 196
Inferior frontal gyrus, 5

Information systems for emergent literacy, 1, 2
    inside-out, 1
    outside-in, 1
Instruction
    small-group, 68, 69
    teacher-directed, 118
    tempo of, 18
    whole-group, 68, 69
Integrated curriculum, 20
International Reading Association, 19, 211
Internet, 22, 24, 156
Intervention programs, 120
Intrapersonal and interpersonal growth, 153
Inventories (see Assessment and evaluation, checklists and inventories)

Jalongo, M. R., 47
Jett-Simpson, M., 112
Journal writing, 69, 94
    math journals, 168
    personal journals, 167
    reflective entries, 213, 218
    response journals and logs, 166
    science journals, 168
Juel, C., 34, 39, 75

Kamberelis, G., 27, 32, 41
Kirby, P., 47
Knowledge of child development, 204
Koeller, S., 156
Kolata, G., 5
Kostell, P., 164
Kostelnik, M. J., 16, 17, 66, 69, 155
Krashen, S., 120, 156
KWHLH strategy, 169
KWL activity, 121

Language
    conventions of, 113
    decontextualized, 32, 78
    nonverbal responses, 120
    processes, 2
    receptive, 191
    samples, 113
    sounds of, 77
Language arts block, 68
Language detectives, 160
Language Experience Approach (LEA), 85
Large, B., 36
Laturnau, J., 7
Learners
    early-to-fluent, 56, 57, 59, 60, 64, 66, 71
    emerging-to-early, 55, 57, 59, 66, 71
Learning disorders/disabilities, 152, 153
    factors in the reader, 152
    factors in the text, 153
    warning signs, 6
Lee, W., 189
Lehman, J. R., 66
Leong, D., 88
Leonni, L., 18, 195
Letter–sound associations, 111, 122, 141
Levin, D. E., 78
Linguistics, 6
Lipton, L., 62, 63, 64, 212, 220

Listening skills
    activities to develop, 114
    comprehension, 118
Literacy
    achievement and, 191
    acquisition, 19, 23, 24, 191, 197
    activities to develop, 114
    comprehension, 118
    early stages or phases, 1, 152
    emerging stages or phases, 1, 2, 6, 110, 152, 207
    functional, 150
    logs and journals, 200
    prerequisite skills, 152
    prior knowledge, 155, 156
    props, 57, 59, 60, 61, 80
Literacy circles, 69, 181–184
Literacy-rich contexts, 111
Literacy rotations, 115–116
Literacy skills
    chaotic family situations and, 152
    emergent, 197
    in reading and writing, 2
    short- and long-term development of, 206
Logical-mathematical connections, 113
Lundberg, I., 36
Lyon, G. R., 6

Maclean, M., 36
Making Words, 132
Marcon, R. A., 17
McAfee, O., 186, 187, 188, 191, 204
McMillon, G., 80
McCormick, S., 5, 118, 119
McFadden, D., 200
McGee, L. M., 30, 33, 34, 38, 41, 42,45, 47, 60, 73, 75, 78, 80
McTighe, J., 173
Mechanics of writing, 212
Memorization, 196
Memory, visual and verbal, 113, 192
Message center, 64
Metacognition, 175, 199
Metacognitive skills, 113, 169, 213
Metalanguage, 33
Middle childhood classroom, 156
Middle childhood years, 149, 153, 185
Miller, D., 59, 151
Mini-workshops and conferences, 66, 116, 152, 156, 189, 191, 200
Mixed-age settings, 20
Many, J. E., 66
Morning message, 68, 160
Morrow, L. M., 45, 66, 150
Movable letters, 132
Mueter, V., 78
Multiage settings, 3, 116
Multilingual classroom, tips for scaffolding language, 120
Murray, B. A., 34, 36
Musthafa, B., 80

Name games, 107
Narrative and expository passages, 197
National Association for the Education of Young Children (NAEYC), 188
National Center for Educational Statistics, 6

National Council of Teachers of English, 211
National Institutes of Child and Human
    Development, 6
National Research Council, 79
Neuman, S. B., 63, 73, 80, 82
Neurophysiology, 113
No Child Left Behind Act of 2001, 23, 203
Nursery rhymes, 102
    repetitions for assessment and, 197, 198
Nyberg, J., 121

O'Brien-Palmer, M., 138
O'Donnell, M. D., 114
Olson, A., 28, 38
Onsets and rimes/word families, 11, 34, 36, 144
Oppenheimer, T., 21
Oral language, 110, 113, 186
Oral reading, 193
Outcomes (see also Assessment and
    Evaluation)
    and authentic assessment and evaluation,
    22
    and children from minority backgrounds
    and high-stakes tests, 22
    and special education classes, 22
    and standardized and normed tests, 22, 23

Palinesar, A. S., 17
Paraphrasing, 156
Parent–teacher conferences, 187, 200
Parents
    communication with, 70
    conferences, 188
    home and school connections, 69
    home environments, 70
    involvement, 119
    portfolios and, 210, 221
    support, 70
Patton, G., 4
Peer conferencing, 165
Peer group, 153
Pelligrini, A. D., 41, 75
Perry, M., 27
Phonemes, 34
Phonemic awareness, 34, 35, 59, 70, 111,
    114, 119, 134, 152, 156, 157
Phonetic approach, 70
Phonetic cue reading, 39
Phonics, 6, 17, 18, 114, 156
Phonograms, 124
Phonological awareness, 1, 6, 18, 34, 70, 114,
    157
    activities, 153
    instruction in, 34, 70, 115, 116, 144
Picture walks, 120
Play sets, 89
Plato, 71
Pocket chart songs and chants, 99
Poems, 57, 58, 70, 125
Poetry, 158
Polakow, V., 26
Portfolios, 117, 199, 209–235
    assessment and, 218
    benefits of, 209, 210
    CD-ROMS, 216
    conference guide/organizer, 222, 223, 226,
        227, 228, 229

conference reports, 213
conferences about, 71, 220
contents, 212
definition and purpose, 209–210
digital, 216
documentation boards (storyboards or
    presentation boards), 221, 230
electronic, 209, 212, 216, 234
evaluation of, 219, 233
goal setting and, 221, 225, 228
implementation, 218
introduction to children, 217
methods of implementation, 209
open-ended questions, 226
oral language samples and, 212
parents and, 233
photographs and, 213
progress charts, 213
response forms, 219
reflection process, 219–221
self-portraits, 218
self-reflection and, 212, 213, 214, 219,
    220, 221
sharing of, 218, 221
showcase, 209, 213, 216, 221, 226
storage and management of, 217
types, 213
VIPs and, 213
working, 213, 209
writing samples and, 212
PowerPoint presentations, 130, 132, 212, 216
Predictable charts, 96
Predicting, 150, 151, 177
Prelutsky, J., 125
Print
    conventions, 111
    environmental, 106
Print awareness, 18, 38, 116
Print production
    mock writing and, 43
    phonemic stage of, 44
    scribble stage of, 43
    semiphonemic stage of, 44
    transitional stage of, 44
Prior knowledge, 151, 156
Problem of the Week, 64
Process writing, 141
Prosody, 126, 150, 156
Puckett, M. B., 188
Punctuation, 111, 141, 152, 160, 212

Read-alouds, 114, 125, 126
Readers
    accomplished, 112
    advanced beginning, 112
    beginning, 112
    consolidating, 112
    disabled, struggling, 58, 118
    emerging, 112
    fluent, 150
    intentional, 151
    transitional, 112
Reader's Theater, 154, 156, 176–177
Readiness point, 2
Reading
    accuracy, 194
    disabilities, 119

finger-point, 74
independent, 194, 198
levels, 197
lists, grade level, 193
neurological components, 5
oral, 194, 202
partner reading activities, 194
readiness, 26
scaffolded learning activities, 194
self correction rate, 194
sustained, silent, 68, 202
Reading around the Room, 98
Reading First grants, 203
Reading Recovery, 119
Reading skills, comprehension and, 111
Reference materials, 197
Reggio Emilia school system, 189
Report cards, 188, 189
Response journals and logs, 166
Retellings, 136
Reutzel, D., 57, 60, 61, 62, 63, 64
Rhymes, 125, 144
Rhythm, 126
Richgels, D. J., 30, 34, 38, 41, 42, 45, 47, 73,
    75, 78, 80
Rimes, 144
Rinehard, S. D., 32
Risley, T. R., 27, 73, 75, 77, 78
Roberts, B., 40
Rodin, A., 4
Roskos, K., 53, 60, 80, 82
Routman, R., 69, 110, 114, 147, 193, 202
Rowe, D., 82
Rubrics, 211
Running record, 119, 193, 195

Scaffolded Reading Experiences (SRE), 156
Scaffolded writing, 88
Scaffolding, 14, 20, 111, 125, 148, 156, 187,
    189, 191
    children with special needs and, 12
    definition, 11
    in emerging literacy, 12
    imaginative play and, 12
    independent performance level, 12
    instructional techniques and, 7
    maximally assisted performance level, 12
Schulze, P., 189
Secret message, 116
Segmentation, 36
Self-appraisal (by child), 199–202
Self-regulation, 116
Self-selected reading, 143
Self-talk, 14
Semantics, 77, 113, 126, 196
Sensitive periods, 6
Sensory deficits, 118
Sentence generation, 197
Shaklee, B., 210, 211, 218
Shanahan, T., 60, 67
Shared reading, 92
Shaywitz, B, 5
Shaywitz, S., 5
Shockley, B., 34
Short story, 158
Siegel, L. S., 36
Single-parent families, 8

DEC 05

Slavin, R. E., 119
Smith, F., 17, 78
Snow, C. E., 27, 35, 77, 78, 115
Social-constructivist theory and
    developmentally appropriate practice, 23
Social-conventional knowledge, 19, 111, 113
Sociocultural influences, 8
Soderman, A. K., 23
Sort, Search and Discover (SSD), 171
Spector, J. E., 191
Speech
    concepts of effective, 114
    cueing systems, 196
    parts of, 196
Spelling, 70, 160, 212
    approximations, 113, 152
    conventional, 157, 197, 198
    invented, temporary, 117, 152, 197
    standard, 44
Spelling pattern recognition teams, 157
Stahl, S. A., 33, 34, 36, 39
Standardized achievement tests (*see also*
    Assessment), 118, 203, 206
    abnormalities in development, 203
    cultural biases, 304
    norm-referenced, 203
    overuse and misuse, 204
    policymakers and, 203
    psychometric properties, 203
    technical and educational inadequacy, 204
    unsuitability, 204
Standardized assessment, status of, 202, 203
Standards for English Language Arts, 27, 211
Stories, reenacting/retelling, 60
Story-writing rubrics, 165
Superior temporal gyrus, 5
Student-led conferencing, 187, 199, 200, 209,
    213, 221, 225, 228
    planning the conference, 229
    preparation for, 226
    role playing, 226, 228
    scheduling conferences, 229
    student and parent reflections, 232
Stanley, N. V., 191
Stanovich, K., 36, 37
Stauffer, R. G., 177
Stefanakes, E., 210, 219
Stewig, J. W., 28, 29, 111
Stone, S., 211, 218
Story mapping, 137
Strickland, D. S., 2, 45, 47
Success for All, 119
Sulzby, E., 27, 32, 41, 45, 79
Summarizing, 156
Surprise Box, 104
Survey, Question, Read, Recite, Review
    (SQ3R), 179

Sweet, J., 39, 47, 74
Smyth, G., 7
Syntax, 77, 113, 114, 126, 196

Tabors, P. O., 33, 73, 75, 77, 78
Take-home portfolio conference,
    230, 231
Talk, narrative and explanatory, 78
Teale, W. T., 27, 32, 41
Television, 117
Tests (*see also* Assessment Tests)
    criterion-related, 203, 211
    diagnostic, 207
    group-administered, 207
    norm-referenced, 203, 211
    paper–pencil, 205
    scores, 187
    spelling, 18
    validity and reliability, 191
Text
    grade-related, 207
    informational, 180
    narrative and expository, 174, 177
Thatcher, R. W., 3
Theatre in a Bag, 59
Theme/concept charts, 139
Themes, 59, 61
Thomas, K. F., 32
Three-way conferences, 230
Tierney, R. J., 174, 204
Tishman, S., 111
Tompkins, G. E., 1, 150, 176
Tone, 126
Torrance, N., 28
Trade books, 119
Transactions, theoretical perspectives
    of, 9
Treiman, R., 34, 35, 36, 42
Tunmer, W. E., 49

Vandervelden, M. C., 36
Venn diagrams, 156, 174
Verbal communication, 110
Visual memory, 111
Visualizing, 150, 151
Vocabulary, 78, 120, 122, 156, 197
    attribute-naming activity for assessment,
        197
    receptive and expressive, 111
    sight-word, 59
Vukelich, C., 82
Vygotsky, L., 11, 12, 59, 110
    acquisition of language, 11
    ADHD and, 13
    cognitive development, 11
    deaf children, 12
    self-regulation behavior, 13

sign language, 13
verbal self-talk, 13

Wagstaff, J., 134
Wait time, 120
Waring, C. C., 5
Weaver, C., 28
Weinberger, J., 70
West, K. R., 189
West, T. B., 37
Whitehurst, G. J., 1, 26
Wigfield, A., 47
Williams, V., 96
Wingert, P., 6, 153
Winograd, P., 188, 205
Word awareness, 50
Word games, 117
Word study, 117, 156
Word wall, 117, 123, 198
Workbooks and worksheets, 18, 19, 70
Work samples, 20, 186, 196, 200, 202
Wortham, S., 22, 153
Writer's workshop, 162–166
    with peer confencing, 162
    story-writing rubrics and, 164
Writing
    alphabetic stage, 197
    anchor papers, 191
    assessment of skills, 198
    attribute-naming as assessment, 199
    consonant stage, 197
    conventions, 117
    developmental inventory of writing skills,
        190
    editing, 152
    fluent, 152
    individual dictation, 117
    journals, 212
    performance assessment and, 191
    plot development, 152
    process, 59, 152, 191
    proofreading, 152
    sequencing story ideas, 212
    topic sentence, 152
Writing center, 196

Xu, S. H., 78

Yale Center for Learning and Attention, 5
Young, J., 80
Ysseldyke, J. E., 203

Zone of Proximal Development (ZPD), 11,
    194
    independent level, 11
    maximally assisted problem solving, 11
Zukowski, A., 34, 35, 36